The World-Wide Web, Mosaic and More

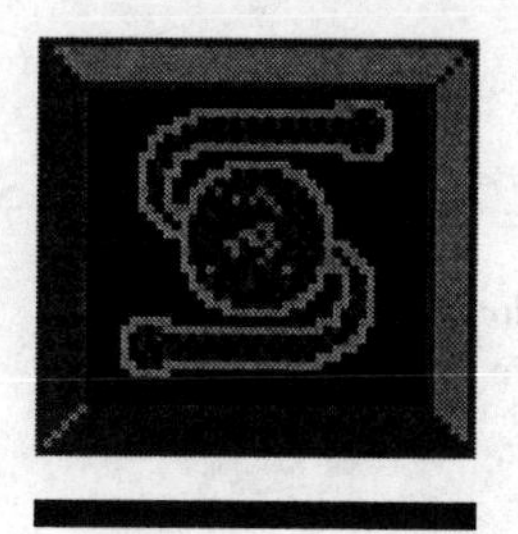

The World-Wide Web, Mosaic and More

Jason J. Manger

McGRAW-HILL BOOK COMPANY
London · New York · St Louis · San Francisco · Auckland · Bogotá
Caracas · Lisbon · Madrid · Mexico · Milan · Montreal
New Delhi · Panama · Paris · San Juan · São Paulo
Singapore · Sydney · Tokyo · Toronto

Published by
McGRAW-HILL Book Company Europe
Shoppenhangers Road, Maidenhead, Berkshire, SL6 2QL, England
Telephone 0628 23432
Fax 0628 770224

British Library Cataloguing in Publication Data
The CIP data of this title is available from the British Library, UK

ISBN 0–07–709132–9

Library of Congress Cataloging-in-Publication Data
The CIP data of this title is available from the the Library of Congress,
Washington DC, USA

12345 CL 97654

Typeset by Ian Kingston Editorial Services, Nottingham
and printed and bound in Great Britain at Clays Ltd, St Ives plc

Contents

Appendices

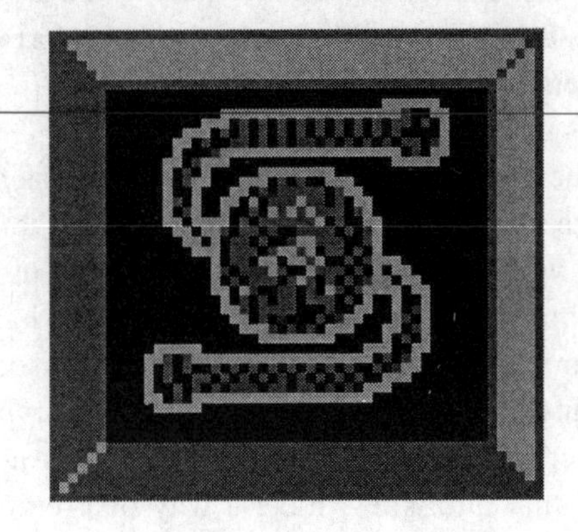

Introduction

Publishing on the Internet is not a new concept; indeed, the publishing of *electronic information* by this particular medium has been established for nearly a quarter of a century – the age of the Internet. So why has interest heightened all of a sudden? Ironically, the Internet has gained nearly all of its public exposure through the *conventional* media. Every newspaper, radio station and television channel has carried Internet-related topics in recent months, and will continue to do so now that the *information superhighway* has caught the attention of the public. Now that service providers are springing up all over the place and the media continue to home in on the more controversial aspects of the Internet, people are waking up to the fact that the Net will be the new mass medium (indeed, multimedia) sensation of the next century. Forget satellite and cable television: the Internet is the thing to watch. One of the main fascinations for media moguls and information publishers alike is that the Internet isn't owned by anybody: it can't be sued and it won't take legal action against you. After all, service providers can't be held responsible for their users, can they? Such a totally anarchistic entity has many possibilities. No equivalent market currently exists that is completely uncensored in this way.

Access to the Net has now been firmly established, and businesses have caught on to the fact that the Internet is basically a big (well, massive) market-place full of consumers just like you and me, and more importantly that it is a market whose consumers are all grouped together in one place, thus making the market much easier to reach and penetrate. Publishing can thus take on many new guises, such as advertising, and (needless to say) the commercially aware have latched on to this fact very quickly indeed. Internet users themselves publish software and information which is shared by the entire community, and all users can benefit from each other's *published* work at no extra expense whatsoever. Advertising costs nothing on the Internet.

A large problem with the Internet lies in its development as a whole. Because so many people have contributed to the design and implementation of the Internet's tools and interfaces, the user is left with a confusing choice of ways in which to access this vast resource. Publishing has thus been sporadic and documents have been provided using a variety of different file-formats, all of which have their own associated tools and interfaces. All of this has recently changed, however, since a new *killer application* has appeared that integrates all of the Internet's resources into just one system and, more importantly, one interface. It seems, at last, that publishers have a way of promoting their work through a single entity, namely *hypermedia*. Hypermedia is related to *hypertext*, a way of combining many different types of medium into a single document. Whereas hypertext allowed the user to cross-reference textual documents with ease, hypermedia offers this and much more besides. A fairly recent development (as recent as 1992) was the *World-Wide Web*, a system designed by Tim Berners-Lee of CERN (the famous Particle Physics Laboratory), which cross-references resources on the Internet for quick and easy retrieval. The original program was completely text-based and its commands were somewhat cryptic and arcane. A graphical browser was desperately needed, and now there is one: Mosaic, the so-called *killer application* that has opened up the Internet to both experts and novices alike.

From a publishing perspective Mosaic and the Web offer many benefits. The graphical nature of Mosaic (it is supported under popular GUIs such as MS Windows on the PC, and X-Windows on UNIX) has undoubtedly been the major attraction to most users. With Mosaic, the user is presented with a completely graphical view of the Internet: a click of the mouse may result in a local hard-disk request or a request to pull a document from a computer that resides many thousands of miles away in another continent. Publishers like Mosaic because it embodies many of the processes that are already very well known to publishing houses generally, such as text mark-up and document layout design.

Then, of course, there is cost. Conventional publishing is a very cost- and labour-intensive process. Thousands of copies of a book must eventually be printed, and leading up to this phase each book must be vigorously proofread (as must Web pages, of course) and then finally typeset. During this process, the text of the book may be contracted in and out to various people for further 'specialist' work. Then the books must be publicized. All of this is vastly easier with Internet-based publishing. On the Web, a single published document is all that is required, and since the actual document is dynamic, it can be updated or corrected with the minimum amount of effort. All of this can be done by one person, the author, and need not involve any third-party. Advertising on the Internet is also much easier – electronic mail can reach potential *customers* all over the world within just a few minutes, and once again, only a single copy of the emailed advertisement needs to be uploaded. Distribution is automatic over the Internet; messages propagate from machine to machine until they have reached all parts of the network.

Finally, there is the ultimate question: will the book be replaced by an electronic equivalent? Many would say that it already has, although I'm slightly more sceptical, being the pessimist I am (one has to be pessimistic with anything electronic). There can be no doubt that a book is more convenient than a personal computer in terms of its portability, availability and cheapness. If I want to see today's news headlines I can do this much more easily by simply purchasing a newspaper. However, in saying this there are cases where the computer user can find the computer more convenient than a paper-based equivalent. If I want to read some Shakespeare sonnets, and perhaps find all the occurrences of the *Dark Lady*, I could simply log in to Project Gutenberg, download a selection of works and then conduct a search electronically on these. Now that's convenience, but I still of course need a computer to carry this all out. When the computer becomes as ubiquitous as the television (it's creeping up faster than you may think), and the superhighway has reached every home, then I might just change my mind, quickly.

Readership

This book will have a wide readership. In a nutshell, anyone with an informational requirement, perhaps with more of an emphasis on creating and publishing sources of electronic information (or at least a means of accessing computer-based information) will want to learn about the Web and the methods of publishing electronic information on the global Internet network. You do not have to be an Internet expert to use the World-Wide Web; indeed, the Web allows transparent access to many popular Internet services such as `ftp`, `telnet`, Gopher/veronica, WAIS and USENET, and all through a common interface. There can no longer be any excuse for not using the Internet because of its complexity. Traditional publishers will also want to investigate the Web as a means of reaching a massive audience of scientists, academics and business people (including, of course, potential customers). Whether you are interested in publishing a product or service, or whether you have a complex information resource that simply needs *humanizing*, Mosaic and the Web are the solutions you require. Mosaic's ability to integrate with many third-party programs allows it to cope with a variety of existing audio, visual and textual formats.

Amazingly enough, you do not even have to be connected to the Internet in order to use a web browser such as Mosaic. As you will learn, it is possible to develop Web documents using Mosaic purely as the *engine* that drives the development process, and which handles all of the different types of medium in your documents. Add-on packages, or *viewers* as they are more commonly known, are used to add this functionality to Mosaic. The PC version of Mosaic has dozens of such viewers, all written by third-party programmers and made available as shareware or freeware. Viewers allow the integration of motion-video, still picture retrieval, audio clips and much more besides. In fact, Mosaic can be used for the creation of a wide range of information-interfaces from help systems right through to presentations and computer-based training packages. Established Internet enthusiasts will want to examine the Web, ultimately because it can save you time actually spent on-line while at the same time reducing the need to remember many dozens of different commands and features of separate Internet tools. Imagine being able to access a Gopher menu or a USENET group graphically, or for that matter being able to explore the Internet with a much greater degree of flexibility generally. Well now you can. Mosaic, and 99% of its add-ons, are all available as freeware (some of the latter are shareware): that is to say that no royalty is asked from the authors of the programs concerned. Couple this with the Internet's free 24 hour access (there are no on-line charges, apart from your local phone calls of course), and you will surely never get a better system with which to publish to a world-wide audience.

What you will learn

Using this book we will teach you the language of the World-Wide Web (HTML, or HyperText Mark-up Language). Since nearly all Web client programs (such as Mosaic and *Cello*) understand HTML, you can design and publish your own electronic literature and then transform it into a complete hypermedia application. We will show you how to install and customize viewers and other information parsers, and how to create stunning and effective Web pages. You will also learn about Mosaic's interface and how it is configured (other browsers are also considered, e.g. *Cello*). Additional information on existing Internet resources is also included to allow interfacing via the Web. Advanced users will want to examine some of HTML's more advanced aspects, such as CGI (Common Gateway Interface) scripting to allow HTML documents to provide the user with keyboard input, and ultimately to allow an interface into a back-end program, such as a database, to be created. Novices and semi-experts will also want to examine the chapter on HTML hypereditors, tools that automate the insertion of HTML tags into documents and make the task of Web publishing that much easier. An extensive set of appendices has also been provided, including an A–Z list of HTML tag references; an A–Z Web Software Guide; an A–Z of interesting Web Home Pages to visit, and an A–Z subject matter guide.

Acknowledgements

My thanks to all the staff at McGraw-Hill UK, particularly Jane Waters, Jenny Ertle, Stephen Rickard and of course everyone else who was involved in this publication. When I initially contacted McGraw-Hill with the idea for this book they said they wanted it completed within three weeks (I always thought they were a crazy lot down at Maidenhead!). However, here is the proof....

Book conventions

All *computerese* text is set in the `Courier` font; this includes Internet host names, e.g. `pipex.net`, IP addresses, e.g. `138.8.8.68`, and the names of all computer commands, filenames and computer output. Various tips and other bits of information are scattered throughout the book; look out for the sections headed 'TIP'.

Jason Manger
Surrey
August 1994

CHAPTER

1

Publishing on the Internet

1.1 What Actually is *Publishing* on the Net?

What is *publishing* on the Internet, and for that matter, what actually is the Internet? Questions such as these are being answered through a system known as the World-Wide Web (or The Web, WWW or W3 for short). Everyone understands publishing in its conventional sense. Books, magazines, newspapers and many other forms of published work are available in abundance. Electronic publishing is a different matter, however. Publishing has always largely been associated with all things paper, and information that has been made available electronically tends to fall into a different class and is largely dismissed by many people as not being *publishing* in the true sense of the word. All this is about to change, however; indeed, it has already changed. The Internet is the world's largest electronic resource, a network of hundreds of thousands of computers that span the globe. Such a resource could really be classed as a country in its own right. With an estimated population of some 25–30 million people (no exact figures are readily available) and a growth rate of some 10% per year, the Internet is the Earth's largest electronic publishing house. After all, everything gets 'published' on the Internet. But is *The Web* the same thing as *The Net*? Well, not really. The Net (or Internet) is the physical communications network, i.e. phone-lines and other telecommunications channels that link the world together. The Web is an application *of* the Internet. It is essentially a program and protocol specification that uses the Internet's infrastructure to communicate.

Publishing, as far as the Internet is concerned, has taken on a whole new meaning. Up until very recently, the most popular methods of publishing information on the Net were achieved through the use of tools such as `ftp` (File Transfer Protocol), WAIS (Wide Area Information Server), Gopher, and the limited capabilities of the textual versions of the World-Wide Web. In fact, all of the above systems suffer from a related drawback, namely that they all shared text-based interfaces. And of course, many still do, depending on your Internet software. Another major drawback with these systems concerns their actual interfaces and the way that information is presented and retrieved: all of them have different ways of achieving this. Significant improvements were forthcoming, however. Gophers could link into FTP sites and even into USENET groups (USENET stands for *Users Network* – a collection of some 9000 topics or newsgroups) and yet none of these popular applications has caused as much discussion, excitement and debate as the Web.

The Web was initially conceived at CERN, the famous European Particle Physics Laboratory in Switzerland, for use by scientists to exchange and share information. The Web's popularity led to its release onto the Internet, and now there is no stopping it. The Web itself is based on a hypertext, or hypermedia, mode of operation in which a single document has embedded *links* to other documents, which can exist locally or anywhere in the world, while at the same time allowing the user to incorporate sound, animations, still pictures, plain text and many other types of medium, all into a single document. The beauty of the Web is that the main core of its operation is left to the underlying protocol, or HTTP (Hyper Text Transfer Protocol). Developers are free to write their own front-ends, or *interfaces*, into the Web, just as long as the protocol implementation is correct. These front-ends, or *clients* as they are known, are growing quickly in number. Clients exist for platforms such as UNIX, PC/MS-DOS and the Macintosh computers. As mentioned, the older WWW interfaces were all textual (telnet to `info.cern.ch` and log in as www to see one now) and relied upon the user to type references in from the keyboard in order to find the information and cross-references that were required. The new generation of Web clients are completely graphical, that is to say that they can be operated through the use of a mouse device and within a GUI (Graphical User Interface) or WIMP (Windows, Icon, Mouse, Pointer) environment.

One such application, *NCSA Mosaic*, has been termed the Internet's *killer application*. Mosaic is a navigational tool that sits on your computer and allows the you to access the Internet through a series of mouse clicks. Images and sound can be pulled into your computer and played/viewed accordingly. Likewise, the you can follow links to other Internet resources with the simple click of a button. All in all, Mosaic is a very intuitive system that seems to fit in very well with the whole concept of the Internet.

Web traffic over the Internet grew by some 300,000% over 1993 with the advent of graphical browsers. Over 3000 Web sites now exist around the world, and growth is expected to be exponential in the next few years. Ubiquitous GUIs such as Microsoft Windows and X-Windows have helped establish Mosaic as the *de facto* standard in graphical Web browsers. As such, Mosaic makes up a large part of this book (although extra coverage is also given to some other popular browsers, such as Cello).

So now you know what the Web and the Internet are and how they are linked together, you may think that's all there is to it. Unfortunately, nothing in life is this simple. Although the Web offers one of the most straightforward ways of publishing on the Internet there is still the *language* of the Web to be learned, i.e. the language that describes how a published document will look through a client browser such as Mosaic. Then, of course, there are other concepts to be learned, such as improving your technique, being resourceful, and getting your work published and publicized. Publishing, ultimately, is all about being creative. Attractive looking Web documents will attract readers and will successfully promote your information. Standards are high on the Net, and this book will teach you how to achieve and even surpass such standards.

1.2 Who are Publishers and what is Electronic Publishing?

Put quite simply, *publishers* are people who make their (or others') work available to an audience, either for profit, or for no personal gain other than for the actual exposure of the work itself. The audience may be very large or very small. What isn't specified is the actual content of the information being published. The majority of published works are inherently paper-based, although there can be no doubt that electronic publishing is gradually encroaching upon our everyday lives. The entire text of many newspapers and similar works has been published on CD-ROM for many years now. The Internet *is* publishing: it has an audience and a method of publishing that is fast and efficient. Any user of the Internet can be a publisher. The most simple method of publishing on the Net is to upload a file to an FTP server so that other users may download the file at their convenience. This act would be classed as publishing if the work being uploaded did not belong to somebody else. To a certain extent publishing therefore implies that the work being distributed must be original. Ultimately, we must not therefore confuse publishing with distribution, even though the two are inextricably linked. Published works also imply some form of permanency, that is to say that they will stay on the Internet longer than items such as email or USENET postings, for example. *Published* works on the Internet include:

- Software (distribution by freeware/shareware authors) is unequalled on the Internet
- FAQs and RFCs (these are self-documenting texts about the *guts* of the Internet)
- All other Internet-works, such as Web pages, Gopher texts and authors' FTP files

Distributed works really include:

- Software not written by the person distributing the item(s) in question
- USENET and email postings (these stay in the system for a short period, although some are archived and original postings could be classed as *published* works, perhaps)
- Any other work passed over the Internet by non-authors

1.3 What is the Language of the Web?

This book is also concerned with a system called HTML, an acronym for HyperText Mark-up Language, which is a subset of an ISO (International Organization for Standardization) standard known as Standard Generalized Mark-up Language, or SGML for short. SGML is a standard that allows authors to define structures for documents (and different document types) and thus to develop mark-up languages to represent these various document types. HTML is the term used to represent both the document type and the language used to construct such documents, whether they be letters, reports or an entire book. HTML is not an *extended* version of SGML: rather it is part of the SGML framework. HTML introduces the concept of 'structured text'. The text for an entire document is marked up using items known as *tags*. Fundamentally, these allow the user to encapsulate parts of a document to change its appearance when viewed (or rather, *parsed*) on the screen by a browser such as the Mosaic program. Tags do much more, however; they can embed images and sounds into documents, as well as creating hyperlinks to other Internet resources such as Gopher, `ftp` and USENET. Learning HTML is a fundamental prerequisite to publishing on the Internet. Work has already started on a new *hypermedia* language called HMML, which will extend HTML's capabilities yet further. Chapter 2 teaches you all there is to know about the key areas of the HTML language so that you can start to write Web documents.

1.4 How can I Publish my own Work on the Net?

In order to publish your own HTML documents on the Internet it does of course make things much easier if you have an actual Internet account. Permanent Internet sites that can afford a dedicated Internet link to their premises can make Web documents available via the use of some Web server software e.g. NCSA's httpd server or the SerWeb program (see Chapter 4 for more information on NCSA's httpd server for Microsoft Windows). Web pages can also be made available via anonymous `ftp`, bypassing the Web's HTTP (HyperText Transfer Protocol) protocol entirely (browsers such as Mosaic mimic the user when initially logging-in to anonymous `ftp` site).

A problem for many users is that their Internet account is established on a *dial-up* basis, that is to say that a user dials into the Internet as and when required. Dial-up access is becoming the most popular method of accessing the Internet, and nearly all service providers offer access through protocols such as PPP (Point-to-Point Protocol) and SLIP (Serial Line Internet Protocol). Dial-up access is cheap, reliable and adequate for most users' needs. The most common dial-up configuration currently in use is the *sub-net* approach, in which customers have their own Internet sub-nodes using the service provider's machine as a base address, e.g. a subscriber to the service provider `demon.co.uk` could have a personal Internet address structured as `myhost.demon.co.uk`.

Renting and Finding *Web Space*

Many service providers offer their subscribers *Web space*, that is, hard-disk space on their Web server machine so that a person on the Internet can access your HTML documents and follow the hyperlinks that you have placed within them. It goes without saying that Web server software is abundant on the Internet. Nearly all (if not all) of the major service providers have a dedicated host for handling Web traffic (refer to Appendices A and G for many examples of Web machines). Renting Web space is a good alternative to running your own Web server since (i) it costs less – many providers offer cheap monthly rates; and (ii) it requires less experience and doesn't involve any considerable technical knowledge; HTML authors can thus get on with actually writing Web material rather than becoming embroiled in administrative duties.

Readers with dial-up connections can run their own Web servers using software that is freely available, although be forewarned that it can be expensive. The reason why is simple: phone bills. The cost of running a Web server via a dial-up connection can be very large, mainly because you have to provide a sustained TCP/IP connection into the Internet in order to allow access to the resources stored on your computer. Web servers must be accessible for long periods of time in order to allow people to access the information you are offering. Some service providers do provide *dial-on-demand* services, whereby the service provider's server will dial your own machine's modem if a request has been made to access your host, although this option can also be expensive to run. You could of course leave your Web server on-line for short periods at a time only; this would cut down your phone usage, although it will of course cut down access to many Internet users in the same process.

The only other alternative to all of these suggestions is to find some free hard-disk space (*Web space*) on an existing Internet host (i.e. not a service provider's machine). You may try mailing an administrator – use the email alias `postmaster` – to see if they would consider carrying your HTML documents. If the host does not run Web server software, i.e. software that runs the HTTP protocol, the chances are that it has an FTP gateway instead. FTP solutions are less elegant than using dedicated Web software, although they do work. Rather than accessing HTML documents using HTTP, the client places an FTP request for the file to be downloaded instead. As soon as the document has been downloaded the content-type of the message (ASCII, HTML etc.) will make the local client launch an appropriate viewer. If the file is in HTML format a browser such as Mosaic should read it into the current window in the normal way, and the file can then be read accordingly. I have even known people who have secretly uploaded their Web pages to a few Internet sites, and then advertised these accordingly. Given the vastness of the Net and the high level of administration involved in running an Internet host, many administrators simply never get round to checking the files on their machines. Then again, there are some hosts that want you to upload files, and contribute work, especially many of the new services that have started up. Look for non-profit-making organizations on the Net (they have a `.org` in their hostname), since these are often after contributions. Refer to Appendix A for a miscellaneous list of Web sites.

Some tips for uploading HTML material

If you have rented some Web space your service provider will doubtless inform you how material is to be uploaded. In the majority of cases, Web pages can be uploaded by traditional methods, such as FTP, and left in a directory area, so they that can replace your existing Web pages. Not many providers will get involved in lengthy editing sessions without a fee being levied, so any changes are best made by altering the document(s) in question and then submitting those that have changed in their entirety. Your service provider may have a routine whereby they will check occasionally to see whether any updates are required, and then install the new pages accordingly.

Alternatively, you may be allocated a *Web account*, whereby you can access your own portion of the server's hard-disk and then make updates as and when you require by uploading the required files etc. Remember also that your service provider's machine may run a different operating system. UNIX-based machines are by the far the most common for Web servers, and these have different naming conventions. Your HTML hyper-references will probably reference files that have the extension `.html` (in lower-case). Such an extension is not valid on DOS, and when you actually come to upload your files you (or the service provider) will alter the names accordingly (the names of the HTML files, not the URLs, that is). You will also have to ensure that any local `file://` resource-types are changed to `http://` so that you access the correct file on the Internet. Many HTML developers use `file://` as a testing mechanism with local files to check out various hyper-links and to implement *stub* documents – dummy documents with no content that are used purely for testing. Of course, if you do not have an Internet connection none of this will apply.

Publicizing your Web Pages

Publishing your work is one thing, publicizing it is another. In order to inform people that your service actually exists there are a number of ways to proceed. Firstly, have a look at the *What's New* Web page at NCSA. This 'advertises' many new services that come into being. NCSA's *What's New* URL address is

```
http://www.ncsa.uiuc.edu/SDG/Software/Mosaic/Docs/whats-new.html
```

Alternatively you may want to place a message on USENET, the Internet's global *bulletin board* service, which many millions of Internet users read. USENET's main Web forum is named `comp.infosystems.www`, although details of any new services should be placed in the related group `comp.infosystems.www.announce`. The group `comp.infosystems.www.users` also discusses many aspects related to HTML/SGML and the Web. Announcements of new Web resources can also be found here occasionally. Finally, you may also want to take a look at the group `comp.text.sgml`.

Another useful medium for publicizing your work is via on-line catalogues. These services carry a wealth of information about other Internet information resources, and since many are Web-based they can also contain hyperlinks to the actual resource itself. Without your contributions these services would simply not exist. An excellent example of an on-line catalogue is CERN's WWW *Virtual Library*, whose URL address is

```
http://info.cern.ch/hypertext/DataSources/bySubject/Overview.html
```

CERN's Virtual Library has many hundreds of entries categorized into different subject groups. Take a look at the URL shown to see how to submit details of your own work. (If this URL fails, try entering just the hostname and browse your way through instead – this goes for all URLs of course). In most cases this will involve writing a smallish HTML file that will describe what you have to offer. The submission of mainstream information that is widely available may not be accepted; ensure that your service is different in some way, and put some thought into your HTML documents; use some interesting features, such as those shown in Chapter 2, e.g. Fill-Out-Forms, in-line images and *imagemaps*, so that your document catches the eye of the reader. Your local service provider may also advertise your Web resource for a small charge. If your Web resource appeals to a certain class of Internet user, browse the USENET hierarchies to see if there is a group specifically aimed at this user group. You can then place a small posting in the group telling people of its whereabouts. If you don't *advertise*, nothing will happen. Advertising on the Internet is a controversial subject at present. It seems that the commercial nature of advertising doesn't fit in very well with the Internet's non-profit-making nature (surely this must be *joke of the year* bearing in mind the killing being made by many service providers). In any case, dedicated USENET groups do exist for commercial advertising. All other advertising relating to *free* Internet services will not be flamed, i.e. criticized. Another excellent on-line catalogue is called *Mother of all BBSs* (MOABBS), which has amassed many hundreds of Web servers in recent times. MOABBS is indexed in an A–Z fashion to make browsing easier. Take a look at its URL at

```
http://www.cs.colorado.edu/home/mcbryan/public_html/bb/summary.htm
```

MOABBS also has many other hyperlinks to other information resources, search indexes and cataloguing software that you may want to examine in the future, but be warned: the Web is highly addictive and it can absorb a lot of time. Appendix G lists many other electronic catalogues that can be used for publicity purposes. Keep an eye out on USENET (`comp.infosystems.www.announce` etc.) for the latest additions to the Web, and of course to see which sites want contributions from people.

1.5 Tips for Web Novices

Two categories of people will mainly want to use the World-Wide Web: (i) *Explorers* – people who don't want to become embroiled in Web technology and who just want to use the Web as an educational tool and perhaps to conduct some personal research; and (ii) *Internauts* – people with sufficient knowledge of the Internet who not only want to use the Web to research information, but who also want to publish their own work and examine some of the underlying technologies that are at work. This book is biased towards the latter class of user, mainly because so much of what is going on within the Web warrants discussion and explanation. As one person on the Net put it, '*This is not Rocket Science!*'. In saying this, however, it does become easy to lose track of the Web's actual purpose, which is ultimately to provide information to the masses. Serious Web developers spend so much time, well, *developing*, that they hardly ever get the chance to read some of the material that has been published, or at least get the time to devote some time to this specific purpose (if you see what I mean).

The Web can be a more than a mouthful, even for the most experienced Internet user. The resource is very, very large and even an entire lifetime wouldn't be enough to examine every aspect of this massively protean resource. Novice users should really start by becoming accustomed with their client-browser (Mosaic or Cello etc.) – read Chapters 3 and 7 for details of both these particular browsers. Keep away from the Internet side of things until you understand your software, and only then attempt a connection.

Another problem for many novices is knowing exactly where to start. There is no *Web home* as such. You do not enter the Web and work your way through to some *end* point, since there is no *end.* That's not to say the Web is infinite – it isn't; it may just lead you around in ever-decreasing circles. NCSA's or CERN's home pages could be considered good starting points, mainly since this is where most of the Web development has taken place. Of course, you may want to find some specific information on a general topic, so an on-line catalogue would be a good place to start (see the end of Appendix G for a list). There are many excellent exhibits on the Web that deal with almost every aspect of human life (and not just computing!) from *Art* to *Zen-Buddhism*. Don't forget that you can also interface to any other Internet resource via the Web, so everything you learnt in my Internet book, *The Essential Internet Information Guide* (you did get a copy?) can be used.

CHAPTER

2

An HTML Primer

In this chapter you will learn how to:

- Understand some of the WWW's basic concepts, such as URLs
- Program in the hypertext language of the Web – HTML
- Import sounds, graphics and animations into your documents
- Create *hyperlinks* to other documents and create cross-references
- Create both hypermedia and hypertext documents

2.1 Introduction to HTML

Put simply, HTML (HyperText Mark-up Language) is a language describing the way in which electronic documents appear when viewed through a WWW client, such as NCSA Mosaic. The majority of Web servers on the Internet understand HTML, and the key to designing and publishing your own work is through a good understanding of the HTML language. The language itself is made up of a series of *tags* which encapsulate parts of the text in a document. The document has no structure imposed on it; it can be a letter, a report, a memorandum or even a book such as this. Other tags are inserted to pull in images and to create hyperlinks to other documents. All HTML files are ASCII, that is to say that they are entered as plain text. You must use an ASCII editor in order to create your HTML documents (MS-DOS version 5 upwards has the `EDIT` program as standard; the standard ASCII Windows editor is `notepad.exe`). HTML itself is a very small language, and as with most languages one can get by satisfactorily with just a smattering of the most essential constructs. HTML is not a page description language (PDL) like PostScript – it is concerned not with the printed page, but rather the *viewable screen*. Using HTML you set out the structure of a Web page as it will appear on the screen to the user. Items such as text emboldening, italicizing, image importation and cross-referencing are all set out in your HTML document. When a browser opens a Web page it parses each line to see how it should display the text. HTML is thus termed a 'mark-up' language, since its documents contain raw text as well as embedded commands that control the make-up of the page. HTML is currently split into three layers of development, each of which is slightly more enhanced than the layer immediately above it:

- **Level 1** HTML is mandatory for all Web clients, such as Mosaic. It handles the ability to create the most fundamental basic building blocks, such as hyperlinks, in-line images, and the most fundamental mark-up and text layout functions.
- **Level 2** HTML is a superset of Level 1. While the actual specification is still being refined within the parameters of the SGML standard, its main addition is the ability to handle *forms*. Forms allow user input to be entered into an HTML document, and Mosaic can safely handle such facilities (without too many GPFs – General Protection Faults, which sometimes cause Windows applications to crash). Forms will be used to allow users to send feedback to a host, and perhaps also to order goods and services and even to make credit card transactions (*secure* HTTP is being implemented for such critical and security-conscious transactions).
- Finally we have **Level 3** HTML, known as HTML+, which is really only a developers' language at the present time. It will include tables and figures and support for mathematical equations (including more complicated font support). HTML+ requires much more work and may not even be an extension, or superset, of earlier HTML layers. See Chapter 4 for more on HTML layer 3.

The Mosaic browser currently conforms to HTML layers 1 and 2. Layer 3 support will clearly become available in the near future. This book is mainly concerned with the first two HTML layers.

▶ TIP

1. HTML files created on a DOS system must have the extension `.HTM` to be read by the Mosaic browser properly (although this can be configured through the `mosaic.ini` file). Under UNIX, HTML files are normally referred to using the extension `.html`. Ensure that files moved from a DOS environment to a UNIX

environment are converted accordingly. Also ensure that the extensions are set in lower-case on UNIX systems.

2. Under DOS, the directory separator is a '\' (UNIX uses '/'). The separator used in HTML should use the DOS version, e.g. '\'.

Before creating your first Web page it is a good idea to examine how HTML actually formats its document. For a start there is no concept of a carriage return code in HTML (other than by explicitly asking for one using an appropriate HTML tag). Lines that are broken up by the pressing of the ENTER key will simply be ignored by HTML. A browser such as Mosaic will expand the line according to the current size of the Window. Codes such as paragraph breaks and line breaks must all be entered by hand. Free-form text is easily made into an HTML document, so starting with a plain ASCII file will enable you to get up and running immediately. A later section of this chapter examines some of the hyper-editors that are available to assist in the writing of HTML documents.

▶ TIP

When creating your HTML files in a Windows environment, open the Mosaic editor in one window and your editor in another. This will allow you to switch back and forth at speed to see how the latest changes to the current file look.

Use the reload icon:

on the toolbar to refresh the current HTML document that is loaded. Make sure you save your HTML file before refreshing in order that the updates can be seen. You don't need to click on the Mosaic window first; clicking on the icon will select the window.

Of course, you could run more than one text editor with a variety of HTML files to aid development. Mosaic is a large program, however, and is hungry for memory – opening more windows will make MS Windows more sluggish on a plain *vanilla* machine, e.g. a 486SX with 4 Mbyte of memory; a 33 MHz 486DX with 8 Mbyte of RAM is a better setup (in fact, more memory in any setup is advisable in order to stop Windows constantly swapping files to disk). Figure 2.1 illustrates the running of an editor and Mosaic side-by-side. Notice the reload icon (highlighted in the upper-left region of the screen), which should be used to update the Mosaic window as new text is added to the document being written.

Apart from using a standard ASCII editor for HTML development, novice HTML developers may want to use an HTML hyper-editor. Refer to Chapter 7 for more details on a range of such tools that are freely available on the Internet.

2.2 HTML Tags

The entire HTML language is made up of a list of *tags*. These encapsulate your Web page text in much the same way as you would add codes in a word processor to control the underlining and

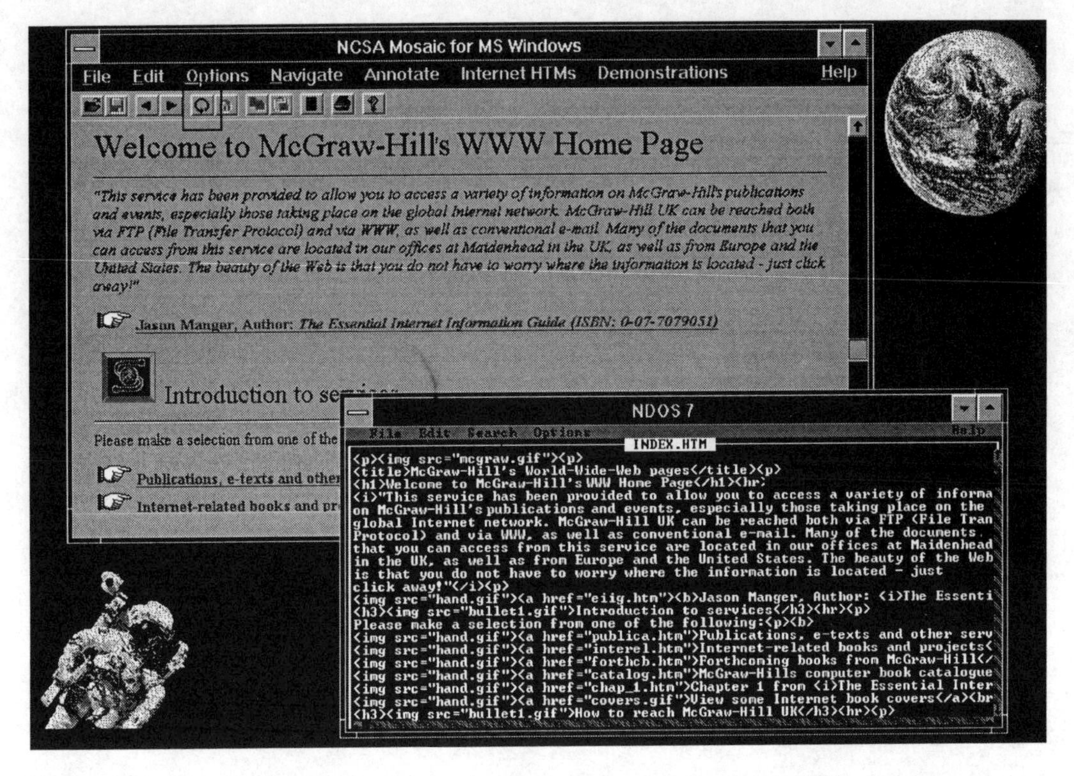

Figure 2.1: Running Mosaic and a text editor in separate windows during HTML development.

emboldening of text. Tags can be identified quite easily since they are strings of text with the characters '<' and '>' around them (left and right chevrons). Tags are used to break text into paragraphs, set out headings, and control emboldening and italicizing of text: basically, everything. All tags, with some minor exceptions, require a starting code and an ending code to tell Mosaic the area of text that we want to refer to. For example, the first part of the text below would appear in italics, and the second part wouldn't:

```
<i>This is in italics.</i>This is not.
```

In this small example, the `<i>` tag starts the italic text and the `</i>` ends it. Thus in Mosaic we would see the text as:

This is in italics. This is not.

Notice that all end-tags start with the characters '</'. Emboldening text, i.e. making text thicker to highlight it, uses similar tags, namely `<b>` and `</b>`. For more information, Appendix E lists all of the HTML tags in general use and provides descriptions of each.

And now to those exceptions: the tags that have no end tag associated with them. These are the end-of-paragraph tag, <p>, and the carriage return tag <br>. The <p> tag comes after some free-form text that you want to make into a single paragraph of text, so there is no </p> code in HTML. The other tag mentioned,
 (or break), simply inserts a carriage return at the point where the tag is mentioned. This can be used to break lines up within a document.

Finally, what about the case of each tag? Luckily, HTML doesn't mind if you use upper-case or lower-case (or even a combination of both) to make tags. Thus <I> and <i> will achieve the same effect, in this case to enable italic text.

2.3 Home Pages

When creating your HTML files bear in mind that the special name `index.htm` (or `index.html` on UNIX) should be used to contain your main HTML document. This *main* document is known as a *home page* and this will be the root document from which all your other HTML documents will be called. Your home page will be the first page that a user will see, so it is nearly always an index to other documents and services. Mosaic will load the HTML file `index.htm` by default (if the default isn't altered, that is). Web servers on the Internet use a variety of names for home pages, although `index.htm` is most common. The initialization file `mosaic.ini` can be manipulated to change the name of your home page. The line in the file:

```
Home-page=file:index.htm
```

shows you the current name in use. The string `file:` on the front of the filename is used by the HTTP protocol to identify either a local file or a remote file (in the case of the latter, an FTP file that resides on another Internet host), as will be explained later in this chapter. You can omit the `file:` prefix in the `mosaic.ini` file if you wish: Mosaic will assume that the file is local, i.e. that it resides on your own hard disk. HTML files that are remote generally start with `http:`, which is basically a request to use the HTTP protocol to download an HTML document to your local machine and then view it. A typical home page is shown in Figure 2.2.

2.4 Titles and URLs

All of the HTML documents that you create should have a main title – see the title of the home page in Figure 2.2 (in the *Document Title* field). Main titles appear in the Mosaic menu under the toolbar (and they can also be disabled from the Options menu in Mosaic). Such titles are used to identify the current document's subject coverage. If the title is to describe the root, or *home page*, ensure words to that effect are inserted. This will help the reader navigate around your hypertext document more easily. Titles are entered into the text between the tags <title> and </title>; for example:

```
<title>McGraw-Hill's WWW Home page</title>
```

will place the title 'McGraw-Hill's WWW Home page' into the title box (note that the 32 bit Mosaic

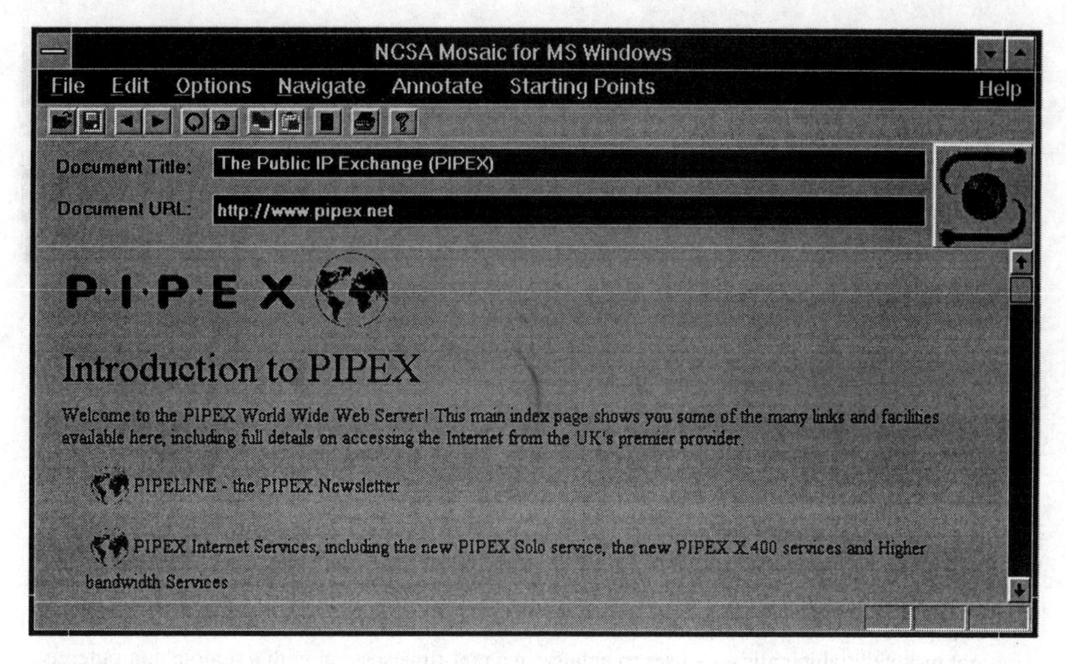

Figure 2.2: A typical home page (at `www.pipex.net`).

version uses the main window title, not a dedicated field). Only one <title> should really be used for a single HTML document. This makes some sense, because it is more logical to keep different topics of information in separate HTML files which can then be called up by the user. In addition, each HTML document should ideally be structured so that, upon entering it, it doesn't seem to have *followed on* from a previous page.

You could structure an HTML file into several different topics (like this particular chapter) with different sub-headings and then insert multiple <title> and </title> as required into each document. This is not advised, however. Mosaic works in such a way that HTML text is *parsed* (i.e. decoded) as it is read into the current window. Text outside the current window is not parsed until you actually use the cursor keys or mouse etc. to move further down into the document. If Mosaic reaches a second <title> construct it will override the original – but then it will not revert to the original if you move back to an earlier part of the text. In other words, the most recent <title> will stay in effect. For this reason it is always best to break your documents up into multiple HTML files, and then use different titles for each of these. When you return from one file its title will be removed and the previous one reinstated. The <title> tags should therefore ideally be placed near the top of a document.

What about URLs? Well this is a large topic, although here are the fundamental concepts. A URL (Uniform Resource Locator) is basically a way for the Web to specify where a particular resource is located on the Internet, while at the same time describing the tool that is required to access it and then finally specifying the actual file's location on a particular Internet host. Files on a local machine may be embedded within subdirectories and may exist on different physical disk drives. This is true of the Web also, except that all of this applies to a particular machine on the Internet, and there are hundreds

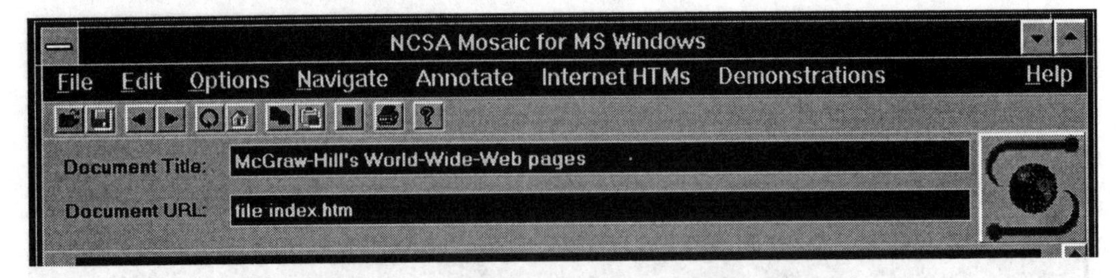

Figure 2.3: The Heading and URL lines in NCSA Mosaic for MS Windows.

of thousands of these. Each machine's file locations will differ widely, so URLs are used to identify where they reside. In general, URLs take the form:

```
resource-type://Internet hostname/path/filename
```

Many `resource-types` are now available, including `ftp:` for an FTP (File Transfer Protocol) server – the Internet's main method of moving files around on the Internet; `gopher:`, a tool for indexing titles from abstracts to allow searching on basically any topic; `telnet:`, the virtual terminal protocol, which allows a user to engage in a real-time session with a remote computer, e.g. an on-line medical database or a chess server; and `news:`, which is used to link into an NNTP (Network News Transport Protocol) to access newsgroups that are part of USENET. Other resource types will doubtless become available in time. URLs allow your document to link with other services and documents on the Internet, bringing a whole new meaning to hypermedia generally. In order to transfer an HTML document from a remote host the resource type `http:` is used. Thus the URL

```
http://www.ncsa.uiuc.edu/Mosaic/Demo/demo.html
```

refers to an HTML file on the Internet host `www.ncsa.uiuc.edu` which resides in the directory called `/Mosaic/Demo`; the file itself is named `demo.html`. A dotted-IP (Internet Protocol) address could also be used in place of a textual Internet hostname, e.g. `158.10.2.22`. Dotted-IP addresses are resolved more quickly in any event, so it can make sense to use them in URLs. On the downside, a dotted address won't of course give any immediate clues as to the whereabouts of the information being accessed. Constructs to reference URLs are discussed later in this chapter. Figure 2.3 shows a typical heading and URL line from the Mosaic program.

When accessing other Internet hosts, mentioning the name of that host's home page is optional. For example, specifying `http://www.microsoft.com` will load a default home page, as set up by the host's server software (server software is discussed in more detail in later sections of this chapter). There is therefore no need to mention the name of any home page in such cases.

URLs on DOS, UNIX, Macintosh and VAX Machines

URLs differ widely. Here are some things to remember. Firstly, UNIX and DOS use different pathname separators. UNIX uses '`/`', whereas DOS uses '`\`'. Any hyper-references that use the '`/`' character will be valid on UNIX hosts, however. The vast majority of the URLs that you will see use this character, since UNIX is the dominant operating system on the Internet. If you are referring to local files on your own machine, use the '\' character to abide by DOS conventions: more on this later. Macintosh users will know that pathnames can include spaces. If you include spaces in a URL each space must be replaced with a code `%20`. The percent sign indicates to HTML that a hexadecimal code follows. 20 (hex) is 32 (denary), and ASCII value 32 is a space. Most punctuation characters also use this hexadecimal notation when specified in URL strings. URLs on VAX machines are different only in that the directory pathnames do not use the separator characters '/' or '\'. Instead, the notation `DEVICE:[x.y.z]file` is used: for example the VAX URL `DUA0:[dir1.files]myfile.htm` would be equivalent to DOS's `\dir1\files\my-file.htm` (the `DUA0:` is a disk drive, the equivalent of `C:\` on DOS).

Another important point concerns UNIX and the tilde character. Some UNIX-based HTML pages on the Web are referred to using a tilde character (~) in the directory part of the URL. On UNIX , the tilde character is a short cut that refers to a user's home directory (it can even be used in UNIX's `cd` command). So for example `~fred` may expand to `/usr/home/fred`. Tildes in directory names shouldn't pose any problems for DOS-based browsers, since the directory expansion is done at the server's end. If your browser doesn't like tildes, simply use the hostname part of the URL (thus loading the system's default home page) and then navigate your way through to the page (this may not be possible if the necessary hyperlinks to the page(s) in question have not been provided, of course. As a rule of thumb, always use a fully qualified pathname to all external HTML files.

One particularly annoying habit of many pages on the Web is the reliance on URL *base addresses*. Many HTML authors provide cut-down versions of URLs that include only the directory location of various files. Browsers such as Mosaic know what hostname they are dealing with from the original URL specified, and therefore do not need to see it in any HTML files that they subsequently parse. If you ever come to save some HTML files to your local machine you may have a very hard time discovering their original locations on the Web, simply because the hostname part of the URL will be absent. This in turn makes the original documents useless, since all the hyper-references and anchor references become invalid. If you are authoring Web documents, always try to use fully-qualified URLs, i.e. those that include the hostname and filename path. Those that don't do this probably have access to their own Web server software via a dedicated Internet connection and are therefore referring to documents without using their own hostname (since, for them, its use is implied; users downloading such files will encounter all manner of problems when they try to load the original document it in order to access some other references embedded within it).

Local URLs

Mosaic can be used locally, that is, without making reference to any external Internet resource. If you are using Mosaic (or another browser) to access local files that exist on your hard disk, a URL of the form:

```
file:///drive|\dir\file
```

or:

```
file:\\\drive|\dir\file
```

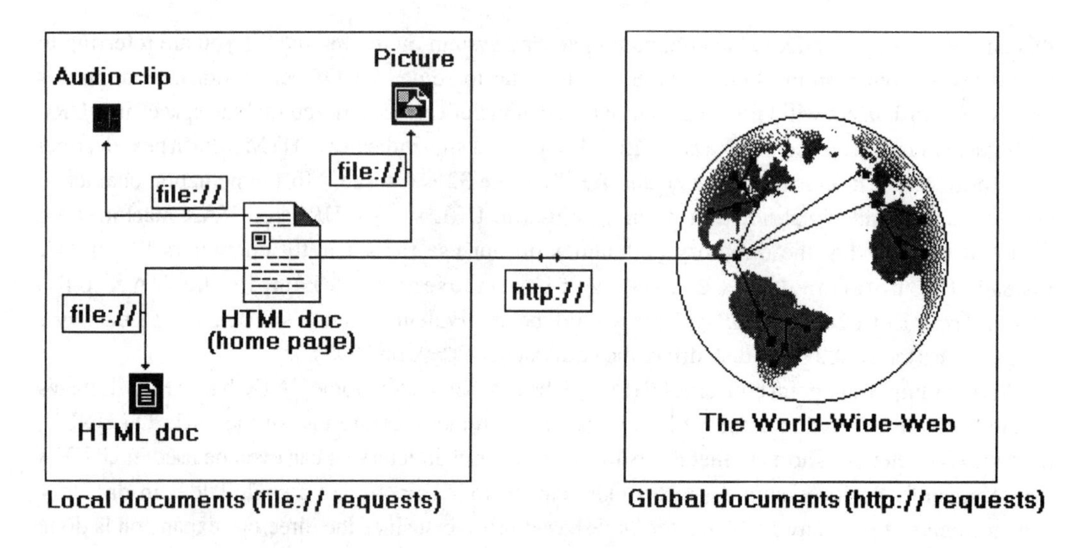

Figure 2.4: Local vs. global file requests.

should be used (note that the pipe character is used after the drive letter). For example, to access the file `index.htm` in the directory `\windows\mosaic` on the `C:` drive of a DOS machine, the URL below can be used:

```
file:///c|\windows\mosaic\index.htm
```

Notice the use of the '`\\\`' and '`///`' which are both valid for local URL references. If you use the '`/`' character in the directory path, however, Mosaic will almost certainly give an error, since this character is not valid as a directory separator under DOS (the '`\\\`' and '`///`' are purely Mosaic-based features).

A URL without any preceding pathname or drive letter is assumed to exist in the current directory, so if you are running Mosaic from `C:\WINDOWS\MOSAIC` and you specify a URL such as `file:myfile.htm`, Mosaic will try to locate `myfile.htm` from within `C:\WINDOWS\MOSAIC`. Figure 2.4 better illustrates the concept of local and global (remote) file request hyperlinks that can exist within a typical HTML document.

2.5 Entering Free-form Text

If you are a newcomer to HTML, one of the best things to do is create some free-form text, such as a simple paragraph, and load this into Mosaic to see what it looks like. Feel free to structure your text so that each line can be viewed within your editor: that is to say use hard returns to break each line. HTML ignores hard returns and will format each line so that it fits within the size of the current Mosaic window. This is done because the user has the opportunity to resize the window, and the text may look a bit strange if it isn't realigned after such a resizing. As a rule of thumb you can lay out your free-form text in any way appropriate, although clearly you will want to break your text up into paragraphs, and this is where you will have to learn some HTML constructs. For example, suppose we entered the following text into our ASCII text editor.

```
NCSA Mosaic is a client browser for the World-Wide Web.
It is a system that allows a user to create and
view hypermedia documents. NCSA Mosaic can handle
images, audio, and even motion video using its in-built and
third-party viewers. Mosaic also allows access to
many other Internet-based facilities such as
ftp, telnet and Gopher.
```

When read into Mosaic the text would appear (according to your window size) as basically:

> NCSA Mosaic is a client browser for the World-Wide Web. It is a system that allows a user to create and view hypermedia documents. NCSA Mosaic can handle images, audio, and even motion video using its in-built and third-party viewers. Mosaic also allows access to many other Internet-based facilities such as ftp, telnet and Gopher.

As can be seen from the result, all of the carriage return codes have been ignored and we have ended up with just a single paragraph of text. In fact, you could enter text with all the line-breaks and structuring you like and Mosaic would simply discard it, or rather HTML would. For this purpose HTML has provided a number of facilities for structuring Web pages, and these are now examined.

2.6 Paragraphs and Line Breaks

A paragraph of text is basically some free-form text followed by the <p> tag. Paragraphs also end with a single blank line. A paragraph can be:

- A single line of text
- A single sentence
- A group of sentences

Note that there is no </p> construct in HTML, so do not encapsulate your text with paragraph tags; simply follow the paragraph with a single <p>. Multiple <p> tags will have no effect. Only the first is taken into account when viewing. In the previous example we demonstrated how HTML joins up lines by ignoring the carriage returns. The <p> in effect inserts the return code that we require, forcing a blank line after the tag. Without using a paragraph tag your document will just be one big paragraph. For example, to see the following Mosaic text on the screen (with the paragraph breaks shown) as:

> NCSA Mosaic is a client browser for the World-Wide Web.
>
> It is a system that allows the user to view hypermedia documents. NCSA Mosaic can handle images, audio, and even motion video using its in-built and third-party viewers. Mosaic also allows access to many other Internet-based facilities such as ftp, telnet and Gopher.

you would need to enter the HTML text as follows:

```
NCSA Mosaic is a client browser for the World-Wide Web.<p>

It is a system that allows the user to view hypermedia documents.
NCSA Mosaic can handle images, audio, and even motion video using its
in-built and third-party viewers. Mosaic also allows access to many
other Internet-based facilities such as ftp, telnet and Gopher.<p>
```

Remember that the insertion of blank lines while in your ASCII editor does not matter. Use them by all means to lay out the text so that it can be understood in its raw form, but bear in mind its interpretation by HTML. The above examples will of course look different on your own screen, bearing in mind the size of the window that Mosaic is running in. An equivalent way of entering the HTML text for the above text is to follow on the text directly after each paragraph break. For example, we could enter the HTML text:

```
NCSA Mosaic is a client browser for the World-Wide Web.<p>It
is a system that allows the user to view hypermedia documents.
NCSA Mosaic can handle images, audio, and even motion video
using its in-built and third-party viewers. Mosaic also allows
access to many other Internet-based facilities such as ftp,
telnet and Gopher.<p>
```

which will achieve the same effect. The disadvantage of this method is that it is slightly more difficult to see where the various tags are placed (in this case the <p> tags) and of course the text does tend to get jumbled up into one mass of characters, with no obvious structure for the person editing the file. In my personal opinion, it is probably better to use the former method, i.e. insert the paragraph breaks as HTML itself would when the tags are interpreted. Both methods are equivalent, however. Another way of breaking a line mid-way is to use the tag `<br>`. This will break the line where the tag appears (exactly the same as a hard return) although it will not add a blank line afterwards. If you want to separate out items (without inserting blank lines in-between) `<br>` is the tag to use. Add a <p> on the final line where you want a final blank line to appear, if required.

2.7 Document Headings

In order to lay out your text as a book-style document, HTML provides different heading settings.

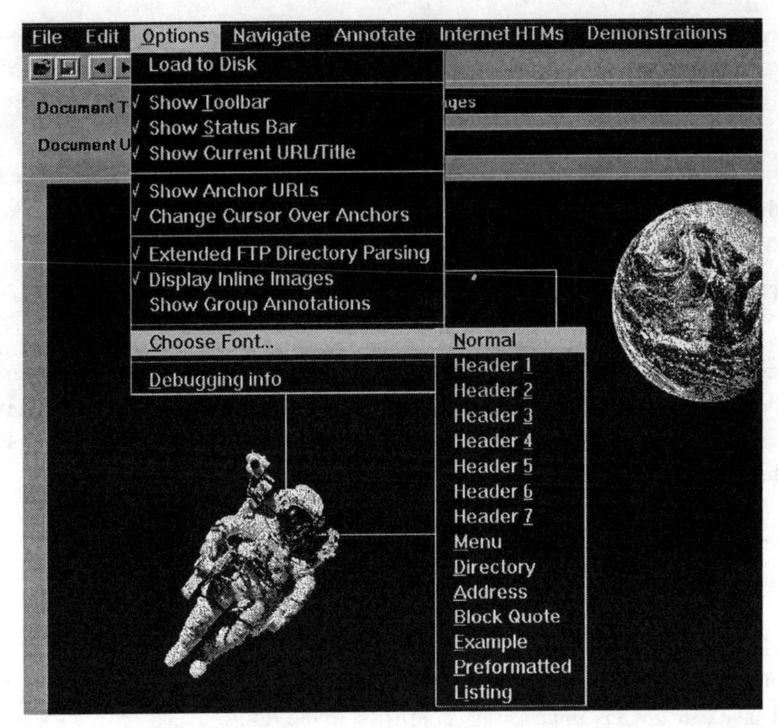

Figure 2.5: Altering Mosaic's headings through the Options menu.

These control the size of the heading text being tagged, and are used to identify the start of new chapter sections just as in this book (e.g. Section 2.7). HTML can use a maximum of six heading levels. In Mosaic you can control how a heading appears by using the Options menu. Figure 2.5 illustrates how the heading selections can be altered under MS Windows. Mosaic will alter its `mosaic.ini` file after any changes have been made. This method of changing the heading definitions allows you to choose fonts (which you cannot do from within HTML) as well as altering the size of the characters at the time. Mosaic provides seven different heading settings, as well as allowing you to alter how normal (untagged) text appears, plus a whole host of other font settings for menus and the like. Mosaic defaults to the Times New Roman font for all of its headings, with sizes starting large at 32 points for header number 1, reducing in size to 16 point for header number 7. Under HTML, the tags for specifying headings are structured as `<h`*n*`>`, where `n` is the heading number that corresponds to the settings in Mosaic, currently 1 to 6. An end-tag must follow after the end of the header text and takes the similar form: `</h`*n*`>`. As the number `n` gets bigger, the headings get smaller. Thus `<h1>` uses the largest font, and `<h6>` uses the smallest. Of course, you can change these to be any size you require. Back in HTML, the actual creation of the header couldn't be simpler. For example, creating an HTML document with the required text and tags could be structured as:

```
<h1>What is NCSA Mosaic?</h1><p>
Mosaic is a system that allows the user to view hypermedia
documents. Mosaic can handle images, audio, and even motion
```

```
video using its in-built and third-party viewers. Mosaic also
allows access to many other Internet-based facilities such as
ftp, telnet and Gopher.<p>
```

When read into Mosaic the text would appear similar to that shown below, with the heading clearly larger than the main text of the paragraph following it:

What is NCSA Mosaic?

Mosaic is a system that allows the user to view hypermedia documents. Mosaic can handle images, audio, and even motion video using its in-built and third-party viewers. Mosaic also allows access to many other Internet-based facilities such as ftp, telnet and Gopher.

Do remember to use the end tag for all the headings you create, otherwise your entire HTML document may appear in the same font as you specified for the header! The ordering of paragraphs and header tags should also be consistent. For example, `<h1>What is NCSA Mosaic?</h1><p>` is correct, but `<h1>What is NCSA Mosaic?<p></h1>` looks a bit strange, even though it will work without problems. Nest your tags properly, and in the proper order, and this will save causing any unnecessary confusion in the future.

▶ TIP

1. A carriage return is implied after a heading tag, so use of the `<p>` construct is not required in this instance. If you do insert a `<p>` it will simply be ignored by the HTML parser. Actually, this is not strictly true, since it depends on the parser. The Cello browser accepts multiple `<p>`s, but Mosaic will not.
2. Start with `<h1>`s and work your way down for each section and sub-section in your document. This adds more structure to the document. Don't be tempted to jump from one header to another out of sequence (it's not the *webiquette*).

And if you are thinking of nesting header tags within each other, don't. It doesn't work at all well in most HTML parsers. This is because HTML, upon encountering a new header tag, will immediately insert a hard return (like an implied `<br>` line break tag), and the end result will probably be that your heading will appear on two separate lines.

2.8 Creating Hyperlinks

One of Mosaic's most impressive features is undoubtedly its ability to link documents together using *hyperlinks*. Hyperlinks, or HyperText References (HRREFS) as they are also known, allow the user to click on an image or a word and then move to a new document, which has further information on the specific term selected. There are many possibilities to this: for example, a user could click on a postage stamp-sized image and call up a full-size version of the same image. Of course, the user may be calling up a local file, or perhaps a file that exists thousands of miles away on a portion of the Internet. With a fast enough modem, this will all be done very quickly, so the actual location of the file will appear transparent to the user. Hyperlinks are mainly used for cross-referencing information, and this section examines how one might go about this task using HTML. All hyperlinks in Mosaic are coloured red and are underlined, by default. Such settings can be changed through the Options menu (and thus in `mosaic.ini`).

Creating Hyperlinks to other HTML Documents

In order to create a hyperlink to another HTML document the `<a href>` tag (hyperlink reference) is used. The syntax of the complete tag that must be placed is as follows:

```
<a href="HTMLfile">LinkText</a>
```

where `HTMLfile` (inside the quotes) is the name of an HTML file, e.g. `chapter2.htm` (including extension), and `LinkText` is some text with which the hyperlink is associated. In Mosaic, this text will be underlined and coloured red (by default that is – it may be different on your own system) and clicking anywhere on these words will make Mosaic load the associated HTML file. Remember to place the end tag, `</a>` in this instance, at the end of the text that you want to make into a hyperlink. For example, we could have the following:

```
<a href="chapter2.htm">View Chapter 2 now</a>
```

In Mosaic this would resemble Figure 2.6.

Placing the mouse cursor over the hyperlink will (if not altered in `mosaic.ini`) change the cursor to a small hand, thus indicating that the mouse is hovering over such a link. Mosaic's status line (if active) will also change to show the user which file is being accessed. Many types of file can be viewed in this way, not only HTML files. The user could pull up an image or just about any other file for which a viewer was available. Viewers and other filters are discussed in more detail within the next chapter. Figure 2.7 illustrates how the cursor and status bar change over a hyperlink.

Selecting a hyperlink to another HTML file, assuming the HTML referenced exists, will result in Mosaic directly loading the file. As the file is being loaded Mosaic tells you its progress at the bottom of the screen on its status line. When launching a hyperlink into another document the document being loaded should ideally have the option of returning to the previous, or calling, document. This is done in much the same way with a `<a href>` tag, but we will alter the name of the HTML file so that we reload the previous document. This *previous* document may be your home

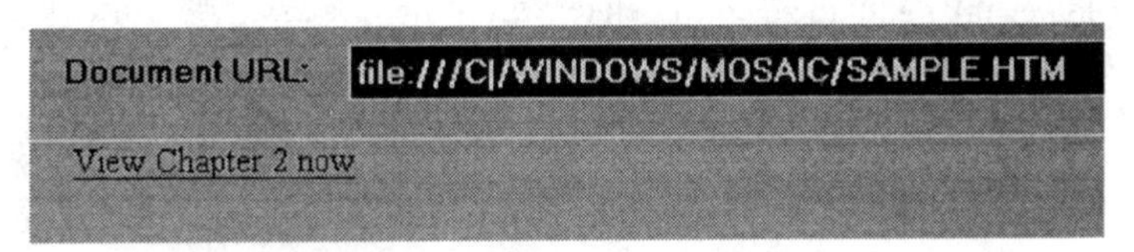

Figure 2.6: A typical hyperlink in Mosaic.

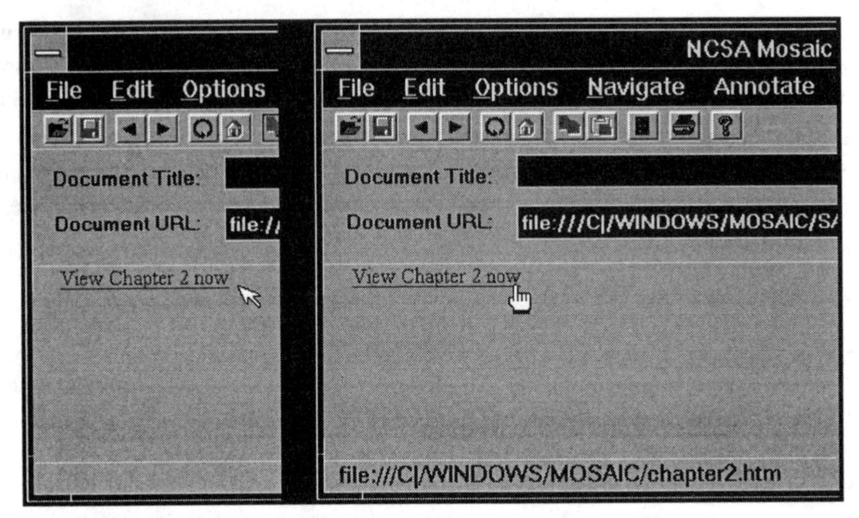

Figure 2.7: Hyperlinks in action (*left*: cursor away from hyperlink; *right*: cursor over hyperlink).

page, or it may not be – simply set it to the previous document that was loaded. When you have finished reading the current document, you can then click and return again; for example, at the end of the file `chapter2.htm` we could have the HTML statement:

```
<a href="index.htm">Return to home-page</a><p>
```

Of course, you can have as many hyperlinks as you require, perhaps creating whole layers of HTML documents and giving the ability to move to any document. Avoid over-complicating your documents if at all possible; two layers of documents should be sufficient for your needs. There are other ways of jumping around documents, using a similar method to hyperlinks known as *anchors*. These allow you to move around within an HTML document (externally also) by indexing various words and then jumping to them in the file.

▶ TIP

You may want to provide an icon for your hyperlink, to emphasize it more on the screen. Your collection of icons and mini-images will increase as you spend more time on the Web. Look to the Appendices for locations on the Internet that have such images to download (free of charge, of course).

In order to insert an icon (a small GIF or X-bitmap only) directly into your `<a href>` hyperlink, add the HTML statement `<img src="filename.gif">` before the `<a href>` statement for example:

```
<img src="hand.gif"><a href="chap2.htm">See Chapter 2 now</a>
```

So far we have only dealt with local HTML files, that is we have assumed that the files you will be referencing exist on your own local machine. If it is your intention to publish your Web pages on the Internet you will have to ensure that the URLs (Uniform Resource Locators) for all of your documents are included; indeed, you may want to reference other published works on the Internet and bring them into your document. The `<a href>` tag becomes much more powerful a concept when you specify URLs in your referenced filenames. Mosaic can reference a variety of different Internet information resources, including:

- Files on anonymous FTP sites (`ftp://` and `file://`)
- Files referenced through Gopher servers (`gopher://`)
- HTML files and images via a World-Wide Web server (`http://`)

In all of these cases you must specify the correct URL to access the file in question. For example, a hyperlink could access a remote HTML file on a Web server using a tag set up as:

```
<a href="http://some.where.com/HTMLfiles/
    index.htm>Internet Papers</a>
```

or a local HTML file could be accessed using a tag of the form:

```
<a href="index.htm>Load Home-page</a>
```

Accessing Gophers, WAIS servers, FTP sites, USENET and telnet-based services requires a bit more understanding, and is dealt with in separate sections later on in this chapter. One point you may like to note is that the HTTP protocol can be used to download many different file types, including in-line images (see next section), and not only HTML files. Chapter 4 deals with the topic of interfacing with other Internet resources in more detail.

Creating Links to Images

Apart from loading external HTML files, you may have a requirement to load an external image into a document. This is done using `<a href>` again, but with the name of the image in question. Handling external images is slightly more tricky than images that are embedded within an HTML document. This is because Mosaic can handle embedded (or *in-line*) images such as GIFs (Graphics Interchange Format files, first developed by CompuServe) and XBMs (X-Bitmap Files, as used by the X-Windows system for UNIX). What Mosaic cannot do, however, is load an external image without the help of a third-party viewer. Microsoft Windows is supplied with all manner of utilities, although a GIF (or X-Bitmap) viewer is not supplied. The `pbrush.exe` program that comes with Windows is only designed to handle native `.BMP` (Windows Bitmap files) and `.PCX` files and so cannot be used for other formats. Mosaic overcomes this problem by allowing the user to configure the `mosaic.ini` file so that an appropriate viewing utility can be used. A popular Mosaic viewer for graphic files is the *Lview31.exe* program, a utility for Windows 3.1 that can view all manner of graphics formats.

Viewers, as mentioned, are configured in the `mosaic.ini` file. If you edit this file, use an ASCII editor and look for the two sections entitled `[Viewers]` and `[Suffixes]`. The `[Viewers]` section has entries which resemble:

```
[Viewers]
TYPE0="image/gif"
TYPE1="image/bmp"
image/gif="c:\windows\mosaic\viewers\lview31 %ls"
image/bmp="c:\windows\mosaic\viewers\lview31 %ls"
...
```

where the `TYPE` definitions identify the various image formats. Following on from these are entries for each image format and a viewer that will handle them properly. If you want to be able to open a separate window for your images you must have a viewer that will work for that particular image format. Mosaic can thus handle any image type, and for that matter any document type in this way. Using this configuration you can load Windows help files (`.HLP` via `winhelp.exe`), ASCII files (`.DOC`, `.TXT` etc. via a suitable ASCII editor) and in fact just about anything. Remember that your viewer programs should ideally be Windows-based. You wouldn't want to exit to DOS momentarily in most cases since this will spoil the overall visual effect of your session, and of course you may corrupt the entire session in the process (exiting to DOS in this way can corrupt the Windows colour palette, among other things).

▶ TIP

1. If you must call a DOS application use the Windows PIF editor (`pifedit.exe`) to try to create a Windowed version of the program (i.e. a 'DOS-box'). This may not always be possible, depending on how the image manipulates the video display, but it's always worth a try. `NOTEPAD.EXE` is a good Windows ASCII editor.

2. My book, *The Essential Internet Information Guide* (McGraw-Hill) has a whole chapter devoted to image utilities available via the Internet, along with descriptions of their various capabilities and their location(s) on the Internet.

3. Never add a `TYPE`*n*`=` style entry for `text/html`. Mosaic may get confused!

As an example, we could structure an image hyper-reference as follows:

```
<a href="telnet.bmp">Load telnet image</a>
```

which would load the file `telnet.bmp` onto the screen in its own window (we could use `pbrush.exe` for `.BMP` images, of course although this particular program is an image editor as well as a viewer, so all of its functionality may not be required). Another advantage of a third-party viewer such as *Lview31* is the fact that it can handle compressed images such as `.JPG`s (Joint Photographic Experts Group). GIF (Graphics Interchange Format) can be handled by Mosaic as an embedded (*in-line*) image, remember. The advantage to external images' use of the `<a href>` tag is the fact that the time overhead for loading the image is taken at the discretion of the user. In-line images take time to load, especially if they are large or if you have a slow modem. In-line images are mentioned in the next section.

The other section of the mosaic.ini file mentioned earlier was [Suffixes]. As the name suggests, this area of the initialization file controls the interpretation of file extensions by Mosaic, and you must add these as required. On a DOS machine you can mention the extensions using upper- or lower-case, but on a UNIX box the case (and length) of file extensions is critical (UNIX users will have a .Xdefaults file etc.). Some typical entries in the [Suffixes] section may resemble the following:

```
[Suffixes]
image/gif=.gif
image/bmp=.bmp,.rle
image/jpg=.jpg
...
```

If an image can have multiple extensions, use a comma (,) after each extension and then place the next extension directly after it (use as many as you like in this way). Remember to start all extensions with periods (.). In the case that Mosaic fails to load an image when you click on an associated image hyperlink, check that the extension is correctly configured in the initialization file, and also that a viewing utility is correctly configured, i.e. that the path to it is correctly stated. Try to use fully qualified path names to all your viewers to avoid any problems. Mosaic will normally give a suitable error when a viewer cannot be found, or if its name is misspelled etc., although corruption in the [Suffixes] section can sometimes lead to it just doing nothing when a hyperlink is activated, simply because the extension of the file in the link is not recognized due to a spelling error. Mosaic may also try to load another viewer if it cannot find a correctly configured alternative.

Finally, a word about image sizes and compression. GIF images are already compressed to their maximum extent (look at the difference between a 256 colour BMP and the same file in GIF format for evidence of this), so they make good candidates for use within an HTML document, either as external or in-line images. JPEG compressed images can be handled if you have a viewer such as *Lview31*, and there are yet further space savings to be made with this option. As a rule of thumb, do not make your images too large; slow modem users may not even want to see the image, remember (and not all of us have V34 modems!). In general, try to make any larger images into hyperlink options, and only include smallish images such as logos and postage-stamp sized diagrams if at all possible. You could give the user a sample of an image by making a smaller version of it available as an in-line image, and then use a hyperlink to the full-sized version of the image. In-line images are discussed in detail below.

2.9 Inserting Images into a Document

External images are one thing. What about internal, or in-line, images? Well, as has already been mentioned, Mosaic has an in-built GIF viewer as standard (it also has an X-bitmap viewer), so images embedded within an HTML document will be expanded automatically, although you can turn off in-line image viewing using the Options menu in Mosaic. The <img src> (image source) tag is used to embed in-line images into documents; for example

```
<img src="telnet.gif">
```

will load the image named `telnet.gif` into the current HTML document. The file is assumed to exist locally within the current directory in this case, although images that reside on remote hosts, and in different directories, can also be referred to. This is done by using a URL in the filename, for example:

```
<img src="http://somewhere.com/images/logo.gif">
```

would make Mosaic load the remote image `logo.gif` at this point and display it in your HTML document. The images in this example have been taken from the Internet site `somewhere.com` and the file itself is located in the `/images` directory of the host concerned. Referring to images in this way is perfectly valid, although it may tend to suffer from the problem of file movement. Because the Internet is a dynamic entity, whose information tends to move about very frequently, be sure to reference images that are unlikely to move, such as some of those on the larger Internet archives and Web servers. If you run your own Web server this will not be a problem, since you will know that the file(s) in question will exist.

Another problem with images is the ability of the client browser to actually view them. Non-Mosaic users may not have a graphical capability, e.g. the textual World-Wide Web clients such as Lynx. Images cannot therefore be displayed, and an alternative arrangement should be made. This alternative can be achieved using the `alt="text"` attribute to allow some alternative text to be displayed instead of the image, for example:

```
<img src="http://somehost.com/gifs/phobos.gif" alt=
    "Moons of Mars: Phobos">
```

would display the text 'Moons of Mars: Phobos' in the case that the image cannot be displayed. This textual alternative does not apply to Mosaic if the in-line image capability is disabled from the Options menu.

Missing Images?

Images that cannot be found (perhaps because the URL is no longer up-to-date, or because the site is down) will be replaced with the Mosaic *Error logo*. This is a small, icon-sized image, which looks like

A similar icon with the word 'Image' underneath it is used when the display of in-line images has been disabled from the Options menu in Mosaic.

Image Alignment

The <img src> tag has three options to align text alongside the current image. These are the align=top, align=middle and align=bottom options, and must be used as follows:

```
<img align=top src="http://some.where.com/logo.gif">
```

that is to say that the words align=... must appear after the word img at the start of the tag. Top alignment will place any adjacent image text pushed up to the top line of the image, whereas middle alignment will line up the image and the text line so that all lines in a paragraph are equal. Bottom alignment places the text towards the bottom line of the image accordingly.

Making an Image into a Hyperlink

Hyperlinks have yet to be discussed, although you can think of them as tags that allow the user to click on a item of text and then be transported to another part of the current document (or to an entirely new document altogether) in order to reference some information. In-line images such as .GIFs (as opposed to textual strings) can be made into hyperlinks so that the user can click on them to move to an appropriate document, or even another image. To do this the <img src> tag is encapsulated by an *anchor* (to be discussed in Section 2.10) which allows the embedded image to be associated with another area of the current document (or another document entirely, as mentioned). For example:

```
<a name=myref href="#ImageAnchor"><img src="telnet.gif"></a>
```

You will now need a tag which looks like <a name="ImageAnchor> (no hash here, note) next to the area (or word/heading etc.) in the current document where you want to be moved to. If you want to move to another document precede the hash with the full document name, e.g. doc_b.htm#ImageAnchor. More information on anchors, specifically the <a name> tag is given below. Images can also be made into hyperlink URLs via the NCSA Windows httpd (a HTTP server) program, which can handle many different types of HTTP request. Using this system you can also create *imagemaps*, which allow different regions of an image to be made into a series of hyper-references to other documents on the Web.

Incorporating Image Animation Files 

If you have the necessary viewing software you can of course incorporate animations into your HTML documents. The main file formats in existence for animations are MPEG (Motion Pictures Experts Group) and AVI (Audio-Visual Interleave). Other formats exist for animations such as .GL, .DL, and .FLI, but not all of them have viewers for the Microsoft Windows environment. Appendix H lists many freeware and shareware animation tools that can be downloaded from the Internet. A significant problem with animation files is their size, especially because audio content may be embedded in the file (although MPEG commonly uses external audio files in many cases, and sound can thus be left out). Downloading small animations is no problem, although some of the realism of the animation will clearly be lost if it is very short. Large animations of decent quality, even those with as little as 150 frames, can be very large (typically over a megabyte). Many animations, such as

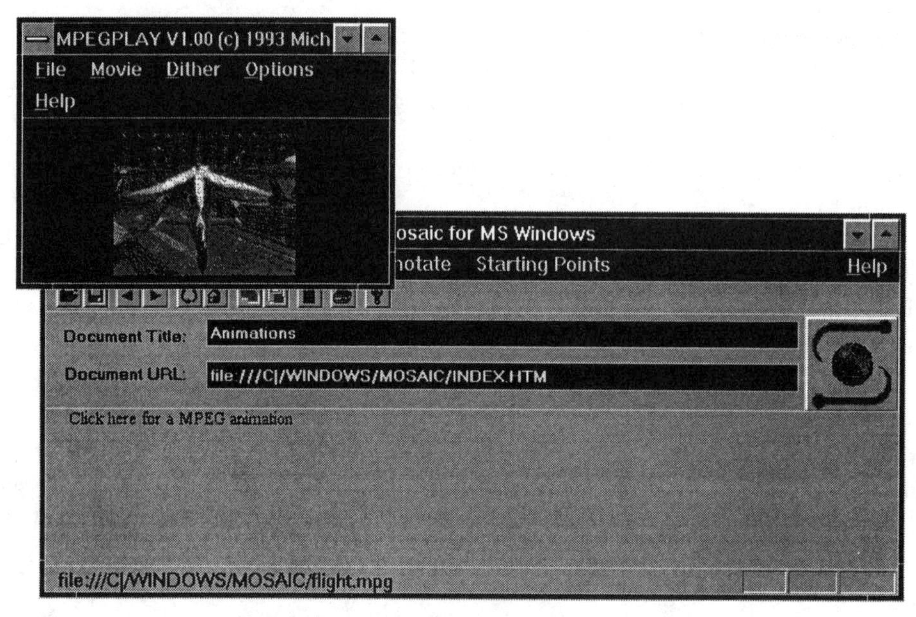

Figure 2.8: Mosaic and an animation running side-by-side.

MPEG, also require significant processor power to deliver realistic effects. Maximizing an image beyond its default size (320×320 pixels is not an uncommon size) can lead to a noticeable degradation in actual image quality.

If you are incorporating animations into your documents you will have to ensure that the appropriate viewer is installed and that the animation is referenced correctly in your URL (if the file resides on an FTP server use `ftp://` or `file://` etc.). Figure 2.8 illustrates Mosaic and the MPEG Player *Mpeg32w* running side-by-side. Animations run better from local disks since they can be loaded very quickly. If you intend to call remote animations (i.e. from an FTP or Web server) ensure the files are small, or at least warn the user that the file may take some time to download.

Refer to the appendices for lists of Web sites where animation files can be downloaded.

Creating Images for use in HTML Documents

A variety of tools can be used to create images, although Windows itself has no in-built support for the GIF format that Mosaic uses for its in-line images. To overcome this problem you can either find a GIF image editor, or use a GIF conversion utility (*WinGif* for example). See Appendix H for other alternatives.

▶ TIP

When creating images for Mosaic using the Windows Paintbrush program you can use the default palette's light grey colour as a background. This will ensure that images blend into the page, rather than 'stick-out' (assuming of course that you want the images to blend in). Images that blend in with the background are also known as *transparent* images. There is a utility on the Internet called `giftrans.exe` that will

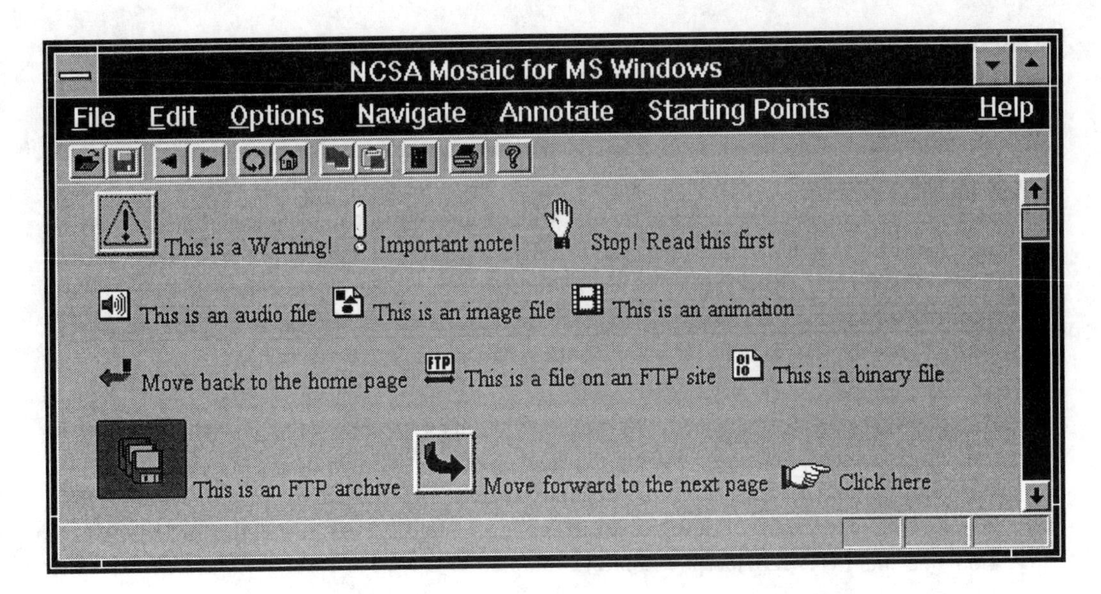

Figure 2.9: Some sample GIF icons for use within HTML documents.

also do this for you. If you use the Windows Paintbrush program be sure to have a GIF convertor at hand, e.g. *WinGif.*

Images themselves are abundant on the Internet. You may want to try FTP sites such as `ftp.funet.fi` and `wuarchive.wustl.edu` in your search for suitable pictures (using Archie with a sub-string search for '`gif`' will also find hundreds of files). The archives previously mentioned collect thousands of images (and icons) for use as in-line images. They arrive mostly in the GIF format (some are JPEGs, so make sure you have a conversion tool such as the ubiquitous `jpg2gif.exe` or `JpgGif`). When incorporating images into your documents, do so liberally. Bear in mind that many people will have slow connections and images can take a while to download. Smallish images are most attractive since they blend in with the text of a document. It is best to go on-line and take a look at a few pages to get ideas, since there is no universal way of laying out images within an HTML document. Figure 2.9 illustrates some of the GIF icons in use within Mosaic.

Windows 3.1 users can of course take screen dumps of icons and then load these into the Paintbrush program in order to make new icons and images.

2.10 Anchors and Cross-references

Anchors allow movement to specific words or titles (i.e. a specific text-string) within a document, as set up by the user (hyperlinks are mostly used to load a new document from scratch). Anchors are invaluable for indexing HTML documents, or for creating glossaries and of course cross-references.

By inserting anchor tags into your document at specific points (mainly after headings and keywords you want to index) you can click on an appropriate index term and then move directly to the relevant area of text that is associated with that anchor tag, even if it resides in another HTML document. In terms of indexing you would tag all of the words that make up the *index*, such as in a contents list or a conventional A–Z index. To create an anchor tag for specific entries the `<a name>` tag is used, as is now discussed in greater detail. Let us deal with anchors for local documents first. The initial step is thus to create an index to all of the sections of your document that you want to reference (that is, move to automatically). This is done by using multiple `<a name>` tags of the form

```
<a name=anchor-name href="#AnchorName">DescriptiveText</a>
```

where `anchor-name` is a unique name for each anchor tag, `#AnchorName` (with an initial hash) is the name for the anchor (an entry bearing the same name – minus the hash – will mark the entry that this anchor belongs to later on in the document), and `DescriptiveText` is some text to describe this entire index item. Be sure to use the end-tag `</a>` to delimit the entire anchor creation entry. Take this small HTML excerpt as a brief example:

```
<title>An HTML Primer</title>
<h2>Index of Contents</h2><p>
<a name=1 href="#FtpAnchor">FTP (File Transfer Protocol)</a>
<a name=2 href="#WaisAnchor">WAIS (Wide Area Information
    Server</a>
<a name=3 href="#TelAnchor">Telnet (virtual terminal
    protocol)</a>
```

On the Mosaic screen these entries will expand into just three lines of text, each of which by default will be coloured red and underlined. Moving the mouse cursor over one of them will result in the anchor name being shown on the status bar, and the cursor will also change shape to a small hand. Now comes the task of placing further anchor tags alongside the later sections of text which you want to jump to when the anchor is activated. This is done with the `<a name>` tag again, mentioning the name of the anchor (here, these are just numbers for the sake of simplicity). For example, if we had a section of a document concerning FTP servers, we could place an anchor tag for this entry nearby, as follows:

```
<a name="FtpAnchor">
<h3>FTP Servers.</h3>
FTP is the Internet's way of moving files around. It is also
the primary method of software distribution over the
Internet.<p>
```

In this small example, which is assumed to be a later part of the same document, the anchor tag inserted as `<a name="FtpAnchor">` relates to a section in a document on ‘FTP Servers’. This tag is not an event in its own right and will not show up in the HTML text. When you click on the anchor tag in the index at the start of the document, as shown in the first example, you will be immediately moved to this part of the document. As many anchors as you like can be set up in this way and you can move anywhere in the document at the click of a button on the appropriate index term. Whereabouts you place the index is up to you, although it makes sense to place it at the start (or at least near the start) of your HTML document, as a table of contents perhaps.

What about anchors to external documents? Well, this is very similar in concept to what has already been explained, in terms of documents A and B. First of all you create a link in the external document that you want to jump to when the anchor tag in document A is invoked (this will be the tag associated with the index or contents list etc.). For example, in document B we could have an anchor reference placed alongside some embedded text as follows:

```
<a name="FtpAnchor">
<h3>FTP Servers.</h3>
FTP is the Internet's way of moving files around. It is also
the primary method of software distribution over the
Internet.<p>
```

Back in document A we can reference this external anchor by using the `<a href>` tag along with some relevant text (perhaps an index, or just a quick mention to the keyword in question – which in this case is the FTP archive `wuarchive.wustl.edu`), for example:

```
There are thousands of FTP sites on the Internet. One of
the best FTP sites known is
<a href="doc_b.htm#wuarchiveAnc">Wuarchive</a>
which specializes in programs for the PC platform.
```

Clicking on the word 'Wuarchive' will activate the anchor and place the user in document B on the line with the string '*wuarchive.wustl.edu*' within it. The only notable difference with external anchors is therefore the addition of the filename (here `doc_b.htm`) and the insertion of a hash (#) after this filename in order to distinguish it from the anchor name. Anchors don't have to be associated with an index, or even a contents page of any description. You can place them anywhere you like to jump around between different parts of a document, just as shown in the example above. Anchors have the advantage over plain hyperlinks in that you can jump to a specific word, and not just to the start of a specific HTML document.

It is also useful to know how to get back to the original document after an external anchor has been invoked. In a local document, where the anchor is just moving you within the same document, you can use the scroll bar to get back to the original position. This of course is not possible with a newly loaded document since we are dealing with a totally different HTML file. If an anchor moves you to a new document, use the *move-back* icon (this is the left-facing arrow icon on the toolbar). This in turn will place you in the previous document. It goes without saying that using this icon for local tags within the same document will not work, simply because the icon only loads the most previous document, and in this context a 'previous document' does not apply.

This subject does deserve a little more explaining though. Many of the HTML constructs, such as `<a href>`, have additional attributes than can be used with them. For example, the `name=` attribute, which we have seen already, doesn't really need to be there at all. In fact this attribute is optional and its use is only required when you want to use the anchor tag itself as an actual destination link. This is very useful to allow the user to return to the area of text most recently called after activating the most previous anchor. For example, take the following HTML extract which uses an anchor within the same document:

```
<a name=myref href="#ImageAnchor">Move to anchor</a><p>

... Main body of text removed to save space ...

<a name="ImageAnchor">
<a href="#myref">Return back again!</a><p>
```

In line one of the above example we have created an anchor called `#ImageAnchor` using the `<a name>` tag as normal. The main body of the document has been removed to save space. The anchor's unique reference name is called `myref` and this has been used in the final `<a href>` tag, thus allowing the user to return to the most recent point before the anchor was activated. This can be useful if a document is large and you envisage that the users may not be able to find the point at which they left after activating the most recent anchor. The motto of this story is this: the `name=` section can be removed in all cases unless you want to use that anchor marker as a reference point to move back to. In such cases the anchor reference must itself have a name, so that Mosaic can identify it and move back to it. If you are using external anchors use the *move back* icon provided by Mosaic. This is much easier than writing another complicated tag, to say the least, although if you want to hard-code the tag simply use the normal routine, that is add the filename before the hash on the returning tag. Figure 2.10 illustrates diagrammatically the concepts behind anchors to local and external files.

Don't forget also that anchors can be used within URLs. For example, you could have an `<a href>` hyper-reference structured as

```
<a href="http://somewhere.com/html/intro.htm#Anchor1">
    Click here</a>
```

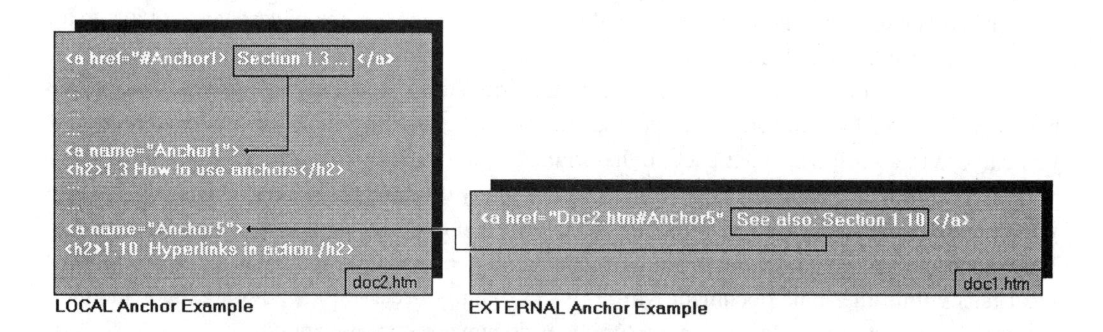

Figure 2.10: Local and external anchors demonstrated diagramatically.

This would insert the clickable hyper-reference '*Click here*', which when selected by the user would load the remote document `intro.htm` and then immediately jump to the `<a name="Anchor1">` entry within the document. If a named anchor does not exist Mosaic (or whichever browser is in use) will simply issue an appropriate warning message and you will be left at the beginning of the document in question.

2.11 Lists and Bullets

Apart from free-form text, HTML allows you to create both bulleted and numbered lists, which are useful for setting out lists of items within a document. For this purpose HTML provides the `<ul>` and `<ol>` tags, for bullets and numbers respectively. The individual items in the list must be preceded by the tag `<li>` (list tag) and the whole list must end with an appropriate end-tag. For example, let us assume we want to create a bulleted list that resembles the following:

- FTP servers
- WAIS servers
- Telnet servers
- Gopher servers

To do this we would have to use HTML's `<ul>` and `<li>` tags in the following way:

```
<ul>
<li>FTP servers
<li>WAIS servers
<li>Telnet servers
<li>Gopher servers
</ul>
```

Notice how the whole `<ul>` (unordered list) tag is finally delimited with `</ul>`. Note also that the `<li>` tag has no end-tag associated with it. In order to create a numbered list in HTML, such as:

1 FTP servers
2 WAIS servers
3 Telnet servers
4 Gopher servers

for example, we would use the `<ol>` and `</ol>` tag combination. Once again, the `<li>` tag identifies each member of the list, as before. For example:

```
<ol>
<li>FTP servers
```

```
<li>WAIS servers
<li>Telnet servers
<li>Gopher servers
</ol>
```

All that has changed in this example is the new `<ol>` tag combination. You should be aware that different browsers may alter the exact characters used for their bullets, such as hyphens (-) for example. If you want to change the size of your bulleted entries, simply encapsulate the entire list with an appropriate <h*n*> header tag (changing the size of the individual bullets is possible by including them in an appropriately sized header tag). Nested bullets of different sizes can also be attractive to set out contents lists and the like; for example:

```
<ul>
<li><h1>1. Section 1</h1>
<li><h5>Section 1.1
<li>Section 1.2
<li>Section 1.3</h5>
</ul>
```

This example uses different heading tags to alter the size of the list. You may want to tab in sub-sections in such lists, and although a smaller heading tag will do this slightly automatically, you should really use the proper HTML alternative, known as a *descriptive list.*

▶ TIP

Bullets can also be made up using an *entity code* of the form `&#ascii-code;`, where `ascii-code` is a numeric ASCII code, thus: `€`. This is a square bullet using ASCII 128.

Refer to Appendix D for a full list of HTML entity codes.

Descriptive Lists

Descriptive lists allow for proper formatting of listed items, specifically with reference to the tabbing of various list items so that they are nested correctly beneath one another. The `<dl>` and `</dl>` (descriptive list) tags are used for this purpose. In addition, the `<dt>` and `<dd>` tags are used to denote a major heading and a minor heading respectively; for example:

```
<dl>
<dt>This is a major heading
<dd>This text below the major heading is set
slightly in (like a tab)
so that the text sits slightly right
of its heading directly above it.
Text can flow on in this way until another
```

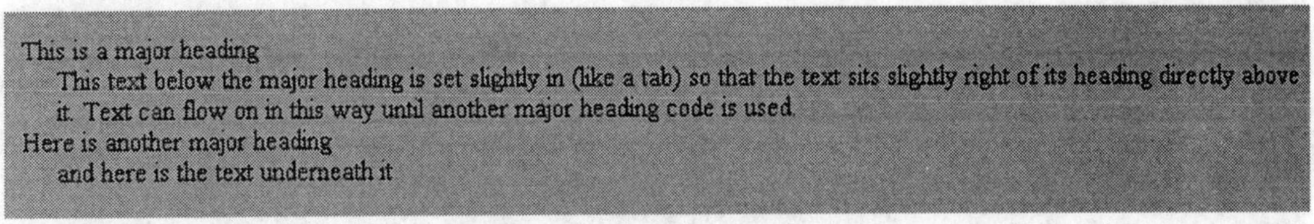

This is a major heading
This text below the major heading is set slightly in (like a tab) so that the text sits slightly right of its heading directly above it. Text can flow on in this way until another major heading code is used.
Here is another major heading
and here is the text underneath it

Figure 2.11: How a descriptive list can be set out under Mosaic.

```
major heading code is used.
<dt>Here is another major heading
<dd>and here is the text underneath it
</dl>
```

Figure 2.11 illustrates how this text would appear under Mosaic.

Descriptive lists can be spaced out by using some <p> (mark end of paragraph) tags after the last line of heading text. This makes them more readable: for example, we could quickly change our previous HTML sample to (note the two new <p> tags after the final line of the <dd> tag):

```
<dl>
<dt>This is a major heading
<dd>This text below the major heading is set
slightly in (like a tab)
so that the text sits slightly right
of its heading directly above it.
Text can flow on in this way until another
major heading code is used.
<p>
<dt>Here is another major heading
<dd>and here is the text underneath it<p>
</dl>
```

We can also add some bullets to each heading (major and minor) by using the <ul> tag, as shown below in a further improved example:

```
<dl><ul>
<li><dt>This is a major heading
<dd>This text below the major heading is set
slightly in (like a tab)
so that the text sits slightly right
of its heading directly above it.
Text can flow on in this way until another
major heading code is used.
<li><dt>Here is another major heading
```

● This is a major heading

◆ This text below the major heading is set slightly in (like a tab) so that the text sits slightly right of its heading directly above it. Text can flow on in this way until another major heading code is used.

● Here is another major heading

◆ and here is the text underneath it

Figure 2.12: Descriptive lists with bullets and enlarged major headings.

```
<dd>and here is the text underneath it
</ul></dl>
```

Going still further, we could use header tags to emphasize the major headings. For example:

```
<dl><ul>
<li><dt><h2>This is a major heading</h2>
<dd>This text below the major heading is set
slightly in (like a tab)
so that the text sits slightly right
of its heading directly above it.
Text can flow on in this way until another
major heading code is used.
<li><dt><h2>Here is another major heading</h2>
<dd>and here is the text underneath it
</ul></dl>
```

Figure 2.12 illustrates the final result, as viewed from within Mosaic.

▶ TIP

Mosaic has a style of text known as '*pre-formatted*' (use the `<pre>` and `</pre>` tags for this) in which all tabs and other white space are interpreted literally, i.e. as they appear in your ASCII editor. This style of text is normally used for program code, although you can change it to be any font you require by using the Options menu in Mosaic, thus allowing codes such as tabs to be kept and incorporated into your HTML files without the need for complex tag codes etc. Use preformatted text for all *computerese* text in your Web pages.

2.12 Incorporating Sound into your Documents

As is the case with images, sound is really just another file format. Under Windows the programs `soundrec.exe` (Sound recorder) and `mplayer.exe` (Media Player) are supplied as standard.

Many third-party sound players are also available from FTP sites all over the Internet. Your Mosaic initialization file (`mosaic.ini`) will tell you which utilities you have installed for various sound formats. The `.WAV` (wave) format is ubiquitous on the DOS platform, and is handled by default from within Windows programs such as those mentioned above. Other sound formats include `.SND`, `.AU` and `.AIFF`. If you are using full-motion video in your Mosaic application, i.e. an `.AVI` (Audio-Visual Interleave) or `.MPEG` (Motion Picture Expert Group, a branch-off from JPEG), sound may be included as a separate file so that it can be played in unison with the motion image. Again, the ability to play sound will depend on the utilities you have access to and more importantly the drivers that you have installed under Windows. Driver configuration is done from within the Windows control panel (`control.exe`) and from there within the *Drivers* icon.

You can play sound through MS Windows in one of two ways: The first is to purchase a sound card, e.g. a SoundBlaster or one of its many clones, while the second is to play all sound through the internal PC speaker. In the case of the latter you will find that some Windows programs, such as `mplayer.exe`, will still eventually require you to use a sound card. Some utilities, however, will play sound files through the PC speaker (`soundrec.exe` is a good example under Windows), so you could install this (it won't play the sound immediately though – it requires the user to press the *play* icon to actually let you hear the sound). Other third-party viewers may play the sound immediately, which is what you may require. The PC Speaker Driver is available free from Microsoft, and from the Internet via NCSA's FTP archive (see appendices). Look at your Mosaic initialization file's `[Viewers]` and `[Suffixes]` sections, for example:

```
[Viewers]
TYPE1="audio/wav"
TYPE2="video/mpeg"
TYPE3="video/quicktime"
TYPE4="video/msvideo"
TYPE5="audio/x-midi"
video/mpeg="c:\windows\mpegplay.exe %ls"
video/quicktime="c:\windows\player.exe %ls"
video/msvideo="c:\windows\mplayer.exe %ls"
audio/wav="c:\windows\soundrec.exe"

[Suffixes]
audio/wav=.wave,.wav
video/mpeg=.mpeg,.mpe,.mpg
video/qtime=.mov
video/msvideo=.avi
```

From this segment of the `mosaic.ini` file we can see that viewers have been installed for a variety of audio and video formats. Video has been included because sound effects are embedded within many video formats (the MPEG format can use external `.WAV` files separately, however). Applications such as Microsoft Video use the audio-visual `.AVI` format which encapsulates both sound and video in one file, so installing a sound format for this should not be required. If you are interested in playing simple sound clips, without any picture content, the simple rule is to ensure that a utility to play your file format is available, and all will work as normal. Be sure to add a suffix for the sound file in the [Suffixes] section. You may have noticed that some suffixes have been carried over from operating systems such as UNIX, which can support more than three characters for a file extension. If the sounds you get hold of are from the UNIX platform you may be able to get away with renaming the file, e.g. .wave to .wav. You can safely remove any extensions which are invalid on MS-DOS from your initialization file. The %lss after the program names are used by Mosaic to substitute a filename argument to the utility in question (not all utilities – e.g. soundrec.exe – accept filename arguments, however, so this must be a consideration when looking for such utilities in the future). Remember, viewers and audio players are not specifically written to run with Mosaic; rather they are written to run in a Windows environment. Mosaic only 'launches' the application to handle each specific file format.

Audio clips can be directly inserted into an HTML document by referencing them locally or remotely. If an audio clip exists somewhere on the Internet, use the <a href> tag with an http:// URL to access the clip, just as you would to access a remote HTML file. For example

```
<a href="http://www.nosc.mil/audio/birdsong.wav">Birdsong!</a>
```

would create a hypertext reference to an audio clip on the Internet site www.nosc.mil (the actual audio file is itself located in the directory /audio as birdsong.wav. Thousands of FTP sites carry audio files. Refer to the appendices for a list of the most popular. Some audio formats are designed for specific platforms, e.g. Sun, rather than the PC, although they can still be converted or even used directly if the correct utility is available through your local configuration. Embedded sounds, as with in-line images, are not yet handled by Mosaic at the time of writing (that is to say that you must have a third-party utility to play audio clips). In order to communicate to the user that an audio clip is available, it is worthwhile getting hold of a small *audio icon* image (must be an in-line image, and thus in the GIF/XBM format) to place within your HTML document. This can be anything you like, although the standard icon resembles:

In order to place this within a document as a hyperlink to an audio clip, simply encapsulate the graphic inside the <a href> tag, for example

```
<a href="http://www.nosc.mil/audio/birdsong.wav"><img
src="audio.gif"></a>
```

which will create the hyperlink, placing a blue frame around the graphic indicating that it is itself a hyperlink reference. This routine is more effective than using text to reference the image because the user can view the icon and thus immediately see that a sound is referenced. In our example tags above, the icon (audio.gif) is assumed to reside locally. This may not be the case, and if you are distributing Web pages over the Internet be sure to reference a Web server that has such icons (see the appendices for a list). This Web server may itself be a service provider who is providing hard-disk space for your Web pages, so in this case you would use their name in any `http://` URL reference, for example:

```
<a href="http://www.nosc.mil/audio/birdsong.wav">
<img src="http://www.demon.net/cyberco/audio.gif">
</a>
```

where `cyberco` could be your *Web account*, i.e. a directory on the provider `www.pipex.net`'s machine for your HTML documents, associated graphics, audio clips etc. All such names will be arranged beforehand with your service provider. Files can be *picked up* from most Internet hosts in this way – although a Web server is the most common method. Here is how you could structure a typical audio clip for use within an HTML document:

```
<h2>Audio Clips</h2>
A typical audio clip can be inserted into
a document such as this by
referencing a small icon to show
the user that a sound is available, and
then referencing the sound using a
hyperlink for example the Windows
<a href="tada.wav"><img align=middle src=
"audio.gif">fanfare sound</a>
can be played by pressing on this icon.
```

In Mosaic we would then see the text as shown in Figure 2.13.

If you are looking for an audio player that will play sound clips immediately, you may want to get hold of a utility called *Wplany* (Windows Play Any sound), which will do this for you. Apart from `.WAV` files, it also handles the `.VOC`, `.AU` and `.SND` formats as well, and it will play sound through the PC speaker if the Microsoft speaker driver is installed under Windows. Another popular utility you may want to use is called *Wham*. All of these utilities are available from the NCSA FTP archive (see the appendices for details of sites for such viewers) and from many other FTP sites on the Internet.

The sound quality of *Wplany* can be vastly improved if you edit your Mosaic

Audio Clips

A typical audio clip can be inserted into a document such as this by referencing a small icon to show the user a sound is available, and then referencing the sound using a hyperlink for example the Windows fanfare sound can be played by pressing on this icon.

Figure 2.13 An embedded audio-clip in an HTML document using a speaker icon.

initialization file `mosaic.ini` and change the `audio/au=` line in the `[Viewers]` section to the following:

```
audio/au=c:\windows\mosaic\viewers=wplany.exe -u -r 8000
```

Change the location of the utility to match your own settings.

If you have a sound card and microphone on your computer system you can of course record all manner of sounds and then and use one as an introduction to a specific document, or perhaps as an introduction to your home page. This is becoming more common on the Internet in an attempt at further *humanizing* documents, and of course to try to move away from the dominant text content of much of the Web.

2.13 Other Tags for your Documents

Now that the most important tags of the HTML language (in layer 1 HTML) have been covered in some detail, here are a few others that can be used to add some extra touches to your documents. Some of the tags in this section have been included to adhere to current mark-up practices, and for backwards compatibility with previous implementations of HTML. It is *webiquette* (that is, Web etiquette) that all HTML documents should ideally start and end with `<html>` and `</html>` tags, and that each HTML document should be broken up into *header* and *body* parts. This has been carried on from the SGML standard out of which HTML was born. The current practice on the Net is to use these constructs, so you may want to incorporate them when finally distributing your documents, although these are not compulsory requirements. Appendix E also lists some lesser-used HTML tags.

Horizontal Rules

The tag `<hr>` (horizontal rule) is useful to mark a horizontal line across the screen (the line is made as wide as the current window will allow). The tag has no end-tag associated with it, and is useful for underlining headings and for marking out different sections of an HTML document. Use it sparingly to enhance your document. For example, we could have the following HTML text:

```
<h1>Welcome to McGraw-Hill's WWW Home page</h1><hr>
Welcome to our World-Wide Web home page. This resource contains
the following information:<p>
...
```

The `<hr>` tag in the example adds a carriage return automatically, i.e. the next line will appear as the start of a new sentence. There is no need to specify a `<p>` (paragraph break) after an `<hr>` – it will be ignored by the Mosaic parser (other browsers may interpret it differently, however, e.g. *Cello*); the carriage return is implied in such instances.

Comment Tags

Comment tags are useful for embedding textual messages in an HTML file. The tag itself is ignored by Mosaic. Use comment tags to document your Web page and to provide details about any special facilities that are included in your HTML document, perhaps version details or author names. The tag takes the format:

```
<!--Some Comments-->
```

and the comment text itself can include white space and tab codes if you require. Use as many comments as you need in a document, although don't overdo their use at the expense of readability. For example, we could have the following single-lined comment:

```
<!-- index.htm revision 1.1 Author: Jason Manger-->
<h1>Welcome to McGraw-Hill's WWW Home page</h1><hr>
Welcome to our World-Wide Web home page. This resource contains
the following information:<p>
...
```

If you want to carry on a comment onto more than one line simply open the tag using <!--, place your text on as many lines as you require, and then follow this (either on a blank line or after the last line of comment text) with a --> end-tag to mark the finish of the encapsulated comment text, for example:

```
<!--
This is a comment that has been carried over
on to more than one line.
-->
```

Address Tags

It is customary for all Web documents to include the Internet email address of the author who wrote the document. Such addresses are normally placed at the end of the document in question. HTML provides the <address> tag for this purpose. While you could of course enter your address using some conventional free-form text, the <address> tag has a special meaning and can be used by the remote system to extract your email address. As an example we could have the following:

```
<address>Author: Fred Bloggs: fred@somewhere.com</address>
```

Note the use of the end-tag </address> to encapsulate the address details. Also note how some additional text can be inserted into the line, rather than just the specific email address by itself.

Header and Body Tags

A convention that is still used today within many HTML documents concerns the *header* and *body* structure of an HTML document. Many authors use the <head> and </head> tags to refer to an area of the HTML document which is known as the *header*. The header typically includes tags such as <title> and </title> and <isindex>, which supplies an input field for the user to enter a search-pattern when interfacing to a back-end program. On the other hand, the *body* of an HTML document is referred to as the place where all of the tags and actual text of the document are stored. This is encapsulated using the tags <body> and </body> respectively. You may also come across the tags <html> and </html> which encapsulate both the header and the body, i.e. the entire HTML document: these are used to indicate to the client program that an HTML-formatted document is being used. All of these tags are optional, although they are worth considering when you come to creating your own HTML documents to keep in with existing mark-up conventions. Here is an example document using the tags described:

```
<html>
<head>
<title>This is a search page</title>
<isindex>
</head>
<body>
<h1>This is a level-1 heading</h1>
This is some text within the body of this example document.
</body>
</html>
```

Entity Names

At some stage you may actually want to insert some literal HTML within an HTML document, e.g. for an HTML training document or tag-reference file. This causes some problems because the < and > characters in the tag definitions will be treated literally, leading to one mass of gibberish on the screen. To overcome this problem HTML provides a number of *entity* names that should be used for this purpose. These take the form of an ampersand (&), followed by a string of characters, followed by a semicolon. For example, the > sign is represented as > (greater than), and < as < (less than). So, to place some literal HTML tags into an HTML document you could code your text as follows:

```
The &lt;img src&gt; tag allows the
insertion of an in-line image, and this
can be encapsulated within a &lt;a href&gt;
tag to make the image itself a
hyper-reference to another document.
```

Many other characters, such as those from the ISO Latin-1 alphabet can also be included. Do not attempt to use ALT-key combinations to try to force ASCII characters into an HTML document: the result may not be what you expected. A full list of entity types can be found in Appendix D. You may also want to try experimenting with the &#*code*; tag also (where *code* is an ASCII numeric code) which allows ASCII characters (including some non-keyboard characters) to be entered directly into an HTML document.

Block Quotes

When inserting some text that makes up a quotation from another source (e.g. from a person) the `<blockquote>` and `</blockquote>` tags are commonly used. Text can flow freely in-between these tags. By default Mosaic uses the Times Roman font for all block quotes, but it is customary to use italics, so you may want to change the default from within Mosaic's Options menu. For example we could have:

```
A modern-day paraphrased quote:<p>
<blockquote>
A mouse in the hand is worth two in the keyboard(!?)
</blockquote>
```

To be quite honest, I haven't found much use for `blockquote` tags (as of yet), mainly since the same effects can be achieved using normal free-form text. Even so, they do have some potential I suppose, bearing in mind that Mosaic can assign a unique font to them. Expect block quotes to be dropped soon.

File Inclusion and Shell Commands

HTML also includes the ability to include external files and even the output of shell commands within documents. However, this feature is only really applicable to NCSA's httpd server program, which has been set up to handle these requests. These tags are thus non-standard SGML. These tags will most probably be dropped and updated as soon as HTML version 3.0 is gradually introduced to the user community. I refer you to the NCSA document

```
http://hoohoo.ncsa.uiuc.edu/docs/setup/admin/Includes.html
```

for more details on file-include tags. The tags themselves are:

```
<inc srv "pathname">
```

which inserts a file into the current HTML document (ASCII or ASCII HTML text only) (for example: `<inc srv "document.htm">`) and

```
<inc srv "|shell-command">
```

which inserts the output of a command into the current document, for example the date or time. On UNIX the `date` command can be used to incorporate the date and time into an HTML document, for example

```
<inc srv "|date">
```

But hold on a minute: all is not lost. PC-Mosaic users can also insert the output of commands into their HTML documents – see Chapter 4 for more details on enhanced DOS shells and returning HTML from CGI scripts. As mentioned, the tags shown above are likely to be dropped in favour of a new alternative, so their use is not really recommended.

CHAPTER

3

Using and Configuring NCSA Mosaic

3.1 Introduction to NCSA Mosaic

NCSA Mosaic is a navigational tool for use with the World-Wide Web, a system in widespread use all over the Internet. Mosaic is available on multiple computer platforms, including UNIX (the popular X-Windows version), Macintosh, and of course the IBM Personal Computer (PC) version, which runs under Microsoft Windows. This chapter is concerned with the Microsoft Windows version of NCSA Mosaic. Windows 95 (aka *Chicago*) will also run Mosaic as a 32 bit application, which should help speed things up considerably. The 32 bit version of Mosaic can be configured to run under Windows 3.1; for this to work you must obtain the Win32s program from Microsoft to upgrade

Windows 3.1, and of course a copy of the Mosaic 32 bit application. All of these topics, including the configuration of Mosaic's initialization files, viewing programs and filters, plus the configuration of the popular Trumpet WinSock package are all covered within this important chapter.

3.2 Installing NCSA Mosaic under Windows 3.1

Windows 3.1 is being superseded by Chicago (Windows 4) as I write, although it goes without saying that there will still be a considerable number of Windows 3.1 users who will still not upgrade. The differences between Windows 3.1 and 4 basically concern performance. The latest version of Mosaic is a 32 bit application which runs under Windows 4 without any problem. Windows 3.1 users may not be able to find the 16 bit version, since, as mentioned, Mosaic has been upgraded. If you are a Windows 3.1 user with a 32 bit copy of Mosaic you will need to get hold of Microsoft's Win32s software, which allows 32 bit applications to be executed. Both Microsoft's and NCSA's FTP server have the software (see the appendices, and below). The first step is of course to install Mosaic and configure the program for optimal use, and this is now discussed in detail.

Installing the Mosaic Program

Mosaic is made up of a series of files that normally arrive as a compressed archive, commonly a `.ZIP` (PKZIP) file on the PC platform. In order to process the file you must decompress the archive using an appropriate utility. PKZIP, and its partner PKUNZIP, which decompresses files, are available on NCSA's FTP site for downloading if you don't have a copy, and, needless to say, the Internet is crammed full of other sites that have this utility. You may want to use a tool such as Archie to search for the string 'pkzip' to find other sources. When decompressing, make sure that you have created a separate directory for Mosaic (don't de-archive the file into the `\WINDOWS` or `\WINDOWS\SYSTEM` directories since you will find it very hard to distinguish which files belong to which program). We suggest that you create a directory called `\WINDOWS\MOSAIC`. Since Mosaic does not come with a setup program, you must carry out the installation manually. The files that you will eventually install will include:

- The Mosaic system itself (the main `.EXE` executable, and DLL files etc.)
- A Windows socket DLL, e.g. the ever popular Trumpet WinSock
- Viewers and filters to allow you to handle text, sound, images etc.
- Optional extras: Win32s (32 bit Mosaic), NCSA httpd HTTP server etc.

If you have not yet installed Windows, do so first. Windows has a very good installation program which will guide you on your way. Assuming you have Windows 3.1 installed make the following directories using the DOS commands outlined below (Mosaic doesn't care what you call them, although you may want to keep to my example). All user input is shown in bold type, and the DOS prompt is the `C:>`:

```
C:\> MD C:\WINDOWS\MOSAIC
C:\> MD C:\WINDOWS\MOSAIC\VIEWERS
```

Two directories have now been created. If you already have a copy of Mosaic you can proceed as below; otherwise you will have to get hold of Mosaic from the Internet. Mosaic is supplied commercially, although its main distribution point is via the Internet. The subsequent installation will load Mosaic's main files into the first directory mentioned. Do this using the DOS command below. I am assuming your Mosaic archive is called `WMOSV2A6.ZIP` (the name will alter according to the version, so alter this name accordingly):

```
C:\> COPY MOSAIC.ZIP C:\WINDOWS\MOSAIC
C:\> PKUNZIP WMOSA6.ZIP
... Mosaic files are now dearchived ...
C:\> DEL MOSAIC.ZIP
```

The first command copies the Mosaic archive (which you have previously downloaded from an FTP site – see the appendices for details of where Mosaic can be downloaded from if you are unsure), while the second de-archives the files using the PKUNZIP program. The ZIP archive can then be deleted – after first being backed up to a floppy disk. Next, run Windows and create an icon for Mosaic. From the File menu select *New* and then *Create a new group*. You don't *have* to create a group window for Mosaics files, although it is recommended since other executables normally come with the Mosaic system, such as the WinSock interface (TCP/IP for Windows, basically) to be discussed in detail shortly, and of course all of your viewers and other filters that you will later accumulate. It is useful to create icons for these to aid your HTML development process. Figure 3.1 shows the steps involved in setting up a typical group for NCSA Mosaic.

Windows will now have a new group called *NCSA Mosaic* in which you can place all the files

Step 1. Create a new program group (Alt-F, N)

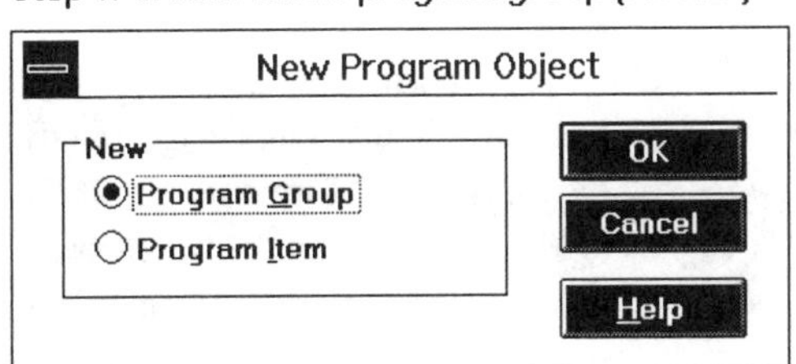

Step 2. Enter a name for the new group e.g. NCSA Mosaic

Program Group Properties

Description: NCSA Mosaic

Group File:

OK

Cancel

Help

Figure 3.1: Creating a new group and entering a group name under Windows.

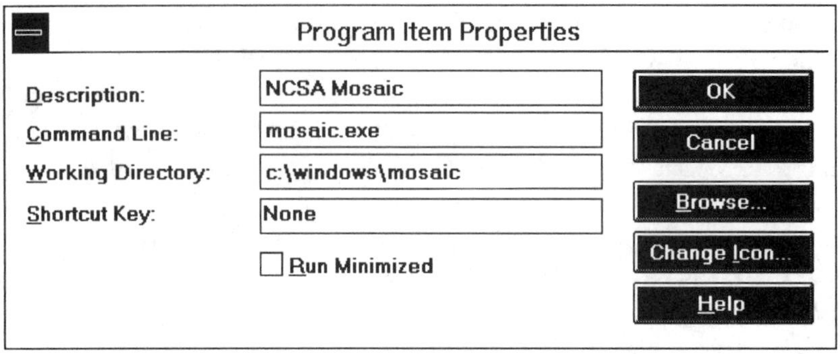

Figure 3.2: Creating a new group entry for `mosaic.exe`.

that are related to this system. The first step is to place Mosaic itself inside the group. Maximize the icon for this new group so that you can see the Window on your screen and then go through the same motions again to install a new file, although this time select the option to create a new file *item*, not a group. Figure 3.2 illustrates the installation of the Mosaic program `mosaic.exe`.

Be sure to specify all of the correct pathnames to the Mosaic program, as shown in Figure 3.2. If Windows cannot find any of the files you specify it will give a warning and you can then re-enter the details. At this stage you can also choose an icon for the Mosaic program. The `mosaic.exe` file contains three embedded icons, of which one can be used. Click on the *Select Icon* button to make a selection, or to see the default icon, or press ENTER (or click on OK) to save the current details. Figure 3.3 illustrates the icon selection screen.

After saving these details the Mosaic group window will have one icon, for the Mosaic program itself. You can repeat this exercise for all your Mosaic-related applications, such as communications tools (the WinSock program), and any viewers or filters etc. Figure 3.4 shows a selection of icons in a Mosaic group window.

You can now run Mosaic if you wish, although to avoid any immediate problems you should configure its initialization file first. Mosaic loads a default home page (an HTML file) called `index.htm`. If this is the first time that you have installed Mosaic it is unlikely that this file will exist, and this will cause a noticeable delay as Mosaic tries to find the file (Mosaic *resolves* all such filenames to see whether they exist locally or remotely, i.e. on another Internet site – the latter will

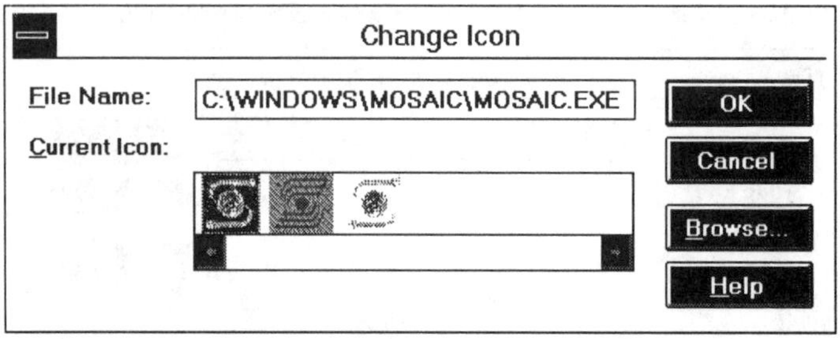

Figure 3.3: Selecting an icon for Mosaic.

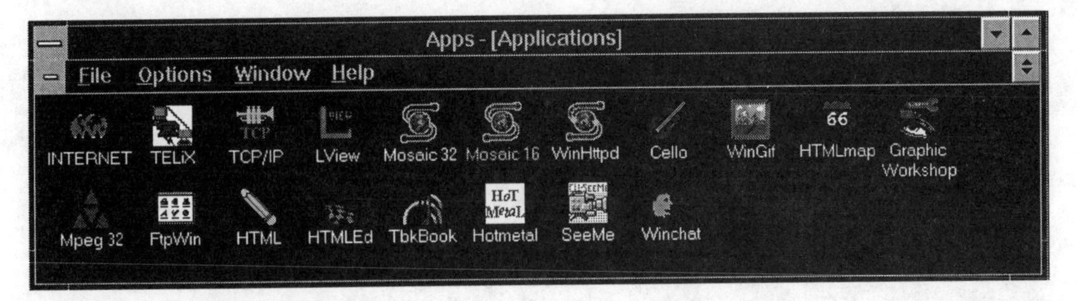

Figure 3.4: A Mosaic group window.

happen if the file cannot be found). Either create an empty `index.htm` file in the same directory as Mosaic or configure the initialization file first.

Configuring the `mosaic.ini` File

Nearly all Windows applications have `.ini` (initialization) files to allow for the fine-tuning of applications. Mosaic is no exception, and nearly every aspect of the system is configurable. The initialization file for NCSA Mosaic is called `mosaic.ini` and should reside in your Windows directory e.g. `\WINDOWS`, and not the Mosaic directory. It is likely that the previous installation phase placed this file in your Mosaic directory, so move it now before proceeding. You can rename the old file to keep a backup; this is important since you may want to refer back to the original file in the future, or even restore the complete file in case of corruption or loss. Also make sure that you edit this file using an ASCII editor. The `mosaic.ini` file is organized as a series of sections with headings in square brackets, for example `[Viewers]`. The main sections of the file are shown below. Differences between the 16 bit and 32 bit Mosaic versions are shown where required, although these are minimal.

- `[Main Window]` Controls the window position and size
- `[Main]` Home page details, your email address and bullet/ruler options
- `[Settings]` Colour of anchors etc.
- `[Mail]` Title for email feedback
- `[Services]` Your NNTP (USENET) and SMTP (email) gateway addresses
- `[Viewers]` The viewers and filters installed on your system
- `[Suffixes]` File extensions which relate to each viewing/filter program
- `[Annotations]` Annotations files (locations etc.)
- `[User Menun]` Customizable user-menus (1 to `n`) to refer to various Web services
- `[Document Caching]` How many pages for Mosaic to cache etc.
- `[Normal Font]` Fonts for headings and text etc.
- `[Heading1-7 Font]` Sections 1–7 for each heading: font details and effects etc.
- `[Menu Font]` Specifies the font used for Mosaic menus
- `[Dir Font]` Specifies the font used for Directory listings in Mosaic
- `[Address Font]` Specifies the font used for hostname addresses
- `[BlockQuote Font]` Specifies the font used for `<blockquote>` text

- [Example Font] Specifies the font used for examples
- [Preformatted Font] Specifies the font used for <pre> formatted text (program output)
- [Listing Font] Specifies the font used for listings
- [Default Spacing] Specifies paragraph breaks etc.
- [Hotlist] URL definitions for QUICKLIST menu entry (*32 bit Mosaic only*)

Within each section are a series of options that control the behaviour of Mosaic (such as setting various parameters). These take the form option=value, e.g. height=466. The following sections examine each section of mosaic.ini and explain the various options that can be used in each section.

[Main Window] Section

The [Main Window] section specifies the default size of the Mosaic window and its starting position (x, y intercept) from the upper left-hand corner of the window. The attributes that can be used in this window include: x, y, width, and height, where x and y are the intercept point of the window, and width and height represent the dimensions of Mosaic's main window. For example:

```
[Main Window]
x=12
y=12
width=798
height=466
```

If you re-size your window Mosaic will update these numbers only if you select the *Save settings* option from its Options menu.

[Main] Section

This section contains a series of options that control the loading of an automatic home page, plus the name of your email address on the Internet, while also specifying a colour scheme for Mosaic. In turn, the following options are available:

Email=*name*

This specifies your Internet email address in the format user@domain, e.g. fred@somewhere.com.

Autoload Home Page=yes|no

This makes Mosaic load a home page upon starting up if set to yes.

Home Page=*name*

Specifies the name of your home page, e.g. index.htm. This can be any name you wish, although if you intend to upload your pages to the Internet your administrator may have to change the name of your home page.

`Display Inline Images=yes|no`
: Determines whether or not GIF or X-bitmap images are displayed within HTML documents. Slow modem users could select `no` to speed things up a bit. Mosaic will place a small postage-sized NCSA image logo (entitled *Image*) to show where the image would have been placed had the option been enabled.

`Grey Background=yes|no`
: Most Web pages on the Internet have a grey background, although if this option is set to `no` a white background will be used instead. Most of the images and icons used on the Web are set against grey backgrounds, so you may want to keep this option set to `yes` in any event.

`Fancy Rules=yes|no`
: Mosaic can draw horizontal lines to break up documents using its `<hr>` tag. Specify `yes` if you want a more attractive line. The alternative is normally just a line of simple dashes.

`Round List Bullets=yes|no`
: Bullets can be displayed as rounded shapes or as dashes. The latter are used mainly for speed purposes, since rounded bullets take slightly longer to render.

`Current Hotlist=`*name*
: Hotlists have yet to be described in detail, although you can think of them as a user-definable list of Web references (URLs) which can be called up at any time, rather than typing them in by hand. Multiple hotlist files can be used, and the *name* attribute specifies which is currently in use.

For example, we could have a `[Main]` section configured as:

```
[Main]
Email="fred@somewhere.co.uk"
Autoload Home Page=no
Home Page=file:index.htm
Display Inline Images=yes
Grey Background=yes
Fancy Rules=yes
Round List Bullets=yes
Current Hotlist=MYLIST
```

If speed is your primary concern, consider the alternative setup shown below:

```
[Main]
Email="fred@somewhere.co.uk"
Autoload Home Page=no
Home Page=file:index.htm
Display Inline Images=no
Grey Background=yes
Fancy Rules=no
Round List Bullets=no
Current Hotlist=MYLIST
```

This alternative speeds things up by firstly by not loading a home page (although it actually may speed things up to include this home page if it is set to point to a frequently used HTML document – this will save users opening the document manually). The other options are configured so that bullets and rules are displayed as quickly as possible. In-line images have also been disabled – this is probably the most noticeable speed improvement within Mosaic.

`[Settings]` Section

This menu is mainly used to control anchor settings, principally their colour and form. The most common options are:

`Anchor UnderLine=yes|no`

As the name suggests, this option controls whether or not anchors (and hyper-references) are underlined on the Mosaic screen. Underlining helps the user to see which areas of the text are references and which are not. If your users have monochrome monitors be sure to enable this option (the next option below will not be relevant in this case).

`Anchor Colour=255,0,0`

This option controls the colour of anchors and hyper-references. The anchor colour may be set to any valid RGB (Red, Green, Blue) colour combination. The RGB values must be separated by commas and can range from 0 up to 255. The default colour is blue or `0,0,255` (Red=0, Green=0, Blue=255), where 255 is the highest colour intensity, and 0 the lowest intensity.

`[Mail]` Section

This section is used if and when you send email back to the NCSA developers (a feature to do this is built into Mosaic's Help menu). Use the option `Default Title=` to contain the textual message that should be placed in the `Subject:` line of the email message when it is sent back to NCSA, for example:

```
Default Title=Feedback on Mosaic
```

`[Services]` Section

The ability to link into USENET is made available via an appropriate NNTP news server address which is specified in this section. An SMTP server (Simple Mail Transfer Protocol – an email protocol widely used on UNIX and hence over the Internet) should also be mentioned, so that email can be sent to the appropriate server for distribution over the Internet. Both of these addresses can be found from your local service provider, although if you have some TCP/IP software already installed and working you should be able to glean the necessary facts from various configuration files (search for strings such as 'nntp' and 'smtp' for example). The options valid in this section are thus:

`NNTP_Server=`*`newshost`*

Specifies the name of an NNTP server, either in dotted-IP notation, or in the normal textual format e.g. `news.demon.co.uk`.

`SMTP_Server=`*`mailhost`*

Specifies the name of an SMTP server, either in dotted-IP notation, or in the normal textual format, e.g. `mail.demon.co.uk`.

Any valid server can be used for these options, although a more local server will benefit you more.

By default Mosaic specifies the NNTP server at the University of Illinois (`news.cso.uiuc.edu`). The SMTP gateway is used purely to allow users to send email back to the NCSA developers (by default this points to an FTPmail address – mail is sent via FTP, i.e. it is uploaded as a file), again at the University of Illinois (`ftp.ncsa.uiuc.edu`).

`[Viewers]` Section

This section is broken down into two subsections, the first of which contains a list of different file types in MIME (Multipurpose Internet Mail Extensions) format. The second subsection contains a list of viewers (or filters) that deal with each respective file type. These utilities are launched by Mosaic after downloading – after an FTP request for example. Entries in the first subsection take the form of a MIME code which is used to specify a file format:

`TYPE`*`n`*`="`*`media-type/file-type`*`"`

where *n* is an ascending number starting at 0 and extending upwards according to the number of file types installed. The `media-type` entries are varied and include entries such as `audio` (sound file), `image` (still image file, e.g. GIF), video (motion video animation) and many more besides, as shown below. The `file-type` entries also take many forms, e.g. `gif` (Graphics Interchange Format), `jpeg` (compressed image, perhaps a GIF) and many others which you can of course add to. The final MIME code could thus be structured as `image/gif` or `audio/wav` etc. Mosaic comes installed with many MIME entries, although the viewing utilities will not accompany Mosaic itself. Some standard Windows applications can be used as viewers, including `pbrush.exe` (for `.BMP` format images), `soundrec.exe` and `mplayer.exe` (for sound/animation), and `notepad.exe` as an ASCII file viewer, for example. Many others, which are resident on the Internet, are documented in the appendices .

The second area of the `[Viewers]` section specifies each MIME type again, as above, but an application (an executable program) is also named as the *viewer* for that particular file type. For example, we could have:

```
TYPE0="image/gif"
...
image/gif="c:\windows\mosaic\viewers\lview31.exe %ls"
```

where `lview31.exe` is an image viewing utility. The `%ls` after each utility allows a filename to be substituted and thus opened by the utility in question. All the viewers you eventually specify must accept a filename in this way in order that the file can be opened. Make sure that all pathnames to each utility are correctly specified, otherwise Mosaic will simply do nothing when you try to launch a viewer (if a mistake has been made in the pathname and/or filename of the utility, Mosaic will give a suitable error message). If you change any entries make sure you exit Mosaic and restart it to make the new settings take effect. Here is a typical `[Viewers]` section in its entirety:

```
[Viewers]
TYPE0="audio/wav"
TYPE1="application/postscript"
TYPE2="image/gif"
TYPE3="image/bmp"
TYPE4="image/jpeg"
TYPE5="video/mpeg"
TYPE6="video/quicktime"
TYPE7="video/msvideo"
TYPE8="application/x-rtf"
TYPE9="audio/x-midi"
TYPE10="audio/basic"
TYPE11="text/plain"
TYPE12="application/help"
TYPE13="audio/au"
application/postscript="c:\windows\ghostview.exe %ls"
image/gif="c:\windows\mosaic\lview31.exe %ls"
image/jpeg="c:\windows\mosaic\lview31.exe %ls"
image/bmp="c:\windows\mosaic\lview31.exe %ls"
video/mpeg="c:\windows\mosaic\mpegplay %ls"
video/quicktime="c:\windows\mosaic\player.exe %ls"
video/msvideo="c:\windows\mplayer.exe %ls"
audio/wav="c:\windows\mosaic\wplany.exe %ls"
audio/au="c:\windows\mosaic\wplany.exe %ls"
audio/x-midi="c:\windows\mplayer.exe %ls"
application/x-rtf="c:\windows\write.exe %ls"
audio/basic="c:\windows\wham.exe %ls"
text/plain="c:\windows\edit.pif %ls"
application/help="c:\windows\winhelp.exe %ls"
telnet="c:\windows\mosaic\trumpet\telw.exe"
```

The final entry for telnet is a special case. Mosaic can make telnet requests via a `telnet://` URL and Mosaic must be told which utility you want to use for such telnet-based activities. Telnet entries do not require a `%ls` argument.

`[Suffixes]` Section

The `[Suffixes]` section is used to identify the many different types of file extension (or filename *suffixes*) that work with the utilities mentioned in the `[Viewers]` section previously described. Each line of this file is a MIME (Multipurpose Internet Mail Extensions) code followed by a list of common filename extensions. Some file formats may have multiple extensions, so Mosaic allows you to specify as many suffixes for one particular file type as you want (each must be separated by a comma, and extensions themselves must be prefixed with a period). Each line of this section relates to the file types in the `[Viewers]` section. You should also be aware that Mosaic uses the very last suffix when writing a file of that particular type to your local hard disk, i.e. when an image or other file is downloaded and viewed. For example, we could have the two entries:

```
[Suffixes]
application/postscript=.ps,.eps
image/gif=.gif
```

which here refer to PostScript files and GIF image files. The first entry allows Mosaic to identify PostScript files by either a `.ps` or a `.eps` extension. GIF images always have the extension `.gif`, so we have inserted this definition also. You may find that some extensions are longer than the three-character limit that MS-DOS imposes. These can be removed – they will be truncated by MS-DOS in any event. A more extensive `[Suffixes]` section could resemble the following (remember that entries for each of these must also be included in the `[Viewers]` section also):

```
[Suffixes]
image/gif=.gif
image/jpeg=.jpe,.jpg
image/bmp=.bmp
application/postscript=.ps,.eps,.ai,.ps
application/help=.hlp
text/html=.htm
text/plain=.asc,.doc,.txt
application/x-rtf=.rtf,.wri
audio/wav=.wav
audio/au=.au
audio/x-midi=.mid
video/mpeg=.mpe,.mpg
video/qtime=.mov
video/msvideo=.avi
```

Entries in the above excerpt are given for the following files: `AVI` (Audio-Visual Interleave – a motion video file format used by Microsoft's multimedia player and by Microsoft's Video for Windows); QuickTime (an animation file format developed by Apple and now available on the PC); `MPEG` (Motion Picture Experts Group) – another audio/visual animation file format; `MID` – an audio file format used with music synthesizers etc.; `AU` – a common audio format used on many platforms such as UNIX and DOS; `WAV` – another audio format used extensively in Microsoft Windows; `RTF` (Rich Text Format) – similar to unstructured ASCII text files but with embedded text-formatting codes retained (also used by the Windows Write program); `ASC` – ASCII plain text files; `HLP` – Windows help files; `PS` and `EPS`, PostScript and Encapsulated PostScript – a page description language for printing documents; `BMP` – an image file format (bitmap) used by Microsoft Windows; `JPG` – taken from the JPEG (Joint Photographic Experts Group), an image compression standard, mainly for GIF images; and finally `GIF` (Graphics Interchange Format) – a ubiquitous compressed image format used on the Internet, originally developed by CompuServe for use on their system.

Many other file formats can of course be handled if you have the appropriate viewing software. For an in-depth treatment of image processing and file formats used on the Internet, see my book: *The Essential Internet Information Guide*, published by McGraw-Hill.

`[Annotations]` Section

Annotations are textual comments that can be attached to documents viewed by the Mosaic program, i.e. HTML documents. Annotations can be attached to local documents and to specific URLs. If, on your journeys on the Internet, you find an interesting resource, you can attach a comment file to the reference using the annotations feature of Mosaic. Two types of annotations are supported: (i) Personal annotations – these are saved on your local machine for reference; and (ii) Group annotations – these are saved on the Web server where you found the current resource, and any annotations made here are saved on an annotation server (currently the NCSA machine `hoohoo.ncsa.uiuc.edu:8080`) has been made available as default. When a group annotation is made to a specific URL, every future reference to that particular URL results in the ability to view the associated annotation. A number of attributes can be specified in this section, including:

`Directory="`*`Directory-Name`*`"`

Specifies a fully qualified pathname of a directory in which personal annotations are kept on your hard disk. This is set by default to `"C:\ncsa\annotate"`, although this can be changed to any valid *Directory-name* on your machine. Make sure this directory exists before using the feature, or else no annotations will be saved.

`Default Title="`*`Title`*`"`

`"`*`Title`*`"` specifies the title displayed when a personal annotation is created. This title is also inserted into an HTML document as a heading to your annotations.

`Group Annotations=yes|no`

Specifies whether or not group annotations are enabled. By default this is set to `no`. If enabled, any comments that relate to the current URL are highlighted and can be shown accordingly.

`Group Annotation Server="`*`Annotation-Server`*`"`

Specifies the name of a group annotation server where your comments can be saved for later reference. `Annotation-server` is initially set to the NCSA server `hoohoo.ncsa.uiuc.edu:8080`. This is probably the only annotations server in existence at the time of writing (`hoohoo.ncsa.uiuc.edu` is an experimental host for NCSA's programs, coincidentally).

Figure 3.5 illustrates the entering of an annotation through Mosaic's main Annotation menu.

Once an annotation has been entered and saved using the *commit* button, the text is written to an external annotation file (the directory location of which is specified in the `mosaic.ini` file using the supplied `[Annotations]` section). All such files are written as HTML text, so they will have an extension of `.HTM`, e.g. `pan-1.htm`. A typical `[Annotations]` section would be:

```
[Annotations]
Directory="c:\windows\annotate"
Default Title="Personal Annotations"
Group Annotations=no
Group Annotation Server=hoohoo.ncsa.uiuc.edu:8001
```

An example annotations file might be:

```
<ncsa-annotation-format-1>
<title>Personal Annotations</title>
<h1>jasons notes</h1>
```

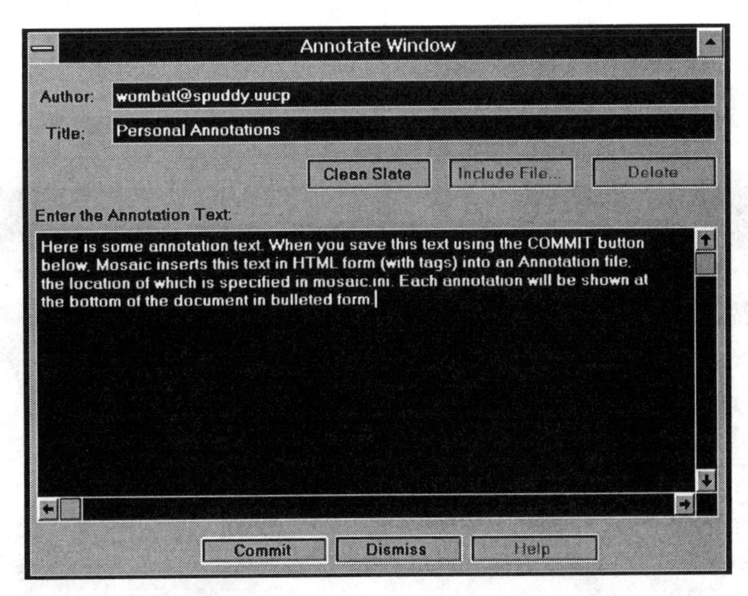

Figure 3.5: Entering an annotation within Mosaic.

```
<address>wombat@spuddy.uucp</address>
<address>Mon Aug 29 12:00:51 1994</address>
_______________________________________________
<pre>
Here is some annotation text as entered by the user.
```

The annotation file is structured as an HTML document with a title, and a header that is set to the value asked for in the annotations window shown in Figure 3.5. The title is taken from the `mosaic.ini` file, as shown previously. Mosaic inserts a date and time stamp for the annotation as well, along with a line separator and then some pre-formatted text that is the actual body of the annotation (notice how the `<pre>` tag is opened but not closed, indicating that all the text beyond this point will be pre-formatted. In order to update an annotation you can do one of two things: (i) edit the annotation file directly using an ASCII editor; or (ii) move to the page with the annotation and then click on the Annotations menu, when the annotation will be shown ready for editing. Figure 3.6 illustrates a Mosaic document and an example annotation. Mosaic places all annotations at the very bottom of the document in which the annotation was made. As new annotations are added to a document, a new bulleted entry is added to the current list of annotations. Mosaic makes a hyper-reference to each external HTML annotation file so that you can click and see its contents.

You may want to use Mosaic's reload icon after adding an annotation, since in some versions of Mosaic (16 and 32 bit) the annotation is not inserted until this is done. All annotations are saved so that when you next run Mosaic they will be inserted automatically. The source HTML document in which the annotation was originally inserted is not altered in any way. Mosaic maintains a log file (called `log`) that stores the name of each annotation and the file it applies to. This file exists in the annotations directory specified in `mosaic.ini`.

[User Menun] Sections

These entries are not really user editable, so do not modify any of the contents unless you are already proficient with Mosaic's menu system. Newcomers should use Mosaic's in-built Navigate menu and

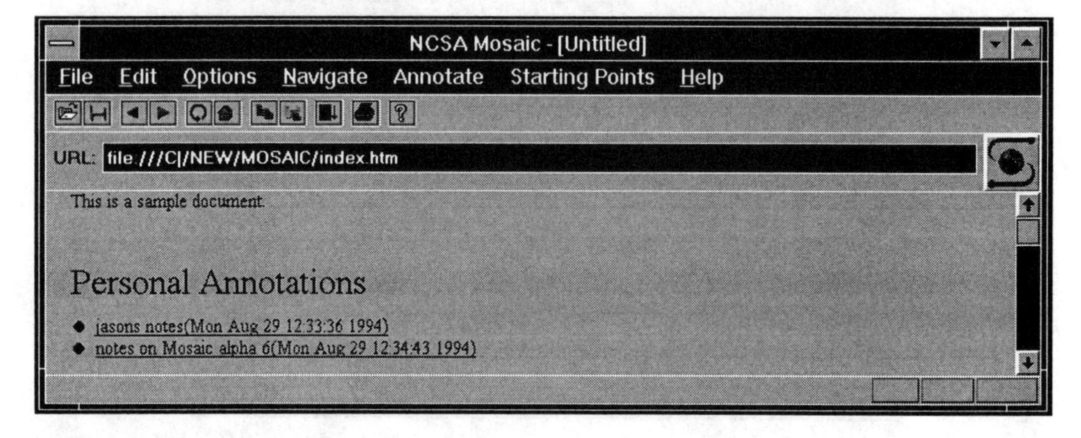

Figure 3.6: How a typical annotation appears within Mosaic.

choose *Menu Editor* to do any editing. Careful editing can be undertaken on some items if you understand the structure of the `[User Menu]` section. User menus allow the user to add new menu items to Mosaic's main system menu and include any URLs that they see fit. One or more menus for all of the URLs you use on a frequent basis can be added to do away with laborious typing sessions. Each menu has a section heading in `mosaic.ini` of the form `[User Menun]`, where `n` is a unique number for that menu (menu numbers should be sequential, e.g. starting from 1 upwards). Within each section, the following constructs can be used:

`Menu_Name=`*`Text-String`*

Specifies the name of the menu as it will appear in Mosaic. `Text-String` should not be enclosed in quotes.

`Menu_type=`*`Type`*

This entry tells Mosaic the level at which the menu resides. Menus can be structured into a hierarchical form. `Type` is most commonly set to `TOPLEVEL`, indicating a menu that exists at the very top of the menu hierarchy in Mosaic's existing menu bar. Mosaic allows the nesting of menus and we refer you to the section later in this chapter on editing Mosaic menus for an in-depth explanation of this facility, which also includes screen dumps of all the salient menus and options.

`Itemn=`*`Text|Type, URL|Menu-Ref`*

This entry can refer to a URL for a specific resource, or it can specify a nested menu that contains further resources. For a simple menu resource definition we could have an entry such as:

`Item1=Microsoft's WWW Home Page, http://www.microsoft.com/`

which would allow the user to click on the first item and then be connected to Microsoft Corporation's World-Wide Web server. Multiple items can be added – simply add an `Item2`, `Item3` and so forth for each resource. If a menu item is not specifying a URL, it must be specifying another user menu. Nested menus are specified using the following form:

`Item1=MENU, User Menu3`

In this case item number 1 in the menu is itself a sub-menu which points to the section entry `[User Menu3]` in the `mosaic.ini` file. `[User Menu3]` could be another series of URLs and/or further menus.

As a slightly longer example, consider the following two menus:

```
[User Menu1]
Menu_Name=Internet HTMs
Menu_Type=TOPLEVEL
Item1=Welcome to the Net,file:thenet.htm
```

```
Item2=History of the Net,file:history.htm
Item3=A Guide to the Net,file:guide.htm
Item4=MENU,User Menu2

[User Menu2]
Menu_Name=My Personal Menu
Item1=Connect to Gopher at info.brad.ac.uk,gopher://info.brad.ac.uk/
Item2=Connect to FTP site at Microsoft,ftp://ftp.microsoft.com/
Item3=Connect to USENET's Beer group,news:alt.beer
```

The first menu in this above example has four items, three of which are local URL references to files on the current machine which are assumed to reside in the current directory, and one of which (the last item) is a sub-menu that leads to the section `[User Menu2]`. This latter menu has three items, of which all are remote URLs to various Internet resources (an FTP server, NNTP server and a Gopher server in this example). For an in-depth explanation of creating user menus in Mosaic refer to Section 3.6. Now you know why it is not wise to alter menu configurations by hand: Mosaic can carry out this task much more easily, and quickly.

`[Document Caching]` Section

Mosaic requires a machine with at least 4 Mbyte of memory in which to run, especially if you are running in enhanced mode. When you open various Web pages Mosaic can cache some so that when you use the *move-backwards* or *move-forwards* icons (the left- and right-facing arrows on the toolbar) to load an earlier Web page the process will be much quicker, since the page(s) will be in memory – Mosaic will therefore not have to make a new HTTP request to fetch the pages from the remote Web server. The ability to cache documents in this way depends on the amount of memory that you have installed. If you specify too many pages, Mosaic will only cache as many as possible. Editable options that can be specified in this section include:

```
Number=nCache
```

where *`nCache`* is the number of documents to cache. To disable all cache activities, simply use 0 as an *`nCache`* value.

> **▶ TIP**
>
> Always try to use an actual disk caching program, such as SmartDRIVE, under Windows. Others are available, e.g. *Ncache* from Norton (Symantec). This will significantly increase the speed of Mosaic for all disk-based activities, such as the reading of larger files (for example in-line images).

Font Sections

Font control is widely customizable under Mosaic. The sections that can be changed include `[Normal Font]`, which refers to all normal free-form text, `[Headingn Font]`, which refers to the in-built HTML tags `<h1>` to `<h6>`; `[Menu Font]` which refers to the font used in Mosaic's menus; `[Dir Font]`, which refers to directory listings; `[Address Font]` which refers to email and Internet hostname addresses; `[BlockQuote Font]` which refers to text inserted using the HTML tag `<blockquote>`; `[Example Font]` and `[Preformatted Font]` which refer to computerese text (e.g. non-proportional fonts for computer program listings, email names etc.); and finally `[Listing Font]` a font used for item lists, one would assume. All of these font sections can be assigned whatever font you like through the Windows interface. A wide range of fonts are available from Arial through to Zapf Dingbats (✿ ✪ ✻ ❈). Simply open the Options menu in Mosaic and choose *Select fonts*. Windows fonts are described in the `win.ini` file under the `[fonts]` section. By default, Mosaic uses the Times New Roman font (TrueType) for all free-form text and headings. Fonts for computerese text are set in the `Courier New` (also TrueType) font. For example, a level 1 heading under Mosaic (using an `<h1>` tag) is defined by default as:

```
[Heading1 Font]
FaceName=Times New Roman
Height=-32
Width=0
Escapement=0
CharSet=0
PitchAndFamily=18
Weight=400
Italic=0
Underline=0
```

The most common and easily editable attributes are now described briefly.

`FaceName=`*`FontName`*

Specifies the name of the font used for this particular item of text. Font names can be found by using the Windows font control utility in the Control Panel or by using Mosaic, of course. Names have to be entered exactly, so watch out for spelling errors.

`Height=`*`heightnum`*

Specifies the height (point size) of the font. Notice that a hyphen (`-`) should prefix the value if only two digits (1–99) are used; therefore `-29` equals 29 points.

`Width=`*`widthnum`*

Specifies the width of the font. If left at 0, the default Windows value for the font is used. Increase the width to alter the appearance of the font within Mosaic.

`Underline=`*`UndNum`*

This setting specifies whether or not a font is underlined, as well as the level of underlining, i.e. the extent of the vertical thickness of the line.

[Default Spacing] Section

This section is used to indicate the size allocated to a line after a paragraph break. The `Paragraph Break=n` option specifies the actual amount in points, where n is the required amount. The default initially allocated by Mosaic is 10. Increase the number as required to add more space in-between paragraphs (and after tags such as <hr> and the heading tags <h1> etc., which insert paragraph breaks automatically). A typical entry could therefore be structured as:

```
[Default Spacing]
Paragraph Break=15
```

This option can be altered and tested without exiting Mosaic. Edit the `mosaic.ini` file in another window, and after saving click on Mosaic's *reload* icon to see the changes take place.

[Hotlist] Section

The `[Hotlist]` section is new to the 32 bit version of Mosaic (the later alpha releases of version 2, e.g. v2.0alpha6). It contains a series of URL definitions that can be called from the *QUICKLIST* entry when the *Open URL* option is chosen from the File menu in Mosaic. The *QUICKLIST* entries in the earlier Mosaic versions were left empty allowing users to specify a URL of their choice (effectively giving them a blank field to quickly enter a URL, rather than selecting one). *QUICKLIST* definitions can be changed through the Navigate menu. Refer to the later section on configuring Mosaic's hotlists for more information. A hypothetical `[Hotlist]` section is shown below.

```
[HotList]
URL0=*Local C: Drive,file:///c|/
URL1=*Mosaic Home Page,http://www.ncsa.uiuc.edu
URL2=*Mosaic Demo Page,http://www.ncsa.uiuc.edu/demoweb/demo.html
URL3=http://cs.indiana.edu/cstr/search
URL4=*CICA Windows Archive,file://ftp.cica.indiana.edu/pub/pc/win3
URL5=*WUArchive,file://wuarchive.wustl.edu/
URL6=*Expo Map,http://sunsite.unc.edu/expo/expo/expo_map.html
URL7=http://rs560.cl.msu.edu/weather
URL8=http://www.ncsa.uiuc.edu/SDG/Software/Mosaic/Docs/whats-new.html
URL9=http://neuromancer.lib.uchicago.edu/david/drfun.html
URL10=http://www.ncsa.uiuc.edu/SDG/Experimental/vatican.exhibits/vex.html
URL11=*Fill-Out Form Example #1,http://www.ncsa.uiuc.edu/SDG/Software/fof.html
```

Notice that a strict specification for each line must be entered. All lines that begin with an asterisk (*) are not direct URLs; rather, they are descriptions that lead to URLs, once chosen by the user. Entries without an asterisk will be looked up directly. Notice how the asterisked entries start with a description, and are then terminated by a single comma followed by the actual URL. NCSA provides some standard URLs, such as access to your local hard disk (as above), and some interesting links to their own home page at `www.ncsa.uiuc.edu`.

3.3 The Trumpet WinSock TCP/IP Package

Trumpet WinSock (Windows Sockets) is a program that allows Windows applications, such as Mosaic, to interface with TCP/IP (Transmission Control Protocol/Internet Protocol), the fundamental communications protocol in use over the entire Internet. WinSock also provides an interface to your modem device which is used to dial into your service provider's machine, establish a TCP/IP connection, and then allow you to run a program such as Mosaic in order that you can gain access to on-line tools such as FTP and telnet. WinSock is a separate program in its own right; Mosaic automatically runs the WinSock program (or rather the *TCP manager*, as it is known), so that an Internet connection can be established.

WinSock itself needs some *tweaking* before it can be installed to work with Windows. This section deals with all aspects of this program's installation and configuration. If you have a copy of Mosaic, but not the WinSock interface, get a copy before proceeding – refer to the appendices to see where to get hold of a copy of the WinSock interface for Microsoft Windows. WinSock may come bundled with Mosaic, so check first (look for the `TCPMAN.EXE` file to see if the WinSock program is already installed).

Configuring WinSock – `TCPMAN.EXE`

Depending on your PC's configuration you will probably be running your Internet connection via a modem attached to serial cable that runs into your PC. A number of protocols exist for running TCP/IP over serial connections, including PPP (Point-to-Point Protocol) and SLIP (Serial Line Internet Protocol). WinSock supports an internal SLIP option to allow programs such as Mosaic to interface with the Internet (the HTTP protocol used by the WWW is carried in TCP/IP packets from your PC and out over the Internet). Your service provider will be able to advise you on how to use Mosaic over a dial-up Internet connection, which we assume is the configuration you are using, simply because it is probably the most popular method of accessing the Internet from the home or workplace. WinSock itself needs to know quite a few things before it can be made to operate with Mosaic. Items such as these need to be specified to WinSock:

- Your service provider's telephone (modem) number and login details
- The communications port to use on your computer
- The IP address of your host, and your service provider's DNS (Domain Name Server) machine
- SLIP protocol configuration details

WinSock's TCP manager is aptly named `TCPMAN.EXE`. You should install it in your Mosaic group, which was created earlier. You will need to install it in order to configure the options above, as well as to use the program when you are connected to the Internet. The `TCPMAN.EXE` icon looks like:

Once you have the `TCPMAN.EXE` icon installed, double-click on the icon to run the program. You will shortly see a screen similar to that in shown in Figure 3.7. At this stage many of the WinSock options are absent and will have to be provided by you during the configuration.

Click on the File menu (or press `ALT-F`) and choose *Setup*. The screen in Figure 3.8 will then appear ready for your details.

The next step is to fill in the various fields on the setup screen. In order to do this you will have to look at your current Internet installation to glean some facts and figures. Each stage of the remaining installation is now considered in turn.

Stage 1 – Run the WinSock Setup Screen

The setup screen contains all of your Internet address details, plus protocol options, and the port setting to use in order to access your modem device. You will have to know the following information before proceeding:

- Your Internet IP address
  This is *your* identity on the Internet, and will take the form of a series of dotted numbers of the form `a.b.c.d` e.g. `158.80.8.68`. Don't confuse this with another **similar** IP address (since there will most probably be others as well).
- The IP address of your DNS server
  This is used to turn textual names into numeric IP addresses, e.g. to turn an FTP address of `assc.com` into `143.127.0.2`. This process is known as *resolving* the Internet address (addresses already in numeric notation are faster since they do not need resolving in this way).
- The serial (COM) port that your modem answers on, e.g. COM2, COM3.
  Your modem will be either an internal or external model. External models plug into a serial port in the back of your computer. This may be named, but they often aren't. Internal modems are configured using an IRQ setting to refer to a particular port (see below).

Your IP address will have been allocated when you initially joined your Internet service provider. It will be written down somewhere (hopefully), or it will be available in a configuration file (try running a setup program that comes with your current Internet installation to find it if you are having problems). The IP address of your own account on the Internet and the DNS server of your host must

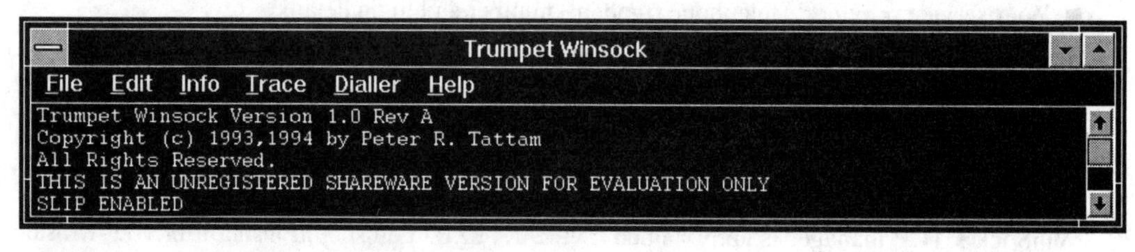

Figure 3.7: The WinSock program's interface.

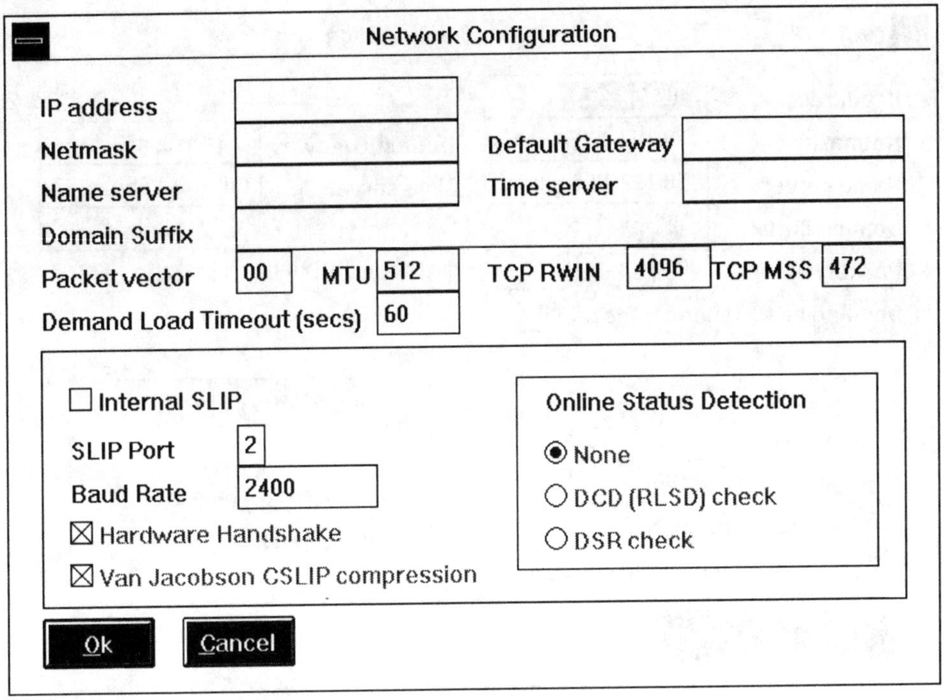

Network Configuration

IP address
Netmask
Default Gateway
Name server
Time server
Domain Suffix
Packet vector 00 MTU 512 TCP RWIN 4096 TCP MSS 472
Demand Load Timeout (secs) 60

☐ Internal SLIP
SLIP Port 2
Baud Rate 2400
☒ Hardware Handshake
☒ Van Jacobson CSLIP compression

Online Status Detection
◉ None
○ DCD (RLSD) check
○ DSR check

Ok Cancel

Figure 3.8: The WinSock setup screen.

be entered. You could get away with specifying another DNS server address, but not another IP address! Once you have entered these two values click on the SLIP option in the lower portion of the Window to enable the Serial Line Internet Protocol mode of operation. Mosaic requires a SLIP interface to function over the Internet – the vast majority of service providers supply such services, so make sure if you contemplating becoming an Internaut.

Next, enter the baud rate at which you wish to communicate using your modem (2400, 9600, 14400, 57600 etc.) and the COM port on which it resides, e.g. COM1 or COM2. If you have not yet installed a modem be sure that it is not placed in a COM port that is already in use by any other piece of software (such as a mouse driver etc.) that may interfere with its operation. Use the `MSD.EXE` (Microsoft Diagnostics) program that comes with Windows 3.1 to see which serial ports are free on your machine. If you use an internal modem read the manual to see which IRQ (Interrupt Request) settings to make, and which jumpers to alter in order to make the modem use a specific COM port. The default values for these nearly always work first time, so a massive reconfiguration is rarely required. You can now save your settings. Figure 3.9 illustrates a typical settings screen that has been completed.

When these options have been saved exit the WinSock program and restart it (you must do this for any changes to take effect). You will now see some additional information in the WinSock screen, typically your IP address details and COM port setting, as shown in Figure 3.10.

All of the options not yet covered in this section will have been given defaults by the WinSock program. These options can be left unchanged – they should work perfectly well with your service

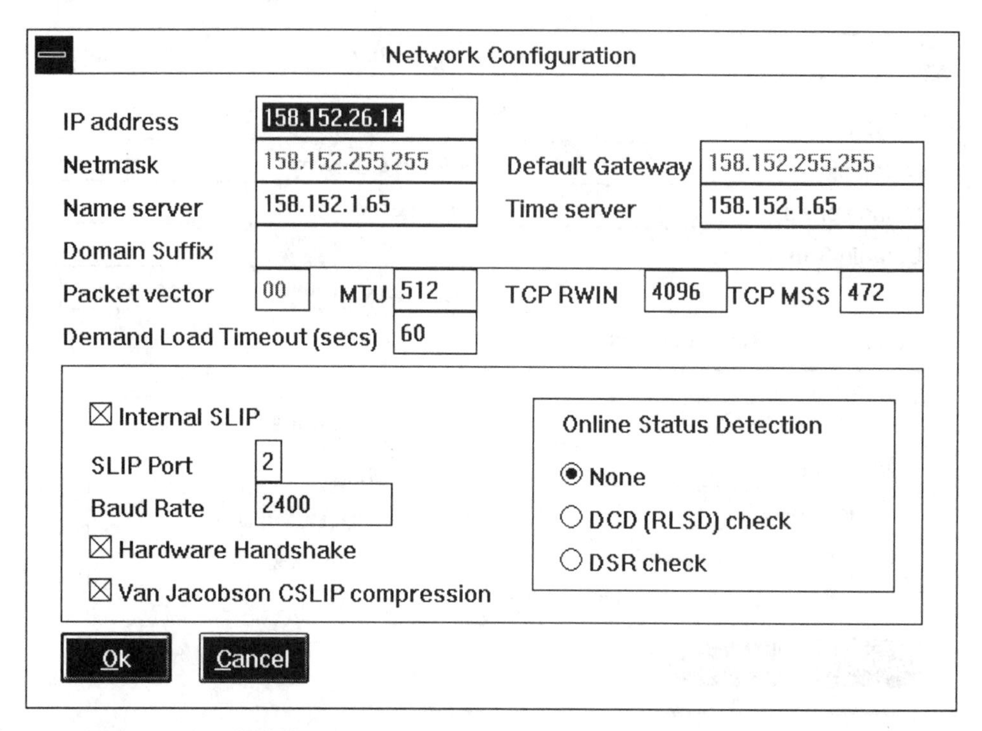

Figure 3.9: A completed WinSock setup screen.

provider's setup. Next you must specify some dialling options. WinSock can be used to dial your service provider's machine in order to set up a TCP/IP connection between you and the Internet.

Stage 2 – Select Modem Dialling Options

When Mosaic is started the WinSock program should be running in the background so that a TCP/IP connection has been established (some versions of Mosaic 2.0 will start WinSock's TCP manager automatically, but if not ensure WinSock is running first). In order to set up the modem dialling options you first decide when you want WinSock to call your service provider. Select the Dialler menu from the WinSock window and click on *Options*, as shown in Figure 3.11.

The three options available are as follows:

```
Trumpet Winsock
File  Edit  Info  Trace  Dialler  Help
Trumpet Winsock Version 1.0 Rev A
Copyright (c) 1993,1994 by Peter R. Tattam
All Rights Reserved.
THIS IS AN UNREGISTERED SHAREWARE VERSION FOR EVALUATION ONLY
SLIP ENABLED
Internal SLIP driver COM2 Baud rate = 2400 Hardware handshaking Compression enabled
My ip = 148.152.26.14 netmask = 158.152.255.255 gateway = 158.152.255.255
```

Figure 3.10: New option settings after restarting the WinSock program.

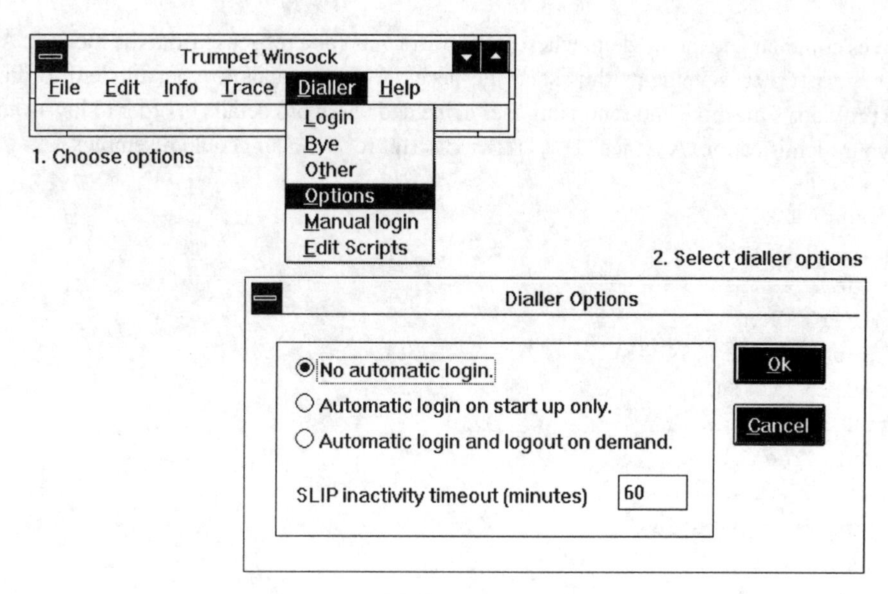

Figure 3.11: The dialling options menu in WinSock.

- No Automatic login
- Automatic login on start-up only
- Automatic login and logout on demand

No Automatic login specifies that when WinSock is started it will not dial your service provider. This may be the optimal setting to specify since you may want to run WinSock just to alter some settings or browse some of the menus, without logging in to your service provider's machine every time. If you do select this option you will have to choose the *Manual login* option from within WinSock's Dialler menu each time that you want to connect to the Internet. *Automatic login on start-up only* is the reverse process of what has just been explained, i.e. when WinSock starts, so does the modem. The final option, *Automatic login and logout on demand*, logs you in and out when WinSock is initially started and when you finally shut down WinSock (either by using the File menu and choosing exit, or by double-clicking on the bar in the top left-hand corner of the WinSock window and confirming the operation to exit).

When you have selected a dialling option, you will have to edit two scripts that are used by the WinSock program. These are used to: (a) dial your service provider's telephone number, i.e. to initiate a connection; and (b) shut down a connection. Both scripts use commands from the Hayes modem command set, along with some other commands which are specific to the WinSock program.

Stage 3 – Edit the `login.cmd` and `bye.cmd` Scripts

The files `login.cmd` and `bye.cmd` are script files used by the WinSock program to control the dialling behaviour of your modem, specifically for dialling in to your service provider's machine and for shutting down a modem connection respectively. Script files under WinSock are made up of two basic commands called `input` and `output`. The `output` command sends a character string, such as a Hayes command, to the modem, whereas `input` waits for a response from the modem. A series of `input/output` statements thus send the necessary commands to your modem to dial your service provider's machine and send your user name and password details in order to log-in and thus prove your identification. A typical `login.cmd` script for a modem could resemble:

```
output ATZ\13
input 10 OK\n
output AT&F&S1\13
input 10 OK\n
output ATDT0813434848\13
input 30 CONNECT
input 30 ogin:
output fred\13
input 30 word:
output fruitcake\13
input 30 otocol:
output SLIP\13
input 30 HELLO\n
```

It is critical that you understand your service provider's log-in prompts before you start fiddling with this file (both script files are ASCII and can be edited via WinSock or by an external editor). Here is that script file again, but with annotations to see what is going on at the local modem and at the remote service provider's machine.

Modem commands	Results
`output ATZ\13`	Send command **ATZ** to wake-up modem and reset it
`input 10 OK\n`	Wait 10 seconds for modem to respond to **OK**
`output AT&F&S1\13`	Send an initialization string to the modem
`input 10 OK\n`	Wait 10 seconds for modem to respond to **OK**
`output ATDT0813434848\13`	Send **ATDT** (attention, tone dial this number) to dial the service provider's modem number
`input 30 CONNECT`	Wait 30 seconds
`input 30 ogin:`	Wait 30 seconds for a `login:` prompt
`output fred\13`	Send `fred` as a user name.
`input 30 word:`	Wait 30 seconds for a `password:` prompt
`output fruitcake\13`	Send `fruitcake` as a password
`input 30 otocol:`	Wait 30 seconds for a `protocol:` prompt
`output SLIP\13`	Send `SLIP` as the protocol required (for Mosaic)
`input 30 HELLO\n`	Wait 30 seconds for a `HELLO` string

It is important to note that an input command is normally *paired* to an output command, so that the commands fed to the modem can be dealt with accordingly. Hayes-compatible modems use commands prefixed with the letters `AT` (known as the AT command-set, a common standard used by nearly all modem devices). AT stands for 'Attention', i.e. wake the modem up to accept commands. Modems respond to commands using the words `OK` (although most can be configured to use numbers – we assume the former in the examples). Note that the WinSock program uses the command `\13` to send a carriage return code (ASCII 13), and this must append all the `output` commands.

The input commands use a similar code, called `\n` which stands for 'new line', so `OK\n` is waiting to receive `OK` on a line by itself, although line 6 is waiting for the word `CONNECT` anywhere in a line (this is because there is no way of knowing the connection speed – the modem may respond with `CONNECT 2400` for a 2400 baud connection, or `CONNECT 9600` for a 9600 baud connection etc.). The `input` command also takes an argument which represents the number of seconds to wait for feedback from the modem, e.g. `input 10 OK\n` waits 10 seconds for an `OK` reply from the modem. Time arguments are useful where you can anticipate a longer delay from the modem (these delays happen mostly at the service provider's end when your connection is up).

As mentioned, you may have to change the login script so that it matches your service provider's login sequence. Log in as normal using your normal Internet software and note down each prompt. It goes without saying that some form of `login:` and `password:` prompt will be used in order that you identify yourself, so be sure to note down the exact prompts used. Some service providers may provide additional prompts, for which you should provide the necessary input and output commands accordingly. For example, the service provider in the example above provides a `protocol:` prompt to which I respond with `SLIP\13` (the string `SLIP` followed by a carriage return to send this string by itself back to the remote machine). This service provider's machine also sends a `HELLO` string to show that the login process has finally been completed. By looking at the `input` prompts it is possible to build up a view of how the service provider's machine responds when its modem number is called. It resembles:

```
Login: fred
Password: fruitcake
Protocol: SLIP
HELLO
```

The entire session, with modem commands, could thus resemble the following. Modem command responses are in **bold** type – all service provider messages have been omitted in this listing.

```
ATZ
OK
AT&F&S1
OK
ATDT0813434848
CONNECT 2400
Login: fred
Password: fruitcake
Protocol: SLIP
HELLO
```

You may have been wondering why some of the prompts in the script file are only partially named, e.g. `ogin:` for `login:` etc. This is frequently done because prompt matching must relate to at least part of a word (known as a substring) in order for WinSock to provide the necessary reply. For example, a service provider may change the log-in prompt from `login:` to `XYZ login:`; thus `ogin:` still matches and the correct response would be given at the correct time. Once you have completed the log-in script, try logging in to your service provider and watch very closely for each prompt to see if everything is okay. A common error made is the omission of codes such as `\n` on the end of response strings. If a modem sends `OK` on a line by itself, use `OK\n`. If a prompt is partially named, don't place any code after the prompt string (as in the case of `ogin:`, and of course `CONNECT`). And if a response to a prompt requires just a single string, place a `\13` after it to send a carriage return, otherwise a whole line may be sent to the remote machine which may confuse it and halt the whole log-in process.

The `bye.cmd` script file is much simpler. It uses a Hayes command to close down the modem connection after a few seconds. It takes the form:

```
sleep 3
output +++
sleep 4
output ATH0\r
```

where `sleep` *n* makes the modem sleep (deactivate itself) for `n` seconds. The string of plus signs (+++) is used by Hayes modems to interrupt the current modem connection and return control to the modem's command level temporarily. A further wait of 4 seconds is done after this, since it can take a couple of seconds for the modem to respond to this interruption. After this the command `ATH0` is given, which is the Hayes command for *Attention, hang up the line immediately*. This is not the most graceful way of closing the connection, but it works. The `\r` (return) command is the same as `\13` to issue a carriage return (otherwise the command would stay on the line, just as it would if you typed it in manually from the keyboard – remember that you are supposed to be emulating the keyboard exactly using such commands).

Some of the newer modems on the market specify that you should use AT to wake up your modem, rather than ATZ, mainly since the latter has the habit of resetting the modem to its factory defaults: something you may not wish to do, bearing in mind that you may have set up some special settings (see below).

▶ TIP

You can edit any script file from within WinSock by clicking on the Dialler menu and then selecting *Edit Scripts*. A window with a list of script files will then appear and you can select an appropriate file to edit (`notepad.exe`, the standard ASCII editor in Windows 3.1 is used to edit the files).

Be sure to **exit** WinSock and restart it to make any changes take effect.

Finally, remember that when you want to shut down your modem connection, use the *Bye* option in the WinSock Dialler menu.

Modem Settings – Some Advice

Many people simply plug in their modem and hope for the best. In most cases, the modem will fire up and connect first time. But is the connection the optimal connection? Here are some quick tips for novice modem users.

Modems employ a feature known as data compression to allow more data to be transmitted over a connection. Your modem probably has a feature called MNP5 (some of the faster V34 modems have MNP10). You may want to disable MNP5 compression, since it actually tends to degrade an IP (Internet Protocol) link. You can disable MNP5 using the AT command `A&K3` (or `AT%C0`) on some models. Make sure also that XON/XOFF flow control is disabled – the RTS/CTS mode should be used (this should disable XON/XOFF automatically, coincidentally). The AT command `AT&K3` will take care of this, although you may have a different command that needs to be issued on your machine. Finally, make sure that your modem operates in an *autoreliable* mode, that is that it tries to make the best connection possible, rather than hanging up if it can't. Normally, the AT command `AT\N3` is used for this (although it may be different on your own model). In non-reliable mode, the modem tries to use MNP5 (or MNP2–4) for a V42bis or V42 connection; otherwise it simply hangs up. Another problem concerning higher-speed modem connections is the ability of the serial port to keep up with the computer. Some of the newer PCs have a UART 16550A serial chip fitted, which can buffer the data received by the modem thus allowing it to pace itself against the computer. Data will be lost if you have a high-speed connection (above 9600 baud) with a normal serial chip and IP will have to keep re-transmitting lost packets, thus slowing down your connection. If you have a UART 16650 chip, be sure to set your communications software to use a high transfer rate, e.g. 19200 baud (your Internet software should have such an option; you may also want to use DOS's `MODE` command to set the baud rate).

Stage 4 – Log-in and Use Mosaic

Once you have configured all of these files you can actually log in and try out Mosaic. Figure 3.12 shows a typical login sequence in operation under Windows. Depending on how you have configured WinSock you may start to dial your service provider's modem number when Mosaic is initially started. If you have selected a manual login, as we suggested earlier, simply maximize the WinSock icon by double-clicking on its icon and then open the Dialler menu and choose *Login* (the similar *Manual Login* option allows you to 'talk' directly to your modem, i.e. enter Hayes `AT` commands to it directly).

▶ TIP

The WinSock program's author, Peter Tattam, has also written a whole host of other utilities, including: TELW (Telnet), a Ping server (checks to see if an Internet host is *alive*), a Chat program (like Internet Relay Chat), plus an FTP interface. Some of these utilities could be used in Mosaic, notably TELW, the Telnet interface for `telnet://` URLs.

```
THIS IS AN UNREGISTERED SHAREWARE VERSION FOR EVALUATION ONLY
SLIP ENABLED
Internal SLIP driver COM2 Baud rate = 2400 Hardware handshaking Compression enabled
My ip = 158.152.26.14 netmask = 158.152.255.255 gateway = 158.152.255.255
Executing script c:\windows\mosaic\login.cmd.  Type <esc> to abort
SLIP DISABLED
atz
OK
at&F&S1
OK
atz
OK
atdT0813434848
CONNECT 2400

gate.demon.co.uk (ttyc1):
demon login: fred
Password:
Protocol: SLIP
fred: IP Address: 158.152.46.144 Running SLIP on ttyc1

Birmingham PoP now in Beta - See demon.announce for more details.
Reading, Sunderland and Yorkshire in beta.

HELLO

Script completed
SLIP ENABLED
```

Figure 3.12: The `login.cmd` script file in action.

▶ TIP

If you already have some Internet software up and running that can use the SLIP protocol, execute this under Windows (in a window by itself), and then configure WinSock so that (a) it knows your IP address; (b) it knows your DNS name, server's IP address etc.; and (c) it has SLIP mode enabled. You can then use your existing Internet software to log in to your service provider without the need for any script files under WinSock. Ensure that you run your Internet software before loading Mosaic. You can then ignore the WinSock icon completely.

Once you have dialled and received the appropriate connection (and the `login.cmd` script has therefore been completed) you can try Mosaic to see if it is working. Try entering a URL by clicking on the File menu and selecting *Open URL*, or press `CTRL-O` as a shortcut to this. Click on the URL field and a cursor will appear. Enter something such as NCSA's home page, `http://www.ncsa.uiuc.edu`. Mosaic should then display a message on its status line similar to *Doing nameserver lookup on www.ncsa.uiuc.edu* and then you should see a *Connecting to HTTP Server* message, followed by *Reading...* and then *Transfering...* messages as Mosaic downloads the required home page. If you see an error box and a message saying that the DNS lookup failed you clearly have a problem. DNS (Domain Name Server) lookups are performed on all URLs in order that a numeric IP address can be found for the Internet site you have specified in the URL. Check the WinSock setup and look at the IP address entry for the name server. It must correctly refer to your service provider's DNS server. We suggest that you ask your service provider for guidance, since this value is not system generated. You may also want to check through all of the IP addresses to ensure that they are correct. Be sure to enter the URL correctly as well, of course, otherwise a warning message will definitely be given.

When you want to terminate your modem connection you can quit Mosaic – causing WinSock to close a few seconds afterwards – although this will depend on your individual dialling options, so if necessary press the ESC (escape) key in the WinSock window to abort the connection or click on the *Bye* item in the Dialler menu to execute the `bye.cmd` script file. You could also use the *Manual Dial* option in the Dialler menu and type `ATZ` to drop the line. If you want to leave Mosaic running and just terminate your modem connection this latter method is what you should use. As a safety precaution, SLIP should time-out after 60 seconds of inactivity (by default) as set in the *dialling-options* screen shown earlier in this chapter.

3.4 The 32 bit Mosaic Version

All Mosaic versions after v2 alpha 3 are based on a 32 bit architecture. Earlier versions are 16 bit applications. 32 bit mode increases Mosaic's performance very well, although it also requires a new installation process and of course there are yet further programs to download and install. The Win32s software is provided free by Microsoft and should be used to allow the 32 bit version Mosaic to run under Windows 3.1. In fact, installing the Win32s software has been designed to enable Windows 3.1 to run any 32 bit application, not only Mosaic. Refer to the appendices for the location of the Win32s software on the Internet. Before proceeding, make a back-up copy of your Windows `system.ini` file, since the installation will make some changes to this. Any changes to Windows `.ini` files ring alarm bells for most users, so make a back-up to avoid any problems.

Installing Win32s for 32 bit Mosaic

The Win32s program arrives as a `.ZIP` file. Unzip the first file into a pre-made temporary directory (assume you call this `\TEMP32`) and you should be left with another `.ZIP` archive and some copyright files etc. This latter `.ZIP` archive must be de-archived using the `-d` option to preserve the directory structure of all the files in the archive (otherwise you will be left with a mass of files in one directory, and the installation will simply fail). After decompressing with the `-d` option you will be left with two directories called `DISK1` and `DISK2`. Now run Windows and from the File menu select the *Run* command and then type in the file to run as `C:\TEMP32\DISK1\SETUP`, where `TEMP32` is the temporary directory in which you de-archived the main PKZIP archive. The Win32s setup program will then run and you will be asked to confirm the go-ahead for the installation. Windows will then copy all of the appropriate files to the `\WINDOWS\SYSTEM` directory. It will also modify `system.ini` to add a line at the very start of the `[386Enh]` section as follows:

```
[386Enh]
device=C:\WINDOWS\SYSTEM\WIN32S\W32S.386
```

This new `device=` command will make Windows load the 32 bit software driver, and will enable you to run 32 bit applications, such as the later versions of Mosaic. The installation of Mosaic has been explained already; the same rules apply here. One thing you may want to watch out for is a conflict between the `mosaic.ini` file on the 16 bit and 32 bit version; they are different (internally speaking), so you may want to make two separate directories for each Mosaic version and run them separately. Be sure to delete all of the files in the temporary directory that you made in order to de-archive the Win32s software – these files are not needed any longer and just take up valuable disk space.

32 bit and 16 bit Mosaic: the Differences

The main differences between the two versions are immediately noticeable. For a start, the main window area is much larger. There is no title field – instead Mosaic displays any `<title>` tagged-text on the actual Mosaic window title bar. Only the URL field is displayed in the 32 bit version (this is now editable also). In addition, the main NCSA logo is much smaller, although it functions in the same way, revolving and animating as Mosaic is busy downloading information and performing DNS lookups. Apart from the text window and the surrounding areas, the real changes are to be found in the menus. Many of the greyed-out items and buttons are now selectable in the 32 bit version. In particular the *Print* and *Print Preview* options are now selectable, as is the *home page* icon in the toolbar. Figure 3.13 illustrates the toolbar and screen area in the 32 bit version of Mosaic.

3.5 Introduction to Mosaic's Interface

By now you should have Mosaic up and running over an Internet connection. The Mosaic program has a variety of menu options and icons, all of which are covered in this section of the chapter. Both the 16 bit and 32 bit versions of Mosaic are slightly different in terms of the features they offer due to enhancements in the later releases of the software.

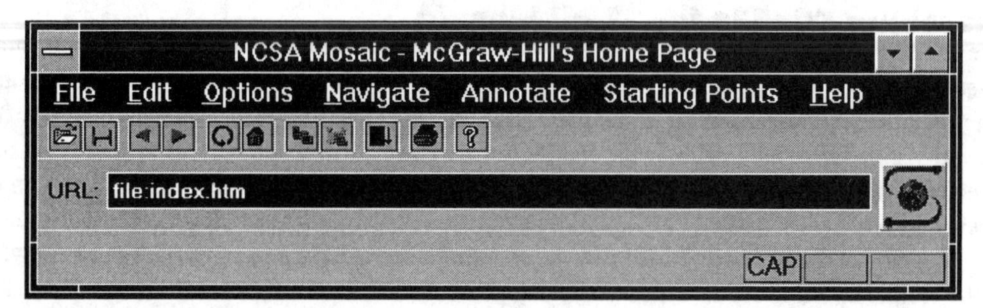

Figure 3.13: The toolbar and surrounding area in Mosaic32.

The Toolbar

The *toolbar* is a horizontal line of icons that are placed along the top of the Mosaic window. These allow various actions in the Mosaic program to be performed, such as printing, reloading pages, obtaining help and much more besides. Figure 3.14 shows the toolbar in the 16 bit version of Mosaic 2.0. Figure 3.15 shows the toolbar in the 32 bit version of Mosaic 2.0. The latter toolbar is virtually

Figure 3.14: The Mosaic toolbar in the 16 bit version.

Figure 3.15: The slightly different Mosaic toolbar in the 32 bit version.

identical albeit for the *home page* icon (icon number 6) which is now reinstated. The colouring of some icons has also been changed in the latter version. Subsequent sections now explain each icon in detail.

Icon 1 – Load a URL 

This icon allows a URL (Uniform Resource Locator) to be entered. URLs are the Web's way of referring to information resources that exist on the global Internet network, as well as also allowing users to refer to local files. URLs take the internal form `type://hostname/path/file`. For example, an FTP (File Transfer Program) URL could look like `ftp://www.mysite.com/gif/icon1.gif`, which refers to a file on an FTP site. Mosaic supplies a window for the URL to be typed in from, and a series of other options allow the user to specify lists of frequently used URLs to be called up to save time. For a more in-depth discussion please refer to Section 3.6, which deals with the File menu in more detail.

Icon 2 – Load-to-disk Feature 

Icon 2 enables the *load-to-disk* feature, which allows files to be stored to disk after a particular URL has been invoked. This icon is not selectable in the 16 bit alpha versions of Mosaic, although an option to load remote HTML and image files etc. to disk is available from the Options menu. The option is also unselectable in the alpha 6 version of Mosaic, but should be reinstated in a future version.

Icons 3 and 4 – Page Movement 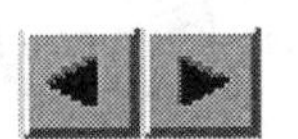

Icons 3 and 4 are the page movement icons. The left-facing arrow allows you to move back through the Web pages recently loaded, whereas the right-facing arrow allows you to move in the opposite direction, e.g. towards more recently loaded pages. These icons can save a lot of time navigating the Web: for example, if you have loaded a Gopher menu you can use these icons to move back and forth to the different areas of the menu, rather than reloading the URL for the home page (or root level menu) etc. The ability to move back and forth in this way is dependent on the number of pages that are cached in memory by Mosaic. The default caching amount is two pages, although this can be increased if you have the required memory. Refer to the section on configuring the `mosaic.ini` file for more information.

Icon 5 – Reload the Current Page

The reload icon refreshes the current page, that is to say it re-reads the page into Mosaic. This option can be used in the development process when you are editing HTML files side-by-side with Mosaic and you want to see your changes, and it can also be used to reload a page if the current window becomes corrupted, e.g. if an area of screen is left blank. Mosaic does have some problems refreshing the screen after windows have overlapped it, so use this option in such circumstances (carefully). I say 'carefully' because if the page to reload has a massive graphic inserted into it, downloading it again may be time-consuming. A better way of refreshing such pages that I have found is to minimize the Mosaic application and then re-open it by double-clicking on its icon.

> **▶ TIP**
>
> If you want to save an HTML file that you are viewing, click on the *record-to-file* feature in the Options menu and press the reload icon: the document will be saved to a filename of your choice.

Icon 6 – Load Mosaic Home Page

The home page icon is used to load the current home page, as set in the `mosaic.ini` file (hence the picture of the small house on the icon in question). To control the name of the home page, alter the `Home Page=` setting in the `[Main]` section of `mosaic.ini`. You can also get back to your home page by constantly clicking on the load previous document icon (the left-facing arrow described earlier), or alternatively by using the *Home* option in Mosaic's Navigate menu. If your `Home Page=` definition is left out, Mosaic will grey out the icon from the toolbar and it will not be selectable.

Icon 7 – Copy Text to Clipboard

Icon 7 copies text marked within a field on the current screen (such as a URL) into the Windows clipboard. User-defined fields, such as those provided by an HTML Fill-Out-Form or an `<isindex>` search document (see Chapter 2 for details on these HTML features) can also be copied to the clipboard. Clipboard features remain limited in both the 16 bit and 32 bit (alpha 6) versions of Mosaic.

Icon 8 – Copy Clipboard Text to Current Document

Icon 8 is used to copy the contents of the clipboard into the current document.

Icon 9 – Find Text

Icon 9 is the *text-search* option, which can be used to search the current document for a search pattern (or string). Case matching is disabled for all searches.

Icon 10 – Print Document 

Icon 10 invokes the print facility, allowing a hard copy version of the currently loaded Web document to be printed. All printer output and configuration is handled through Windows, including printer selection. The 32 bit version of Mosaic has a *Print Preview* option you may be interested in trying out (although it seems a bit buggy in the alpha 6 release).

Icon 11 – On-line Help 

The final icon is used to summon the Windows help program (`winhelp.exe`) for on-line help with the Mosaic program. The help file `mosaic.hlp` may not be bundled with the early alpha versions of Mosaic, however, so this option may not be fully available (it doesn't come with the v2.0alpha6 version either).

The Mosaic System and Interface

The Mosaic system is made up of a series of menus and options that are now explained in greater detail.

The Document Window and Surrounding Area

Figure 3.16 illustrates the Mosaic document window (the 16 bit version) and surrounding area. The document, or text window, is a resizeable window in which the current HTML document is rendered,

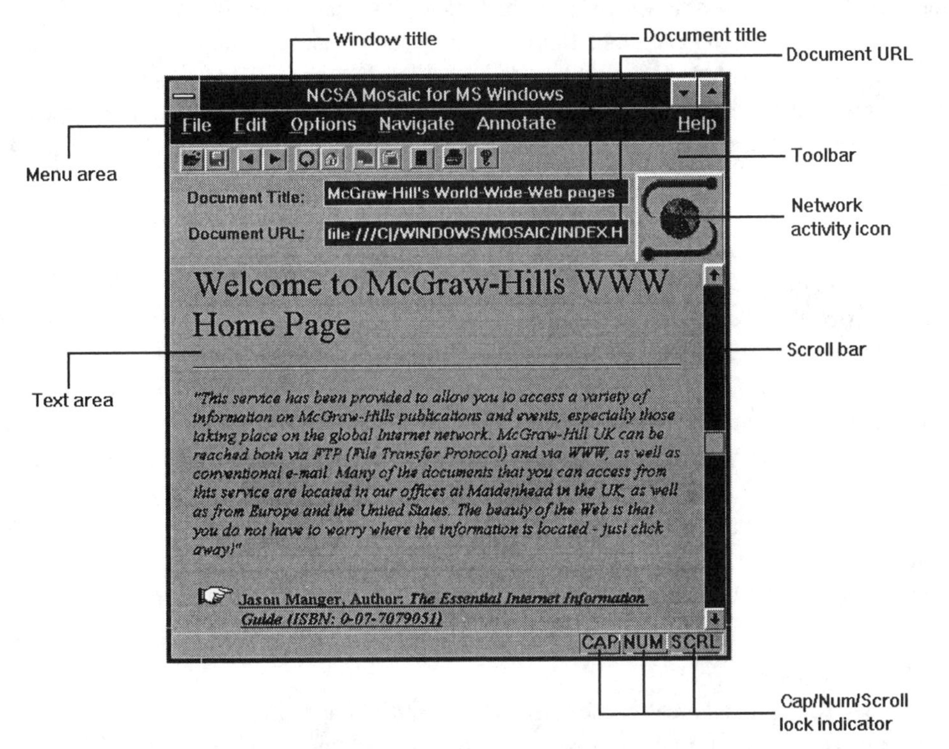

Figure 3.16: The Mosaic text window and surrounding area.

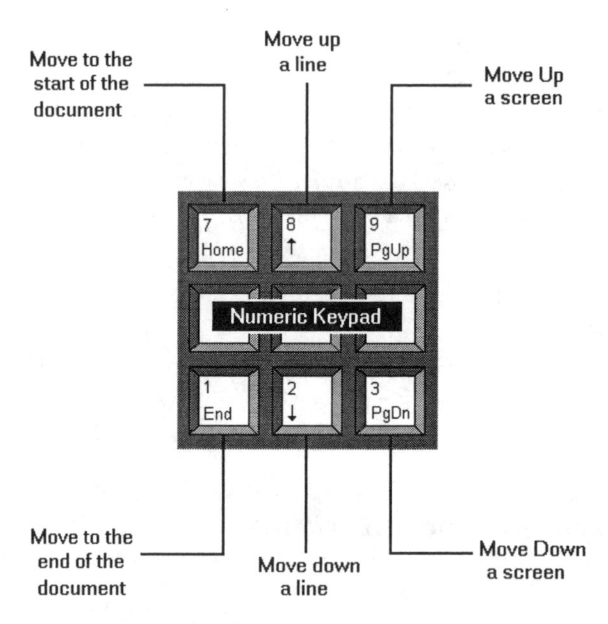

Figure 3.17: The numeric keypad keys for navigation

i.e. graphically displayed. Text is automatically scaled to fit within the window whenever it is resized by the user. The very top of the screen holds the Window title, and below this are the various menus, arranged horizontally from left to right. Below this is the toolbar and then the document viewing area. The very last line is the Mosaic status bar, which is used to display any system messages, such as the progress of a file that is being downloaded. The large icon in the top right-hand corner of the Mosaic window is the network activity icon. This picture of the globe revolves and flashes as data is being pulled from the Internet to your computer, or if a DNS (Domain Name Server) lookup is being performed. When the icon stops animating nothing is being accessed. While the icon is active no mouse or keyboard activity is allowed.

To move around the document the vertical scroll-bar can be used. Clicking within the bar will move the text within the window up or down accordingly, or you can *drag* the scroll-bar button to the position required (remember that the length of the scroll-bar represents the size of the current document (lengthways), so, for example, dragging the button to the bottom of the bar is the same as moving to the end of the document.

The 32 bit version of Mosaic doesn't use a *Document Title* field: instead, it places all HTML titles in the main window title bar, which saves a considerable amount of space.

Many other keys can be used to move around within a document. The numeric keypad has many movement keys, shown in Figure 3.17. Be sure to have the `[NUMLOCK]` key disabled when using the numeric keypad for document navigation within Mosaic or nothing will happen.

The Title and URL Bars

Two of the most important areas of the screen are the title bar and URL bar. When you open a new document it is customary for it to have a title to tell you what you are actually viewing. This will be provided using an embedded HTML tag within the document itself (called `<title>` – see Chapter

Document Title: McGraw-Hill's World-Wide-Web pages

Document URL: file:///C|/WINDOWS/MOSAIC/INDEX.HTM

Figure 3.18: A typical title bar and URL bar.

2 on the HTML language). Documents do not have to display a title, although without one the user would not be able to ascertain the subject matter of the current document. Ensure that when you come to design your own Web pages your own titles are as descriptive as possible. The 32 bit version of Mosaic uses the main window title as a title bar, rather than using a dedicated field as in the earlier 16 bit alpha versions. Only the URL bar is retained in the later 32 bit versions of Mosaic.

The URL bar show the current Uniform Resource Locator. URLs show the host that you are connected to and the type of information being browsed, as well as the location of the file that is being browsed. If you wish, the URL and title bars can be hidden through use of the Options menu (this gives more room for the actual text of the current document). The information in the title and URL bars cannot be changed manually (nor deleted), although text can be highlighted (do this by positioning the cursor on the start of a word and dragging the mouse with the left mouse button depressed over the text you want highlighted) and then copied to the Windows clipboard. Clipboard activities are limited in the early Mosaic versions, so using this feature does not have much demand. Figure 3.18 illustrates a typical title and URL bar as seen from within Mosaic.

3.6 The Menu Bar

The menu bar consists of a series of sub-menus which control the operation of the entire Mosaic program. User-definable menus can also be added to this menu bar to add further functionality to the system. Each menu is now discussed in its own section.

The File Menu

The *file* menu (`ALT-F`) has the following options. To select an option click on it using the mouse, or move to the item with the up/down cursor keys and press ENTER. Many options also have additional keys to select them – see below. The following menu options are available:

- Open a URL (or `CTRL-O`)
- Open a Local file (or press L)
- Save Window Position
- Print (or press P)
- Print Preview (or press V)
- Print Setup (or press R)
- Document Source
- Exit (or press X)

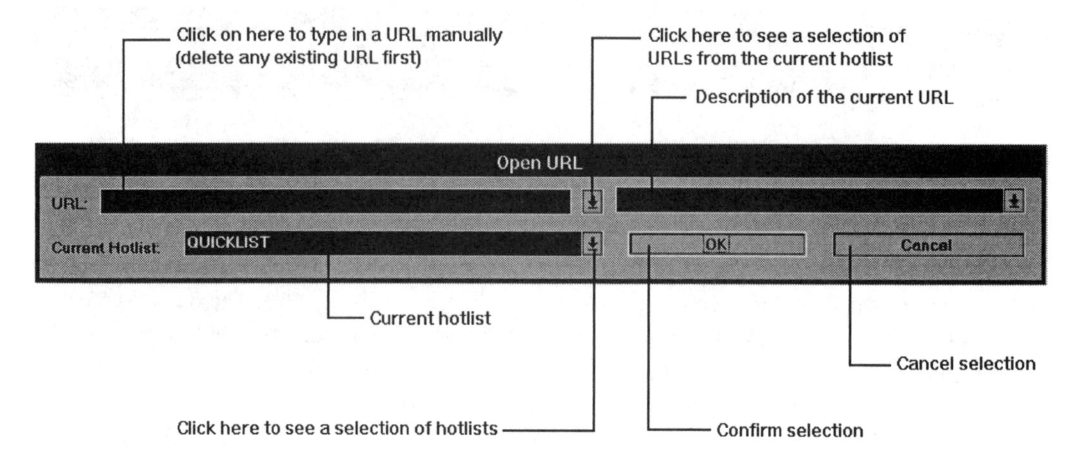

Figure 3.19: Selecting the *Open a URL* option.

Opening URLs

The first option, *Open a URL*, allows the user to enter or select a URL (selection is performed via a *hotlist*). Hotlists are Mosaic's way of allowing the user to store frequently used URLs in a file so that they can be called up from a menu. Hotlists save the user from typing in URLs by hand. In the process this also helps reduce the chance of making any typing errors. Selecting this option results in the window shown in Figure 3.19 being displayed.

When clicking on the URL field there may or may not be an existing entry already in the field. This will depend on which hotlist is activated. The 16 bit version of Mosaic provides an entry called *QUICKLIST*, which is basically an empty record which will allow you to enter a URL by hand, i.e. without clearing away any existing text from a field. The 32 bit version of Mosaic stores some new URL entries in the *QUICKLIST* entry through use of the new `mosaic.ini` file section called `[hotlist]`. You can click on the hotlist selection *QUICKLIST* button (the small down-arrow on the quicklist field) to access this option. When selecting URLs you can do this in one of two ways, namely:

- Select a URL description to call up the required URL
- Select a URL directly

The first method requires that you simply click on the small down-arrow icon on the URL description window. A list of descriptions will then be shown (Figure 3.20). Select the item that interests you and the URL for it will be placed in the URL field. You can then click on OK and Mosaic will connect to the host (via the Internet) to download the file you have requested. Using URL descriptions is beneficial since many URLs do not convey the actual content of the resource being addressed (unless they are really very specific, e.g.

```
ftp://www.microsoft.com/pub/doc/htmlguide.htm
```

unlike a URL such as `http://rs560.um.edu/index.htm`, which could be anything).

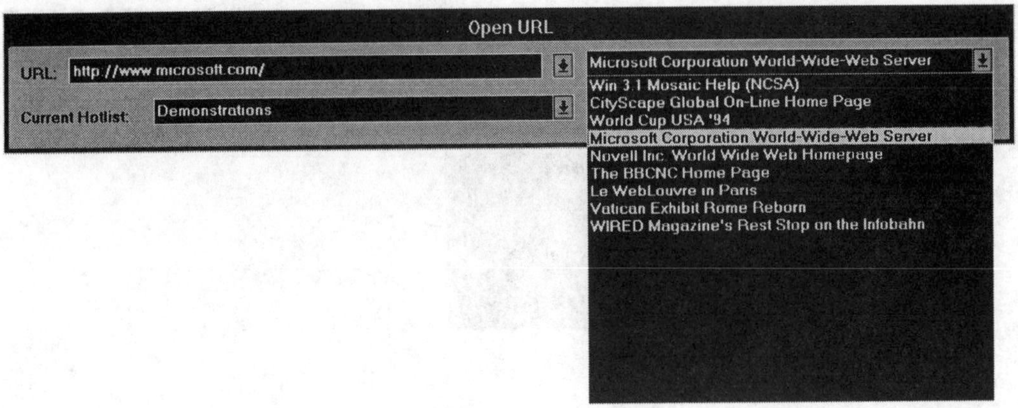

Figure 3.20: Loading a URL via a descriptive list.

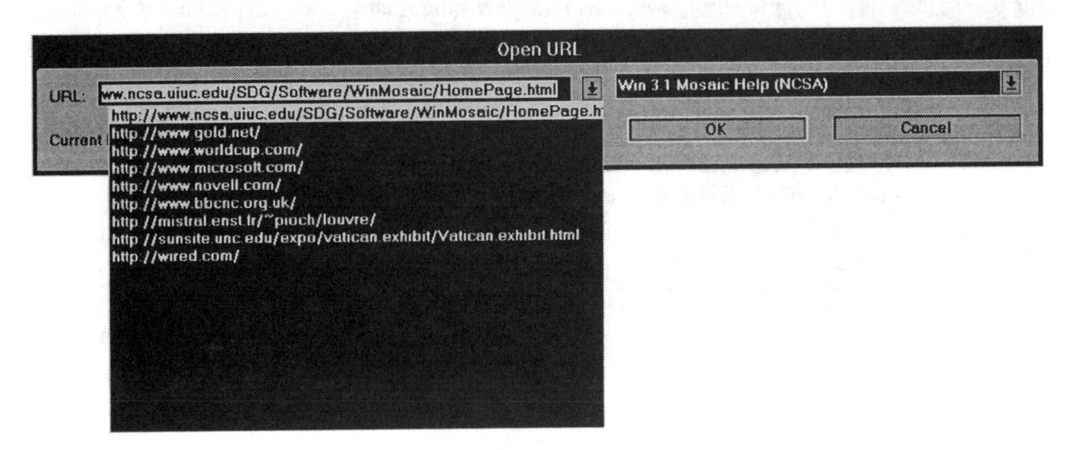

Figure 3.21: Loading a URL from a list of existing URLs.

The second method of loading a URL is to select an actual URL entry, rather than looking through a descriptive list on the screen, as shown above. To do this, simply click on the down-arrow icon on the URL field (the first field in the top left-hand corner of the screen) and a list of URLs will be displayed. As you move through each URL a single line of descriptive text is shown to the right of the field, as shown in Figure 3.21.

If the URL you require exists in another hotlist, click on the down-arrow icon in the hotlist field and a list of current hotlists will be displayed. Click on one to load it and then Mosaic will display the first URL and description in the fields provided. You can now select the URL using the methods previously described. Figure 3.22 shows the loading of a specific hotlist. Creating hotlists is the topic of a later section.

Opening a Local File

The second option in the File menu opens a local document that resides on your local hard disk. Any type of document can be opened (or *viewed*) according to the viewers and filters installed within the

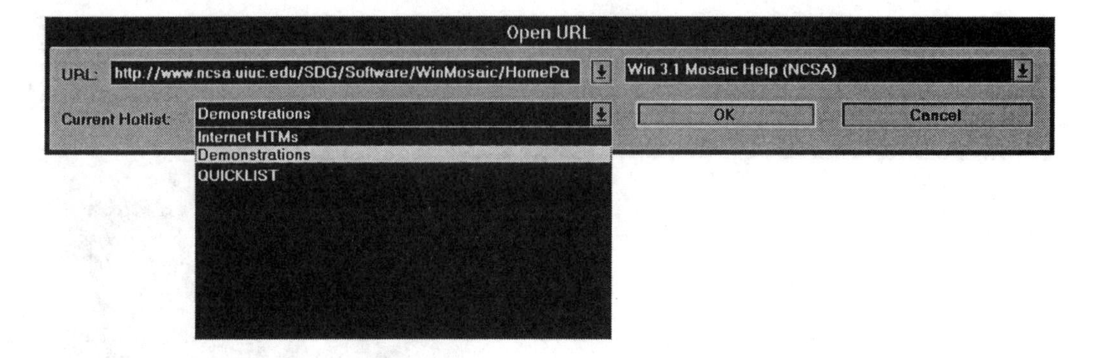

Figure 3.22: Loading a new *hotlist.*

[Viewers] section of the mosaic.ini file. When selecting the option a list of all the files in the current directory is displayed. Click on the file that interests you, or click on the '..' entry to load the parent directory (if applicable). If Mosaic recognizes the file by its extension, that is it matches it using the [Suffixes] section of the mosaic.ini file, the utility that deals with that file will be launched. If the file being selected is an HTML file Mosaic loads and parses the file as normal.

> **▶ TIP**
>
> If you load a local HTML file that has been downloaded from the Internet, the chances are that it will contain references to external URLs. Mainly these will be images that are embedded into the document, and which you don't have any control over the loading of. Mosaic may try to resolve these references (time-consuming), even though you may not be logged-in to the Internet. This will eventually result in an error from Mosaic. Disable in-line images to disable such images. You may also want to view the file with an ASCII editor instead in order to save time (if you are in a hurry).

Loading files locally is the only way of looking at an HTML document when you are not logged-in to the Internet. Use it for development purposes and for browsing any files retrieved from the Net. Users without Internet connectivity will clearly use this option regularly.

Saving the Window Position (User Preferences)

When Mosaic starts up it reads the [Main] section of the mosaic.ini file. This section contains the x, y coordinates of the upper right-hand-side of the Mosaic window, as well as the width and depth of the current window. All these settings can be saved so that the next time Mosaic is run it will use the coordinates previously saved. Move the window and size it to your desired requirements before clicking on the option to save the new position. In the 32 bit windows version this option can be found as *Save Preferences*, which as well as saving the window position, will also save any user menu settings.

Printing Options

The printing options allow a hard copy of the current document to be sent to a printer. The early alpha versions of Mosaic have not implemented any of the printing options. In the 32 bit version of Mosaic the *Print* option dumps the current document to the printer as set up to work in your current Windows configuration. The current printer configuration can be changed through the *Print Setup* option in this menu, which is what all Windows applications link to in order to change the current printer settings. The *Print Preview* option allows the user to view the document as it will be printed (i.e. in a WYSIWYG format). This option is only available in the later 32 bit versions of Mosaic.

Document Source

This is another feature not implemented in the early alpha versions of Mosaic. It allows the current HTML document (the *document source*) to be viewed in its raw form (with embedded tags). Other Web browsers, such as *Cello*, have similar features. This feature is not available in the early alpha releases of Mosaic, although the 32 bit version has the facility. Figure 3.23 shows the *Document Source* command in action.

Exiting Mosaic

The final option in the File menu closes down the current Mosaic window and shuts down the program. No confirmation check is made, so you will be exited immediately.

The Edit Menu

This is the smallest menu in the Mosaic system. It contains the options *Copy* and *Find*. The *Copy*

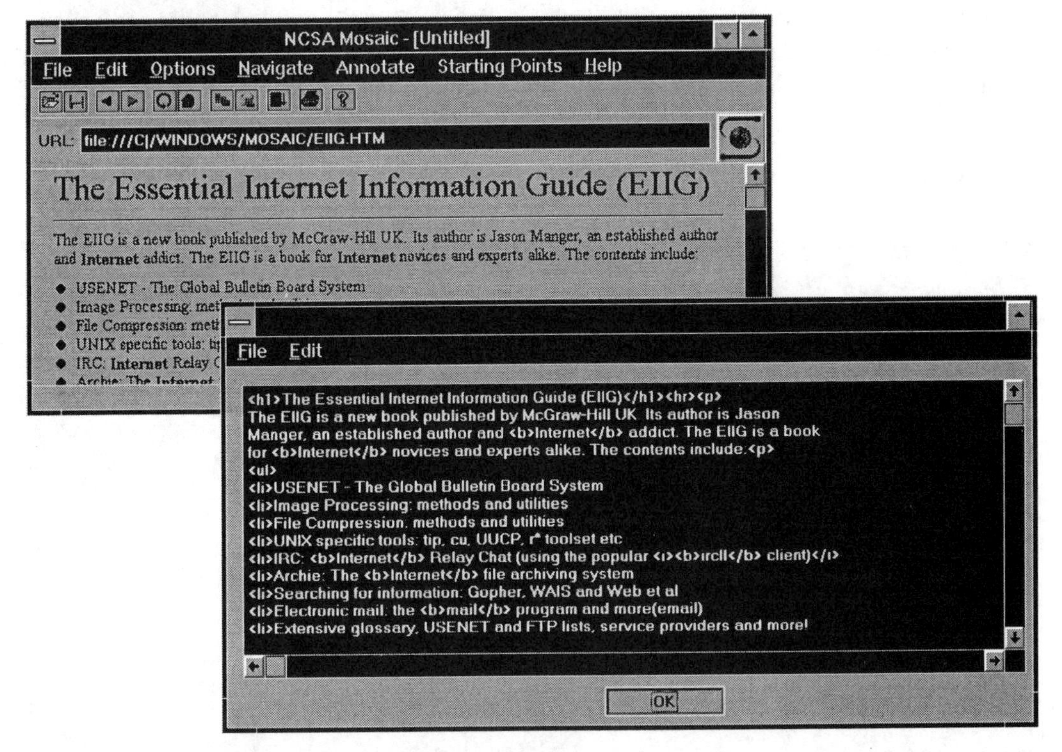

Figure 3.23: The *Document Source* command in action.

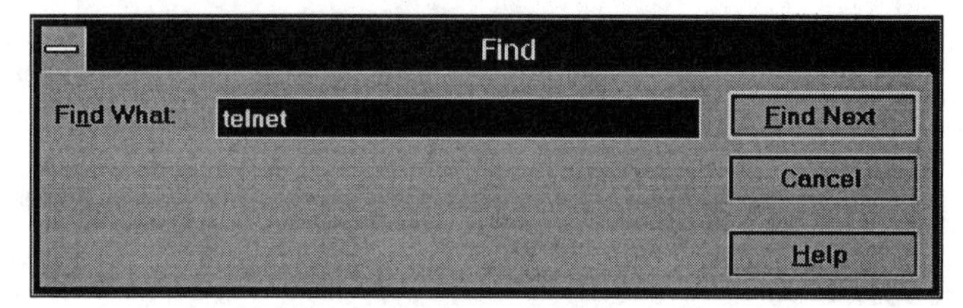

Figure 3.24: Entering a search string (to find the word 'telnet').

option allows a portion of highlighted text to be copied to the clipboard. Text from an HTML document (in the document window) cannot be copied, although all field values can – which include annotations (to be discussed) and email messages to be sent to the NCSA developers. The *Find* option, as the name suggests, allows a search to be conducted on the current document. All searches are case-insensitive and substring patterns are used: for example, entering 'net' will match 'Inter**net**' and 'tel**net**", as well as 'TEL**NET**", and 'INTER**NET**' (in upper-case). When selecting this option Mosaic provides a window for you to enter a search string. Enter the string and press ENTER to start the search. Figure 3.24 illustrates the string input field and a sample search pattern of 'telnet'.

If the search string cannot be located within the document Mosaic will warn you, as shown in Figure 3.25. If Mosaic finds a match it moves the document so that the line on which the pattern was found is the first line in the document window (move the search window out of the way if it obscures the view). To find the next occurrence of the string click on the *Find Next* option in the search window. If no further matches are found in the remainder of the document Mosaic warns you. Searches can only take place over the current document and any hyperlinks within a document are not followed.

The Options Menu

Many of the most useful options of the Mosaic program can be found in this menu. The options available to the user are as follows:

- Load to Disk
- Show Toolbar (or press T)
- Show Status Bar (or press S)
- Show Current URL/Title bar
- Show Anchor URLs
- Change Cursor Over Anchor

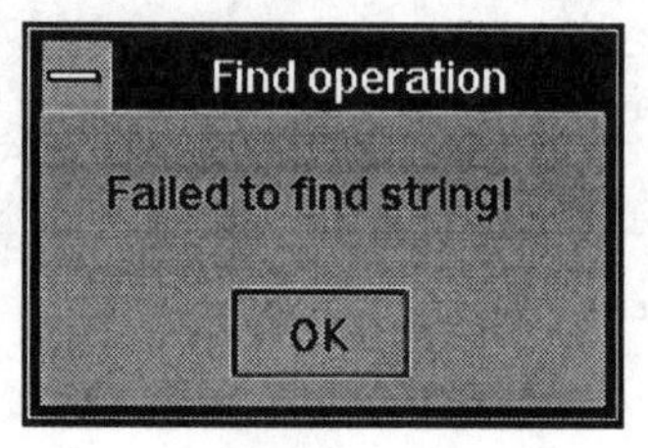

Figure 3.25: *Search pattern not Found* window.

- Extended FTP Directory Parsing
- Display In-line Images
- Show Group Annotations
- Change Font
- Debugging Information

All of the menu-items mentioned above are *yes/no* type options. Mosaic places a small tick by the side of those options that are enabled (those that are not ticked, or *checked*, are therefore not in use). Click on an item to enable it, and click on it again to disable the option. Each item in the menu is now discussed in more detail.

Loading Files to Disk

This option is very useful, for without it none of the documents downloaded from the Internet will ever be saved for you to refer back to. On your travels through the Web you will pick up hundreds, perhaps even thousands of files (images, sounds, HTML documents and the like), and it would be impractical to load everything to disk by default – you would very quickly run out of hard disk space. Mosaic therefore allows you to turn on disk-loading so that certain files can be saved to your local hard disk. This option can be tricky to use, so bear these points in mind first:

- You cannot enable the option in the middle of the file-transfer, which makes sense, otherwise you would end up with only a partial version of the file.
- Plan your loading activities carefully, so that the loading option is enabled before you decide to follow a hyperlink to a particular file
- Only *files* of information can be downloaded, so you cannot grab an item such as a Gopher menu or an FTP directory structure, since these objects are not *downloadable* items in the true meaning (Mosaic will ignore such objects while file loading is enabled).

When enabling the file-loading option Mosaic prompts you for a filename in which to save the current file that is being accessed. Since many of the files you will be accessing are UNIX-based, some filenames will not be valid (any file that has over 8 characters as a filename, and over 3 characters as an extension is not valid in MS-DOS). Mosaic may therefore truncate the name of file for you automatically. In most cases the files you access will have names that are perfectly valid under MS-DOS, but you can of course alter the name of the file if you wish. In some special cases, such as during a search operation on a veronica or WAIS server, Mosaic can insert some strange characters into a filename. If the filename in question contains any non-alphabetic characters, enter a completely new name to be safe. Mosaic will warn you if a name is not valid, however. After a file has been downloaded to your disk the only indication that you will have that the file has been transferred is the absence of the *Transfering* message on the bottom of the screen. If you intend to view some documents again be sure to disable the disk-loading option, otherwise Mosaic will keep asking you for filenames to save all the documents you open!

Another very important point is worth bearing in mind when you have just saved a remote document to your local hard disk: avoid immediately loading the file as a local document in order to view it. This sometimes has the effect of exceeding the page cache (the number of pages that you can refer back to in Mosaic's document history buffer without issuing another time-consuming remote URL request), and even deleting the base address of the current URL – this *base address* refers to the current Internet hostname where the file you requested resides. Files are sometimes specified in a hyperlink without using a hostname in the URL (which is generally a bad idea, so avoid doing this when designing HTML files – **always** use the full URL in all references). Mosaic knows which host you are currently connected to and it would normally just insert the hostname automatically. If a local document is loaded you may run the risk of losing the hostname reference to a particular series of files. The only way to get over this is to use the *load previous-page* icon (the small left-facing arrow in the toolbar), and if this doesn't work re-load the page again using the appropriate URL.

▶ TIP

You can load a local HTML file (only) by selecting the *Open a URL* option in the File menu and entering:

```
file:filename.htm
```

For example, `file:index.htm` would load the local file named `index.htm`.

Show/hide Toolbar

The second option in the Options menu toggles the toolbar on and off. Disabling the toolbar will give you slightly more room on the screen for viewing documents, but beyond this not much else besides.

Show/hide Status Bar

The status bar, which appears along the bottom of the Mosaic document window, can also be hidden from view using this option. Status bar messages inform you when downloads are taking place, the names of anchors, and which lock keys are enabled, e.g. Caps Lock, Num Lock.

Show/hide Current URL/Title Bar

The title bar and URL bar can be toggled on or off using this feature. Disabling these options will increase the document window size considerably. Note that since Mosaic32 does not have a title bar, only the URL line can be disabled in the 32 bit version.

Show/hide Anchors/URLs

Anchors are references to other parts of a document located either locally or externally. Mosaic highlights all anchors and URL hyper-references using a blue (by default) colour, while also underlining the anchor concerned and updating the status bar with the name of the reference as the cursor passes over it. If you enable this option the status bar is not updated with the anchor name, although the colour and underlining defaults are retained.

Change Cursor Over Anchor

Mosaic changes the cursor shape from an arrow to a small hand when the cursor is placed over an anchor (or hyper-reference). The cursor shape will not be altered over anchors if this option is enabled.

Extended FTP Directory Parsing

This option toggles extended FTP directory parsing, which in plain English means that whenever Mosaic is browsing an FTP site's file system (using a URL like `ftp://ftp.kodak.com` for example) and *extended* mode is enabled, icons are used instead of bullets to represent directories and files. Icons are not selectable, i.e. they are not hyperlinks; both methods still use conventional hyper-references to actually get to the files they are indexing.

Display/hide In-line Images

In-line images can be embedded within HTML documents. These are still images which are either in the GIF (Graphics Interchange Format) or XBM (X-Windows Bitmap) image format. Downloading images can be time-consuming for users with slow modems. This option can thus be used to disable the downloading of such images. If image display is disabled, Mosaic places a small postage-stamp sized icon (the NCSA Mosaic Logo) in place of the original image.

Show/hide Group Annotations

Annotations, as the name suggests, are small snippets of information provided by the user and which reference a particular URL. Comments can thus be placed alongside URL references so that the user has some further information on the resource in question. Annotations come in two flavours, *group* and *personal*. Group annotations are stored on a central server machine on the Internet for a particular URL, whereas personal annotations are stored locally on the user's hard disk. This option enables and disables Mosaic's feature to show when a particular group annotation (not a personal annotation) is available for a particular URL. Annotations will be discussed in more detail later.

Choosing Fonts

Nearly all of the fonts used in the HTML language can be customized, including *normal* text, headers, block-quotes and so forth. The font face, size and other attributes such as underlining and italics can also be configured through this option. Mosaic provides you with a list of text styles that can be changed when you initially select the option, as shown in Figure 3.26.

When you have decided which text item to change (e.g. a header) Mosaic calls up another window in which you can change the font's size and face etc., as shown in Figure 3.27, which is altering the font definition for a level one heading (this is accessed through an HTML `<h1>` header tag).

Debugging Information

Mosaic can track many system events to aid debugging when things go wrong. The ins and outs of tracking protocol traffic and tracing system events is beyond the scope of this book. System developers will mainly be interested in these options; novices should leave them alone.

The Navigate Menu

This menu contains a number of options that concern moving between documents and creating and manipulating URLs. The basic options in the Navigate menu are:

- Move backwards

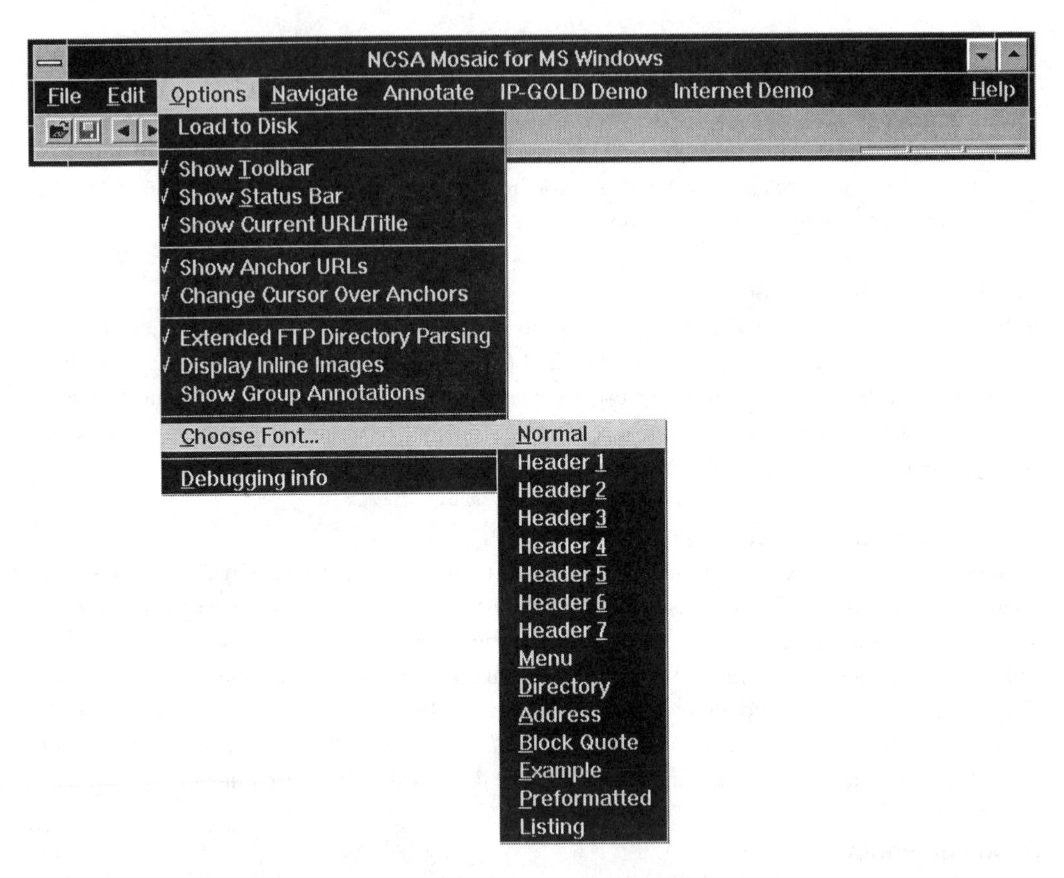

Figure 3.26: Selecting a font type to change.

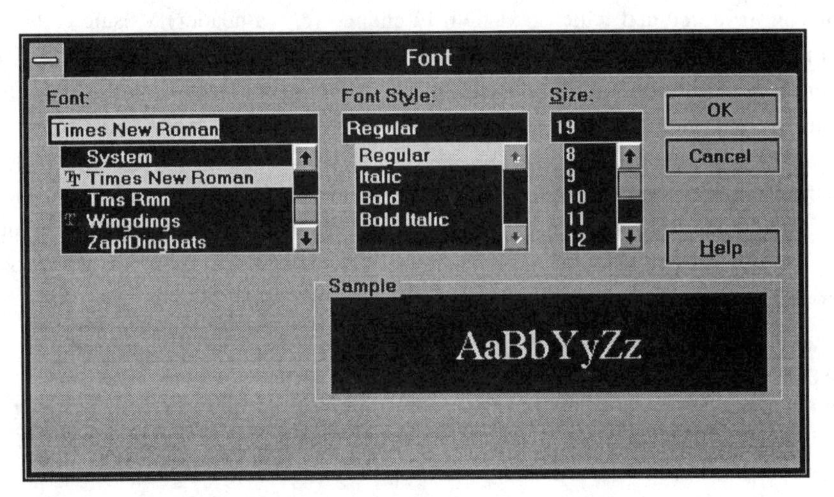

Figure 3.27: Changing a font's attributes.

- Move forwards
- Reload
- Home
- History
- Add current to hotlist
- Menu editor

Move backwards and *move forwards* allow movement back and forth between pages already loaded by Mosaic into its memory cache. These functions are also duplicated in the toolbar. The *reload* function is also another duplicate for the reload icon in the toolbar; this simply reloads the current document into Mosaic and is used if the screen is corrupted, or if you are developing HTML alongside Mosaic and want to reload the current document to see any changes. The *home* option moves you back to the home page associated with the current URL (the small icon of a house in the toolbar replicates this function). The *home* facility is not available in some of the early alpha releases of Mosaic, e.g. v2alpha2. A useful function which is not found in the toolbar is the *history* function, which displays all of the URLs entered during your Mosaic session, including any local files that have been loaded. You can click on any of the URLs displayed to load (or reload) that particular URL, which saves you from manually re-entering such details. Figure 3.28 illustrates the history window in action.

The final two commands relate to Mosaic's hotlists. The option *Add current to hotlist* places the currently selected URL into the current hotlist. The *menu editor* option allows you to create your own hotlist menu structures. Hotlists are a powerful short cut feature and are discussed in more detail below.

Creating and Editing Hotlists

Hotlists are used by Mosaic to allow frequently used URL definitions to be made available as menu options, so that they can be called up from the menu bar, or from the *Open a URL* option in the File menu. Hotlists are created and edited using the *Menu editor* option in Mosaic's Navigate menu. Selecting this option results in a screen similar to that shown in Figure 3.29. All hotlists are stored in the Mosaic initialization file `mosaic.ini` when your hotlist modifications are saved.

The screen itself is split into two areas, the left-hand side referring to menus (or *hotlists*) that have already been created, and the right-hand menu representing the items in each menu. The four buttons along the bottom of the screen control the insertion, copying, deletion and editing of the menu's various items. *Items* in this case refer to the menu names, the items in each menu (names of various URLs) and the *type* of item. Menu items can be configured to be menus or sub-menus. In Figure 3.29 it can be seen that item *Jason* is set in slightly further than the item *Internet HTMs*. In this context the item *Jason* is therefore classed as a sub-menu, rather than a menu item, i.e. an item that is a selectable URL. Menus and sub-menus that have more than one item in them are identified by a hyphen (-) as the first character. The *QUICKLIST* hotlist has no items in the early Mosaic versions, and in this mode allows the user to enter a URL manually. The 32 bit version of Mosaic has a number of URLs in the *QUICKLIST* that can be used.

Any of the existing menus can be clicked upon with the mouse to show their internal structure. The simplest menu consists of a series of URL descriptions. When a menu is clicked upon the items

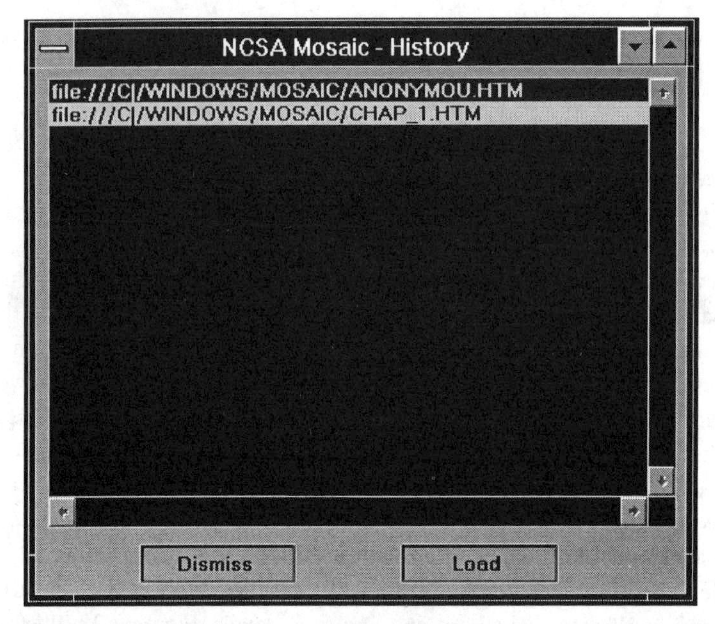

Figure 3.28: The Mosaic history buffer (Navigate menu).

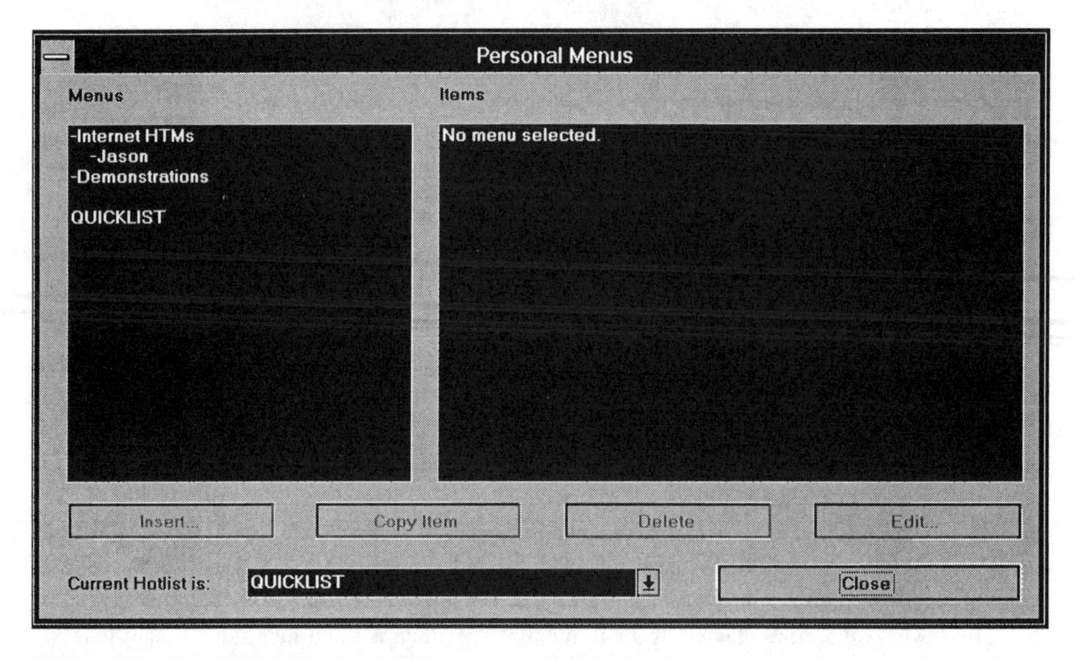

Figure 3.29: The Mosaic menu editor screen.

are shown in the right-hand window. Clicking on an item allows you to edit it, although the supplied buttons can also be used for this purpose. Figure 3.30 illustrates a typical menu with five items. These are some popular URLs of services found on the Internet.

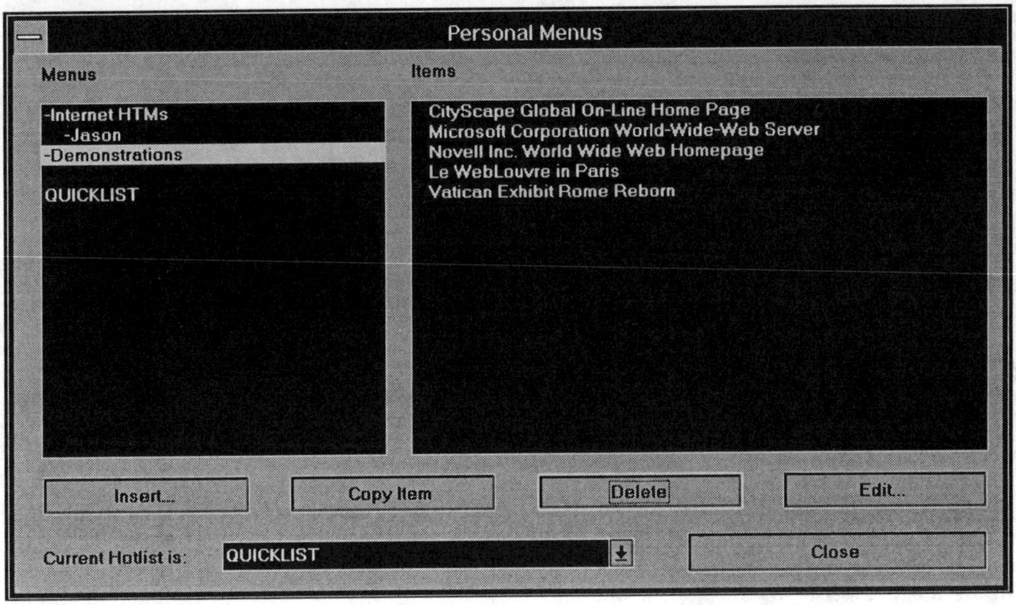

Figure 3.30: Selection of the menu *Demonstrations*.

Creating a New Menu

To create a new menu it is probably easier to work in the left-hand window, since this is where the current menu structure is displayed (either window can be used, however). Also ensure that you are in the correct location for the new menu. The location of the new menu you will be creating will be either relative to another sub-menu (i.e. it will be placed beneath an existing menu) or it will be created as a *top-level menu*. In Figure 3.30 the currently selected menu is *Demonstrations*. If we now click on the *Insert* button a new item will be added. The item can either be another menu, or it can be an additional item in the current menu. Since the *Demonstrations* menu item is itself a menu Mosaic would assume that we wanted to add a new item or sub-menu to the existing menu. Mosaic also allows an item called a *separator* to be created; this is basically a straight line used to break up and distinguish separate groups of menu items. If you want to create a completely new menu that is not part of an existing item, simple click on the empty line in the left-hand window. Mosaic will then allow you to add a new menu after you click on the *Insert* button. Figure 3.31 shows the result of clicking on the *Insert* button while the *Demonstrations* menu is selected, and then selecting the *menu* radio-box option.

As soon as the *insert* option is chosen Mosaic displays a window that allows either a *menu*, *item* or *separator* to be created. In Figure 3.31 the menu option has been chosen. Mosaic then asks you to supply a name for the menu, and the name *Trial menu* has been typed for purposes of the example. Clicking on the OK button then returns you to the previous window, where the new menu will be displayed accordingly. Since our new menu was created within the *Demonstrations* menu it will be placed underneath this entry, as shown in Figure 3.32.

Notice how the new menu has been inserted in both windows. bear in mind that the right-hand window lists all of the items that will actually be seen when you click on the *Demonstrations* hotlist

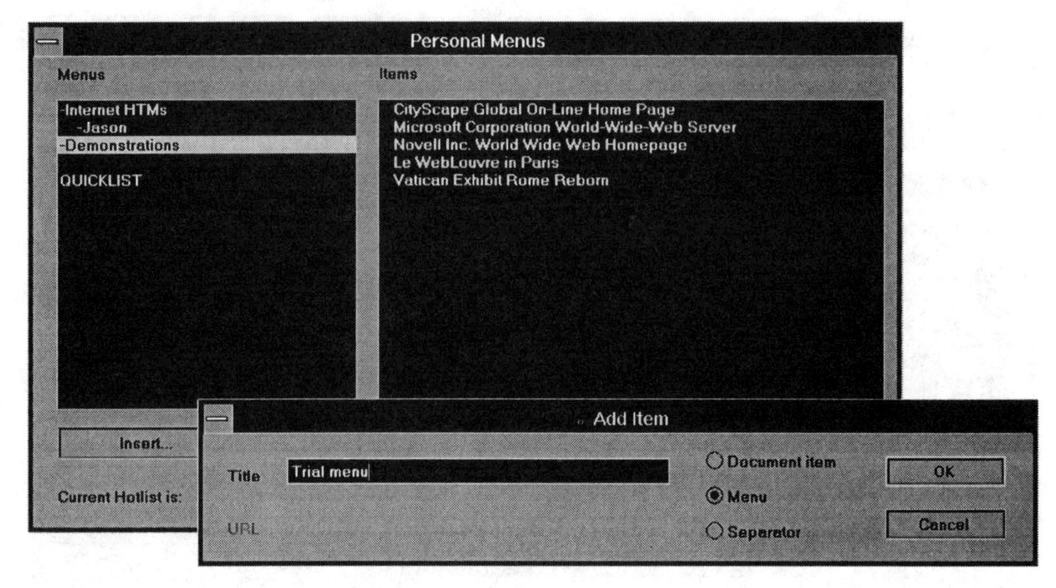

Figure 3.31: Creating a new menu item.

menu. Mosaic shows you the structure of your menus in the left-hand window (although, alternatively, you could have carried out this whole exercise using the right-hand window in just the same way). Notice also how Mosaic distinguishes menus from normal URL description items; the > in front of the menu tells you that this entry will lead to yet further items of interest. You could, of course, add further sub-menus to existing sub-menus to structure URLs into different classes.

Menu creation is pretty straightforward. What about individual items within a menu?

Creating a New URL Item Description

Once you have created all of your menus a time will come when you will have to place some URL descriptions within them: after all, this is the whole purpose of using hotlists – namely to call up frequently used URLs. Once again, the creation of a URL description will require you to decide the menu in which you want the description to actually appear. Items can be only be created within existing menus or sub-menus. Click on the menu in which you want an item to appear and then click on the *Insert* button. Mosaic will than allow you to create an *item* (as opposed to a *menu*). Once this radio-box is selected two fields will be provided, one for a textual description of the URL, and the

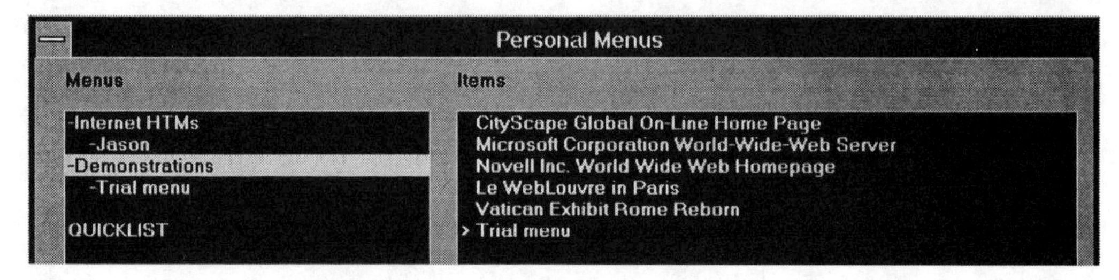

Figure 3.32: The newly created *Trial menu* (partial screen view).

second the URL itself. No validation is carried out on URLs entered into the system, so any mistakes will have to be rectified at a later stage. Figure 3.33 illustrates the creation of a URL and associated description for the NCSA Web server `www.ncsa.uiuc.edu`, home of Mosaic.

In Figure 3.33 our newly created *Trial menu* menu option has been clicked upon. Mosaic shows that there are no items in the menu because the right-hand window is empty. We can now enter the details as required. Remember that you must enter the full URL name, so precede any host names with `http://` if you are downloading images or HTML-files etc. Use other resource-types as required, e.g. `gopher://`, `telnet://` and so forth. In the 32 bit version of Mosaic a new `mosaic.ini` section called `[Hotlist]` has been added which allows URLs to be added to the standard *QUICKLIST* entry. This is discussed in detail within Section 3.2.

Editing an Existing Item

To edit an existing item simply click on the appropriate menu or URL description and then click on the *Edit* button. Mosaic will then display a window with the URL description and name for you to change. If the item you select is a menu, you can change its name (although not its position). If the item selected is a URL description you can change the URL itself or the textual description that accompanies it.

Deleting an Existing Menu

Deleting options must be carried out very carefully: deletion of a sub-menu will result in the deletion of all the items (and any sub-menus) within it. Mosaic will therefore ask you whether or not you want to delete in a *recursive* manner before proceeding. If you select not to delete recursively many of the existing menu structures within `mosaic.ini` can become *orphaned*, that is to say that a sub-menu may not have an associated parent menu (a sub-menu that can never be called even though the

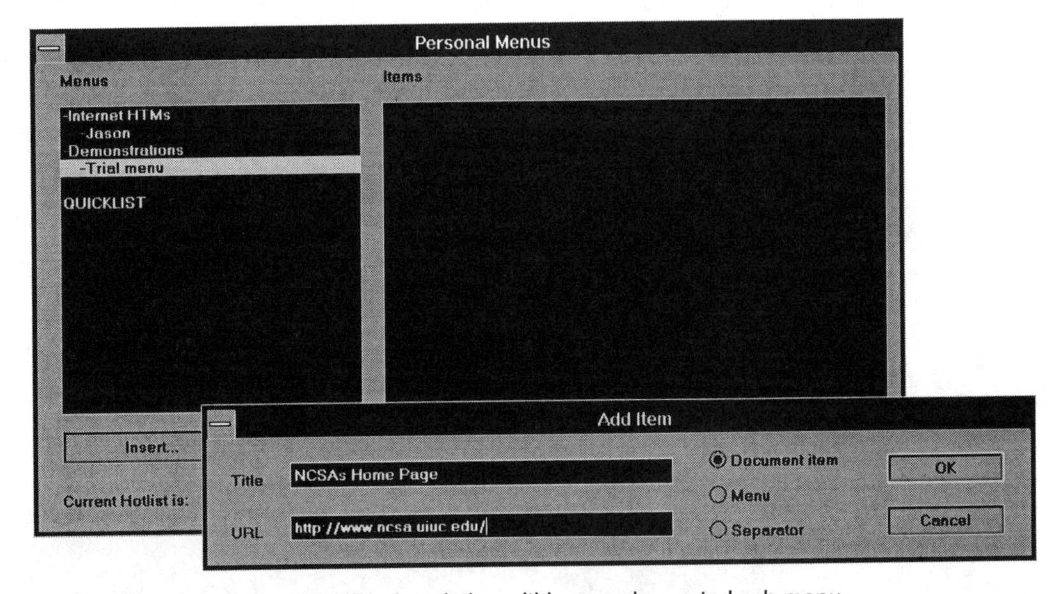

Figure 3.33: Creating a new URL description within a newly created sub-menu.

definitions for it still exist in the `mosaic.ini` file). You will have to hand-edit the `mosaic.ini` file to overcome this problem. In fact, it's worth having a look at what has been done to the initialization file after any hotlist modifications, since Mosaic does have the nasty habit of placing newly created menu definitions all over the place within the file, rather than in any specific order. Refer to Section 3.2 for more details on the structure of hotlists within the `mosaic.ini` file.

Using Separators

Aside from menus, sub-menus and URL definitions, there are also *separators*. These are inserted into your hotlist menus to separate various menu options, perhaps in an attempt to categorize various URLs. Separators are non-clickable items, so although you could in theory create your own separators using any characters from the keyboard using a standard URL item, this wouldn't be wise since Mosaic would treat it as a valid URL if you clicked on it accidentally, which would then result in a failed DNS name lookup.

CHAPTER

4

Advanced HTML concepts

4.1 Introduction

Layer 1 HTML is mainly concerned with marking up text and controlling the layout of the document as it will appear on screen. Beyond layer 1 HTML the user has to step outside of the realm of the browser and deal with different entities entirely, such as Web servers and other external programs. One of the most advanced areas of HTML concerns Fill-Out-Forms (FOFs), or just *forms* as they are known in the HTML community. Forms are a very important concept, since without them the World-Wide Web would only deal in one-way traffic. Forms allow user input to be included within an HTML document, which can then be transmitted to a remote Web server on the Internet. The information transmitted could be anything from a simple textual message (the Web equivalent of an email) or it could be something more complex, such as an encoded *query string* that sets out the parameters for a search of a database or other file, returning any results in a format such as ASCII or marked-up ASCII, e.g. HTML format.

This chapter introduces forms in context to the NCSA httpd server, which runs under Microsoft Windows (or *WinHttpd*). WinHttpd has been provided so that users can run their own Web servers on the Internet via a suitable TCP/IP connection. It is also possible to run WinHttpd on a local machine for development and testing purposes, i.e. where the client browser and WinHttpd server processes are running on one machine. The WinHttpd software brings many new facilities to bear, one of these being Fill-Out-Forms, and another called *Imagemaps* (in-line images with multiple hot-regions, or hyperlinks, embedded within them). In this chapter you will learn how to:

- Create Fill-Out-Forms using the HTML `<form>` construct
- Interface Fill-Out-Forms with remote Web servers using the Common Gateway Interface (CGI)
- Use standard MS-DOS batch files as CGI server scripts
- Use extended DOS pre-processors (Norton DOS) as alternatives to `COMMAND.COM`
- Create advanced CGI scripts using a dBASE-like fourth generation language (4GL)
- Create *Imagemap* event-regions to launch hyperlinks and other URLs

The NCSA WinHttpd software has one major advantage for PC users, namely its ability to use standard MS-DOS batch files as a means of interfacing a client to a remote Web server. As you will come to see, however, the standard MS-DOS pre-processor (or *shell*) lacks the real power and functionality to handle complex string manipulation functions. For this reason we have devoted some parts of this chapter to an alternative called NDOS (Norton DOS). NDOS is one of the best alternatives to `COMMAND.COM` currently available. In fact, it is left to the developer the *language* in which they choose to implement server scripts. As you will learn, just about any language can be used that has the facility to access DOS environment variables (this is the basis of the CGI standard).

4.2 Inserting Forms and User Input into your Document

HTML forms are themselves very easy to create, as we will show in this chapter. However, a form by itself is completely useless unless the data entered into it can be transmitted and used by a process located elsewhere (commonly this process, or server, will be located remotely). Setting up a server to deal with a form requires some additional expertise, however.

Many of the current form server programs are written in the programming language C, although there are exceptions (versions come in other UNIX languages such as `perl` and `awk`, for example). In fact, most of the development within the form-processing arena is being carried out on the UNIX operating system at the time of writing. This section starts by looking at the required tags that are used to create forms, while the later part of this section examines some programs (mainly DOS batch files and some simple 4GL programs) and concepts to deal with form-processing. If you are not a programmer (or developer) forms are a concept that you may want to bypass for the time being, at least until they become a concrete addition to the overall HTML language. A knowledge of MS-DOS batch files and a dBASE-like language would be useful for readers contemplating this section.

HTML Form Tags

A form is an area on the Mosaic text window that has one or more fields that allow the user to supply input from the keyboard. Once a form has been filled, the data can be sent to a destination server. Most commonly this will be a HTTP server on another Internet host. This HTTP server will be able to deal with the forms you send because it will have a dedicated program to check the data that has been sent (typically this includes checking the number of fields sent, their length and type etc.). What is actually done with the data depends on the context of the whole operation. A form could be used to send email to a person for example, in which case your form would contain some fields for the recipient's email address, and a field area in which to enter the message.

Clearly, you cannot send just any form to a particular server; the person who wrote the Web page that includes the form will also have tailored the server to receive information from this particular form. The `<form>` and `</form>` tags are used to encapsulate your actual form layout. Within these tags are a series of additional sub-tags called `<input type>` tags. These contain details such as the data type of the input field (text, numeric, check-box etc.) and the name of the field (so that it can be identified when finally sent to a server). Finally, an `<input type>` tag must be provided to actually submit the form to the remote server. You are free to place whatever text you wish around each tag so as to tell the user what input is required. You may also want to break these up into paragraphs for neatness.

Form Tags

To create a form area use the `<form>` and `</form>` tags to mark out the required area. Place your individual field definitions, and any text required, in-between these tags (field tags are discussed below). The `<form>` tag takes the form

```
<form method="cMethod" action="cScript">
... fields ...
</form>
```

where `cMethod` is the method actually used to transmit the form to the remote server. Currently the `POST` and `GET` methods are most widely used within HTML forms. A description of the main posting methods for form handling are discussed later after the field types that can be used in a form have first been explained.

Form Text Fields

Text fields allow the entry of alphanumeric data, that is letters and numbers (and punctuation symbols etc.). The form of the tag is:

```
<input type="text" size=nSize name="cName">
```

where `nSize` represents the width (in characters) of the field, and `cName` is a unique fieldname for this entry. For example, we could create a character field to hold a person's name using the tag:

```
<input type="text" size=40 name="Fullname">
```

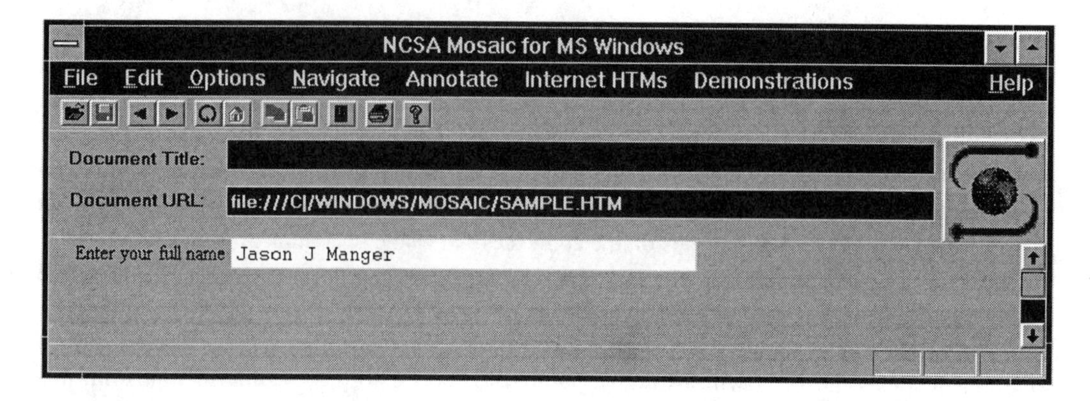

Figure 4.1: A simple text field.

This small example would place a 40 character field on the screen at the exact position it was mentioned in your HTML document. This wouldn't mean anything to the user without some additional text of course, so add some as follows and don't forget to place a `<form>` and `</form>` around the outside of the tag, otherwise the field will not appear. The URL in this example is fictitious. Using such a URL may not please Mosaic (click on the *Ignore* box if an error appears while you are developing your forms off-line).

```
<form method="GET" action="http://somewhere.com/cgi/postform">
Enter your full name
<input type="text" size=40 name="Fullname">
</form>
```

On the Mosaic screen this will resemble that shown in Figure 4.1. In order to enter some data into the field you must first click on the field using the mouse. A cursor will then appear and you can enter some text, as shown.

The example shown will in fact do nothing, apart from allowing you to enter some data, since there is no way to actually *submit* the data to the (fictitious) remote server mentioned in the form tag. To do this we must use another `<input type>` tag, but using the special `type="submit"` attribute instead. A form submission tag takes the form:

```
<input type="submit" value="Text string for instructions">
```

where the value option specifies some text that will be inserted into a button for the user to click on in order that the form data can be submitted to the server in question. We can thus extend our previous example as follows:

```
<form method="GET" action="http://somewhere.com/cgi/postform">
Enter your full name:
<input type="text" size=40 name="Fullname">
```

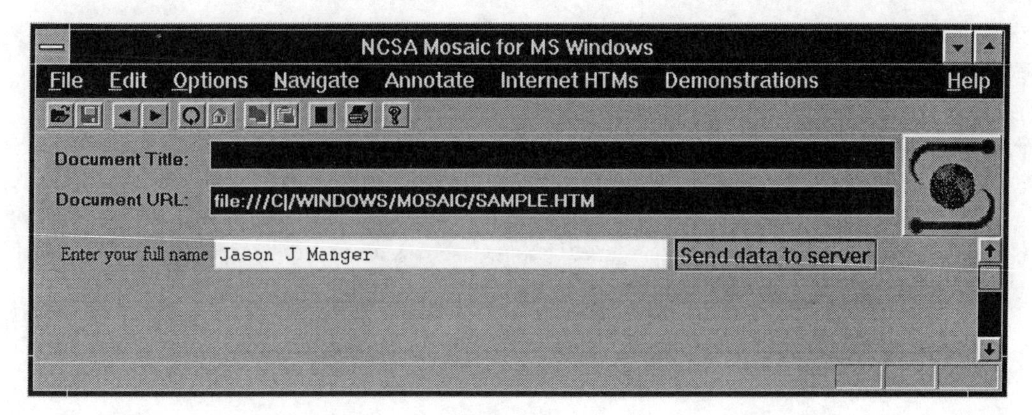

Figure 4.2: Text field and submit button.

```
<input type="submit" value="Send data to server">
</form>
```

which, on screen would resemble the form shown in Figure 4.2.

If you want some *default text* in a text field, simply quote the `value=` attribute along with the text you require (the user can of course delete the text if necessary). For example, we could allocate a default year to a field as follows:

```
<input type="number" size=4 value="1995" name="TheYear">
```

Defaults are useful since they speed up form entry, especially when the values in some form fields stay the same.

Form Numeric Fields

These are constructed exactly the same as text fields, and they appear exactly similar except for the fact that only numeric data can be entered. Change the `type` entry to `number` for numeric fields. Do not use numeric fields for details such as phone numbers, since many such numbers include hyphens and even other characters. Use numeric fields for monetary amounts, e.g. salaries and any numeric quantities. For example, we could have the two-field form (which borrows some tags explained earlier in the previous section):

```
<form method="GET" action="http://somewhere.com/cgi/postform">
Full Name:
<input type="text" size=40 name="Fullname">
Salary:
<input type="number" size=5 name="Salary">
<hr><input type="submit" value="Send data to server">
</form>
```

In this example, a five-digit field has been provided for a salary figure, and a 40 character field for a person's name. Both fields appear on one line since there are no paragraph (<p>) breaks.

Form Check-boxes and Radio-boxes

Check-boxes allow *yes/no*-type replies to be forwarded or recorded. Each check-box is a small square which if clicked on is filled with a small cross to indicate that it has been selected. One or more check-boxes can be enabled at any one time. Use check-boxes for multiple responses. The `<input type>` tag for a single check-box takes the form:

```
<input type= "checkbox" name="cName" value="cDescription">
```

where `cDescription` is some text that describes what the check-box represents (for the server machine to use), and `cName` is the system identifier for the family of check-boxes in your form. Note that each system identifier (the `name=` part of the tag) should ideally be the same if you are using multiple check-boxes – different ones can be used for check-boxes, but not for radio-boxes, since the latter can only return one option, whereas check-boxes can return multiple choices. You will also have to supply some free-form text for each check-box, so that users know what they are clicking on. For example, we could use a series of check-boxes for part of a questionnaire on the Internet:

```
<form method="GET" action="http://somewhere.com/cgi/postform">
Which Internet tools do you use? <p>
<input type="checkbox" name="cquest" value="Telnet">Telnet
    server<p>
<input type="checkbox" name="cquest" value="FTP">FTP server<p>
<input type="checkbox" name="cquest" value="WWW">WWW server<p>
<input type="checkbox" name="cquest" value="WAIS ">WAIS server<p>
<p><hr>
<input type="submit" value="Send replies to server">
</form>
```

In Mosaic, this would resemble the screen shown in Figure 4.3. If you want your check-boxes on a single line remove the <p> paragraph breaks from the HTML document in the previous example (as shown in the next example with radio-boxes).

Radio-boxes are similar in appearance to the check-box already discussed, except for the fact that radio-boxes are rounded and that only one selection can be made from a sequence. Use a `type="radio"` attribute to create each radio-box and use `value=` attributes to name the contents of the box. Radio-boxes should be used in cases where only a single reply (from a choice) can only be selected. For example we could have:

```
<form method="GET" action="http://somewhere.com/cgi/postform">
How do you wish to pay?
<input type="radio" name="rquest" value="CHEQUE">Cheque
<input type="radio" name="rquest" value="PO">Postal Order
```

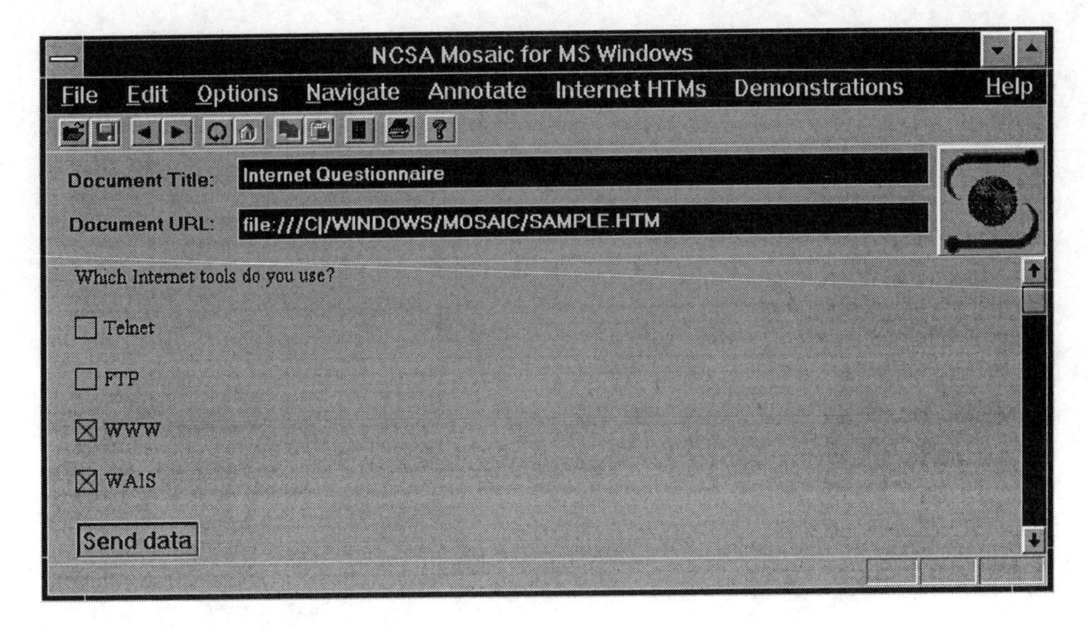

Figure 4.3: A simple check-box form.

```
<input type="radio" name="rquest" value="CC">Credit Card
<input type="radio" name="rquest" value="CASH">Cash payment
<p><hr>
<input type="submit" value="Send reply">
</form>
```

In this example the user should be able to select only one method of payment. A radio-box is thus the field type we require. This example would result in the screen shown in Figure 4.4 (the selections being all on one line this time to save screen space).

Section 4.3 contains more on posting methods, server variables, and finding out how to determine whether or not a check-box or radio-box has been activated.

▶ TIP

If you want to check a radio-box automatically, use the 'checked' option in the tag, for example:

```
<input type = "radio" name="r1" value="name" checked>
```

Form Text Area Fields

A text area field is basically a character-based field that extends over more than one line. Such fields are useful for entering free-form text that is larger in nature. Two new tags called `<textarea>` and `</textarea>` are used to create the field. The field also has two additional attributes called `cols=`

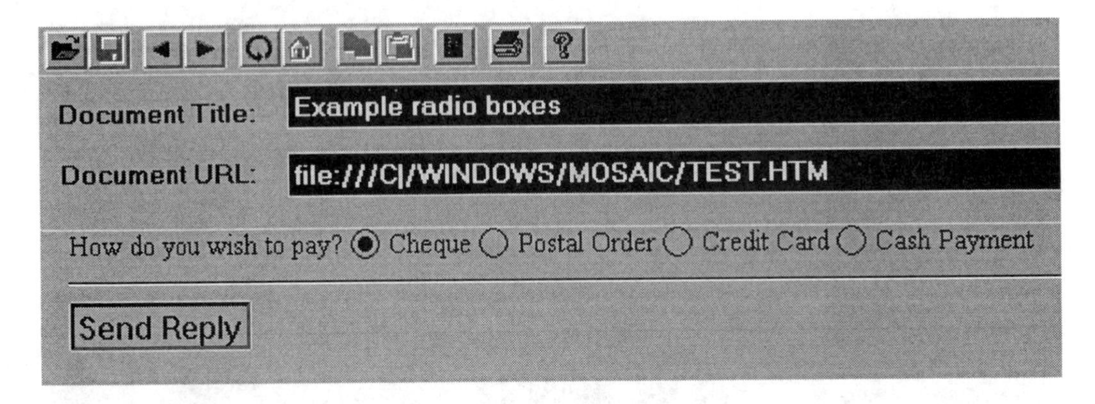

Figure 4.4: A simple radio-box form.

and `rows=` to allow the size of the field to be specified (in terms of the number of rows and columns, one column being a single character wide and one row being a single line deep). For example we could have the HTML excerpt:

```
...
<textarea name="freeform" rows=4 cols=50></textarea>
...
```

which would create a field with 4 rows (depth) and 50 columns (width). To place some default text in the window, place it in-between the two tags, for example:

```
...
<textarea name="freeform" rows=4 cols=50>
Here is some default text.
</textarea>
...
```

Remember that all `<textarea>` tags must be within `<form>` and `</form>` tags. As an example of a form using a text-area field we could therefore have the following:

```
<form method="GET" action="http://somewhere.com/cgi/postform">
Comments:
<textarea name="Comments" rows=4 cols=50><hr>
<input type=submit value="Send reply">
</form>
```

In fact, even though we have specified 4 rows and 50 columns in the example, Mosaic will allow this area to be exceeded. If you continually type in text from the keyboard Mosaic will not insert any soft returns, so the text just continues onwards, scrolling horizontally along the field. This cannot be

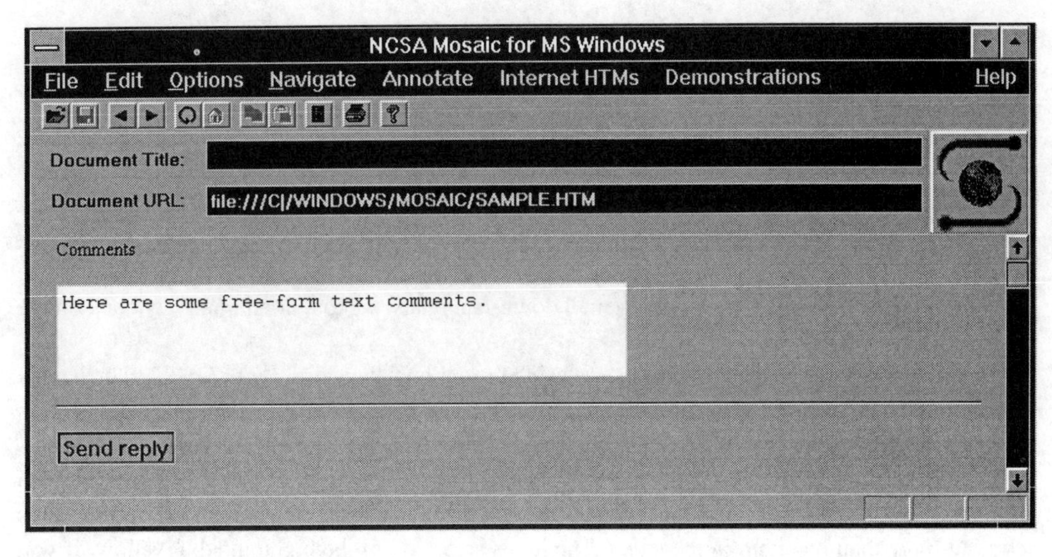

Figure 4.5: Example free-form text field.

done vertically, however – Mosaic will strictly enforce the number of rows. Figure 4.5 illustrates the resulting Mosaic page from the example above.

Form Selection-boxes

Forms can also make use of selection-boxes, in which a value can be returned from a scrolling menu of existing options. This feature makes use of the `<select>`, `<option>` and `</select>` tags, which are in turn embedded within your `<form>` and `</form>` area. The simplest selection-box is constructed using a series of tags such as

```
<form method="GET" action="http://somewhere.com/cgi/postform>
<select>
<option>Apples
<option>Oranges
<option>Pears
<option>Bananas
<option>grapefruit
</select>
</form>
```

which would create a small bar in your document resembling that shown in Figure 4.6. In order to

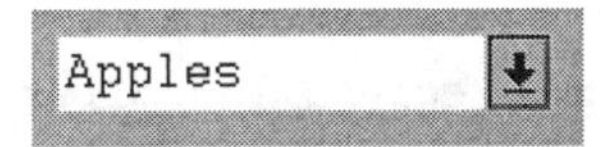

Figure 4.6: Example selection box (default).

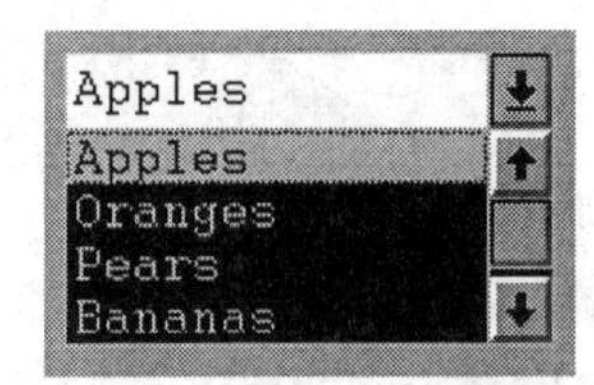

Figure 4.7: Extended selection box.

select other items in the box click on the small down-facing arrow icon, or alternatively click on the box itself.

This selection-box can be increased in size using the optional keyword '`multiple`', which must be mentioned within the `<select>` tag, e.g. `<select multiple>`. When this extended version of the tag is used we end up with a selection-box that resembles that shown in Figure 4.7.

The extended size of the box is not the only change, however, since the `multiple` attribute also allows the user to *drag* the mouse (keep the button down when dragging) over multiple options, thus selecting more than one item in the menu. The items selected will be highlighted in yellow. If you want a particular item to be selected automatically (and highlighted) when a selection box appears, place the word `selected` in the corresponding `<option>` tag; for example:

```
<form method="GET" action="http://somewhere.com/cgi/postform>
<select multiple>
<option>Apples
<option>Oranges
<option>Pears
<option selected>Bananas
<option>grapefruit
</select>
</form>
```

would highlight the item *Bananas* in the list. If the selection box did not have the `multiple` option enabled this item would still appear as the first item seen. If you place more than one `selected` option in the list Mosaic simply highlights each entry that you have tagged. Finally, if you need to increase the number of rows in your selection list, use `<select size=`*n*`>` where `n` represents the number of rows (or lines) to display in the list.

As an example of a form that uses some simple text and radio-box elements, consider the HTML file shown below. This form implements a simple supplier's order sheet, with areas for details such as names, addresses, order quantities and descriptions, plus payment methods (implemented as radio-boxes).

```
<!--Example supply/order form-->
<title>SUPPLIER'S DETAILS</title>
<form method="GET" action="/cgi-bin/supplier.bat">
<pre>COMPANY NAME:                    CUSTOMER NAME:<p></pre>
```

```
<input type="text" size=40 name="custname">
<input type="text" size=40 name="compname"><p>
<pre>SALESPERSON'S NAME:</pre><p>
<input type="text" size=40 name="salpers"><p>
<pre>SUPPLIER'S ADDRESS DETAILS:       CUSTOMER'S ADDRESS
DETAILS:</pre><p>
<input type="text" size=40 name="addr1">
<input type="text" size=40 name="cusaddr1"><p>
<input type="text" size=40 name="addr2">
<input type="text" size=40 name="cusaddr2"><p>
<input type="text" size=40 name="addr3">
<input type="text" size=40 name="cusaddr3"><p>
<hr>ORDER DETAILS<p>
<pre>QUANT         ORDER DETAILS         UNIT COST  TOTAL</pre>
<!-- Order details-->
<input type="number" size=3 name="qno1">
<input type="text" size=40 name="desc1">
<input type="number" size=8 name="qcost1">
<input type="number" size=9 name="qtot1"><p>
<input type="number" size=3 name="qno2">
<input type="text" size=40 name="desc2">
<input type="number" size=8 name="qcost2">
<input type="number" size=9 name="qtot2"><p>
<input type="number" size=3 name="qno3">
<input type="text" size=40 name="desc3">
<input type="number" size=8 name="qcost3">
<input type="number" size=9 name="qtot3"><p>
<hr>METHOD OF PAYMENT:
<!--Method of payment-->
<input type="radio" name="rad" value="cheque">CHEQUE
<input type="radio" name="rad" value="po">PURCHASE ORDER
<input type="radio" name="rad" value="cod">C.O.D
<input type="radio" name="rad" value="cc">CREDIT CARD
<hr>
CARD NUMBER: <input type="text" size=1 name="ccnoa">
<!--Credit card field-->
<input type="text" size=1 name="ccnob">
<input type="text" size=1 name="ccnoc">
<input type="text" size=1 name="ccnod">-
<input type="text" size=1 name="ccnoe">
<input type="text" size=1 name="ccnof">
<input type="text" size=1 name="ccnog">
<input type="text" size=1 name="ccnoh">-
```

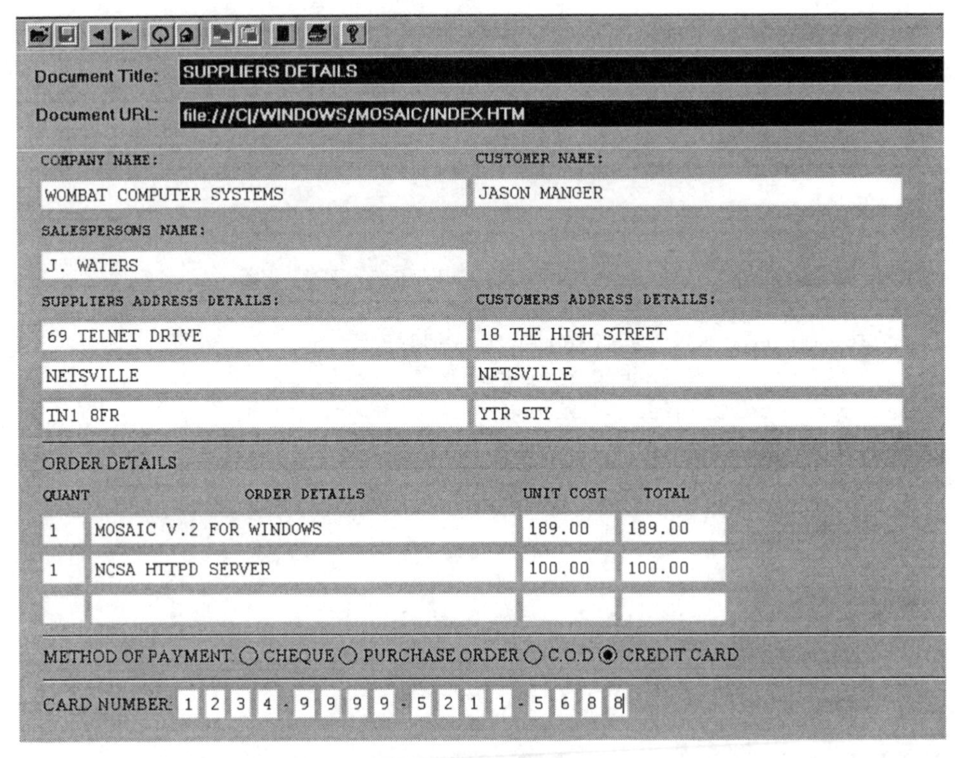

Figure 4.8: How our example form looks within Mosaic.

```
<input type="text" size=1 name="ccnoi">
<input type="text" size=1 name="ccnoj">
<input type="text" size=1 name="ccnok">
<input type="text" size=1 name="ccnol">-
<input type="text" size=1 name="ccnom">
<input type="text" size=1 name="ccnon">
<input type="text" size=1 name="ccnoo">
<input type="text" size=1 name="ccnop"><p>
<input type="submit" value=" Send details to server ">
</form>
```

A large problem with forms is their size – they can consume quite a large area. To use the full area of the screen you can place fields side-by-side (simply leave out the <p> paragraph break at the end of the field in question). Credit card numbers can be entered using a single field, although using multiple text fields (with one-character widths) looks particularly attractive and resembles the layout used in many paper-based forms. Bear in mind also that the larger your form, the larger the query string will become. Figure 4.8 illustrates how the form shown in the next example looks when viewed through Mosaic.

Note the hyphens (-) inserted in-between the credit card numbers to break up the fields. The use of <pre> tags to insert field titles is also useful, since Mosaic will then print all white space, thus allowing you to set two text strings apart from one another.

▶ TIP

1. When using the preformatted tag </pre> for *computerese* text be sure not to use the <b> tag on the start of a sentence that has itself been tabbed-in or centred etc. Mosaic will ignore any leading white space and place the text at the start of the leftmost column. To overcome this problem place some normal text before the emboldened item(s).

2. Mosaic has the horrible habit of insetting a carriage-return (like a <p> paragraph break) after every </pre> preformatted end-tag. This means that `Courier` font text cannot be embedded within a sentence without the line being broken. Try to avoid embedding preformatted text within sentences until a fix is released that cures this particular problem.

Providing a Form Deletion Function

Many of the forms in existence on the Internet provide a *reset* function which erases all of the entries in a form. You may also want to provide such a feature. To do so requires use of the `<input type>` tag with a `type="reset"` attribute. For example you could have:

```
<input type="reset" value="Delete all fields">
```

which will create a button labelled *Delete all Fields*, which when clicked on will do just that.

4.3 Interfacing to Web Servers – NCSA WinHttpd and the CGI

Since this book is concerned with MS-DOS and Windows-based software we will first examine the writing of some server scripts using the recently released NCSA httpd (HyperText Transfer Protocol Daemon) server, a fully fledged Web server that runs under Microsoft Windows. The NCSA httpd program accompanies this book on disk, and is also available from many archives on the Internet – see the appendices for details. The NCSA httpd program can be run locally on a single PC, although this is clearly not the point of using the software, albeit for testing purposes. The httpd program is a server implementation and should ideally listen on a TCP/IP connection for people requesting Web documents, images, audio clips and the like. The NCSA httpd server is based on a standard known as CGI, or Common Gateway Interface.

CGI is a means of interfacing external servers, such as HTTP servers, with Web clients so that items such as forms can be transmitted and dealt with. As you know, a form by itself has no use whatsoever if the data you place in it cannot be sent, decoded and processed by some server entity. The process of sending and decoding such data is embodied in the Common Gateway Interface standard. We will return to the subject of the CGI and form transmission methods in a later section of this chapter. You can run the httpd program locally, however (even without an Internet connection), to test out the program's various features, and of course to write CGI-compliant scripts. CGI is needed in order to carry out such functions as

- The storage of data from a client-form on a remote server
- To program event-driven systems, such as hot-regions within an in-line image
- To facilitate two-way communication over the World-Wide Web

The NCSA httpd program allows you to do all of these things while (most importantly) allowing you to run your own Web server on the Internet so that clients can access and retrieve published documents.

When we talk about CGI there are mainly two items of interest that concern us: (i) the CGI script that has been called from within a form in the client's document; and (ii) the *back-end* program, normally an executable file that is called from the script which is able to parse or process the data passed from the client. In many instances the script and back-end are one and the same thing, depending on whether or not the script can handle the parsing of the client's data satisfactorily. DOS is not very good at parsing information, since its string-handling functions are basically non-existent. UNIX is much better suited to handling such parsing operations, since its *shells* (many are available, e.g. Bourne Shell, C-Shell) have all of the functionality required, and of course they can interface with many other standard UNIX text-processing tools such as `perl`, `awk` and `sed`. Because of the limited nature of many DOS shells it is better to call a back-end program from within the script. This back-end could be written in any high-level language that has been compiled as a standalone executable utility, e.g. C, Visual Basic or FoxPro. Parsing can then be handled with ease, using all of the available facilities of that particular language. Later sections of this chapter examine MS-DOS, Norton DOS and a high-level programming language called *Icon* as a means of implementing CGI scripts.

Installing the NCSA httpd Server

When you obtain the program de-archive it (the program is zipped with PKZIP, and you will need version 2.04g of PKUNZIP). Make sure that you also use the `-d` option to preserve the original directory structure of the files; a whole mini file system will be created. Call the main directory into which you copy the archive HTTPD, e.g. `C:\HTTPD`. When the program has been de-archived you must configure it, or at least keep the default settings (these are commented out to start with). In addition, the NCSA httpd program requires a Windows socket interface (such as the Trumpet WinSock version 1.1 or later). This may have come with your Mosaic archive, although if not grab it from the Net: see the appendices for details. Configuring the rest of the program is very well documented within a series of HTML files that you can read with Mosaic. We recommend that you keep all the default options – simply de-comment them. One important point concerns the amount of environment space you have allocated under Windows. Edit the Windows `system.ini` file and look for the section entitled `[NonWindowsApp]`; change the `CommandEnvSize` setting to `8192` (bytes), or increase this even further if you have enough memory.

▶ TIP

VERY IMPORTANT: When running your server machine locally, e.g. on your own

PC (for trial purposes) do not use the *LOAD LOCAL FILE* option in Mosaic since this will by-pass the server. Select the File menu and *Open a URL* and then enter

```
http://localhost
```

which will route all requests through the server (ensure the NCSA httpd is running first). Your HTML home page (`index.htm`) should then be loaded.

Creating CGI scripts using the NCSA httpd program requires the use of a special Windows PIF (Program Information File) named `hscript.pif`, which you may want to examine. This PIF file calls your command pre-processor (normally `COMMAND.COM`, although better shells are available, e.g. Norton's NDOS) as held in the DOS environmental variable `COMSPEC`. This in turn is used to execute a CGI script. Commonly this script will be a DOS batch file (`.BAT`), although `.EXE` and `.COM` files can also be called. Because many CGI scripts are DOS batch files, they themselves must run in the DOS environment, and not in a fully fledged Windows environment with nice boxes, buttons and other widgets (although it is possible to utilize the features of Windows CGI on the servers through more advanced programming languages such as Visual Basic or FoxPro for Windows).

The whole implementation of DOS-based scripts running under Windows can be slightly complicated to understand, although you will get the gist of things when we some to some examples. You can of course try the examples out yourself with the NCSA httpd program running on your own machine (through the server, not through Mosaic *locally* remember, so use the *localhost* URL as shown in the tip above). Some of the file locations can be tricky to configure when you specify URLs. This is because the httpd program is configured to use an automatic document path of `c:\httpd\htdocs`. All the documents you reference in a URL must therefore be quoted *relative* to this directory. For example, your `index.htm` home page is **not** referred to using the URL:

```
http://localhost/httpd/htdocs/index.htm
```

but instead just the shortened version:

```
http://localhost/index.htm
```

since the system already assumes all document URLs are specified relative to the `c:\httpd\htdocs` directory. You can change the `DocumentRoot` variable in the `c:\httpd\conf\httpd.cnf` file to alter this default setting if you require. The `localhost` string can be replaced with your own numeric IP address if your Internet connection is up and running. People who are not placing their server on the Internet should always use `localhost`. If you wanted to offer your server to users on a temporary basis, through a dial-up connection for example, you could dial into your service provider to establish a TCP/IP connection and then run the httpd server with your IP address. This can be a bit impractical, however. People could of course then issue a URL such as `http://yourhost/` accordingly (the file `index.htm` is used as a default home page).

The two entities in this client–server scenario are thus the Mosaic browser (the client) and the remote server machine (in this case we are assuming the NCSA httpd program is taking care of server requests, although in reality it could be a UNIX-based server running a variety of scripting tools). Client programs can issue a huge array of information requests, perhaps something simple like a file download request, or something more complicated, such as a search operation for example. Clients send messages to the server that contain just the minimum amount of information for the server to process the request. Scripts are themselves called from an HTML document using the `action=` part of the form tags, e.g. `<form action="URL">`. The URL specified in the `action=` part stores the name of the script to be executed; for example:

```
<a href="http://somewhere.edu/cgi-bin/mailscrpt.bat">...</a>
```

or, likewise:

```
<a href="/cgi-bin/myscrpt.bat">...</a>
```

The second form of the URL, shown immediately above, should be used for those people that are running Mosaic and the NCSA httpd server on one machine locally, i.e. for testing purposes, or if you do not have a Internet connection. The name `/cgi-bin` is in fact a special alias that refers to the directory `\HTTPD\CGI-DOS` on your hard disk. This is where all of your CGI scripts must be stored if you use the default `/cgi-bin` location – which we recommend to avoid any further, complicated, configuration. So to recap: when you install the NCSA server edit the `\HTTPD\CONF\ACCESS.CNF` and `HTTPD.CNF` files and uncomment all of the suggested default values. Your CGI scripts (such as DOS batch files) must then be kept in `\HTTPD\CGI-DOS`, although you call these in your form's `action=` part using the special directory name `/cgi-bin/filename` where `filename` is your batch file script. The NCSA server accepts '\' and '/' as directory separators.

URLs for UNIX- and DOS-based scripts are slightly different, mainly because DOS machines use the extensions `.BAT`, `.COM` and `.EXE` for executable files. UNIX requires no such extensions, so you can quickly see which type of machine you are connecting to. Also, don't worry about accessing a UNIX script from a DOS client (or vice versa) – it will work. The HTTP protocol running within the server on the remote machine will run the script in *that* environment, and will only pass back the results. In such instances, where the client is requesting a script, the server will create a series of environmental variables which contain all of the information that the server needs to carry out the client's request. The CGI v1.0 specification is largely made up of these variables and their various usages (all of which are discussed below in detail). Windows has a problem in that it cannot pass such variables to a DOS process, so it must create a script known as a *jacket script* in which the necessary commands to create the CGI environment are made prior to invoking the remote script. Script files also make heavy use of file redirection (using the > and >> operators). All of the DOS-based batch file script files pass their data via redirection using this method.

Requests that send information to a server result in the client placing its data in a temporary file which itself is connected to the standard input of the remote server. Information is thus fed across as and when required. Retrospectively, information from the server's standard output (results of searches and/or files being downloaded) are placed in a file which is connected to the client's standard input.

Posting Methods: GET versus POST

Forms must specify an action= field that points to a script file on a server machine that will handle the form request. The main posting methods currently in use are GET and POST, but when should each be used? The use of each type will depend entirely on the server script that is reading the data from the client. In the GET method an environment variable called QUERY_STRING is created that holds the encoded data from the submitted form. The server script must therefore be able to examine the environment variable and deal with it accordingly, i.e. store it in a database, use it to conduct a search, or pass it on to another tool, such as a Gopher or WAIS server. The QUERY_STRING variable passed using the GET method resembles:

```
name1~value1&name2~value2
```

where name1 and name2 (up to name*n*) are the names of each form-field (set using a name= attribute within each form-field – discussed below). Each name and value *pair* is separated by an ampersand, spaces are converted into plus (+) signs and all non-alphabetic and numeric characters are converted to a hexadecimal value of the form %nn (for example, a colon would be translated to %3A – 3A is 58 in decimal, and ASCII value 58 is a colon)

The POST posting method is used to send the form data using the *standard input* (or *stdin*), a term coined on UNIX that refers to the location from which a program obtains its input. By default this is normally the keyboard, although it can be redefined – so for example the standard input could arrive from a file. When the POST method is specified the script program examines its internal keyboard input buffer, since all the data arriving using this posting method will be from the client's form (the NCSA httpd program still creates the QUERY_STRING anyway, so you could still access the data using a POST-like method). The complete query string is sent using the standard input so your script program must capture the input stream and then process it accordingly. The input stream will resemble:

```
name1=value1&name2=value2
```

where name1 and name2 (up to name*n*) are the names of each form-field (again, these are set using the name= attribute of each form field). Each name and value pair is separated by an ampersand and the = sign is used to separate the value from the form-field name (as opposed to a ~ in the GET method). The system variable CONTENT_LENGTH is also created – this contains the length of the query string sent. All of this may seem confusing: after all, it is. Both of these methods are examined in greater detail later with actual examples. As a simple rule of thumb you can think of POST as using equals (=) characters and GET as using tildes (~), although don't forget that POST creates a QUERY_STRING variable to pass its form data, and GET reads the standard input to get the same details. Scripts that use both these methods are examined later.

The second attribute in the <form> tag is cScript, which actually names a server script that will process the form-data that the client is sending. This takes the form of a normal URL string, for example http://somwhere.edu/ht-bin/formscript, where formscript is the program that will examine the form and extract its data. If you are developing in the DOS environment this will be a standard DOS batch file, e.g. myscript.bat. The script could exist locally, in which case you should simply quote a URL similar to that of `http://path/file`, making sure that the `path` and `file` point to the location of the required script. It goes without saying that only form and script developers will know such details, since they are creating them, although this is not strictly true since many forms are provided by authors at reachable URLs so that you can use their services, e.g. an SMTP (email) or an NNTP (USENET) server.

Dealing with Radio- and Check-boxes

When a form containing a check- or radio-box is sent to the server, the server will know which item has been selected since the name of the item will be *flagged*. For example, in the radio-box excerpt in Section 4.2 we had a simple form containing just four radio-boxes (only one of which can be selected). If we therefore clicked on the radio-box with the `value=` setting configured as *CASH* and then submitted the form, the server would set the `QUERY_STRING` (containing the encoded form data) as:

```
rquest~CASH
```

where `rquest` is the name of the radio-box (set using the `name=` part – these must all be the same in the case of a radio-box since only one option can be selected) and ~ (tilde) is the separator character used by the `GET` posting method – the `POST` method differs in that it uses an equals sign. Aside from radio-buttons, a check-box could of course have multiple options selected. Using the check-box in the example within Section 4.2 we could send the following to the server after submitting a form:

```
cquest~WWW&cquest~Telnet
```

which shows that the user has selected two check-box items (namely *Telnet* and *WWW*). If no boxes are selected nothing at all will be placed in the `QUERY_STRING` variable (radio- and check-boxes will not place their identifier names in the `QUERY_STRING` variable when they are left unselected, unlike normal textual fields).

In reality a form will contain more than just radio- and check-boxes; it will probably contain many other fields, such as text and numeric fields. How you deal with a radio/check-box value depends on your application. Typically, these are used to control the behaviour of the server program that is dealing with the form: for example, we could have a radio-box to set a male/female flag. Some pseudocode for a typical server database program could then resemble the following:

```
open database
add a blank record
replace database->name  with name~fred+smith
replace database->address with address~28+High+Trees+Netsville
replace database->phone  with phone~123+4567
if ( radsex~male )
    replace database->sex with "Male"
else
    replace database->sex with "Female"
endif
```

This small pseudocode example shows a simple information update operation where some fields from a submitted form are placed into a database on the server. Rather than using a text field for a person's sex, a radio-box can be used instead. The server script tests the radio-box value `radsex` to see whether it is set to `male` or `female`, and then the database is updated accordingly. The parsing operation to extract the actual form values has not been shown in this example – this will depend on your own server language implementation. The form that submits this data would therefore resemble:

```
<form method="GET" action="http://somewhere.com/cgi/getdata">
Please enter your details:<p>
Name: <input type="text"    name="name"><p>
Address: <input type="address" name="address"><p>
Phone: <input type="phone"   name="phone"><p>
Sex:
<input type="radio" name="radsex" value="male">Male
<input type="radio" name="radsex" value="female">Female
<p><hr>
<input type="submit" value="Send data to server">
</form>
```

There are clearly many other instances where check- and radio-boxes can be used. The important point is that your back-end script can *parse* such values and distinguish which items are input fields and which items are actually check/radio-boxes. A later section of this book examines some actual programming examples for parsing the data submitted by forms.

CGI Variables

The Common Gateway Interface uses a number of other environment variables in which values for the current client request are kept. The *jacket script* that was mentioned earlier sets all of these variable and than passes all details over to the server. A typical jacket script could therefore resemble the following:

```
SET SERVER_SOFTWARE=NCSA/V1.3Pre (MSWindows)
SET SERVER_NAME=138.8.8.68
SET SERVER_ADMIN=postmaster
SET GATEWAY_INTERFACE=CGI/1.1 DOS (experimental)
SET SERVER_PORT=80
SET SERVER_PROTOCOL=HTTP/1.0
SET REQUEST_METHOD=GET
SET HTTP_ACCEPT=C:\TMP\HS166134.ACC
SET SCRIPT_NAME=/cgi-dos/dbsearch.bat
SET OUTPUT_FILE=C:\TMP\HS166134.OUT
SET QUERY_STRING=find~sgml
SET REMOTE_ADDR=127.0.0.1
c:\httpd\cgi-dos\dbsearch.bat find~sgml
```

Notice the last line, which is the name of the server script being called along with any arguments (these are the actual encoded data transmitted by the form). All of the variables mentioned above are now discussed briefly. Any of these variables can be used from within your CGI scripts and/or back-end program accordingly. They are set as soon as the server executes the script file that is called by the client. Some of the variables are specific to Microsoft Windows only, and are marked as such.

CGI Default Variables

The following CGI variables are always created by the httpd program, irrespective of the posting method in use by the form.

`SERVER_SOFTWARE`

This variable contains the name and version of the information server software that is answering the request (and which is also running the server gateway). The Windows httpd program sets this as `NCSA/V1.3Pre (MSWindows)`.

`SERVER_NAME`

This variable contains the server's host name, i.e. its DNS alias, such as `machine.myhost.com`, or the equivalent numeric IP (Internet Protocol) address, e.g. `138.8.8.68`.

`GATEWAY_INTERFACE`

This stores the revision version number of the CGI specification to which this server complies. Windows httpd version 1.3Pre complies with the CGI version 1.1 specification.

`OUTPUT_FILE`
(Windows only)

This variable points to the name and location of the file on the client's machine that is used to hold the script output from the server, and could be used within a *back-end* to refer to the data.

CGI Request-specific Variables

The following variables are specific to the client request.

`SERVER_PROTOCOL`

A variable that holds the name and revision number of the information protocol that the current client request made. This will be the value `HTTP version 1.0` in httpd v1.3.

`SERVER_PORT`

Contains the port number on which the server accepted the client request. This is set to `80` on nearly all Web servers (a commonly agree port number adopted for HTTP servers world-wide), and a default of 80 is suggested by the httpd installation program. Some servers on the Internet are using other port numbers, e.g. 8080.

REQUEST_METHOD

A variable containing the posting method with which the client request was made. For the HTTP protocol the valid types are GET and POST, both of which were discussed in detail in the previous section. A CGI back-end or server script could use this value to control which type of parsing was required.

HTTP_ACCEPT

These are the MIME types (file formats) that the client will accept, as given by HTTP headers. The variable is set to the name of a temporary file with the .ACC extension. For example, the MIME type for ASCII text is text/plain. All MIME types are set up in the files mosaic.ini (for Mosaic) and /http/conf/mime.typ (for httpd).

PATH_INFO

Contains extra path information, as specified by the client. Scripts can thus be accessed by a *virtual pathname*, followed by additional information at the end of the path. The extra information is kept in this variable. Decode this if it comes from a URL before it is passed to the resulting CGI script. For example, if a URL was structure in a hyper-reference as http:/host/dir1/script.bat/dir1/dir2/file then the part of the URL /dir1/dir2/file could be the file the script has to access, and should thus be decoded by the server (this extra path information is the actual value held in the variable).

PATH_TRANSLATED

This variable provides a translated version of the PATH_INFO variable. This is used for virtual-to-physical path mapping. Virtual paths are relative to the directory set up by the server (/httpd/htdocs is the default in Winhttpd 1.3).

SCRIPT_NAME

A virtual path to the script being executed. For example, /cgi-dos/myfile.bat refers to the batch file that resides in /httpd/cgi-dos/myfile.bat since /httpd is the default directory in which httpd expects to find all its system files.

QUERY_STRING

Stores the information sent by the client in a form or in the <isindex> document (and is also the text which follows the ? in a URL .

REMOTE_HOST

Stores the hostname of the client making the server request. If the server does not have access to this particular data, it should set REMOTE_ADDR and leave REMOTE_HOST unset. If you are using httpd locally, i.e. client and server on one machine, the `REMOTE_ADDR` variable is set to the default IP (Internet Protocol) address of `127.0.0.1`.

REMOTE_ADDR
: Contains the IP (Internet Protocol) address of the client making the request to the server.

CONTENT_TYPE
: This variable is set for queries which have some attached information, e.g. the `POST` method used in a form. It contains the MIME type of the data being sent back to the client, e.g. `text/html` for an HTML document, or `text/plain for plain text.`

CONTENT_LENGTH
: A numeric value representing the length of the actual message content (such as a query string) as passed by the client to the server script. This value is useful when the `POST` posting-method is used.

CONTENT_FILE (Windows only)
: Contains the name of a file which itself contains the content data sent by the client to the server, such as a query string from a form, or an `<isindex>` search string. The exact number of bytes (or characters) in this variable is contained in `CONTENT_LENGTH`.

The most common variable that you will use in your CGI script is most definitely `QUERY_STRING`, which is created in all instances (in the Windows httpd, at least) after a form or other search field has been executed by the client. Query strings always arrive as one line and must be parsed by the server script (or *back-end* program) accordingly.

Command Line Variables

If your data is **not** arriving from a form, but is instead arriving from a document with an `<isindex>` tag (this provides an input window for some search text and then sends it to the server – as discussed below), the command line argument `%1` will hold the entire query string. The same variable is also set to the value of the query string if a form using the `POST` posting method is being used by the client.

Using `<isindex>` Documents

HTML documents that have an `<isindex>` tag within them are used to provide the user with a *front-end* into a search system, i.e. your batch file script. A small window is provided into which a search string can be entered (the client translates all spaces in the string into plus signs). A question mark is then added to your batch file's URL along with the entire search string, before the batch file is re-invoked and processes the data accordingly. Your batch file must detect whether or not any search arguments have been passed in order to call an HTML document with an `<isindex>` tag so that the user can actually enter some text. The only other way of specifying a search string is to use a URL of the form:

```
<a href="http://host/cgi-bin/myscript.bat?findthis">
```

where `findthis` is the search string. This is not a very good method since users cannot enter a search string of their own choosing because it is hard-coded into the HTML document. The alternative is to set up your batch file to check the DOS variable `%#`. This variable contains the number of arguments passed to the batch file and can be used to see whether or not a search string has been passed. An `<isindex>` document translates a search string into a series of words separated by plus signs, for example the input text *the quick brown fox* is converted into the DOS variable `%1` as:

```
the+quick+brown+fox
```

which is easier to decode – just replace all plus signs with spaces, and extract accordingly. If the `%#` variable is zero (no search string passed) we would call an external HTML file that has the `<isindex>` tag within it, and perhaps some instructions to the user. This is done via the special line in the batch file called `Location:` which refers to the HTML file, e.g. `Location: http://host/cgi-bin/isindex.htm`. When users have entered a search pattern they are returned to the batch file and the search can take place. An example of this is given in the following section.

File Transfer Queries

At this point it is worth showing an example script. The example below is an MS-DOS batch file that allows a client to request a file from a server machine. The file in this instance is `AUTOEXEC.BAT`, which is conveniently found on nearly all PCs. The task in this example is therefore to create a simple script to download an ASCII file from a remote server to the current machine (if you are using httpd locally you will still see the outcome).

```
set OUTFILE=%OUTPUT_FILE%
echo Content-type: text/plain > %OUTFILE%
echo.                          >> %OUTFILE%
type c:\autoexec.bat           >> %OUTFILE%
```

Firstly, the variable `OUTFILE` (arbitrary name) is created using the DOS `SET` command, and is assigned the value of the variable `OUTPUT_FILE` (DOS variables must be enclosed in percentage signs if you want to extract their internal values in this way). `OUTPUT_FILE` is a reserved variable created by the httpd program; it contains the name of a temporary file in which the results from the server are sent back to the client. The next two lines of the script are critically important. The first of them is a MIME file type. MIME is an acronym for Multipurpose Internet Mail Extensions – you have dozens of them in your `mosaic.ini` file in the `[Suffixes]` section. MIME extensions tell the client (Mosaic) what file type it is being sent back from the server, e.g. GIF image (`image/gif`),

HTML document (`text/html`), ASCII document (`text/plain`) and so forth. In our example the text will be a sequence of simple ASCII characters (MIME type `text/plain`). The string '`Content type: `' must also be included (the space after the colon is optional) in front of the MIME extension. The second line in the script must always be blank: the command `echo.` achieves this.

If you are unsure about a MIME extension simply refer to your `mosaic.ini` file to see some examples of various file types. You can also refer to the MIME configuration file `mime.typ` in the `/httpd/conf` directory of your newly installed system, which has a much longer list of MIME extensions. Remember that each command that produces some output for the client must be redirected to the `OUTFILE` variable that is created on the first line. You can call this what you like as long as everything tallies up to this variable. Notice how the first redirection symbol is a > (overwrite/create file). Since we are creating the temporary file for the first time we can get away with this; be sure not to use any subsequent >s, however, since you may overwrite your temporary file. The remaining >> symbols simply append data into the same file. And so finally the temporary file would look like the following, after being written to disk:

```
Content-type: text/plain

@ECHO OFF
smartdrv /q
path=c:\utils;c:\batch;c:\dos
prompt $p$g
```

which in essence is a very small `AUTOEXEC.BAT` file. The blank line in the example output was provided by using a period immediately after the DOS `ECHO` statement. If you are using MS-DOS earlier than version 5.0 you will not have this feature. Do not use `ECHO` by itself, since this will result in a message indicating whether or not echoing is on or off – instead use an entry such as `ECHO " "`, or even `ECHO` *`<ALT-32, ALT-255>`*, where *`<ALT-32, ALT-255>`* represents a space and then a blank printing character (make sure that a space comes before the *`<ALT-255>`*); the `<ALT>` represents the pressing of the ALT key (as if you didn't know). The very last line uses the standard DOS `TYPE` command to display our file (`AUTOEXEC.BAT`, in this example), which is also redirected into the temporary file in the same way. Ensure that the location of the file is fully qualified, i.e. the exact path from the root directory to the file is given so that the file can be found on disk.

This example is redundant for all intents and purposes, since you can transfer any text file, HTML document or image directly using a suitable URL. The power of this type of script is the use of the `Location:` string, which replaces the `Content-type:` definition. If you wanted the server to access a particular file automatically (rather than you specifying the exact URL) simply structure your script as:

```
set OUTFILE=%OUTPUT_FILE%
echo Location: http://host.com/files/text.txt > %OUTFILE%
echo.                                         >> %OUTFILE%
```

which informs the server to grab the file specified by the URL `http://files/text.txt` for the client. You can also specify a file on an FTP, Gopher or WAIS server using the URLs: `ftp://`, `gopher://` or `wais://`.

Form-based Server Queries

We have seen how forms are created within HTML. What about interfacing them with a server script so that the data in the form can be used? This is an area in which a great deal of development is taking place on the Internet. It doesn't really matter which program is used on the server just as long as the data in the client's form can be processed (or *parsed*) without any problems. When the client processes a form and the user clicks on the *submit* button the form data is sent across to the server in an internal form which the server must be able to decode. There is no special (or *standard*) program that decodes the form data that has been transmitted; programs have been written in a myriad of scripting languages, e.g. `perl`, `awk` and `sed` (on UNIX), and even high-level languages such as C, BASIC and Icon (the latter is examined later on in this chapter). UNIX shell scripts and DOS batch files can also be used. As an example, take the following HTML form:

```
<form method="post" action="http://somewhere.com/cgi-bin/dbsearch.bat">
<b>Person search</b><p>
Search on:
<select name="what">
<option selected>Name
<option>Title
<option>Address
<option>Phone
</select><P>
which:
<select name="how">
<option>contains
<option>is exactly
</select><P>
the following:
<input type="text" value="value"><p>
<input type="submit" value="Start searching">
</form>
```

This example form resembles that shown in Figure 4.9.

Our sample form allows the user to enter some details about a person so that the person can be searched for in a database to extract an email address or to obtain a phone number etc. At this stage the database is undefined, as is the program (or script) that is going to decode the data sent through the form. Depending on which item the user clicks the httpd program will create a *query string*, which is sent to the server script. In this case the server script is called `dbsearch.bat` (a DOS batch file) that resides on the Internet host `somewhere.com`). The form contains two selection bars: the first decides what item we are searching on as a key to finding the person (name, title, address, phone number), while the second provides a method of searching: a substring search, or an exact search. A

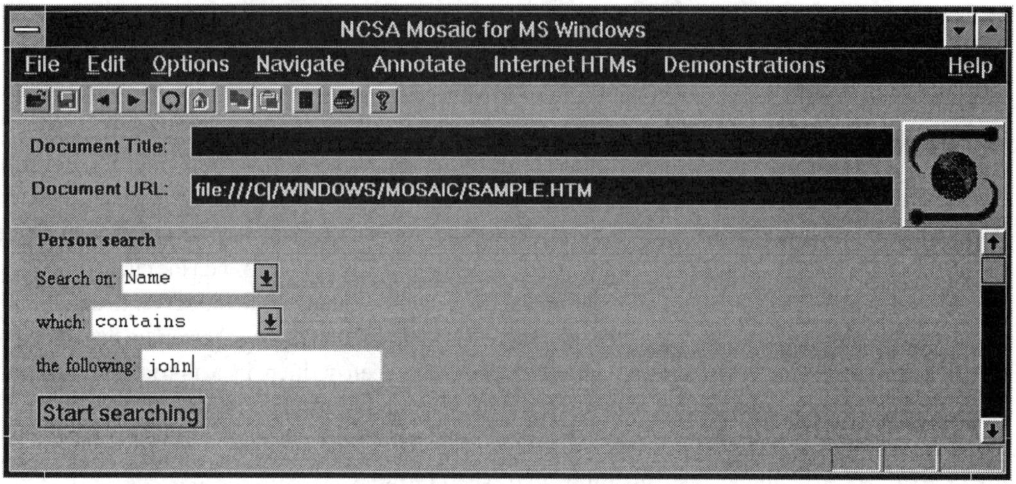

Figure 4.9: The form in our previous example.

text field has been provided at the end of the form (called `value`), which allows a string to be entered, e.g. a name, title, address or whatever. If the user now selected option *Name* from the first bar, and *contains* from the second bar, this implies that the input field would contain a name, e.g. *john*, and that the user would be searching for a person in the database whose name contained the string *john*. This might match a first name or a surname, depending on how the database was structured. The httpd client would now send the following query string (assuming the `POST` posting-method was in use):

```
what=Name&how=contains&value=john
```

which all relate to the options in the form selection areas. Ampersands (&) are placed after each field entry. This type of coding is specific to forms using the `POST` method, as well as `<isindex>` searches. If the `GET` posting method was used the query string would have all = signs replaced with tildes (~), for example:

```
what~Name&how~contains&value~fred
```

The final part of the query string is the actual value being searched for, in this case *john*. Multiple values could be returned here. Another valid query string could be transmitted as:

```
what=Phone&how=is+exactly&value=0761908777
```

which specifies an exact search for the phone number `0761908777`. This number, if found, should identify a single person immediately, although a query string of:

```
what=Phone&how=contains&value=0628
```

would conduct a search that matches `0628` in the phone field of the database, thus finding all people who live in that particular telephone area. Multiple values would clearly be returned here if there were more than one person sharing this number (although this will depend on how the database is searched: `0628` could exist *within* a number and not as a prefix, for example, so you may want to add a *starts with* option into your form and then make the database search look for the text at the beginning of a line when it sees this option). An important point to note concerns the entry of blank spaces. For example, if you entered a name *john bloggs* the space would be changed to a '+' (plus sign), so the entire query string would resemble:

```
what=Name&how=contains&value=john+bloggs
```

This is also true for form *options* as well. In the previous example form we have an option *is exactly*, which would be sent in the query string as `is+exactly` – so decode this appropriately. Mosaic also converts all special characters, such as punctuation symbols, to the hexadecimal format `%nn`, so for example a colon (`:`) in a query string is replaced with the hexadecimal value `%3a`, or ASCII value 58, which is a colon. This hexadecimal conversion takes place for `<isindex>` query strings as well. If a URL contains such special characters they are also converted into hexadecimal notation in this way. For example, the query string `fred smith:38` could arrive at the server as:

```
what=fred+smith%3A38
```

The script that handles these query strings must first get rid of those ampersands, replace the plus signs with spaces and separate the actual query into its component parts (as well as deal with any hexadecimal characters, of course!). It must then decide how to act on the results it has been passed, e.g. store them or use them as the basis of a keyword search. Ultimately this may mean passing the data to a program that you have written that parses the query string into something that can be used by a search tool, or even a database back-end. Now you know why DOS batch files are not the best things to use as CGI scripts, since string manipulation is not one of DOS's key features.

Some of the DOS shell alternatives, such as Norton DOS (NDOS) have much better string manipulation features, although the process of parsing such strings would still be laborious. The NCSA httpd server sets a number of environment variables that contain all of the data required to handle the client's request.

Textual Search Queries using `<isindex>` Documents

Apart from form input, you can also carry out queries to remote server scripts by entering search patterns via Mosaic in a single text field. This can be done using the special tag called `<isindex>` which makes Mosaic supply an input window for the search string you require. When you enter the search string, it is simply added to the URL (like a query string in the forms shown earlier) and is sent off to the server. When a batch file script is called within a hyper-reference you can make the batch file control whether or not a search pattern is included by adding a ? to the batch file name and then placing the search string you require. For this type of script you will need: (i) a simple HTML file that has the `<isindex>` at the very top of the file, or near to the top at least; (ii) a batch file script that examines whether or not a search string has been specified, and if not to invoke the HTML file previously mentioned – the batch file script will also have to carry out the actual task you require. Under DOS it is possible to use filter commands such as `FIND` to locate some text within a file (UNIX has the more powerful `grep`, `egrep` and `fgrep` tools); (iii) an HTML file with a hyper-reference to call the batch file; and lastly (iv) a simple ASCII file to search.

First of all create a simple HTML file with a hyper-reference to the batch file. Assume the batch file is called `finddata.bat`. We could therefore have the single HTML line:

```
<a href="/cgi-bin/finddata.bat>Search for a person's email
    address</a>
```

Now create a small HTML file, perhaps called `isindex.htm`, with the `<isindex>` tag, as follows:

```
<isindex>
<title>Search for email addresses</title>
<h2>Enter a person's name to search for</h2>
This file allows you to carry out a
search for a person's email name
using their first or last names.
Enter your search name below and
press ENTER.
```

Next, create the batch file `finddata.bat`, as shown below:

```
set of=%output_file%
if NOT %#==0 goto showqry
rem No query, so signal the server to call
rem the HTML isindex document
rem so that the user can enter a search string:
echo Location: /isindex.htm > %of%
echo. >> %of%
rem Generate a plain text report for the user:
:showqry
echo Content-type:text/plain > %of%
echo. >> %of%
echo Here are the details you requested: >> %of%
echo. >> %of%
rem type c:\httpd\cgi-dos\datafile | find /i
rem "%QUERY_STRING%" >> %of%
```

The first line of the batch file, as ever, sets a temporary variable into which all output is redirected to the server. Next the batch file tests how many arguments were sent to the server (the DOS variable `%#` stores this numeric value). If a search string hasn't been sent along (it won't have been, although you can do so by appending a *?searchstring* to the URL that mentions the batch file), the file `isindex.htm` is launched using the CGI `Location:` directive mentioned earlier. This file allows the user to enter a search string from the keyboard and then the batch file is reactivated again at the next point to do the actual processing of the request. At this point we are returning data to the server, so we have to include the two compulsory header lines, namely `Content-type:` (MIME type) and then a blank line. The MIME content type for this request will be `text/plain` – nearly all such scripts using the Windows CGI must return ASCII scripts because of the DOS environment (note that you couldn't return a nice HTML file in this instance because the angle-brackets of the HTML tag language would interfere with DOS's redirection symbols. Ouch!). Next we output a line of text telling the user that the results are ready, and then we arrive at the actual command that accesses the required data for the user. In this example the `TYPE` command has been used with a simple ASCII database (as shown below) which is then piped into the `FIND` command (the `/I` option makes the search case-insensitive, by the way), and the results are written out to the server's temporary file.

Your `mosaic.ini` file's `[Viewers]` section will have a viewer for the `text/plain` type such as `notepad.exe`. This viewer will be used to view the results accordingly. The ASCII database that is also required is called `datafile` and for the sake of the example is a simple list of user names and email addresses in the format shown here (you can add what you like just as long as each person's details appear on one line, such is the way the `FIND` command works):

```
jason          wombat@spuddy.uucp
president      president@whitehouse.gov
fred           fred@somesite.somewhere.edu
```

To initiate a search the hyper-reference shown earlier would be clicked on. The batch file would then be called, and since no search-pattern was mentioned in the URL the `isindex.htm` file is loaded, allowing the user to enter a search string. As soon as one is entered the batch file is re-entered and the `FIND` command goes to work on the value of `QUERY_STRING`, the system variable that holds the search string previously entered. Any lines that match the search string are output and redirected to the server in the process. Back at the client end an appropriate viewer is launched for the ASCII file and the user would see the results. Remember, to bypass the `isindex.htm` file, simply structure your URL as:

```
<a href="/cgi-bin/finddata.bat?president>Search for the President</a>
```

where `?president` represents the search string you want to use. You won't of course be able to control the search string's contents; hence the provision of the `<isindex>` tag within a separate file to initiate such searches. I would imagine that there are not that many DOS-based scripts in existence, such is the horrid nature of the DOS environment generally. Systems such as UNIX have been bought up entirely on a *software tools philosophy*, in which many dozens of useful commands are available for script processing. UNIX is also more flexible in terms of its redirection capability; there is no need to keep specifying >> statements on every line, as in DOS. UNIX tools such as `perl` are available for the MS-DOS platform. The biggest problem with using DOS as script parser is really down to its string-processing capabilities. Because an `<isindex>` document encodes the data it sends by replacing all spaces with '+' signs (as well as changing all non-alphabetic and non-numeric characters to hexadecimal notation) our example script would not work if we submitted the full name of *Joe Public* since `Joe+Public` would not be matched, even in a case-insensitive search using the DOS `FIND` command. This small problem could be remedied by making sure that our data file stored names in the form *firstname+lastname*, although this is a bit impractical.

Saving the Data from a Submitted Form

It's all very well mucking about with ASCII files using the simpler DOS filter commands. These are so limited in their use that they are hardly ever used in the vast majority of CGI scripts. Instead, many programmers write their own *back-end* programs and then call these from a batch file directly. Take the simple example of a form that requests a user to enter their name, address and a phone number. How could we store this in a more structured database? When considering a system to do this you should ensure that: (i) the program is DOS-based; (ii) that it has the ability to compile a source-program into a DOS executable format, i.e. it is has a *compiler* and *linker*; and (iii) that it extracts environment variables from the current shell. The last item is clearly very important, since CGI communicates all of its values through environment variables.

Alternative DOS shells (e.g. Norton's NDOS) offer many additional functions although these are still of course DOS-based and at the end of the day they will only run as a DOS batch file within a DOS window. A high-level language such as one of the dBASE clones, e.g. Clipper, or even perhaps Visual Basic, would be ideal since these systems can create standalone executable files, which in turn can use all of the features of the host program, e.g. string processing, database storage, searching and manipulating data, and of course in the case of Visual Basic *et al.* the Windows environment. Take the HTML form below as an example. This invokes a batch file called `dbstore.bat` which in turn invokes a program written in a fourth-generation language (4GL) called *Clipper*. The DOS-based version is used for our examples. Clipper uses an English-like language (similar to the original dBASE dialect) and you can compile its source code programs into DOS `.EXE` format. Clipper has many dozens of functions that make it much more suitable to string processing. It is also a proper data storage system and records are organized using relational tables (organized as rows and columns).

```
<TITLE>FORM EXAMPLE</TITLE>
<H2>Storing The Data From Forms</H2>

Here is a simple set of text fields.
Fill them in and press the "Start
Search" button. The server script will
then invoke a program to extract
the data from the QUERY_STRING variable and
then store this in a dBASE
compatible database.<P>

<FORM METHOD="GET" ACTION="/cgi-bin/dbstore.bat">
<B>Enter details:</B><HR>
Name:     <INPUT TYPE="text" SIZE=30 NAME="name"><P>
```

```
Address: <INPUT TYPE="text" SIZE=50 NAME="address"><P>
Phone:   <INPUT TYPE="text" SIZE=20 NAME="phone"><P>
<INPUT TYPE="submit" VALUE=" Submit Details ">
</FORM>
```

Three fields are provided in the form above. When all details have been entered the submit button sends the data off to the CGI batch file `dbstore.bat`. Since the posting method of the form is `GET`, the httpd server will receive a query string of the form:

```
name~Fred+Bloggs&address~29+High+Street+Netsville&phone~123-456-789
```

which represents a hypothetical person's name, address and phone number. The batch file mentioned in the form's `ACTION=` statement (`dbstore.bat`) is structured as:

```
set of=%OUTPUT_FILE%
echo Content-type: text/plain                        > %of%
echo.                                               >> %of%
echo Your request has been dealt with, thank you. >> %of%
c:\httpd\cgi-dos\stordata.exe
```

Choosing an appropriate MIME type for the `Content-type:` in this instance could be tricky, since we may not actually be returning any actual *data*, although when you think about it the user at the client end of the connection may want to see a message instructing them that their request was dealt with by the server. The text in the third DOS `echo` statement will do this – a viewer on the client's Mosaic system should be configured to load a Windows editor or other ASCII viewer for this. The last line in the batch file is the actual program that is going to handle the form data that has been submitted. This points to an executable program, and you will notice that is output is not redirected. This is because the program does not send any output in this instance. We could do away with the user message in the above example and have the program display a line of text to the same effect. If this were the case you would have to redirect the output (httpd may give a warning error otherwise).

The language (or rather, the *compiler*) used to create the `.EXE` is left up to you. In the next example I have used the Xbase language that comes with the *Clipper 5* database system (a popular database compiler formerly from Nantucket, and now Computer Associates). I apologize to all the purists who may expect some C examples, but Clipper should appeal more to novices, since its language is English-like and is fairly simple to understand. Clipper is a structured programming language that is not unlike some of the BASIC dialects. It also borrows some concepts from C, although not the ability to create small executables, alas. However, it has all the functionality to handle strings and environment variables, and much more besides. The actual source code, or, in CGI parlance, the *back-end*, resembles the following:

```
// Clipper v5.01 back-end to process the
// CGI QUERY_STRING variable
```

```
// and store a submitted name, address and phone number into a
// dBASE compatible .DBF database file. I am assuming a GET
// posting method (must remove "~", "&" and "+" signs).

// Define some variables:
static cName, cAddress, cPhone, nFirstAmp, nFirstTilde,
    cQString
// Open the example enquiry database (FULL pathname note) and
// get a copy of the QUERY_STRING variable:
use c:\httpd\cgi-dos\enquiry new
cQString := getenv("QUERY_STRING")

// Parse the string to get the name:
nFirstTilde := at("~", cQString)
nFirstAmp   := at("&", cQString)
cName       := alltrim(substr(cQString, nFirstTilde+1, ;
                abs((nFirstAmp-nFirstTilde)-1)))
cQString    := substr(cQString, nFirstAmp+1, len(cQString))

// Parse the string to get the address:
nFirstTilde := at("~", cQString)
nFirstAmp   := at("&", cQString)
cAddress    := alltrim(substr(cQString, nFirstTilde+1, ;
                abs((nFirstAmp-nFirstTilde)-1)))
cQString  := substr(cQString, nFirstAmp+1, len(cQString))

// Parse the string to get the phone number:
nFirstTilde := at("~", cQString)
nFirstAmp   := at("&", cQString)
cPhone      := alltrim(substr(cQString, nFirstTilde+1, ;
                len(cQString)))

// Update the database:
enquiry->(dbappend())
replace enquiry->name  with strtran(cName,"+"," ")
replace enquiry->address with strtran(cAddress,"+"," ")
replace enquiry->phone  with strtran(cPhone,"+"," ")
```

The salient functions to note from this program are `getenv()` and `substr()`; `getenv()` simply fetches an environment variable, here `QUERY_STRING`, which holds the formatted query string from the client, and `substr()` is the Clipper substring extraction function. The database is opened using Clipper's `USE` command (the database is called `ENQUIRY.DBF` and its location **must** be fully qualified, not partially qualified, or the CGI script will crash). The database has three fields, called `name`, `address` and `phone`, all of which are character-type fields sharing the same size as mentioned in the `SIZE=` declarations within the form that submits its data to this program. When the query string arrives, it is fetched from the environment into the program and stored as a variable called `cQString`. We can then go to work extracting the constituent parts of the string to get the name, address and phone number. Query strings using the `GET` form-posting method are value-pairs structured as `variable~value` and separated by an ampersand (`&`), where `variable` is the form variable associated with that item of data (i.e. the `name=` part) and `value` is the actual data as entered into the form field. We must therefore firstly look for the first tilde (~) and ampersand, and simply extract what is between them. This will be the person's name. In Clipper this would be done using the three statements:

```
nFirstTilde := at("~", cQString)
nFirstAmp   := at("&", cQString)
cName       := alltrim(substr(cQString, nFirstTilde+1, ;
               abs((nFirstAmp-nFirstTilde)-1)))
```

Take the earlier `QUERY_STRING` value of our example:

```
name~Fred+Bloggs&address~29+High+Street+Netsville&phone~123-456-789
```

The task begins using the Clipper `at()` function, which returns the numeric position of a character within a string (thus the variable `nFirstTilde` would be set to 5 because the first tilde appears at position 5 in the query string), and the variable `nFirstAmp` would be set to 17 using the same method. Now we can extract the value between character positions 5 and 17, which is *Fred Bloggs*. The result is then placed in a variable called `cName`. The same process is done again to extract the address and phone number. After each extraction the query string is cut down to get rid of the part already dealt with (this makes string processing considerably easier, since there is only one tilde and ampersand to deal with). The last item extracted is the easiest, since we do not need to search for a final ampersand, simply because there isn't one. All query strings have plus signs (+) instead of spaces, so these should be removed. This is done using the Clipper function `strtran()` which is all self-explanatory. Finally, we must save the values sent to us. A new record is added (*appended* in Clipper parlance) to the enquiry database using the `dbappend()` function, and the final `replace` statements update the fields in the newly created record with our extracted values. This CGI back-end could in theory be written in any language, such as C, BASIC or any other high-level language for that matter. The choice of language must reflect your own needs. The whole point is that this Clipper program could have been a Windows version of the same program. A later program in this chapter also shows how you can return HTML rather than plain old ASCII text.

At the server end of things everything will be very quiet. No message will have been shown that some data has arrived, and the server administrator (perhaps yourself) will only know that an access has been made to your system because the httpd icon will animate itself briefly during the database access (an MS-DOS httpd shell will also flash up quickly as the jacket script is run). However, you could write another little program (DOS users will run this in a windowed DOS-box, perhaps with its own icon and associated PIF file) that examines the database for new updates, perhaps beeping or showing a brief message to indicate that some new data has arrived. The Clipper program below does just this (to see this working on your own machine run this program in its own DOS box and then submit the form to the server).

```
// Sample Clipper program to watch for updates to the enquiry
// database and display any new details that arrive.

OldCol := setcolor("w+/b,,n")
cls
use c:\httpd\cgi-dos\enquiry readonly
OrigRecs := enquiry->(reccount())
? "WAITING FOR NEW DATA TO ARRIVE"
?
? "Records in database: "+alltrim(str(reccount()))
?
? "Waiting for new data. Press <ESC> to quit ..."
do while (inkey() != 27)
    use c:\httpd\cgi-dos\enquiry readonly
    NumRecs := enquiry->(reccount())
    if (NumRecs != OrigRecs)
        goto bottom
        tone(700,2) // Beep!
        ?
        ?"NEW DATA HAS ARRIVED AT "+time()
        ? replicate("-",70)
        ?
        ? "Name    : "+enquiry->name
        ? "Address : "+enquiry->address
        ? "Phone   : "+enquiry->phone
        ?
        ? "Records in database: "+alltrim(str(reccount()))
        ?
        ? "Waiting for new data. Press <ESC> to quit ..."
        ?
        OrigRecs := NumRecs
       loop
    endif
enddo
setcolor(OldCol)
cls
```

The Clipper ? statements are analogous to `printf()` in C, or `PRINT` in BASIC. The program runs in a loop until the ESC key is pressed, constantly checking the `ENQUIRY.DBF` database for new records. New records are appended to the bottom of the database so all we have to do to see the new data is jump to the bottom of the database (`go bottom` in *Clipperspeak*) and then print the field details directly from the database. The program then waits until another record is added *ad infinitum*, or at least until the ESC key is pressed or your hard disk blows up, whichever happens first.

Returning Results as HTML Documents

Let's face it: ASCII files are horrible. Returning search results as HTML files is a much better solution, since no extra viewing utility has to be loaded – Mosaic handles everything. If you want your application to output the results of a database search or other *lookup* function, this can be done be in a number of ways. One method is to write a back-end that parses the query string and then creates all the HTML results as a series of text strings, all of which are then written out to a temporary file (with an `.HTM` extension to be accurate). When the back-end program terminates it passes control back to the batch file script from which it was originally called. The script then invokes the DOS `TYPE` command on the temporary HTML file previously created, and the output is redirected to the server in the normal way: task completed. Try to avoid placing calls to DOS functions in your programs. Such methods are unreliable: they can create new shell environments and any CGI variables may not be made available. The redirection of the actual output may also be tricky to implement since the < and > characters must be quoted, and the quotes themselves will appear within the HTML document, which doesn't look very nice, to say the least.

The scripts and programs below implement a simple acronym database that can be searched through a pre-supplied `<isindex>` document. The user can submit an acronym to the server and be sent back a suitable reply as an HTML document (use `text/plain` for ASCII feedback, for example). Since an `<isindex>` search allows input with spaces, we will treat these as separate search patterns, that is separate acronyms, for the sake of the example; e.g. the input `dos gui` is converted by `<isindex>` to `dos+gui`, which we will use to search for the two acronyms 'dos' and 'gui'. As an added bonus we will return the results in HTML format, something we can do now that it is possible to escape DOS batch files as a means of parsing such queries. The batch file script that we will use for this example is shown below; it will be called using a suitable `<a href>` hyper-reference within another HTML document in the normal way when the user clicks on the reference.

```
set of=%output_file%
if NOT %#==0 goto shoquery
echo Location: /demo/acindex.htm   > %of%
echo.                              >> %of%
:shoquery
c:\httpd\cgi-dos\acserver.exe
echo Content-type: text/html       >> %of%
echo.                              >> %of%
type c:\httpd\cgi-dos\tempfile.htm >> %of%
```

The file `acindex.htm` is a simple HTML document with an `<isindex>` tag. It will be called to allow the user to enter a search pattern. This file is called when no search arguments are passed to the batch file (tested using the `IF` statement with the DOS `%#` variable). In fact, you may want to get rid of this `IF` statement and always call the file, because it goes without saying that user input will always be required in such instances. The back-end program is then called (`acserver.exe`) which parses the `QUERY_STRING` variable, and conducts a search of an acronym database using the extracted words from the query string. The important thing to note from the back-end program is how it creates the HTML file that contains the results. Results, in this case, are the definitions for the acronyms selected. Of course you could return anything, such as an image (or *imagemap* – see the next section), sound, or even a hyper-reference to a another Internet resource altogether. Let's keep things simple for the moment, however. Finally, we have a DOS `TYPE` command, which simply displays the results to the client. Because the MIME type `text/html` has been used, Mosaic will automatically read this into the current window (no viewer is needed – make sure you **only** have a `text/html=.htm` entry in your `mosaic.ini`'s `[Suffixes]` section). If you want to view the text in its raw HTML form (with tags) change the `Content-type` to `text/plain` and an ASCII viewer, if defined, should be loaded.

The back-end program itself (again written in Clipper for DOS, a very *convertible* language, so convert as required) resembles the following:

```
// Clipper Acronym server back-end.
// Parse the QUERY_STRING returned from
// the <isindex> document and find the acronyms.
// Return data as an HTML
// file (MIME: text/html).

// This is where the HTML file will be written on disk:
#define TEMPFILE "c:\httpd\cgi-dos\tempfile.htm"

static fd, cString, PlusPos, ThisWord, Acronyms := {}

// Create the temporary results file:
fd := fcreate(TEMPFILE,0)

// Open the acronyms database:
use c:\httpd\cgi-dos\acronyms new

// Parse string to extract individual acronyms:
cString := getenv("QUERY_STRING")+"+"
do while !empty(cString)
     PlusPos := at("+", cString)
     ThisWord := alltrim(strtran(substr(cString,1,PlusPos),"+",""))
     // Strip out any duplicate acronyms:
        if (ascan(Acronyms, ThisWord) == 0)
        // ascan() returns 0 if not found:
        aadd(Acronyms, ThisWord)
```

```
    endif
    cString := substr(cString,PlusPos+1,len(cString))
  enddo

  // Get acronym definition and convert into HTML.
  // Write this into a temporary file. The batch file
  // will type this out when we exit this back-end program:
  for n := 1 to len(Acronyms)
    dbgotop()
    locate for alltrim(lower(ac_name)) ;
      == alltrim(lower(Acronyms[n]))
    if found()
      // Create an HTML entry for this acronym:
      AcNam := alltrim(upper(ac_name))
      AcDes := alltrim(ac_desc)
      fwrite(fd, "<title>Here is your Acronym Server Reply</title>")
      fwrite(fd, "<h2> &AcNam </h2><hr>")
      fwrite(fd, "&AcDes")
    else
      // Didn't find this acronym!
      NoAc := alltrim(upper(Acronyms[n]))
      fwrite(fd, "<h2>&NoAc</h2><hr>")
      fwrite(fd, "Sorry. No definition could be found for this ";
      + "acronym.<p>")
    endif
  next
  fclose(fd)
```

The database in the example is a standard dBASE `.DBF` file with the two fields, `AC_NAME` and `AC_DESC` representing the acronym name and description respectively. The HTML tags in the results for a typical search are simply written out along with any variables. This makes the task of creating the HTML file much easier and straightforward, since there is no output redirection involved within the program, unlike a DOS batch file. You will notice from the batch file that the `TYPE` command is of course redirected, otherwise the results would never be seen (this would also cause an httpd server error). Many enhancements can be made to this program; indeed, just about anything can be accomplished within the limits of the back-end program's capabilities, that is.

Users sending check- and radio-box data to the server will parse this in just the same way as has been shown – there is, after all, no real difference in the actual concept here, although you will want to use a form rather than an `<isindex>` document (the `QUERY_STRING` variable will still be used here).

Using Forms without Input Fields

One aspect of Fill-Out-Forms that you have not have considered is the provision of a *submit* button by itself, i.e. a form with no user input whatsoever. This could be very useful to allow a user at the client end of the HTTP connection to call a remote script which could then pass back some results. Such *results* will not be items such as search results, since the user hasn't input anything in the way of search strings (the server will have created an empty `QUERY_STRING` variable as well, of course); rather, the results will be documents that have already been processed by the server. They could be newsletters, an electronic-magazine (an *e-zine*), or just about any item of information held as a file on the server machine. So why would we want an empty form? The main reason is to provide a user-definable button. No other *button*-producing tags are currently available in HTML, and these can help to make a document look more attractive (the alternative is a normal `<a href>` hyper-reference to an HTML file). Take the two example forms in the HTML document shown below (you can have as many forms as you like within an HTML document if you need multiple buttons) which allows two different files on the server machine to be downloaded by the client at the click of a button. The `get=` posting method has no relevance in an *empty form*, although you could enter a valid method to stop the browser crashing unexpectedly.

```
<title>Newsletters</title>
Please select a newsletter to view.
If you want to save the file
please make sure that your <i>record-to-file</i>
feature is enabled before making your selection.<p>

<FORM METHOD="get" ACTION="/cgi-dos/test1.bat">
<INPUT TYPE="submit" VALUE=" Download our 1993 newsletter ">
</FORM>

<FORM METHOD="get" ACTION="/cgi-dos/test2.bat">
<INPUT TYPE="submit" VALUE=" Download our 1994 newsletter ">
</FORM>
```

The two CGI script files are the DOS batch files `test1.bat` and `test2.bat`; these simply output an HTML file for the client to see. If you want the client to see an ASCII file instead, be sure to use a MIME type of `text/plain` instead. The batch file `test1.bat` is shown below; `test2.bat` is similar except for the fact that it displays a different file. Since the batch files return HTML text the files being displayed must be pure ASCII and have the `.HTM` extension.

```
set of=%output_file%
echo Content-type: text/html    > %of%
echo.                           >> %of%
type c:\httpd\htdocs\news93.htm >> %of%
```

Of course, the result of a button-click could activate any valid URL, not just a batch file script or other back-end program. We could call a Gopher server, read some USENET news, or connect to an FTP server to download a specific file from anywhere on the Internet; for example, we could have a button to download a file from an FTP site using a form definition structured as follows:

```
<FORM METHOD="get" ACTION="ftp://ftp.microsoft.com/pub/win32s.zip">
<INPUT TYPE="submit" VALUE=" Download the win32s software ">
</FORM>
```

Using Hidden Fields in Forms

The `<input type...>` tag also allows the special type called `hidden` to be used. When this attribute is specified, the input field is not shown. This in turn can be used to send configuration data to the server, such as plain text or even the value of an environment variable. Take the simple form below as an example:

```
<form method="get" action="/cgi-bin/demoscrp.bat">
Full name:
<input type="text"  name="personname" size=40><p>
<input type="hidden" name="secret" value="Some hidden text"><p>
<input type="submit" value=" Send data "><p>
</form>
```

This form provides one text field and a submit button. The `hidden` field shown carries the value *Some hidden text* by default and is never seen by the user. In fact, 'hidden' fields would be a slightly incorrect description, since Mosaic and many other browsers have *Document Source* features that will reveal the value of any such fields. So, never include sensitive data that you do not want revealed, e.g. passwords. One thing you cannot do with a conventional text field is provide a default value that is itself an environment variable. If you do, all you will see is the literal variable name. The actual encoding of environment variables is done at the server's end of the connection when the client submits a form to it. If the server then spots an environment within a hidden field using the `value=` attribute (this is the main condition that must be satisfied) it will then replace the variable with its own value and then send this back to the client within the standard CGI `QUERY_STRING` variable. If the variable is not recognized the server will omit the entire entry, so essentially a blank field is returned.

You may just want to place some plain text in the hidden field which could be used by the server when parsing the `QUERY_STRING`. Different forms called from the same server could use a code in the hidden field that names a particular database to be updated, or which names an email alias to be informed when the form is filled in (UNIX users will be able to make use of this facility more easily since they can parse the query string and just pipe it into the standard UNIX `mail` program). Many other uses of hidden fields are of course possible, and will depend on your own requirements as a form developer. Section 4.4 shows how Norton's NDOS can be used with a hidden field to some advantage.

4.4 Alternative DOS Shells – Norton DOS

If you do not have access to a compiler such Clipper or Visual Basic, or do not want to learn such an extensive language from scratch, you may want to purchase a new DOS pre-processor. The standard DOS pre-processor, `COMMAND.COM` is only adequate for the most simple search-and-display operations. Norton DOS (NDOS), a commercial product, is a much better alternative. Installing NDOS as a CGI script is very easy: in fact you don't have to do anything to the httpd program. However, make sure that your CONFIG.SYS file has a

```
SHELL=C:\norton\ndos.com
```

statement within it (change the name of any directories according to your own machine, of course) so that NDOS.COM is used instead of COMMAND.COM.

This section examines how an alternative DOS pre-processor, namely Norton's NDOS, can handle parsing operations in the CGI environment. Among NDOS's features are an extensive set of extra system environment variables which hold everything from the date and time right through to variables that hold the current drive, CPU status information, memory amounts and much more besides. Norton's string-processing capabilities are much more developed than COMMAND.COM's; NDOS provides a wealth of functions, such as @INDEX[string1,string2] which returns the position of string2 within string1 (or -1 if string2 is not found). A substring extraction function called @SUBSTR[string,start,nlen] also exists (the same as Clipper's, in fact) which returns a substring, starting at the position start and continuing for nlen characters. Dozens of other useful functions are available. In order to extract a query string from an <isindex> document, or from a fill-out-form (FOF) we could use these functions accordingly. For example, a QUERY_STRING of:

```
emailname~fred@somewhere.com
```

could be extracted using the NDOS @substr and @index functions as follows:

```
SET NAME=%@substr[%QUERY_STRING%,%@eval[%@index[%QUERY_STRING%,~]+1]]
```

which would set the variable NAME to fred@somewhere.com by taking the substring value of the variable QUERY_STRING from the first occurrence of a tilde (~) character up to the end of the string. The +1 simply ensures that the tilde is not included (by moving on one character). The @EVAL function allows us to evaluate a numeric expression – the +1 would be echoed literally otherwise, which is not what we require. In numerical terms our SET command above would look like the following when submitted to NDOS

```
SET NAME=%@substr[emailname~fred@somewhere.com,10]
```

noting that the last argument to @SUBSTR is in fact optional (in which case NDOS uses the length of the string being examined). Longer query strings with multiple items (such as those from HTML forms) will require function nesting. This still becomes quite long-winded, even with NDOS. The best way of approaching this is to *chop up* the QUERY_STRING into smaller parts by using copies of the string. For example, a QUERY_STRING with the value:

```
formfield1~fred&formfield2~fred@somewhere.com
```

would require the NDOS commands below, which firstly take copies of both portions of the string, and then assign these to the variables FIELD1 and FIELD2. The batch file then extracts the data from these accordingly.

```
SET FIELD1=%@substr[%QUERY_STRING%,0,%@index[%QUERY_STRING%,&]]
SET FIELD2=%@substr[%QUERY_STRING%,%@eval[%@index[%QUERY_STRING%,&]+1]]
SET DATA1=%@substr[%FIELD1%,%@eval[%@index[%FIELD1%,~]+1]]
SET DATA2=%@substr[%FIELD2%,%@eval[%@index[%FIELD2%,~]+1]]
```

The variables DATA1 and DATA2 now hold the actual contents of the fields submitted by the client's form, e.g. fred and fred@somewhere.com. These scripts can be written in a number of other ways, although it makes sense to keep each line quite short, otherwise the nesting becomes very hard to read. One problem we haven't dealt with yet using NDOS is the use of plus signs in spaces within fields. If you remember, the client sends the form data in an encoded string, with all spaces replaced with +s. Getting rid of such characters can be achieved by using a simple loop, for example:

```
@ECHO OFF
rem Strip +'s from a query string ***
set myfile=%@unique[]
set n=0
:loop
if %@eval[%n]=%@len[%QUERY_STRING%] goto exit
if "%@substr[%QUERY_STRING%,%n%,1]" == "+" goto notok
:ok
echos %@substr[%QUERY_STRING%,%n%,1] | tee /a %myfile%
set n=%@eval[%n%+1]
goto loop
:notok
echos %@char[255] | tee /a %myfile%
set n=%@eval[%n%+1]
goto loop
:exit
```

This batch file uses a number of NDOS functions to weed out the strings of data between any plus signs. The first line creates a unique file to hold the results, using NDOS's @UNIQUE function. After this a loop is set up which repeats until every character in the QUERY_STRING variable has been examined (the numeric variable n is tested against the length of the string using the NDOS @LEN function. In-between the loop structure are the actual testing statements, which see whether the current character is a plus sign. If it is we simply print a blank space (*ALT-255*) instead. If a plus sign is not scanned we print the current character from the QUERY_STRING variable. The n variable is incremented (increased by one) in all such instances so that we can test whether or not to exit the program. The NDOS TEE command has been carried over from UNIX – as have most of the best tools. It is a very useful tool that stores the intermediary output of a batch file command (or other DOS command) and places it in a file specified by the user (the /a option makes TEE append the data to the file, rather than overwriting it). The normal >> operation will not work in this instance, hence the use of the TEE command. Because individual characters are being output by the program, the normal ECHO command is not used because it will output a carriage return, thus forcing each character onto a new line. NDOS's ECHOS command is therefore used, which omits the output of a carriage return code. All of the existing code is standard MS-DOS.

Now that the QUERY_STRING has been parsed and the plus signs removed, it is left to you what is actually done with the results. In our small NDOS example the query string was written to a file. This file could be opened by another suitable back-end program and the results processed accordingly. Of course, if another back-end program was being used this might actually be able to handle the parsing operation better than NDOS (this wouldn't be an understatement – I find parsing is still long-winded with NDOS).

Incorporating Norton Variables into HTML Documents

Norton DOS has a number of useful system variables which can be included in a server's HTML file for the client to be returned upon executing a form or <isindex> request. The most useful are the date and time, or %_DATE and %_TIME respectively. For example, we could take the very simple example script file below:

```
set of=%OUTPUT_FILE%
echo Content-type: text/html                   > %of%
echo.                                          >> %of%
echo The time on the server machine is: %_TIME >> %of%
```

This would display the time on the server machine to the client. Since this is bound to be different according to the server machine's whereabouts (bearing in mind that the Internet crosses many different time-zones) such time strings are hardly ever used. Dates are (slightly) more reliable however. The example batch file script above is not really of any great use since you will clearly want to incorporate some other text in the file (text that will change, according to the requirements of the client, e.g. search results). Therefore you will have to incorporate the %_TIME variable in your HTML file that is either output to disk with all of your tags etc. (as shown earlier in the Clipper CGI scripts that use the DOS TYPE command for example), or by incorporating the HTML tags in the batch file itself – as is discussed in the next section. Another useful NDOS variable includes %_DOW (day of the week). Many of the existing variables return information specific to the Norton DOS setup and the server's machine – these are not very beneficial to the HTML scriptwriter, unless you wanted to return details of (say) the CPU and disk storage statistics of the server machine (not very useful to say the least).

Unfortunately, when sending a form to the client you cannot set the value= part to any DOS variable in order to use this as a default value within a normal text or numeric field (although you can return variable values as text within an HTML document).

Incorporating Norton Variables into Hidden Form Fields

A short while back we examined hidden form fields. NDOS can make some use of this facility via its built-in environment variables (as can any DOS variables, not that any of the standard DOS variables are of much use). If a Norton system variable was embedded within an `<input type..>` tag with the `value=` attribute set to `hidden`, for example using NDOS's `%_TIME` variable as:

```
<input type="hidden" name="time" value="%_TIME">
```

this could be used so that when the client submits a form containing the hidden field above, the `%_TIME` variable will be changed to the current time (in the form `hh:mm:ss`) which could then be extracted from the `QUERY_STRING` as a time-stamp to indicate when the form was actually transmitted, or rather submitted.

Overcoming COMMAND.COM's Redirection Problem

The standard MS-DOS pre-processor, `COMMAND.COM`, has a serious problem in store for all HTML developers in that it cannot use the redirection symbols < and > within an `ECHO` statement. Since these symbols are used within HTML tags, this clearly inhibits the user from incorporating them in a batch file script to return marked-up HTML text. Norton DOS overcomes this problem by introducing an *escape character* that is used to precede the redirection symbol, thus removing its special usage under DOS. The Norton `SETDOS /Ec` command sets the escape character that you want to use, where `c` is the character, e.g. a bracket '`(`' or colon '`:`'. For example, `SETDOS /E:` uses the colon as an escape character. Place the `SETDOS` command in your `AUTOEXEC.BAT` (or the NDOS equivalent `NSTART.BAT`).

Remember that it doesn't matter which version of DOS the *client* is running, and whether or not they have an enhanced shell such as NDOS running, since the server is simply using the features of NDOS to make script-parsing and the actual output of any results to the client that much easier. All the variables and other features in a server's batch file script are parsed by NDOS and expanded into the results required *before* being sent back to the client. The client only sees the raw data and isn't concerned with the software used by the server that actually returned it. This is a common misconception about using a different pre-processor that you should now understand more clearly. After defining a suitable escape code character you can include HTML tags within the standard DOS `ECHO` command. Assuming our escape character was '`{`' (set with the NDOS command `SETDOS /E{`) we could now have a batch file with embedded HTML tags structured as:

```
set of=%output_file%
echo Content-type: text/html                    > %of%
echo.                                           >> %of%
echo {<title{>A directory listing in HTML format{</title{> >> %of%
echo.                                           >> %of%
echo {<pre{>                                    >> %of%
dir                                             >> %of%
echo {<pre{>                                    >> %of%
```

In this example we have simply provided some sample output using the DOS `DIR` (Directory) command. All output is still redirected as normal, but now we can directly include our HTML tags in the same file (albeit, *escaped* with the appropriate character to avoid conflicting with DOS's redirection symbols). Since the listing is computer-text, the `<pre>` tag (pre-formatted fixed-pitch text) has been used for the font.

▶ TIP

I have known some DOS scripts to fail because the output from the batch file is not being echoed to the console (`CON` device). Using the DOS command `CTTY CON` (direct all output to the console, i.e. the screen) cured the problem. Place this command in your `\NSTART.BTM` (NDOS's own `AUTOEXEC.BAT`) so that when NDOS is run, the command is executed. Alternatively, place it in your actual batch file script (if you encounter such problems, that is).

NDOS also has a batch file construct called `TEXT..ENDTEXT` which can be used to encapsulate some simple ASCII text. No variables can be included in the text (at least with NDOS v7.0) unfortunately, so tags cannot be included. You can, however, use these commands to include just raw textual data. Any tags you need can be specified before the appropriate statements, for example:

```
set of=%output_file%
echo Content-type: text/html > %of%
echo.                        >> %of%
echo {<pre{>                 >> %of%
text                         >> %of%
Here is some pre-formatted text that runs onto
multiple lines. This is another clever feature of
the NDOS pre-processor.
endtext
echo {<pre{>                 >> %of%
```

The `TEXT..ENDTEXT` statements are beneficial since you don't need multiple output-redirection symbols after every line. The `TEXT` statement must itself be redirected, however, otherwise a httpd server error will occur.

Modifying the `httpd.cnf` File

If you want to run a DOS-based program as a scripting language you can simply mention it in the batch file that is called by the form or `<isindex>` document hyper-reference, as we have shown already. You can however also change the PIF file that the httpd server uses, so that a different program *engine* is used for script processing, perhaps Windows-based rather than DOS-based. To do this requires some knowledge of the file `httpd.cnf` which resides in the `\HTTPD` directory. By default the `HSCRIPT.PIF` file uses the value of `%COMSPEC%` as a script file interpreter. This standard DOS variable is normally `COMMAND.COM` (or if `SHELL=` is set to a different value in

CONFIG.SYS, a better alternative such as NDOS.COM can be used). Rather than altering HSCRIPT.PIF, it is better to create an alternative .PIF file that mentions the name of the program you want to use, e.g. the QBASIC (Microsoft Quick Basic) program, or a Perl interpreter, or of course something more advanced, such as Visual Basic. Taking Visual Basic as an example, you could create a VB.PIF file and reference this through the httpd.cnf configuration file which is now discussed.

The httpd.cnf file contains a number of start-up defaults for the httpd server program. Among its many options are the variables ShellExec and ShellExecOption. ShellExec names the PIF file that you want to use as a CGI script interpreter (or indeed the name of any valid executable if you want to bypass the PIF file). PIF files are mainly used in order to control DOS-based programs running under Windows, e.g. to make sure they use their own window etc. ShellExec will default to HSCRIPT.PIF if not included in the configuration file. ShellExecOption is normally /C, which is an argument to COMMAND.COM (or NDOS.COM etc.) that you want to execute a command, such as a batch file or other DOS executable (this would be a batch file if using the default HSCRIPT.PIF file) and then return immediately to the previous shell. Clearly, the /C option will be invalid for any program other than the standard DOS pre-processor, so it must be omitted through the configuration file. For Visual Basic we could therefore insert the lines:

```
ShellExec VB.PIF
ShellExecOpt ""
```

into the httpd.cnf file (at the bottom of the file perhaps). This in turn informs the httpd program to use VB.PIF as the main CGI *engine*. The program that *follows* in this instance will be a Visual Basic program. The VB.PIF file must point to the name of the main Visual Basic executable, e.g. C:\VB\VB.EXE. This will be the program called in your form or <isindex> script using a <a href> hyper-reference. Similarly, any other program can be called in a PIF file of your choosing, although this method does of course have the drawback of having to modify the WinHttpd configuration file to achieve all of this. Some programs may need additional parameters to work properly – you can include them directly in the PIF file, or in the httpd.cnf file using the ShellExecOption variable. The former method is recommended since it is generally easier to modify the values using the supplied Windows PIF editor pifedit.exe.

Using a Different Scripting Interpreter – *Icon*

Many UNIX tools, such as sed, awk and perl have been moved to other environments, such as DOS, and make very good scripting languages. Another tool, *Icon*, has also been developed and shares many of the features from UNIX tools, such as those previously mentioned. Icon is a structured, high-level language that borrows many of its features from C. A version for Microsoft Windows is being developed and will allow CGI server scripting to take on a new lease of life. Because Icon is not a DOS shell, it can return HTML text without using a third-party DOS pre-processor. It also compiles its files to .EXE format and you can finally do away with DOS batch files as form scripts. Icon is available from the FTP site cs.arizona.edu in the /icon directory. The DOS version is in a subdirectory of this named binaries/msdos-386 (for 386/486/Pentium-based machines). Get all of the .EXE files in this directory and you can start to develop some CGI programs. The benefits of using Icon are really down to two things: (i) its executables are very small, which makes distribution and storage much easier, as well as speeding up the execution of your program; and (ii) Icon's string-processing functions are second to none – and string-parsing is probably the trickiest area of CGI scripting (as you now know!).

The main programs that you will have downloaded are `icont.exe` and `iconx.exe`. All the icon source programs that you eventually create should have an `.ICN` extension and must be edited and saved using an ASCII editor. The `icont.exe` program is basically a compiler and linker rolled into one. It can create an executable version of your program if you use the `-X` option in the following way:

```
icont -X filename.icn
```

The `-X` stands for *make executable*, although an object version (a non-`.EXE` in an internal tokenized format) of your program can also be made if you use the `-I` option (interpreter option). If you use the `-I` option an `.ICX` file will be produced and you should use `iconx.exe` to execute this file. The `.EXE` files created using the `-X` option are not standalone applications in the true sense; Icon will need to find the `iconx.exe` program in the DOS `PATH` to ensure that an Icon executable can be run. Compiled and interpreted versions of programs are useful to the developer, since in the case of the latter development time can be decreased since the overhead of creating an executable version of the file is removed. If you are creating very small CGI scripts then this overhead will be very small indeed – so small in fact, that you will probably see no noticeable difference in speed between either of these methods. Another useful option for `icont.exe` is `-E` to check the syntax of an Icon program. As mentioned, make sure that `iconx.exe` is installed in a directory that is contained within your DOS `PATH` listing so that it can be found by the NCSA server when it executes the script. You will not have to alter any settings in the NCSA httpd server itself since Icon is a DOS executable and can be called satisfactorily using your DOS pre-processor (e.g. `COMMAND.COM /C ICONT.EXE iconprog.exe`).

We can't hope to teach you all of the Icon language, so you are advised to look in the `/doc` subdirectory of the FTP site given earlier in order to thoroughly learn the facilities offered (the document `tr90-6.doc` serves as a good introduction to Icon's capabilities, and lists many program examples). Readers may also want to check out the USENET group `comp.language.icon` for all the latest developments and contributions, or purchase *The Icon Programming Language* by Griswold and Griswold, published by Prentice-Hall. As mentioned earlier, Icon borrows much from the C language, and many of its functions are similar to C. Icon's control structures are also similar to C, so if you have any C programming experience you are well on your way to understanding Icon.

The most fundamental Icon functions are: `write(text)`, which outputs a line of text and which is analogous to C's `printf(string)` function, or Clipper's `?` statement; the `read()` function, which returns a line from the standard input, like C's `fread()` function; and `find(s1, s2)`, which returns the position of string-1 (`s1`) in string-2 (`s2`) – this is the same as Clipper's `at()` function, if you remember. Conditional statements in the Icon language include the ubiquitous `if (condition) ... then action` statement, which is used to carry out one or more actions depending on a variable condition. Icon's variables are themselves assigned using the `:=` operator. Icon also supports a `while` and `every` looping structure to allow multiple passes over a series of files, arguments etc. One important thing to remember is that Icon statements must be enclosed in at least one procedure, just as in a C program using the `main()` function. Like C, Icon also uses the function name `main()` to refer to the first procedure that is called when the program is executed (notice the `end` declaration that terminates the procedure). Other procedures can also be defined which also take arguments, just as with C and Clipper. Seen below is a very simple Icon program (assume it is called `typfile.icn`) that copies everything fed to it to the screen:

```
procedure main()
  while read() do
     write()
end
```

Compile this program to an `.EXE` file using the command `icont -X typfile.icn` and then run the executable. Nothing happens. This is because the program is reading from the standard input device, the keyboard by default (in fact this runs exactly like UNIX's equivalent of DOS's `TYPE` command, `cat`, the concatenate program). If you type some characters and press ENTER they will simply be echoed back to you. Icon's `read()` function is used to read a line of text from a file. If the file is not specified, Icon defaults to the standard input file, the keyboard (just as is happening now when you use the program). Icon's functions do not have to actually specify what they are reading and writing since this is automatically set to the standard input and output streams in the case of `read()` and `write()`, i.e. the keyboard and console (DOS `CON` device). The `write()` function in the example is acting on the `read()` function's input. In order to use this program with an external file we would have to use DOS's redirection feature, for example using a command of the form:

```
typfile < c:\autoexec.bat
```

which would display the entire contents of the `autoexec.bat` file. The `read()` function automatically stops reading the input stream when the end of the file is reached, i.e. no more data exists to be read.

I think you now have a basic understanding of how `read()` and `write()` work, so let's briskly move on to an Icon CGI script example (see next section) that can be used with a Mosaic form. The Icon CGI script below uses the standard input (*stdin*) stream mechanism to write a query string sent by the client to an external file. Scripts that use the *stdin* must have their data submitted by a form using the `POST` method. If you specify a `GET` method with a script that is expecting input from the standard input, the NCSA httpd server may give an error, or it may simply do nothing at all. Our sample Icon script does the following: first it opens a file for writing using Icon's `open()` function, and uses the file mode `wa`, which stands for *write* and *append* (we will want to write to the file, and append details to it rather than overwriting it on subsequent occasions). The next few `write()` functions simply output some HTML text, which is then displayed back on the client's screen. HTML tags are not a problem here, you will have noticed. The script than uses the `read()` function to read from *stdin*.

Omitting the `Content-type:` Declaration

Here are some additional points to bear in mind that apply to all CGI scripts. Since Icon executables are very compact, and they handle the *stdin* and *stdout* streams faultlessly, we can do away with a DOS batch file to invoke the script, and let Icon so this directly, i.e. by mentioning the `.EXE` file instead of the `.BAT` file in the `action=` part of the `<form...>` tag. If a script program displays some output it must set up a MIME type, e.g. `text/plain` or `text/html`. If the script does not provide any output you can do away with the normal `Content-type:` line, although you must output a single blank line to tell the server that the program has completed its task. Our example, below, displays some HTML text, so the `Content-type:` lines are kept. Here is the Icon script in its entirety (the #s are comments in Icon, as in UNIX shell scripts):

```
#
# Sample CGI script for a POST method form. This script reads
# from stdin and writes all data to an external file.
#
procedure main()
  local line, ofile
  ofile := open("datafile.txt", "wa")
  write("Content-type: text/html")
  write()
  write("<b>Results stored OK!</b>")
  while line := read() do
      write(ofile, line)
  close(ofile)
end
```

A salient feature to note in this script is the use of a file descriptor in the `write()` function. Since the `write()` function can also be used to write data to an external file (in the example our file descriptor is the variable `ofile`, which is assigned to our output file, you will notice) we must specify this descriptor in any `write()` command that needs to reference such a file. In this instance the query string submitted on the standard input is being saved to the file `datafile.txt` (note: this will be saved in the directory pointed to by the NCSA server's PIF file `hscript.pif` – commonly this is `C:\TEMP` so you may want to change this accordingly). The `local` statement declares some working variables that are local to the `main()` function. Icon also supports the (dreaded) `global` declaration for variables that have scope over every function in an Icon program. As you would imagine, the `close()` function simply closes our output file. Ensure you have closed all open files to avoid corruption to the file. The actual HTML form that submits some data to this script could be as simple as:

```
<form method="post" action="/cgi-bin/iconprog.exe">
<input type="text" size=20 name="aname">
<input type="submit" value=" Submit data ">
</form>
```

where `iconprog.exe` is our Icon script above. A sample query string that could be saved in our data file could therefore resemble:

```
aname=Some+sample+data
```

where aname is the name assigned to the first (and only) field in the example form shown above. If other form fields were evident, their data would also be added to the query string as normal. As mentioned earlier, you may not want to return any output text, i.e. HTML, to the client. Returning ASCII text is a hassle since the client will have to launch an appropriate viewer, which may take a while to run. In this case simply omit the Content-type: line and leave the blank line, e.g. a write() statement, at the appropriate point (you must leave a blank line otherwise a server error will occur), for example:

```
procedure main()
   local line, ofile
   ofile := open("datafile.txt", "wa")
   write()
   while line := read() do
       write(ofile, line)
   close(ofile)
end
```

Icon has all of the features that allow it to read from the standard input as well as reading DOS environment variables. We have seen how the standard input stream can be captured using the read() function. DOS environment variables are handled using a function called getenv(var), where var is the variable name in question (this is the same in Clipper, coincidentally). The getenv() function is normally associated with GET scripts, since this does not use the standard input to send the query string to the server. Instead it simply sets the variable QUERY_STRING. Forms that use the GET posting method are simpler to write, since they simply involve a line of code to grab the variable. The POST method is mainly provided since many tools (notably those running under UNIX) support the standard input stream as a way of obtaining data. Some tools may not of course have the ability to capture an environment variable. Take the sample HTML form:

```
Enter some text:<p>
<form method="get" action="/cgi-bin/iconprog.exe">
<input type="text" size=20 name="aname">
<input type="submit" value=" Send ">
</form>
```

This form uses a GET posting method in conjunction with a simple text field. An Icon script to grab the QUERY_STRING variable from this form could therefore resemble:

```
#
# Sample Icon CGI script to read the QUERY_STRING variable and
# write this to an output file.
#
```

```
procedure main()
    local qs, ofile
    ofile := open("datafile.txt", "wa")
    # Write a blank line to tell server we've finished.
    write()
    qs := getenv("QUERY_STRING")
    write(ofile, qs)
    close(ofile)
end
```

When the form field is filled with some data and submitted the Icon program will this time examine the variable `QUERY_STRING`, as set by the server automatically when this posting method is used. Both programs are therefore equivalent in terms of the way they write query strings to a file in order to save some form data. What we haven't done yet, however, is to actually parse some query strings with Icon.

▶ TIP

If your script files return server errors such as '*Error Response From Server*', you should check the `.OUT` files created by the NCSA httpd program. These will contain any output generated by the script, plus any output from the script interpreter program, e.g. Icon or Clipper. You may find that a file cannot be opened (always use fully qualified names if possible) or that you have run out of memory etc. The `.OUT` files are placed in the directory named in the `hscript.pif` file (this is found in the `\HTTPD` directory).

To parse strings using the Icon language you may find these snippets of information useful before you begin. Sub-strings, i.e. parts of strings, are accessed using the form `string[x:y]`, where `x` is the starting point and `y` is the ending point (this is analogous to Clipper's `substr(string,x,y)` function). Strings start at position 1, and not 0 as in some languages. The use of sub-strings to handle query strings from forms is very useful, to say the least, and without this feature string processing would be very difficult, if not impossible, to achieve. All variables in Icon are in fact one-dimensional arrays, that is to say that a variable `mystring` with the value `"hello+there"` would be represented internally so that `mystring[1]` would be equal to "h", `mystring[2]` would be "e", `mystring[6]` would be "+" and so forth. C also shares this similarity, although pointers have to be used to access arrays and this in turn can tend to turn many users off the idea. Icons arrays are much easier to set up and process.

Functions which have a particular usefulness in string parsing include `find(s1,s2)` which returns the array position of string `s1` within string `s2`, so in the context of our previous example, `find("+",mystring)` would return 6. If the `find()` function fails the statement within which it was called will inherit this failure also. Inheritance is an object-orientated concept. Novice users may simply wish to allocate a zero value to a variable and then use the `find()` function as follows in order to make things easier to understand, since `find()` doesn't return any numeric value. If the string being searched for is larger than a single character, `find()` returns the first position of the character that was found.

```
# A simple way to use the find() function.
procedure main()
local newpos, astring
...
newpos := 0
astring := "The+quick+brown+fox"
newpos := find("quick", astring)
if (newpos == 0) {
   ...
   ... string not found code goes here
   ...
}
...
end
```

Icon also provides a string-scanning facility, which takes the form

```
string ? expression
```

where `string` is the subject string (i.e. the string to be scanned) and `expression` is some code that performs the scanning function. If the code requires more than one line, open a section using { and } (as done in C also). For example, the code below performs a string scan that simply outputs every character to the screen on a separate line.

```
procedure main()
local qstring
qstring := getenv("QUERY_STRING")
qstring ? while write(move(1))
end
```

The `move()` function is used to move about within a target string and return a substring accordingly. For example, the statement:

```
string ? move(1)
```

would move one character forward within a string and would return that character – although it wouldn't actually be printed to the screen unless a `write()` function was nested around it, as in the example program. To pass through an entire string the `while` construct has to be used: for example, the statement

```
string ? while write(move(1))
```

would move through the entire variable `string` and write every character to the screen (as used in the previous program), whereas:

```
string ? while write(move(3))
```

would write every three-character sub-string to the screen. If the string wasn't a multiple of the size specified in the `move()` function the remaining characters will still be shown.

Parsing GET Form Query Strings

The sample Icon script below (`iconform.icn`) can be used in conjunction with a form that uses the GET posting method. This script will parse a form that contains two fields. A detailed description of the script appears after the listing. An HTML form used to send data to this script could resemble:

```
<form method="GET" action="/cgi-bin/iconform.exe">
<!--These field names can change as required-->
<input type="text" size=40 name="fld1">
<input type="text" size=40 name="fld2">
<input type="submit" value=" Send data ">
</form>
```

The Icon CGI script itself resembles the following:

```
#
# Icon CGI script to extract two form fields of the form:
# field1~value&field2~value ("+" signs will be extracted).
#
procedure main()
  local qs, t1, t2, field1, field2, i
  qs := getenv("QUERY_STRING") || "&"
  t1 := qs[find("~",qs)+1:i := find("&",qs)]
  t2 := qs[i+1:0]
  field1 := strip_plus(t1)
  field2 := strip_plus(t2[find("~",t2)+1:0-1])
  write(field1)
  write(field2)
end

# Strip out + signs.
procedure strip_plus(string)
  local counter
  counter := 0
  string ? {
      while (tab(upto(~""))) do {
```

```
            counter := counter + 1
            if (string[counter]=="+") then
              string[counter] := " "
            move(1)
        }
    }
    return(string)
end
```

First, the script uses the `getenv()` function to store the CGI `QUERY_STRING` variable, and then performs some string parsing to return the two field values as the variables `field1` and `field2`. The `||` is Icon's string concatenation operator – it simply adds a string to the end of another string. When parsing strings it is useful to have a start and end-point character to refer to in order to extract various parts of a string. If a form submitted the `QUERY_STRING` value as:

```
name~jason+j+manger&phone~12345678
```

we can immediately see that two fields have been sent by the ampersand in the middle that separates them. It would be easy to extract the first field value, since we know where it ends, i.e. at the ampersand (&). However, the second field is harder to extract since it isn't delimited (terminated) with any character whatsoever. We could fidget around adding some code to check for a null character or end-of-line, although an easier way is to just append a character using the `||` operator as soon as `getenv()` loads the variable. Now our query string would resemble:

```
name~jason+j+manger&phone~12345678&
```

and we have two ampersand characters that identify the end of each field. The start of each field is easy to match, since `GET` forms use the tilde (~) character. Now all we have to do is extract the characters between the tildes and the ampersands and then take out any plus signs. The program does this by first creating two temporary variables (`t1` and `t2`) that hold these sub-strings, as shown below:

```
t1 := qs[find("~",qs)+1:i := find("&",qs)]
t2 := qs[i+1:0]
```

The variable `t1` uses the `string[x:y]` feature described earlier to extract the first sub-string field, although instead of using a literal number (which would be impossible anyway since the string will clearly change in each form submission!) the `find()` function has been used to find the character positions of the first tilde and ampersand. Since `find()` returns a numeric value representing a character position it can be used directly within Icon's `[x:y]` sub-string field. The '`+1`'s make sure that we move on a character after finding the appropriate tilde or ampersand so as not to include it in the extracted string. Notice the use of a variable (`i`) in the first line of the code shown above. This has been done so as to keep a note of the first ampersand position in the query string; this value can be used since the next character after the first ampersand is the second field. So far, variable `t1` is set to the value:

```
jason+j+manger
```

and `t2` is set to the value:

```
phone~12345678&
```

Variable `t1` can now have its plus sign removed, although variable `t2` still needs some processing to remove the name of the form-field that has been prefixed to it. To do this is very simple, since we can simply use the `find()` function to locate the tilde, and then embed this within a substring (`[x:y]`), as before. This is done using the Icon statement

```
field2 := strip_plus(t2[find("~",t2)+1:0-1])
```

Ignore the `strip_plus` for the moment. As we can see, the `t2` variable is structured so that the sub-string between the first character after the tilde and the last character before the final ampersand is extracted. One important point regarding Icon's `[x:y]` substring feature is the use of the value zero (0). If used, Icon simply returns the entire string. Thus `0-1` returns the entire string minus one character, the ampersand in this case, since we don't want this in the final result. The resulting string in the context of our example is therefore:

```
12345678
```

which is a hypothetical phone number, although this will depend on the form and could in fact hold any value (this CGI script will parse any two field values passed to it). Our script doesn't do much with the field values passed. In reality, you might want to store these to a file (perhaps they make up some order information, or a registration perhaps), or perform a search operation. Some simple `write()` functions have been used in the script to display the field values. The `strip_plus` that is nested within the `write()` function is in fact a separate user-defined procedure which takes out all of the plus signs in the query string, as shown below. Procedures are useful to break up large programs, and to make programs more *reusable* (a function could be called by many different parts of a program, rather than writing the same code many times, for example). Procedures (or *functions*) are common to most programming languages, including C, Pascal and even BASIC (*subroutines*).

```
procedure strip_plus(string)
  local counter
  counter := 0
  string ? {
      while (tab(upto(~""))) do {
         counter := counter + 1
         if (string[counter]=="+") then
```

```
                string[counter] := " "
            move(1)
        }
    }
    return(string)
end
```

The procedure `strip_plus()` is called with one argument, namely a string to remove the +s. Thus, when we issue the statement `strip_plus(t1)` we are in fact passing the variable `t1` to the `strip_plus` procedure. This is how the procedure works. It starts by defining a counter variable (`counter`) that will be used to keep track of the movement through the string passed to the function (held in the variable `string`, which is the main argument passed to the procedure). We then undertake a string-scan operation on the argument passed and examine every character in turn. This is done by the `while (tab(upto(~""))) do` statement. The `tab()` function is used to set a character position within a string and then return a substring from the previous position to the next (this will be the same when the loop starts, so the first character will be examined. The `move(1)` function ensures that we move a single character at a time through the entire string. Icon keeps track of sub-strings automatically using `tab()`, so there is no need to define any further variables as in other languages. The `upto()` function is used to loop up to a certain point and then exit, as specified in its argument, which is the somewhat cryptic `~""` string of characters. The tilde ~ is Icon's *not* operator (C and Clipper have `!`). Don't confuse this with anything to with the CGI string; it isn't in this instance. Icon uses the `""` to refer to a *null string* or an (empty-string). *Empty* to Icon does not mean a string such as `"  "`; the string must have no white space, i.e. `""`.

Null values are useful for determining when an end of a string has been reached, as in the case of the value that has been passed to the `strip_plus` function. The statement `(tab(upto(~"")))` `do` is therefore really saying '*return a substring up to the point where a null character is found and then exit*'. The rest of the statements simply use Icon's array features to examine successive (single) characters. When we enter the `while` loop in the procedure, we are in fact examining each character of the argument passed to the procedure. In our example, variable `t1` is the value `jason+j+manger` which is in fact an array stored as: `t1[j]`, `t1[a]`, `t1[s]` and finally `t1[r]` (that is, `t1[1]=="j"`, `t1[2]=="a"`, `t1[3]=="s"` up to `t1[14]=="r"`. A string can have its internal characters changed simply by assigning them literally using the `:=` (assignment) operator, as shown in the program.

The small Icon script below has been designed for use with a `GET`-based form that contains a single field. It could also therefore be used with an `<isindex>` form (although note that no parsing of any hexadecimal values has been included). This listing is different in that it performs some validation to see if the submitted field is empty, and it returns some HTML text to the server. It also writes the field data into a temporary file. Note that the script assumes that the first field is called `field1`; alter this accordingly. As before, an explanation of this script follows the listing.

```
#
# QUERY_STRING Icon CGI parser for a GET query string. This script
```

```
# handles a form that submits one field: name~<name>
#
global qs, field1, til
procedure main()
  local qs, ch, counter, secpos, ofile
  counter := 0
  # Load the QUERY_STRING variable:
  qs := getenv("QUERY_STRING")
  # Oops! no field value passed. Return a warning message.
  if (qs == "field1~") then
    {
     write("Content-type: text/html")
     write()
     write("<title>Error</title>")
     write("<b>You did not supply a name. Please re-enter it.</b><p>")
     write()
     stop()
  }
  # Take out any "+" signs:
  qs ? {
    while (tab(upto(~""))) do {
       counter := counter + 1
       if (qs[counter] == "+") then
         qs[counter] := " "
       move(1)
    }
  }
  field1 := qs[find("~", qs)+1:0]
  ofile := open("datafile.txt", "wa")
  write(ofile, field1)
  close(ofile)
  write("Content-type: text/html")
  write()
  write("<title>Results received</title>")
  write("</b><p>Your results were received by the server.</b>")
  write()
end
```

This script uses many of the Icon constructs explained in the previous program. The salient features to note from this listing are the use of HTML tags embedded within `write()` functions and the check for a submitted field that is empty. If you submit an empty form the query string will simply store the name of each field along with a tilde (for the `GET` posting method, that is). You can check this accordingly using a statement such as that in this program for a single field:

```
if (qs == "field1~") then ...
```

For multiple fields simply use a statement such as:

```
if (qs == "field1~field2~field3") then ...
```

which checks for three empty fields.

Scanning External Files

If a search string submitted to a server is to be used as a search string Icon can be used to return the search results. The files that Icon can scan are limited to plain ASCII files, although because its string-handling facilities are mature, you can break up the file into different *fields*. The next CGI script acts as a simple email lookup program. The file it scans is called `datafile.txt` and is structured as:

```
wombat@spuddy.uucp      =Jason Manger   >12345-6789
js@somewhere.com        =John Smith     >12345-6666
fbloggs@fred.edu        =Fred Bloggs    >54544-8888
```

Notice how the = and > characters have been used to identify the last two columns in the file (the first column can be identified simply because it starts at column 1). The form used to submit a value to our script resembles the following, containing just a single field and a submit button:

```
<title>Email name lookup service</title>
Please enter an email name of the form name@host:<hr>
<form method="get" action="/cgi-bin/search.exe"><p>
<input type="text" size=40 name="mailname">
<input type="submit" value=" Send ">
</form>
```

The Icon script that receives the information from the above form resembles the following:

```
#
# Example Icon CGI script to perform a simple lookup
# operation on a file.
#
procedure main()
  local fd, line, qs, ss
  fd := open("datafile.txt", "r") # Open the search file
  qs := getenv("QUERY_STRING")    # Original query string
  ss := qs[find("~", qs)+1:0]     # Extracted search string
  while line := read(fd) do {
    if (line[1:find(" ",line)] == ss) then {
```

```
        write("Content-type: text/html")
        write()
        write("<title>User Lookup Result: OK</title>")
        write("User lookup result<hr>")
        write("<b>" || ss || " </b>is<b> " ||
          line[find("=",line)+1:find(">",line)-1] || "</b><p>")
        write("Phone: <b>" || line[find(">",line)+1:0] || "</b>")
        write("")
        stop()
     }
   }
   write("Content-type: text/html")
   write("")
   write("<title>User Lookup Result: Failed</title>")
   write("The user <b> " || ss ||
     " </b> could not found in the database.<p>")
   write("")
end
```

This form is very simple. It starts by opening the database shown earlier. Make sure that this is in the **same** directory as the directory specified in the `hscript.pif` file or else the program will fail – normally this is `C:\TEMP`, the value of the `%TEMP%` variable, so you may want to change this accordingly. You could use the Icon concatenate operator (||) to add on a fully qualified pathname (this is a good idea in all cases in fact), for example:

```
fd := open("C:\DATAFILE\" || "datafile.txt", "r")
```

which would assume that the database can be found as `C:\DATAFILE\DATAFILE.TXT` (don't put in any spaces of course, or the filename won't be found).

The script starts (as is always the case with `GET` forms) by examining the `QUERY_STRING` variable to extract an email name. Since the email name will arrive in an encoded form, for example

```
mailname~wombat@spuddy.uucp
```

the string is parsed using the `find()` function to get rid of the form field preamble. The parsed string is then held in the variable `ss` (for *search string*). Next, the program uses a `while` loop in conjunction with the `read()` function to read successive lines from the database. This happens until the end of the file is reached. An `if` statement then checks the value of the search string (`ss`) against the email alias that appears in the database. The email alias is extracted using the expression:

```
line[1:find(" ",line)]
```

which returns a sub-string containing all the characters from column 1 up to the column with the first space (which itself marks the end of the field). If a match is made the program simply outputs some sample HTML text that prints the user's human name, along with his or her telephone number. Other fields can be added of course. The individual fields are themselves extracted using Icon's sub-string expressions with nested `find()` functions that seek out the = and > characters that are used in the database as field markers. Of course, if a file marker is missing or incorrectly typed the program may return some spurious data.

Summary

This section has shown some of Icon's capabilities. It has many, many more, however. We refer you to the references mentioned at the start of this section (both on- and off-line) for further information. Enough examples have been shown that should allow most scripting and parsing requirements to be undertaken.

4.5 Creating Imagemaps

Imagemaps are a feature that has sprung up all over the Web. An imagemap is basically an in-line image (such as a GIF file) inserted using the `<img src>` tag but which also includes the special tag-option `ismap`, which makes the image *selectable*. Imagemaps allow the user to click on portions, or *hot-regions*, of an image and then launch an associated hyperlink. This has many uses, including:

- Clicking on different parts of an image to explain its constituent parts, e.g. for an anatomical diagram
- Allowing users to click on a map to view various town and city information (these are abundant on the Internet)
- Constructing a menu out different parts of an image.

In HTML we would start by having a hyper-reference constructed as an in-line image, for example:

```
<a href="/cgi-win/imagemap.exe/mymap">
<img src="/demo/images/jason.gif" ismap>
</a>
```

where `imagemap.exe` is the name of the imagemap handling program (this is stored in the `\HTTPD\CGI-WIN` directory), and `mymap` is a reference to a special map file definition that holds the details of all the hot-regions in the image. This map file is stored on the server machine. Creating an imagemap requires the use of a special imagemap program and an HTTP server program that actually supports imagemaps. The Windows NCSA httpd server that is discussed later in the book has this capability built in. When an in-line image is classed as an imagemap using the special `ismap` option, clicking on a portion of the image that is a hot-region (normally these are visible rectangles, circles or other polygons such as triangles) will send a message back to the server containing the name of the imagemap and the cursor location on which you clicked. This takes the form:

mymap?70,150, where 70,150 is the x,y cursor coordinate, and mymap is the imagemap file. The server then refers to an imagemap reference file that contains all the x,y coordinates that make up the various *hot-regions* of the image. If the cursor position falls within such a region, an associated URL is launched. This is commonly an HTML document, but could of course be anything from an FTP server to a Gopher. The following steps must be followed in order to create an imagemap. We assume that you have the NCSA Windows NCSA httpd server program installed and running.

Stage 1 – Creating the Actual Image

The first step is to actually create an image for use as an imagemap. You can do this from scratch, although you may find a picture that has already been drawn instead (these are abundant on the Internet). The images themselves must be in the GIF format or at least a format that Mosaic can use as an in-line image. You can create the image with any tool that you like. The Windows 3.1 Paintbrush program pbrush.exe will create .BMP (Windows Bitmap) files, but not GIF files, unfortunately. However, the *Lview31* program will read and convert .BMPs to .GIFs, as will the DOS utility bmp2gif.exe, which is also on the disk. Refer to the appendices for the locations of other popular utilities. However, we advise you to stick with the Windows Paintbrush program for the moment, since it has one very important feature, namely the ability to show the current cursor position (select the last item in the View menu to enable this). This feature is critical for imagemap design, since without it you cannot ascertain which areas will be used for each hot-region. When you edit or create your image you must note down the x,y coordinates for each area (or shape) accordingly.

Rectangular hot-regions are by far the easiest to create because they require only two sets of x,y coordinates, the first representing the upper left-hand corner, and the second the lower right-hand corner of the rectangle. A circle also takes two sets of x,y coordinates, the first representing the centre of the circle, and the second representing the radius of the circle (get a coordinate of any tangent). Polygons, such as triangles and other multi-sided objects, use as many coordinates as are required – simply note down the x,y coordinate at the start and end of each line, and carry on in a clockwise direction (ensure the shape is *bounded*, i.e. it is a fully enclosed region). The server will recreate each region according to the x,y coordinates in order to see whether the cursor position that you clicked in the client image falls inside any hot-regions. Figure 4.10 illustrates the Windows Paintbrush program in action with the cursor location feature in action. Some examples of shapes are also given in the diagram for reference.

Once you have created your image and noted down the various cursor coordinates for each hot-region you can proceed to configure the Windows httpd server to accept imagemap requests. If you have installed the httpd server and kept all of the default directories during the configuration of the program (advisable) you can use the examples literally; otherwise, change the directory locations accordingly. All of the files are ASCII, so use an ASCII editor to make any changes.

Stage 2 – Configure the imagemap.cnf file

The file imagemap.cnf resides in the directory c:\httpd\conf (as installed by the NCSA httpd). Each line of the file contains the name and location of an imagemap file that has yet to be created. The file being referenced here will contain the x,y coordinates, or *hot-regions*, and their associated URLs. The syntax for each entry in the imagemap.cnf file is:

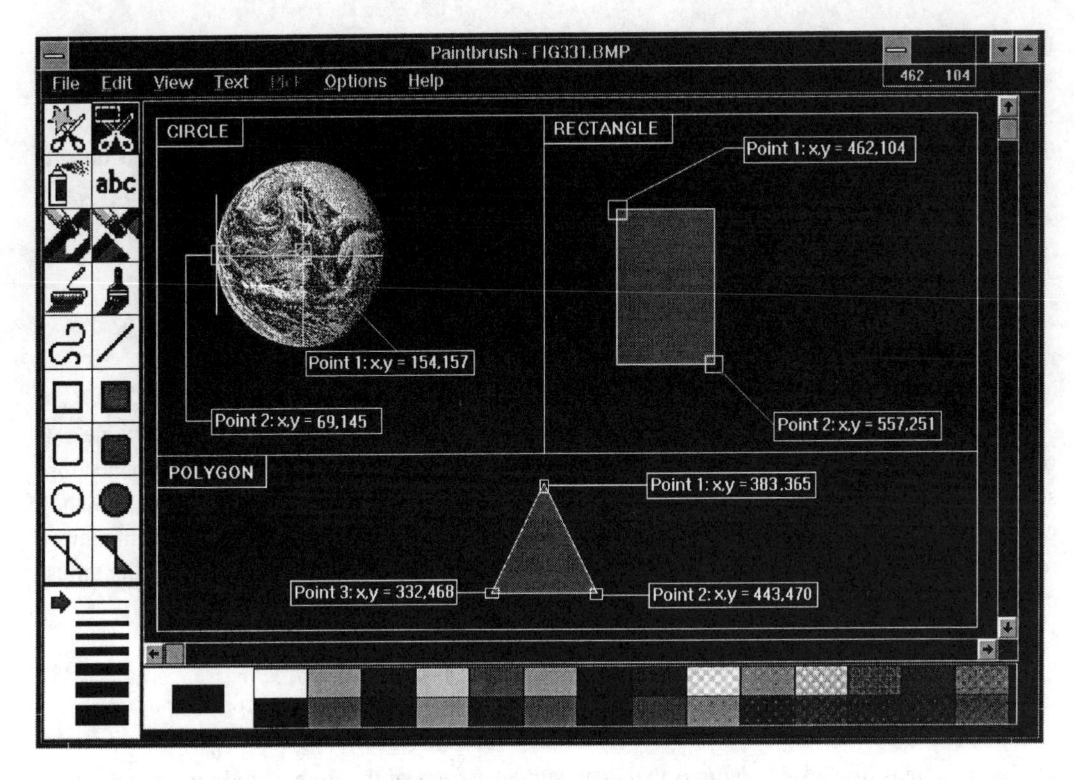

Figure 4.10: The Windows Paintbrush program and cursor position window.

```
mymap : c:\httpd\conf\maps\mymap.map
```

where `mymap` is a name for this entry (this will be used in your hyper-reference to the imagemap within an HTML document) and `c:\httpd\conf\maps\mymap.map` is the name of the map file that contains the cursor coordinates of each hot-region in your image, as mentioned.

Stage 3 – Create a `.map` File for your Image

Now we can create the map file referenced in the `imagemap.cnf` file shown previously. For the purposes of the example we have called this file `mymap.map`. Each line of this file takes the form:

```
Shape URL X,Y-Coordinates
```

where *`Shape`* is one of `poly` (polygon – a triangle or other multi-sided object), `circle` (a circle), or `rect` (a rectangle).The *`URL`* value is normally the name of an HTML document to call when that shape is clicked upon: for example, we could have the URL `http://ahost.com/file.html` for an HTML document that exists on another Web server, or just `http:/dir/file.html` for a local file on your own server. Alternatively, it could also be a request to start a Gopher server, e.g. `gopher://hostname`, or indeed any other service using the appropriate URL, e.g. `ftp://` or `news://`. The final field (*`X, Y-Coordinates`*) is a list of `x,y` coordinates that describe where the current shape (i.e. *hot-region*) is located within the image. Each set of coordinates must be separated by at least a single space. A special shape-name of `default` should also be used so that a mouse-click on an area not within a hot-region will call a file or other URL that is required (no coordinates are required for this entry). A sample map file that calls a series of HTML documents could therefore resemble:

```
default    /demo/noregion.htm
rect       /demo/rec1.htm254,50 360,136
rect       /demo/rec2.htm90,156 192,260
circle     /demo/circ1.htm462,104 462,50
```

This map file has three hot-regions, two of which are rectangles and one of which is a circle. All of the imagemap processing is of course taking place at the server's end of the network connection, so if you reference any HTML files, as above for each hot-region, be sure to create them so that they can be sent back to the client accordingly. If you want to send an image back to the client simply reference the image in your URL, e.g. `http://hostname/dir/image.gif` (the client must clearly have a viewer for the image format being sent back).

(The most extensive imagemap that I have seen to date resides at the URL:

```
http://white.nosc.mil/future_pc.html
```

and has hundreds of clickable *buttons* that deal with all aspects of the Web including general topics as well as those concerned with the Internet. Check this one out (although be warned – there are a good dozen imagemaps on this page).)

Figure 4.11 illustrates a typical imagemap structure. The rectangles will be the hot-regions in this case.

Of course, some images may require hot-regions that are not rectangular. Examples here include maps where different regions, such as counties or states, will be used as hot-regions. In order to create an imagemap for this type of picture you will have to select the shape type `poly` (which stands for polygon, a multi-sided object). Take Figure 4.12 as an example imagemap. This is a picture of Europe, as viewed from a nearby satellite. It is broken down into a number of countries, each of which will be a separate hot-region. Remember to work in a clockwise direction when assigning `x,y` coordinates to polygon shapes, and ensure that you know where you have started from – choose a significant point and remember it. Eventually you should end up with a closed region, although absolute accuracy is not required (you could even use a rectangle around a country if you are not too concerned with the accuracy of the imagemap).

An imagemap file for the picture in Figure 4.12 could therefore resemble that shown below. Now the user could click on a country and see an appropriate HTML file. Notice how each URL in the example has been structured as an HTML file with the name of each country in order to achieve this. The entire list of `x,y` coordinates has been shortened to save space (there were about 30 of them for the UK at least).

```
default /demo/nocountry.htm
```

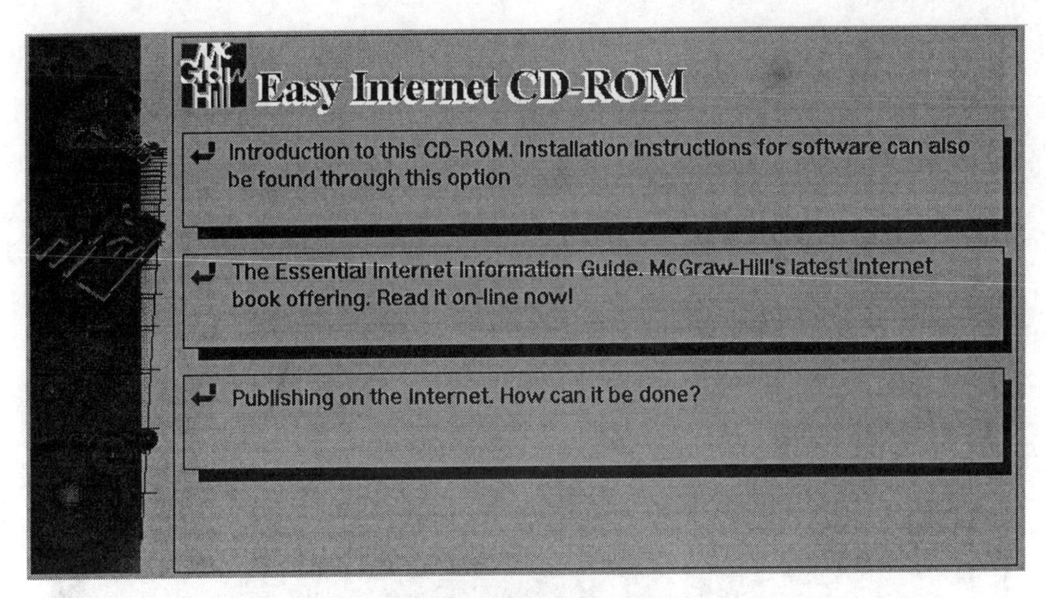

Figure 4.11: A typical screen for use as an *imagemap* (with three rectangular hot-regions).

```
poly    /demo/britain.htm  267,84 276,78 285,77 291,73 285,76 ...
poly    /demo/italy.htm   ...
poly    /demo/france.htm   ...
poly    /demo/spain.htm   ...
```

In the case of maps such as these, which originate from a satellite, you can come up with some interesting ideas. The imagemap could point to other images (via an appropriate URL), and could be used to show the user a *near* real-time weather map of a particular country. Weather images are abundant on the Internet. Many Web hosts update their images as each new picture becomes available via satellite. Since the locations of such images are held constant, you could point each hot-region at the URL of an image for a certain country. You may want to look at the URL at Imperial College London on:

```
http://src.doc.ic.ac.uk/11/pub/weather/images/
```

which contains weather maps of various regions around the world, e.g. `eur.gif` for Europe. By adding the appropriate filename to the URL you could give access to an up-to-date image for a particular country. The easiest way of doing this to keep the imagemap file simple and just point it to a normal HTML file. This HTML file, e.g. `britain.htm`, could then resemble the following:

```
<title>United Kingdom</title>
You have clicked on the United Kingdom.<p>
Click <a href="http://src/doc.ic.ac.uk/11/pub/weather/images/uk.gif>here</a>
```

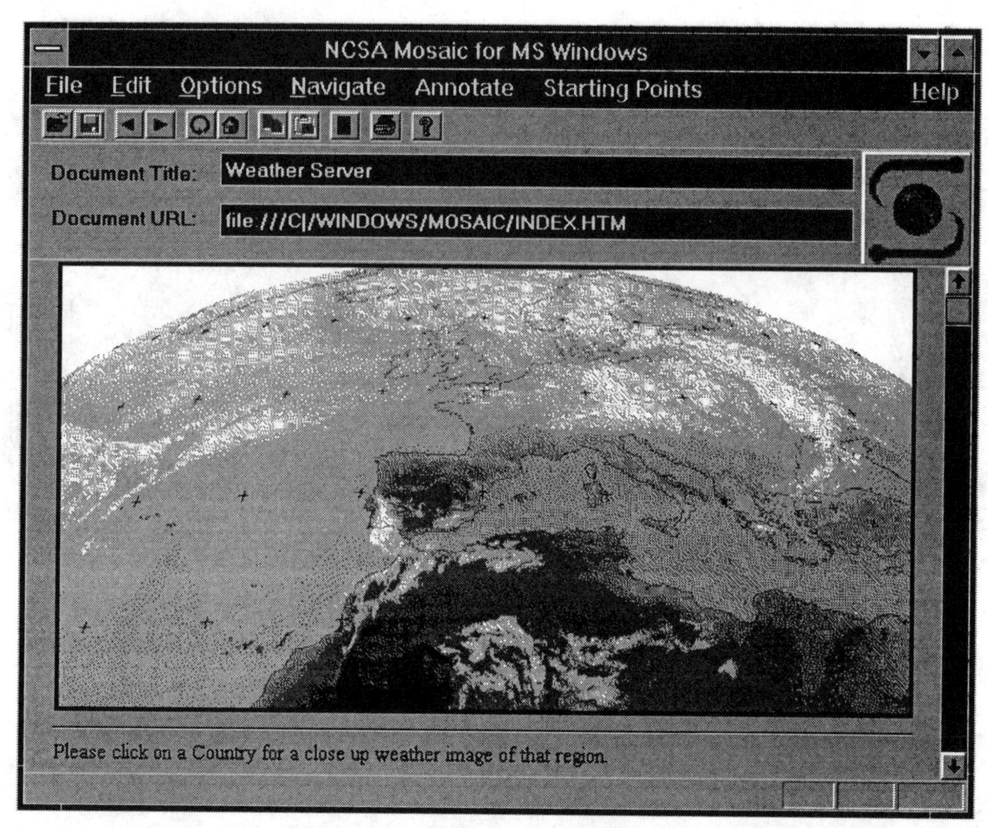

Figure 4.12: An imagemap structured as a picture of Europe with hot-regions as countries.

```
to see an up-to-date picture of this region now.
```

Clicking on the hyper-reference '*here*' would thus call the server at `src.doc.ic.ac.uk` and retrieve the file `uk.gif`. You must have a GIF viewer installed in this instance, e.g. *Lview31* or *WinGif* – see Appendix H for a list. Many other things can be done of course, such as inserting the picture as an in-line image directly into the HTML document using an `<img src>` tag. Before you use such image references always log on with a browser and see just exactly where the file resides (and in the process make a quick note of the exact URL). Remember to place a default entry in your imagemap file so that any mouse-clicks outside any of your hot-regions result in an appropriate message.

Check out the URL:

```
http://tns-www.lcs.mit.edu/cgi-bin/mapmaker
```

for details of the new *MapMaker* service, which automates the design and layout of imagemaps automatically (using polygon structures). This URL requires a form-based browser such as Mosaic version 2.0.

CHAPTER

5

Interfacing to other Internet Services using HTML

5.1 Introduction

HTML can interface to a variety of other Internet services, including FTP servers, Gopher servers, `telnet`-based resources, WAIS databases and even USENET groups (via an NNTP server). Files made available on any of these systems can be downloaded into your HTML document while you are on-line. Providing links to external Internet services from within an HTML document allows you to browse on-line databases, conduct searches for specific items of information, and of course, to access the Internet through a completely graphical interface without having to learn any arcane commands. A document is only as good as its hyperlinks, so be sure to reference as many relevant services as are required within your document. In this chapter you will learn how to:

- Interface HTML documents to USENET via an appropriate NNTP server
- Interface HTML documents to Gophers, WAIS and other indexing tools
- Conduct a `telnet` session with a remote Internet host

Mosaic uses a URL (Uniform Resource Locator) to tell it which type of Internet resource is being referenced, along with the Internet host on which the resource resides, followed by its exact path and filename.

HTML itself supports the following main URL resource types:

- FTP (File Transfer Protocol) – `ftp://` or `file://`
- Gopher and WAIS Servers – `gopher://` and `wais://`
- NNTP Servers (for USENET retrieval) – `news://`
- Telnet-based resources – `telnet://`

By far the simplest to use is `ftp://` (or `file://`), mainly because hostname and filenames are easy to specify in URLs and are well understood from the file system structure that files such as these use. It goes without saying that some resources will not be *files* as such, e.g. a telnet-based resource. Services such as `news://` and `telnet://` are less frequently used, and in any event their use is somewhat different from accessing a file using a tool such as FTP, which is specifically designed for the job. Of course, USENET articles are stored as files on news servers in any event, so the concept is *physically* the same at least. Direct use of the `wais://` URL is also limited; many WAIS servers are currently accessed indirectly via a Gopher index, although WAIS servers with their own URLs are gradually appearing – see Appendix B for some examples.

Referencing FTP Servers

Mosaic can pull a file from any FTP site on the Internet. To reference an exact file from an FTP site one must clearly know: (i) the name of the FTP site; (ii) the directory where the file resides; and (iii) the name of the file (a tool such as *Archie* has already been designed to locate such information, and is in widespread use on the Internet). Be sure to quote the exact name of the file, including different character cases (upper- and lower-case characters will matter if a file resides on a UNIX box). Using the `ftp://` resource type it is possible to reference any type of file, be it an HTML document, an image or a sound clip. As an alternative you can load an FTP site's entire file system and browse it using Mosaic's graphical interface. For an example of the former method we could have an HTML `<a href>` hyperlink tag constructed as:

```
<a href="file://www.pipex.net/incoming/goodmorning.au">
    Greeting!</a>
```

which references an FTP site called `www.pipex.net`. The file we are accessing in this instance is an audio clip in the `.AU` format. Clicking on the hyperlink '*Greeting!*' would make Mosaic look for the file accordingly. If an appropriate audio utility is installed, the audio clip will be played as soon as it has been transferred to your machine. The URL resource type `ftp://` can also be used interchangeably. A normal FTP request requires the user to log-in literally as user *anonymous* and then provide a full Internet email address as a password (although some do allow just a name and @ sign, e.g. `fred@`); for example:

```
fred@somewhere.com
```

Mosaic does this automatically for you so all of this is transparent to the end-user. File transfer then begins, and a count of the number of bytes as they are being transferred is shown on the status bar at the bottom of the Mosaic window. If the file does not exist Mosaic will give an appropriate error message. If the URL is okay, that is the file exists, Mosaic will display a '*Transfering file*' message on the status line and the file will be written to your hard disk. If a viewer is installed for that particular file it will be launched as soon as the file is downloaded. See Chapter 2 for more on file viewers and their configuration.

▶ TIP

You can browse the entire hierarchy of an FTP site by shortening the URL to just the name of the FTP site. This will allow you to browse the remote FTP server's file system and then download the files you require. For example, a URL of:

```
ftp://ftp.ncsa.uiuc.edu/
```

will load a root directory for this site, i.e. you will be placed at the very top of the file system (in the host's *root* directory (`C:\` to DOS users)).

Anonymous FTP is normally thought of as the only way in which files get transferred across the Net. Of course this is not the case. Many files are transferred using *conventional* FTP, so that authorized users of a particular machine on the Internet can access their files. This requires a valid user name and password to be specified. Anonymous FTP servers only store *publicly available* files, not the files of authorized users. In the case where an FTP server does store such files, anonymous users will only have access to directories with the appropriate read permission, e.g. `/pub`. If you are an authorized user of a host, and you wish to connect to your own account via FTP, use a URL of the form:

```
ftp://username:password@hostname.domain
```

where `username` is your user name (on UNIX this will be commonly stored in the `/etc/passwd` file) and `password` is your personal password. The `hostname.domain` part refers to your machine's Internet host name; for example we could specify

```
ftp://fred:nettastic@hostname.domain
```

to log-in as user `fred` with password `nettastic`. This form of URL has one glaring problem, namely the use of an easily viewable plain-text password! This sort of URL is therefore hardly ever used. To overcome this problem, simply remove the `user:password` part of the URL and you should be prompted for a user name and password accordingly, thus preserving the security of the system concerned.

Referencing a USENET Group (via an NNTP Server)

Mosaic can also reference NNTP (Network News Transfer Protocol) servers so that USENET groups can be browsed while you are on-line. This can be useful if your document has an associated newsgroup so that users can see if any relevant material is available. The news server that is used will be found in your Mosaic initialization file. To specify a news URL simply structure it as:

```
news:alt.beer
```

where `alt.beer` is the USENET group that we are interested in (you can omit the normal '`//`' prefix from the URL if you wish). Mosaic would then make the news request and shortly you would see a screen similar to that shown in Figure 5.1. Each USENET (email) posting is then tagged by Mosaic as a hyperlink back to the actual message on the news server, and clicking on an appropriate message will result in it being displayed as HTML text. In the case of the second URL method, Mosaic relies on a default NNTP server that is specified in your `mosaic.ini` initialization file. Look at your file under the `[Services]` heading and you should see an entry entitled `NNTP_Server=`, which names the news server that your information provider uses, for example:

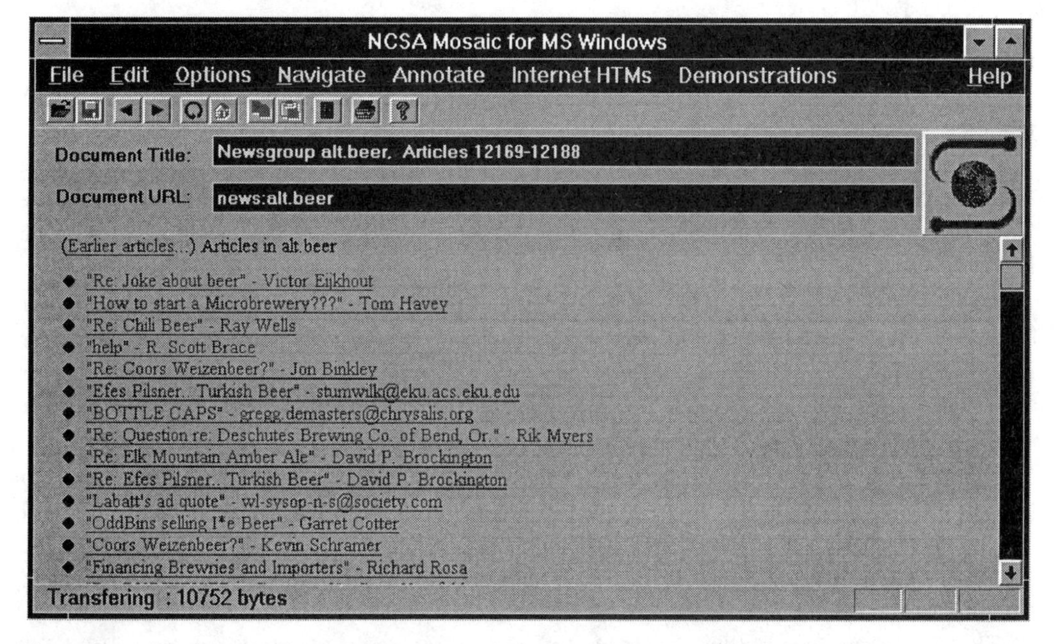

Figure 5.1: The Mosaic system browsing a USENET group.

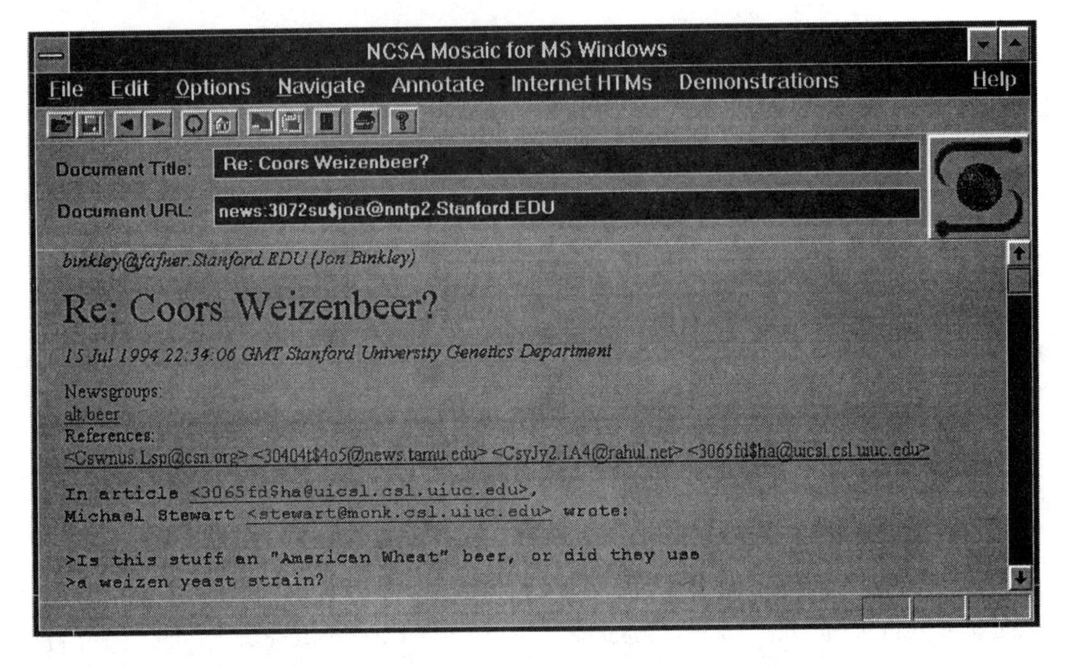

Figure 5.2: Reading a typical USENET message.

```
[Services]
NNTP_Server="news.demon.co.uk"
```

If you are unsure as to which name to use, ask your service provider. Alternatively you can of course quote any valid NNTP server in your initialization file, and that will be used by Mosaic (clearly, a more locally situated news server will serve you best, in order to speed things up). A default NCSA news server that can be used is quoted in `mosaic.ini`).

As Figure 5.2 shows, Mosaic loads just a screenful of messages at a time. You can click on the '*Earlier articles*' hyperlink to go back further in time (Mosaic loads the most recent postings). Figure 5.3 illustrates a typical screen when a message is clicked on and loaded. You can move back to the listings by using the '*Previous screen*' icon on the toolbar (the left-facing arrow in the toolbar)

Wildcards such as * cannot currently be used to match specific USENET groups and/or hierarchies: for example, you couldn't specify a URL of `news:alt.*` to load only the `alt`ernative USENET hierarchy. There is also no current method of specifying a different NNTP news server other than through your initialization file (although both of these problems are being addressed back at NCSA for future releases of the Mosaic program).

When viewing USENET groups using the * wildcard Mosaic shows two figures by each newsgroup name, which are the total number of number of articles in each group, and the current article number that is selected. USENET articles arrives in their thousands and are purged from the system as time progresses. Thus when clicking on a specific newsgroup you will be placed on an arbitrary article number, namely the first article in the group that is available. If you `telnet` to an NNTP news server directly (this is possible on most service provider's machines, since USENET

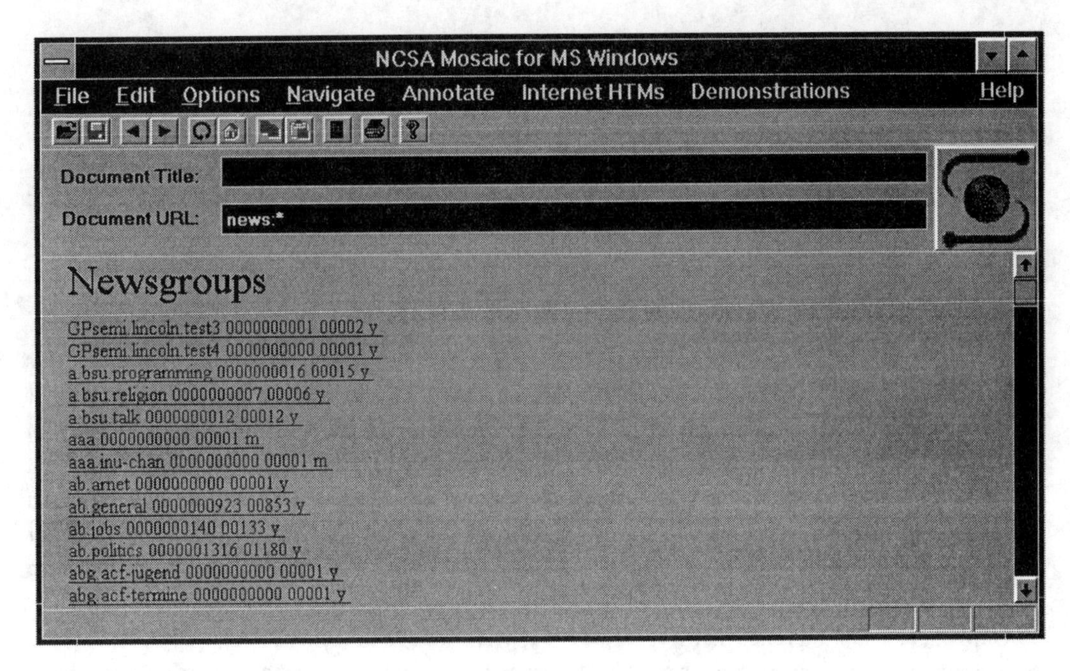

Figure 5.3: Specifying the URL `news:*` to load all USENET hierarchies.

news is mostly handled by a separate network machine commonly called '`news`', which answers on port 119), use the command `NEWSGROUPS` to list all of that news server's newsgroups (a very long list – beware). The command `GROUP`<*name*> (where <*name*> is the USENET group) is the group-loading function, while the commands `NEXT` and `LAST` move you back and forth between articles. You can view USENET news in this way using a textual interface under Windows via a third-party telnet program, e.g. NCSA's *WinTel* program (see appendices for its whereabouts on the Internet), although this is not nearly as nice, or indeed convenient, as specifying a `news://` URL within an HTML document directly. You may also have noticed that some news servers provide additional hyper-references within an article. These are normally the message-id and/or email address. Clicking on these will provide further information on the items referenced.

Referencing a Gopher Server

Gopher servers can be called up from within an HTML document so that they can be browsed, or an individual resource retrieved. Gopher is a file referencing tool not unlike Archie in many respects (the reader interested in referencing an Archie server from within an HTML should look at the Web resource called `http://hoohoo.ncsa.uiuc.edu/`), where files from all over the Internet are referenced by title (although not internally via strings that are embedded in a document's body). Hundreds of Gopher servers are available on the Internet (see the appendices for a list of popular servers that you can access in your documents). When specifying a Gopher server in your HTML document, as a hyperlink, you can structure your URL as either:

- Pointing to the top-level (the *root*) of the Gopher server; *or*
- Pointing to the fully-qualified pathname to a file on a Gopher server.

Specifying Top-level Gopher Menu URLs

In the case of the first method a URL could be quoted simply as a hyperlink reference in your HTML document, as follows:

```
<a href="gopher://consultant.micro.umn.edu/">Gophers Home</a>
```

which would load the top-level menu of the Gopher at `consultant.micro.umn.edu` (Gopher's home, coincidentally). The user would then be presented with a series of menus from which further selections can be made. Gopher organizes files hierarchically, just like a conventional file system under MS-DOS or UNIX. Some references in a Gopher menu will end at a document (this may exist anywhere on the Net – Gopher will FTP the file for you or will telnet to the resource, depending on which type of resource it is), while some selections will lead you to further file system areas, or *subdirectories*, in file system speak. Figure 5.4 illustrates a typical Gopher root menu called from within Mosaic.

Gopher can itself reference many different file types, although documents (ASCII and binary) are most abundant. Mosaic uses a series of different icons to let you know what each particular resource is. The resource may not be *tangible* at all: for example, it could be a telnet link to a remote Internet server, in which case Mosaic would use the telnet protocol to call the resource (ensure you have a

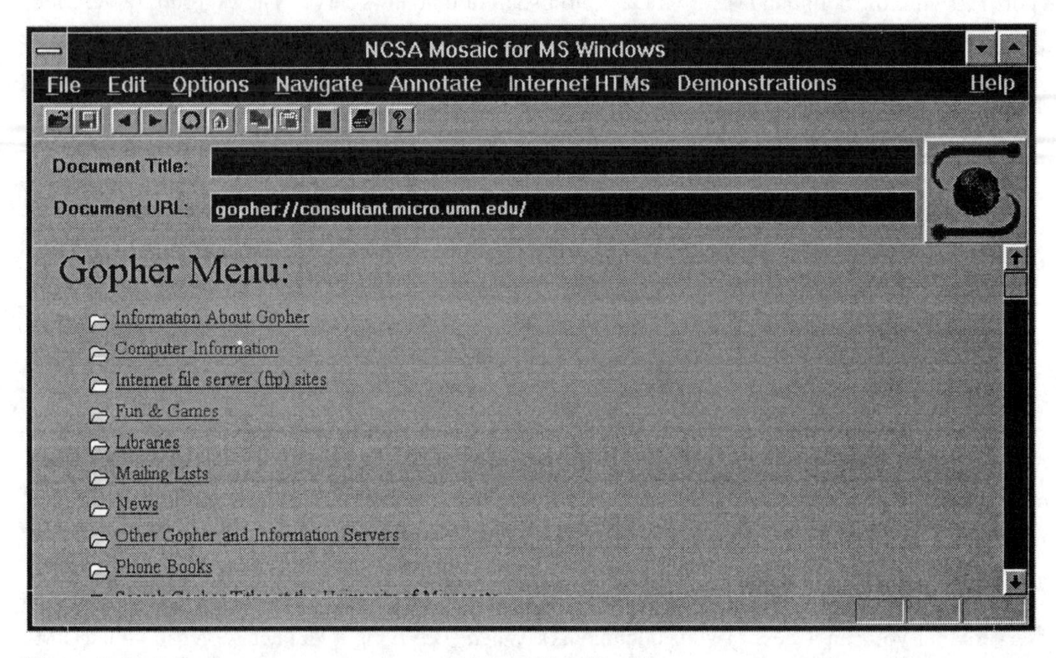

Figure 5.4: A Gopher root menu accessed from within Mosaic.

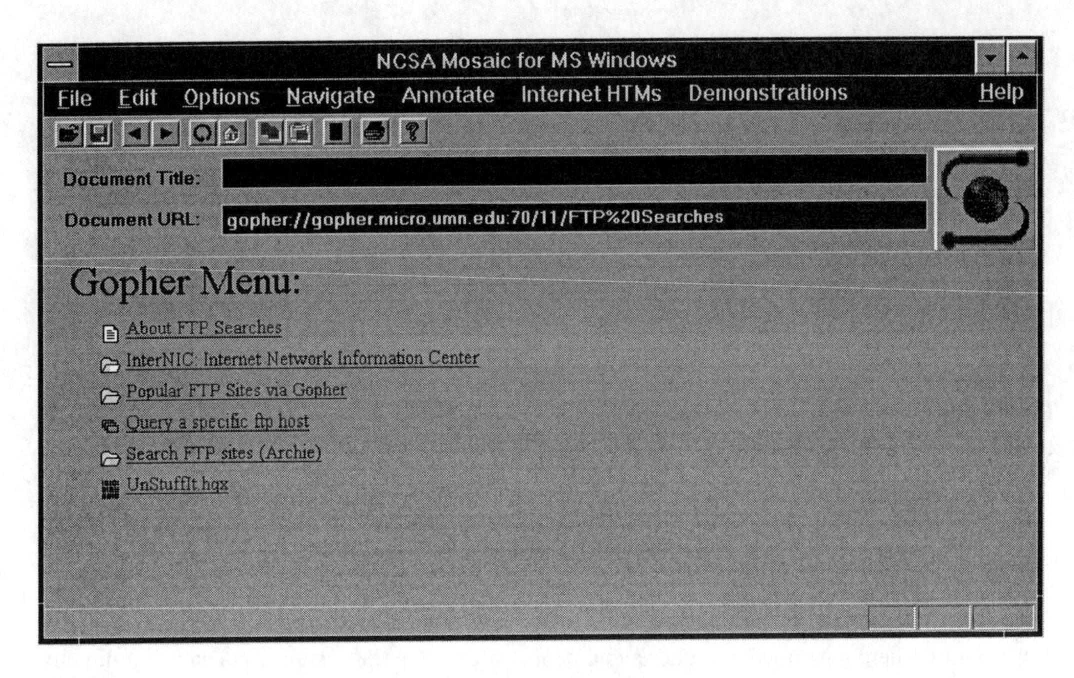

Figure 5.5: A selection of different file formats and resources.

`telnet` utility installed on your system for this purpose – see Chapter 2 for more details). Figure 5.5 illustrates some typical icons that you may see on your travels in *hyperspace*:

As can be seen from Figure 5.5, resources can be both Internet tools and documents alike – the screenshot shows a screen after clicking on the *Internet File Server* hyperlink previous to this. In fact, all Gopher items become hyperlinks under Mosaic, so pointing and clicking replaces all of the normal keystrokes for accessing Gopher menus through a textual interface. One of Gopher's best aspects is its ability to allow searches in *Gopherspace*. Gopherspace is a collective term describing all of the known Gopher servers in existence. Because individual Gopher servers contain localized information, for example pertaining to a local campus of a university or college, the information you require may not be on the Gopher you eventually access. For this reason a tool called veronica was created in order to allow searches to be made across hundreds of known Gopher servers to find the information you require. Veronica servers can be found within many Gopher menus (although not all Gophers) and if you are conducting a search this is the option to go for (gopher sounds like 'go for', hence its name: '*go for information...*'). Figure 5.6 shows some common Gopher icons.

▶ TIP

When downloading ASCII files Mosaic will launch an editor for the file automatically so that you can view it (look for the entry `text/plain` in your `mosaic.ini` file in the `[Viewers]` section. It would help if an editor, rather than a file viewer was used, since then you can save all such files. If you want to use a DOS-based editor create an entry using `PIFEDIT.EXE` and make it use a window, rather than the whole screen. Then specify the `.pif` file you have just created as the utility to launch (not

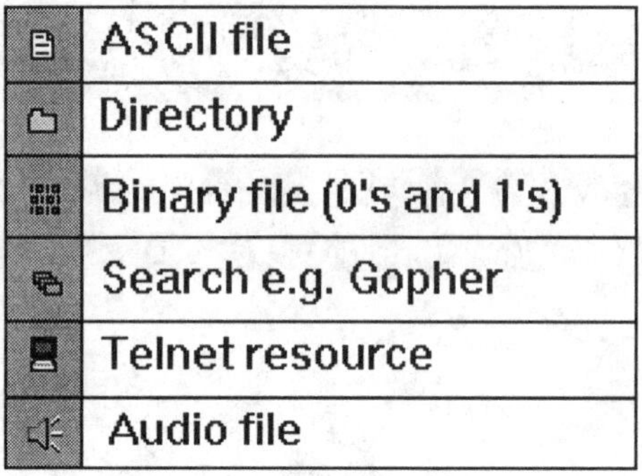

	ASCII file
	Directory
	Binary file (0's and 1's)
	Search e.g. Gopher
	Telnet resource
	Audio file

Figure 5.6 Gopher icons in common use.

the utility itself). You can of course use `NOTEPAD.EXE`, the ASCII editor that comes as standard with Windows 3.1 as an alternative.

Specifying Full Pathname URLs

If you know where a particular Gopher menu item is stored in a file system you can call it directly, rather than loading the top-level menu page from Mosaic. This is slightly trickier, however, since the names of such directories are not shown until you actually follow a hyperlink and the URL is updated on the screen. If you are developing applications that require searches using the Gopher system simply take note of the URL on the screen when you gain access to a search item, e.g. a veronica hyperlink. For example, Figure 5.7 shows a local Gopher server that I use quite frequently (`info.brad.ac.uk`). The option to search for documents on this menu is located within the menu called *Other Information Servers* (it may be different on other servers note, although the description will be similar). In Figure 5.7 the very last hyperlink in the list is the one we are interested in, since it seems to offer access to some external information servers.

▶ TIP

If you access a conventional text-based Gopher, use the = command (equals sign) on an item to tell you the exact location of the item. This is analogous to a URL under Mosaic, and can be used to allow you to make note of the exact whereabouts of files and search tools to integrate into your Web documents at a later date.

On clicking on the last hyperlink item in Figure 5.7 we would be are taken to a number of options (these are stored in the Gopher directory called `/11`, as you can see from the URL). The port number of 70 in the URL is a default used by most Gopher servers. It can be omitted from your URL in such instances (unless your Gopher answers on a specific, non-standard, port number). Figure 5.8 illustrates the next menu that we would see. It consists of a number of options, although we are interested in a veronica search in this example. Searches can be identified by the small layered icon in the diagram, which stands for a *search-related* operation (e.g. Archie file search, Gopher search).

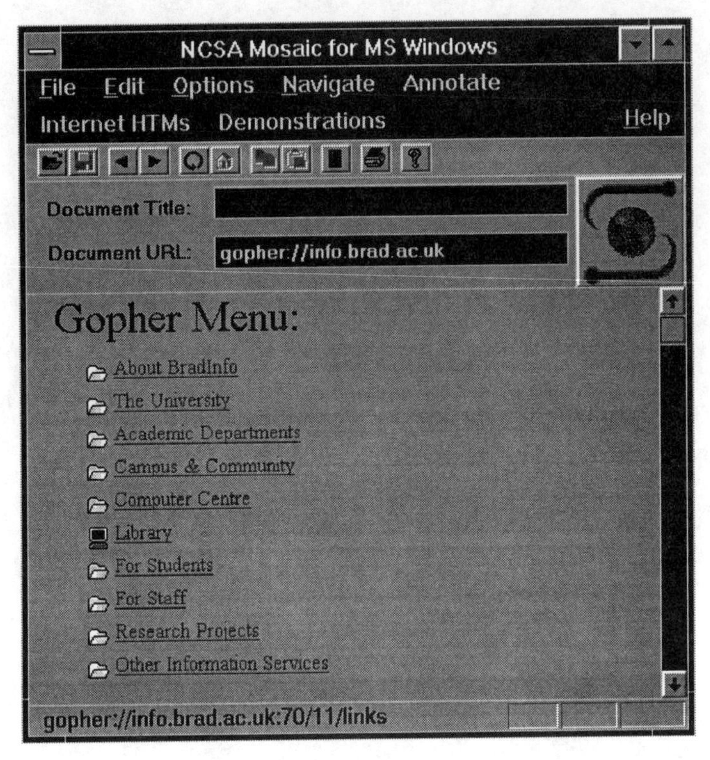

Figure 5.7: The Gopher menu at the Internet host `info.brad.ac.uk`.

Common search links will allow you to hunt for people via the X500 protocol (in essence an electronic mail protocol), or search local Gophers in one country, as in the case of the United Kingdom in Figure 5.8. We are now very near to finding the URL we require to access a veronica server. You may of course want to note all the URLs of search tools shown in menus such as these for future reference in your documents. This will also save you presenting a top level menu to your users, saving them the hassle of navigating such menus. Clicking on the veronica hyperlink then results in a screen in which you can enter am *index-term*, that is a string of characters that you want to search for in Gopherspace (that is, most of the Gophers around the world). This is shown in Figure 5.9. Notice the area above the status line, which allows entry from the keyboard.

More importantly, we have also found a URL at which we can conduct veronica searches directly, namely `gopher://veronica.sunet.se:2347/7`, a gopher server that answers on port 2347 in Sweden ('`.se`' is the country code suffix for Sweden). In the example I have supplied a search string of 'HTML' to find all documents related to the HyperText Mark-up Language. The veronica server obliges and provides a series of entries in which the string 'HTML' has been found (the case of the search string is ignored). The references found for us exist on FTP sites scattered all over the world, and we have found all of them in just a few seconds! All we have to do now is click on a hyperlink that interests us. If any entries scroll outside of the window simply use the side-bar to move down to any items that you require. Since most of the documents that are accessible are ASCII documents (a few binary files may be available, e.g. compressed files or utilities), Mosaic will

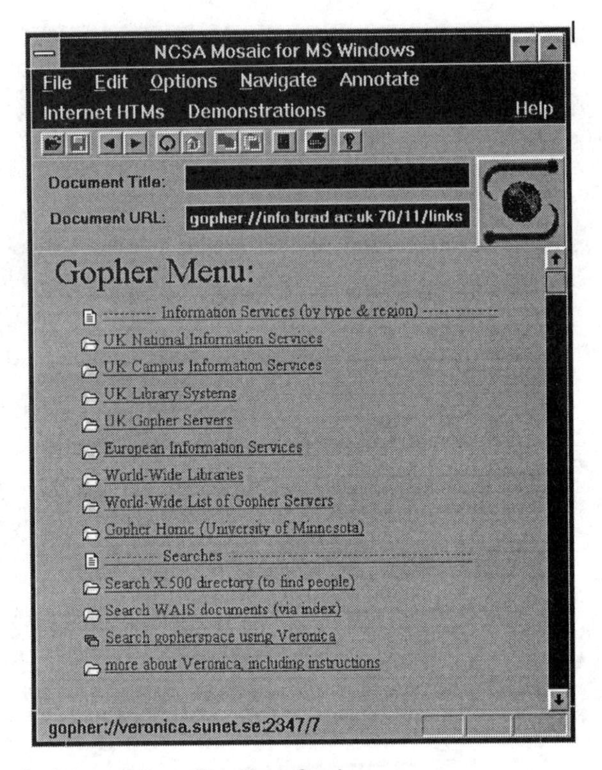

Figure 5.8: Some typical search hyperlinks in a Gopher menu.

download the file and launch your ASCII editor on the file when it is fully retrieved according to the filename extension. You can then save the file (Mosaic will supply a name, although this can be changed if you wish). For this reason it is important that your ASCII file viewer has a *save-file* feature. Figure 5.10 shows the results screen mentioned.

Well now you know how to find that elusive URL: simply search for the service using Gopher (via the Web or using a gopher client, or a gopher server via `telnet`) and then make a note of the hyperlink that offers the search: in this case a veronica server was referenced at `gopher://veronica.sunet.se:2347/7`. In an HTML document we can use this URL reference to help users search for other documents via an appropriate hyperlink, for example:

```
<a href="gopher://veronica.sunet.se:2347/7">
    Conduct a Search</a>
```

This hyper-reference would allow a user to click on the words 'Conduct a Search' and then be connected directly to the Veronica server mentioned. Many other servers exist apart from this one. Refer to the appendices for a list of servers that can be linked into your HTML documents.

To speed up your searching you can bypass all user input of search terms by placing a

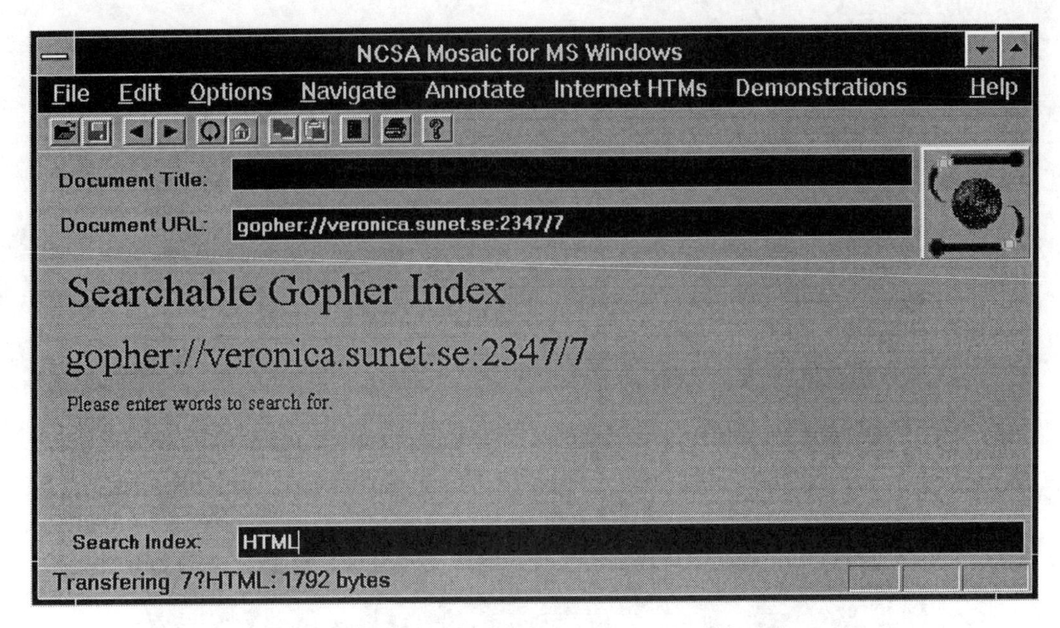

Figure 5.9: Entering an index term (or search string) to locate related documents.

question mark (`?`) after the URL and then follow this by the actual search string that you want to find. For example:

```
gopher://veronica.sunet.se:2347/7?html
```

would search for the string 'html' (upper and lower cases) on the host specified, here `veronica.sunet.se`. This type of search is termed a *hard-coded* search, since the user cannot specify the search string manually.

Referencing WAIS (Wide Area Information Servers)

WAIS is another Internet tool that is made up of a series of source databases, the contents of which are indexed (as opposed to Gopher which relies on indexed *titles* of documents). With WAIS you can search a database for a string and then examine parts of the database that contain any matches. Many different databases exist on WAIS and more are constantly being added. Databases exist for specific USENET groups, as well as many general topics, such as drugs and medical data, religious topics, computer software, agricultural news, aeronautics, and in fact a massive array of different subjects ranging from the everyday to specialist usage. The first versions of WAIS were text-based applications. Graphical clients did become available though, under systems such as X-Windows. The text-only versions of WAIS can be cumbersome to use, so it makes sense to use a graphical interface. Many servers are springing up all over the Internet that offer WAIS-searching facilities (see Figure 5.8 for an example hyperlink in a Gopher menu) and these can be used in a URL to allow the user to search a specific WAIS source database. While WAIS has not been implemented with the type of

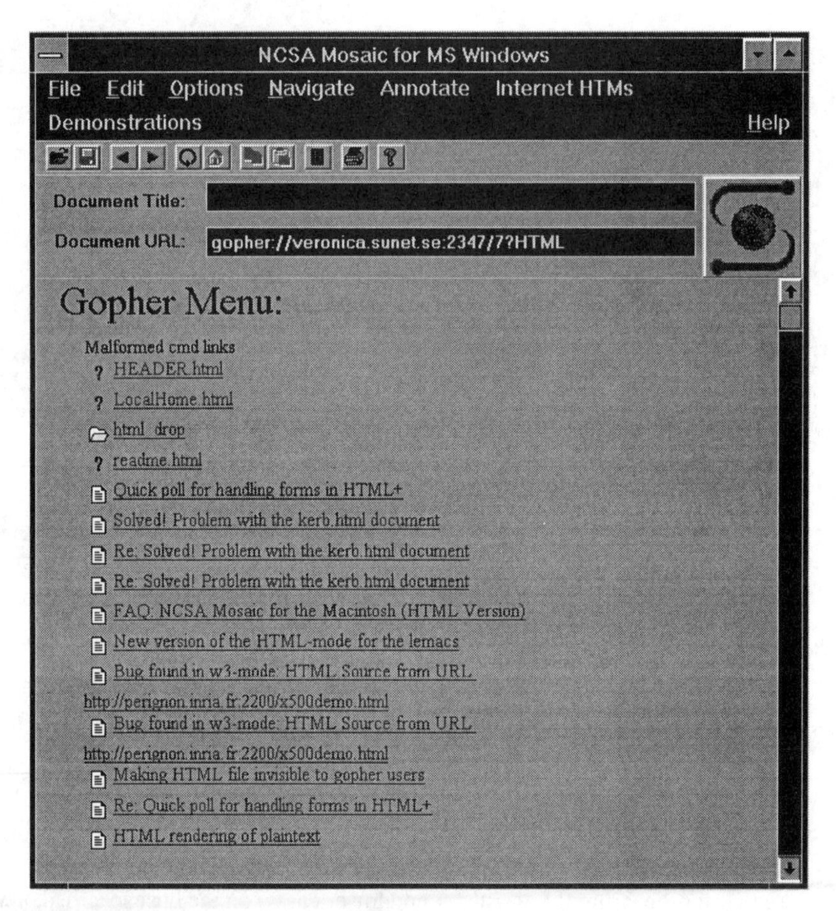

Figure 5.10: Results for the search string 'HTML'.

success that Gopher has received via the Web, it is still searchable on some Web servers that have a link to the program. See the appendices for lists of Web pages that have WAIS interfaces.

As mentioned, WAIS databases are structured as individual files, called *sources*. Such files end with a `.src` (for source) extension; for example `acronyms.src` is the common acronyms database on WAIS. Dozens of others are available and are ordered in an A–Z fashion. Your first link into WAIS is in fact normally via an A–Z index. In the text-based WAIS systems a list of sources will first be shown to you. Mosaic presents you with a list of references organized as a series of icons named A through to Z which index the subjects contained, e.g. 'A' for *acronyms*, *abortion*, *aboriginal studies* and so forth. Figure 5.11 shows a typical Mosaic page for a WAIS index. Notice the entry for `directory-of-servers.src`, which is itself a source database that acts as a guide to all the source databases on the WAIS server (and different WAIS servers have some variations in the actual sources they carry, although these are minor).

In order to use WAIS one must select a source database and then search this using a keyword. In order to select a source database it is most likely that you will click on a letter corresponding to the

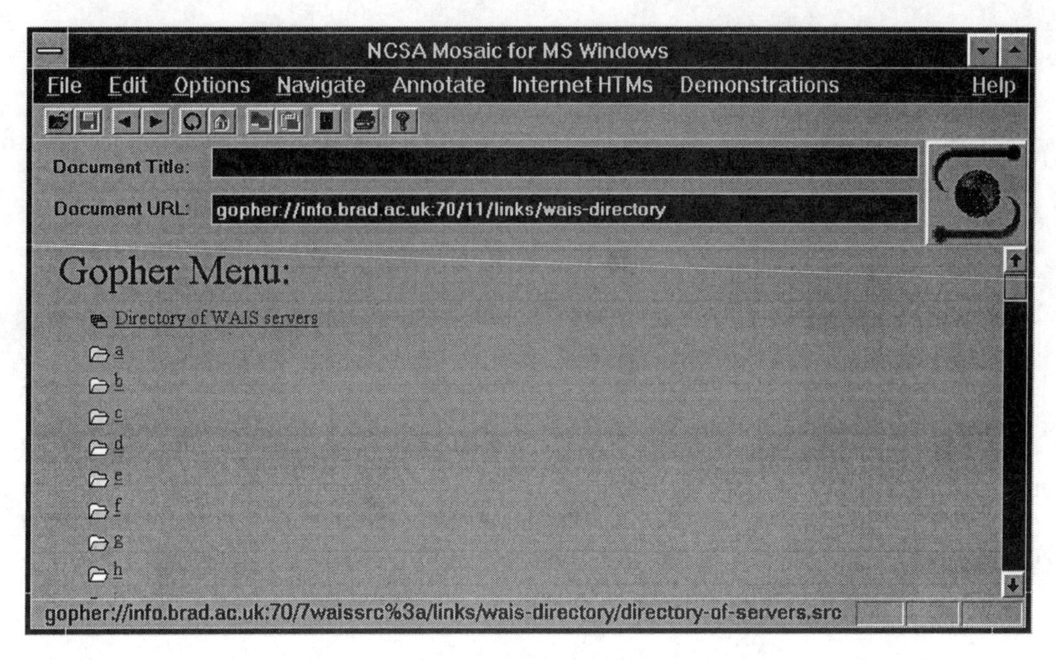

Figure 5.11: A typical A–Z WAIS index.

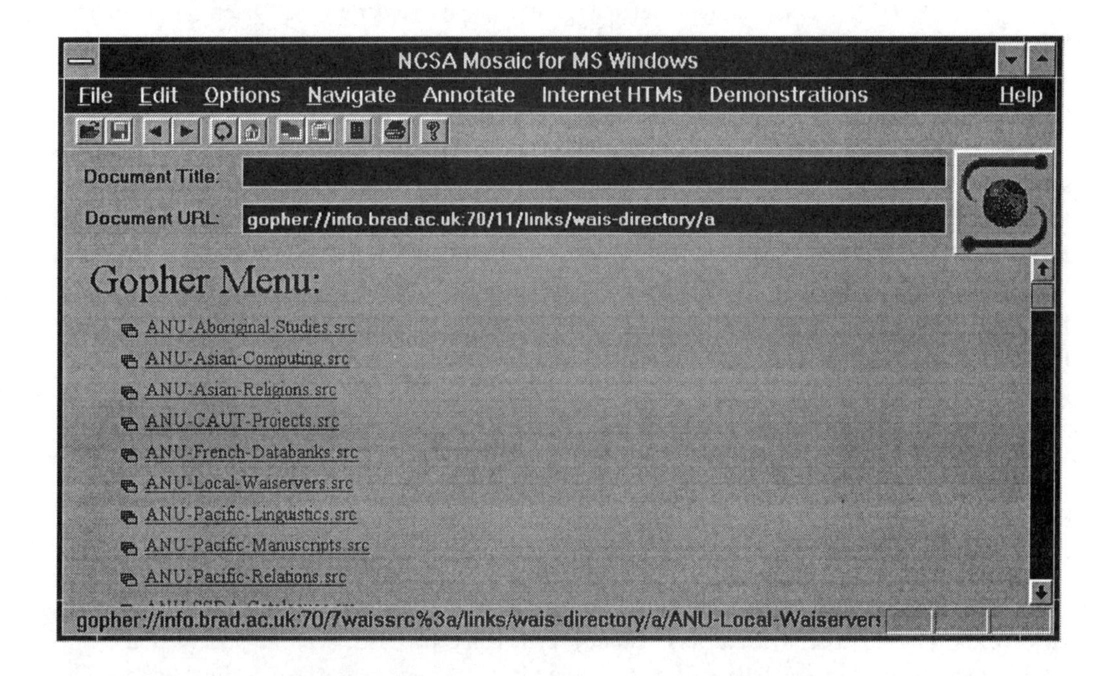

Figure 5.12: Source WAIS databases under the letter 'A'.

subject that interests you, for example 'A' for acronyms. Clicking on a letter, as in Figure 5.11, results in a list of source databases which you can access.

Selecting a letter from the above menu thus leads you to a list of sources, as shown in Figure 5.12.

You will have noticed from Figure 5.12 that every source is in fact a search index (note the icon); there is nothing you can do with a source database other than search it. Source databases are not individual files; rather they contain embedded links to thousands of documents on FTP sites all over the Internet, and perhaps to Gopher server entries and even other WAIS sources. When you have searched a source all documents that contain the search string will be shown as hyperlinks, and you can click on the link to access the requested file. From this point onwards the entering of search strings and the retrieval of results is really all self-explanatory.

Many WAIS services are provided through Gopher servers anyway (Gophers can access WAIS and FTP data with ease). Whether or not you access a Gopher server to get at a WAIS database is irrelevant; the process will be transparent to the user if you specify the URL correctly. Don't forget that the URL can be extended to include the names of source databases, and that URLs can also contain embedded search strings using the ? character. For example we could specify the source database on Aboriginal studies as a hyper-reference in an HTML document as follows:

```
<a href="gopher://info.brad.ac.uk:70/7waissrc/links/wais-directory/a/
    ANU-Aboriginal-Studies.src?australia">
Search for Australian Aboriginal facts
</a>
```

In this small HTML extract our hyper-reference uses a Gopher server's WAIS gateway to search the WAIS source called `ANU-Aboriginal-Studies.src`. The characters `?australia` placed at the end of the URL initiate an immediate search for all references to the word 'australia' (case insensitive). Of course, you can omit this if you wish in order to allow users to type search strings of their own. The URL is starting to look bit long, you may have also noticed. This is mainly due to the fact that WAIS sources tend to have long names. Remember that in order to get the URL you need to enter Mosaic and load up an appropriate URL (you can type URLs in directly under Mosaic's File menu to save time). This will probably mean entering the name of a Gopher server using the `gopher://` resource type (most WAIS indexes are accessed by Gopher servers at the time of writing) and then trace the menus until you find a WAIS hyperlink. You may want to trace this even further to find the appropriate source database. In the HTML example above these reside in the directory called

```
/7waissrc/links/wais-directory/
```

followed by a letter in the range a–z (lower case to match the exact directory) and then the name of the source database. Other servers will of course use different file system areas for their WAIS details.

Note that all special characters within a path name or URL, such as punctuation symbols, are converted to the format `%xx` by Mosaic, where `xx` is a hexadecimal (base

16) number. All such numbers should be replaced with their ASCII equivalents accordingly, e.g. `/7waissrc%3a` becomes `/7waissrc:` (hex 3a is decimal, or ASCII, 58, which is a colon) so that the correct directory can be found. Most scientific calculators have a hex (base 16) to denary (base 10) converter. And no, I'm not going to show you how to convert these numbers manually!

▶ TIP

Macintosh machines. If you are using a URL to reference a Macintosh machine, be aware that directory names can have spaces in them.

To allow for this use the special hexadecimal code `%20` (ASCII 32 – a space) to represent each space in the URL (you can thus tell which URLs refer to Macintosh machines). As an example we could therefore have the URL:

```
gopher://gopher.host.edu/11/Other%20Information%20Servers
```

When any documents have been found and you click on an associated hyperlink for that item, Mosaic will launch an ASCII file viewer to allow you to see the file. I'll emphasize again that you must specify an ASCII editor (not an ASCII viewer such as the `TYPE` command under DOS) in order that you can save all the documents you eventually access. WAIS does not download the document to disk as such (like FTP does); rather it downloads it to a buffer, i.e. an area of memory, where it is then displayed. Whether or not you save the file depends on your individual Mosaic configuration. Readers may be interested to know that there are a variety of WAIS client programs for the PC that are Windows-compatible and which can be used in conjunction with Mosaic, although not as part of it. See the appendices for details of such programs.

Referencing Telnet Resources

Telnet is a program found as standard on all UNIX systems. It is the virtual terminal protocol, a program that allows a user to log into a remote machine (perhaps on the Internet) and then use it in real-time just as if the machine was being used locally. Telnet copies all of the output generated by the remote host and passes it over the network to your machine for this purpose. Mosaic uses the URL resource type of `telnet://` when you want to contact an Internet host. Many thousands of telnet-based servers provide information that you can query in real-time. Examples include medical databases, game servers, Internet Relay Chat servers (IRC servers allow multiple users to hold conferences on-line), and of course many Gopher, WAIS, Archie and other standard Internet tools are available via telnet for those people without a local client. As such, using telnet from within Mosaic bypasses its graphical interface to a large extent. Telnet services differ enormously and there is simply no easy way of allowing Mosaic to interpret an interface (such as a menu) and then turn this into a graphical representation. Services such as FTP and Gopher are simple because their interfaces are uniform across the entire Internet network. This is not the case with telnet-based services, which may link to all manner of programs and interfaces.

Including telnet hyper-references in your documents allows the user to jump into the Internet's *raw mode* of operation temporarily. If an HTML document was concerned with medical matters, you could provide a reference to an on-line medical database via telnet, and they can use the system immediately. Of course, if an alternative Gopher interface was available you could specify a Gopher URL (`gopher://`) and use a prettier interface altogether. Unfortunately, many such services have yet to be *Gopherized* in this way and you may have still to access a service via telnet. If you need to find sources for on-line telnet-servers you can obtain one of the many Internet guides to help you, or of course you can purchase my book, *The Essential Internet Information Guide*, and read the appendices, where hundreds of such entries are all marked out for easy reference. So how does one use telnet under Mosaic? Well, for a start you must have a telnet client installed under Mosaic. A common client is the Windows program `TELW.EXE` (Telnet for Windows) which is available on-line (see the appendices). This program opens a window when you reference a telnet URL and then starts the session specified. Because you are in the Windows environment you can jump back to Mosaic whenever you like. Multiple telnet sessions are also available, so you could in theory be in more than one telnet session at a time. To install a telnet client requires you to: (i) have the program at hand; and (b) to mention it in your `mosaic.ini` initialization file. Look for the line `telnet=` under the `[Viewers]` section, where you should see the name of the appropriate utility. Be sure to provide the exact location of the file so that it can be found. When you install all your Mosaic viewers, do so in a separate directory and then point to this accordingly, for example:

```
telnet="c:\windows\mosaic\viewers\wintel.exe"
```

Telnet URLs are specified slightly different, mainly because there is no filename associated with the resource, unlike FTP, Gopher and WAIS for example. URLs can use dotted-IP addresses (these are slightly faster to resolve) or a normal textual address can be used. For example, we could telnet to the National Archaeological Database using the URL in the following HTML hyper-reference:

```
<a href ="telnet://cast.uark.edu">
    National Archaeology Database</a>
```

Telnet undergoes a phase of user identification before it allows access to a remote system. This is handled by the remote system, not Mosaic. The Mosaic/telnet program you use simply copies the characters from the remote session (as do all `telnet` programs) over to the client for you to see. You will be required to enter a user name (and sometimes a password) to access the service you have called in the URL. In the case of the example URL above, the user name `nadb` must be entered (for the National Archaeological DataBase) as soon as a connection has been established. A URL cannot contain a user name and/or password combination (yet) so this must be entered by hand at the appropriate prompts. Remember that you are conversing with a remote system in this mode. Depending on the service you are calling you should see some form of identification, such as a machine name and welcome message, and then a prompt such as `login:`. Most of the systems that you will telnet to will be UNIX-based. UNIX identifies a user using a program which is actually called `login`; this program presents the prompt `login:` for you to identify yourself (`login` also checks your password, if required, and then finally allows you entry to the system if all details are valid).

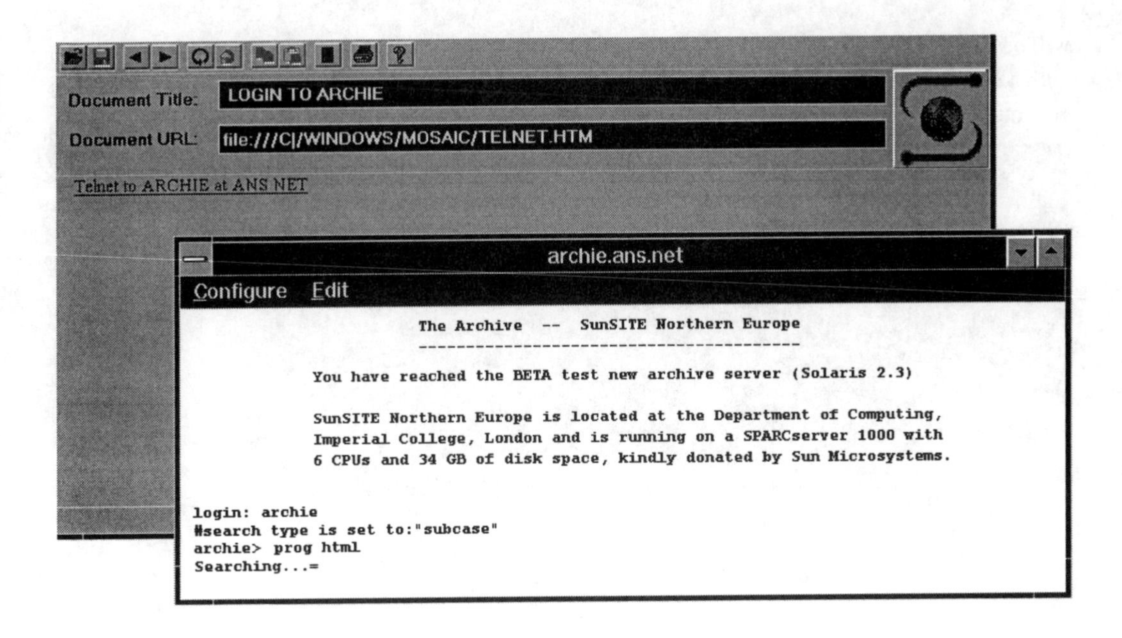

Figure 5.13: The NCSA *WinTel* program in action.

▶ TIP

Some implementations of telnet require the user to press the carriage return key in order to wake the system up. This is because the UNIX `login` program requires this (`login` is called by `telnet` to carry out user-identification). Pressing the `CONTROL` key and `ENTER` together may also work, as will the clicking on the Windows telnet application in some cases.

NCSA's *WinTel* program is a bit buggy; better alternatives are available. See the appendices for details of the WinSock package (this has a version called `TELW.EXE` which is more refined and less bug-prone).

Figure 5.13 illustrates a typical login session with a remote telnet server at the Internet site `archie.doc.ic.ac.uk` (a popular Archie server at Imperial College, UK).

NCSA *WinTel* can also be run as a standalone application, so that it is run from an iconized state with an existing TCP/IP connection. The WinSock system is needed for this; *WinTel* will call this when the program is run in its standalone mode, and will also request a `telnet`able host for you to actually call.

Connecting to Telnet from a Gopher Menu

Some Gopher menus have telnet links embedded within them. In the text-based mode of Gopher an entry will have the characters `<TEL>` after it to indicate this. Under Mosaic a small icon of a computer will be used instead. When choosing a telnet link from a Gopher menu you will normally be presented with a user name to log in with. The message takes the form of a standard Windows warning box and you must click on OK (or press ENTER) to acknowledge the message before proceeding. If the message is not displayed, log-in with the user name (and password) that has been published.

CHAPTER

6

The Cello Browser

6.1 Introduction

Apart from Mosaic, another Web browser has been drawing attention on the Internet recently, namely *Cello*. Cello was developed at the Legal Information Institute (LII) at the Cornell Law School, USA, by Thomas Bruce. Cello performs much the same task as Mosaic, although its interface is very different. You may want to try Cello as an alternative view on the World-Wide Web. In this chapter you will learn how to:

- Use Cello's interface and menu commands
- Configure Cello's `cello.ini` file
- Identify the essential differences between the Mosaic and Cello browsers

In the case of the last item here, use this chapter to explore each program and note their various features. You may find that one program has a feature that could be useful in a particular setting as opposed to the other. Of course, the best solution is to use both browsers, and have the best of both worlds. Each browser marks up its HTML slightly differently, so the actual appearance of the text on screen may be a deciding factor in which application to eventually use. Here are some of the more important differences between Cello and Mosaic that may help you choose which program to choose:

- Cello cannot (yet) handle fill-out forms (FOFs) for server interaction and CGI scripting. It is essentially a level 1 HTML browser.
- Cello has no toolbar, unlike Mosaic.
- Mosaic is a 32 bit program, while Cello is currently a 16 bit Windows application
- Cello has built-in Telnet support (so that no third party *viewer* is needed).
- Mosaic's document source features are limited to showing HTML; Cello can strip out HTML tags and allow the file to be saved in this form to disk.
- Cello has limited *hotlist* (URL shortcut) facilities and menu-nesting.
- Mosaic has no in-built colour support for fonts etc. Cello has colour support for most HTML constructs, such as headers.
- Cello has specific local file support options configurable through its `.ini` file which stop time-consuming nameserver lookups when working in local-disk mode only.

Of course, some disadvantages can become advantages if viewed from a slightly different perspective. Since Cello is a 16 bit application you do not need to use the Win32s software to allow it to run under Windows 3.1 – as is currently compulsory with the later 32 bit versions of Mosaic. The Win32s software is a large and memory-hungry program; you may have found that you cannot run other Windows applications once it is loaded (try some clipboard activities on a 4 Megabyte machine and you will soon get the picture). Cello's in-built telnet support also adds a nice touch to the overall program. NCSA's own telnet contribution, *WinTel*, is rather buggy, and in a nutshell is horrible to use (although better alternatives are available, e.g. WinSock's *TELW*). You can install your own telnet client under Cello if you wish.

Mosaic's main advantage over Cello is that it has a more 'professional' feel about it, and since it was developed by the people who themselves basically invented the Web, you know that it will get the job done without too many problems. In the main, Cello is a level 1 HTML parser; Mosaic is already at level 2 HTML (and level 3 can only be a whisker away). Cello therefore tends to appeal more to the novice HTML developer.

Installing the Cello Program

The main Cello archive is maintained at the Cornell Law Institute's FTP site on the Internet host `ftp.law.cornell.edu`. You will find the Cello archive in the `/pub/LII/Cello` directory as `cello.zip` (a PKZIP compressed file). Cello is also available from numerous other Internet FTP sites around the world (see the appendices). Once you have downloaded the archive make a directory for Cello, e.g. `\WINDOWS\CELLO`, and place the `.ZIP` archive in this directory. Next, run `PKUNZIP.EXE` on the archive and you should be left with the files that comprise the main Cello program. Make a back-up of the `.ZIP` file before proceeding and then delete the `cello.zip` file from your hard disk to free up space. The main Cello executable currently occupies over half a megabyte of disk space.

You will now have to enter Windows (you could have done all of this under Windows, of course) and create an icon for the file `cello.exe` that came as part of the archive. As always, a Web browser needs some form of TCP/IP interface to function correctly. Cello tries to launch the WinSock DLL for this purpose, so ensure that all of the necessary WinSock files are also in Cello's directory, e.g. `TCPMAN.EXE` and `WINSOCK.DLL`. It is a bit annoying to have to keep on duplicating copies of WinSock with every browser, although there is no other way of making the program find just one copy other than installing every Web browser in one directory that contains the necessary WinSock files (not advisable!). The icon that Cello uses is a small picture of a cello (the instrument, that is). Double click on the icon and the program will shortly start. If you receive an error saying that the network had not been found simply ignore it; Cello has just tried to make a TCP/IP connection and you probably haven't established a modem connection yet (depending on how WinSock is configured to dial into your service provider's machine).

Cello's Interface

The first difference that you may notice with Cello's interface is that it doesn't have an extensive toolbar, as in the Mosaic program. Cello's menus are considerably well-stocked, however, and it has some nice features buried away. Figure 6.1 shows the Cello program when it is initially started. A small copyright notice is displayed when first starting the program; click on it to remove it from the screen.

The only icons that are shown on the screen are placed on the upper left- and right-hand sides of

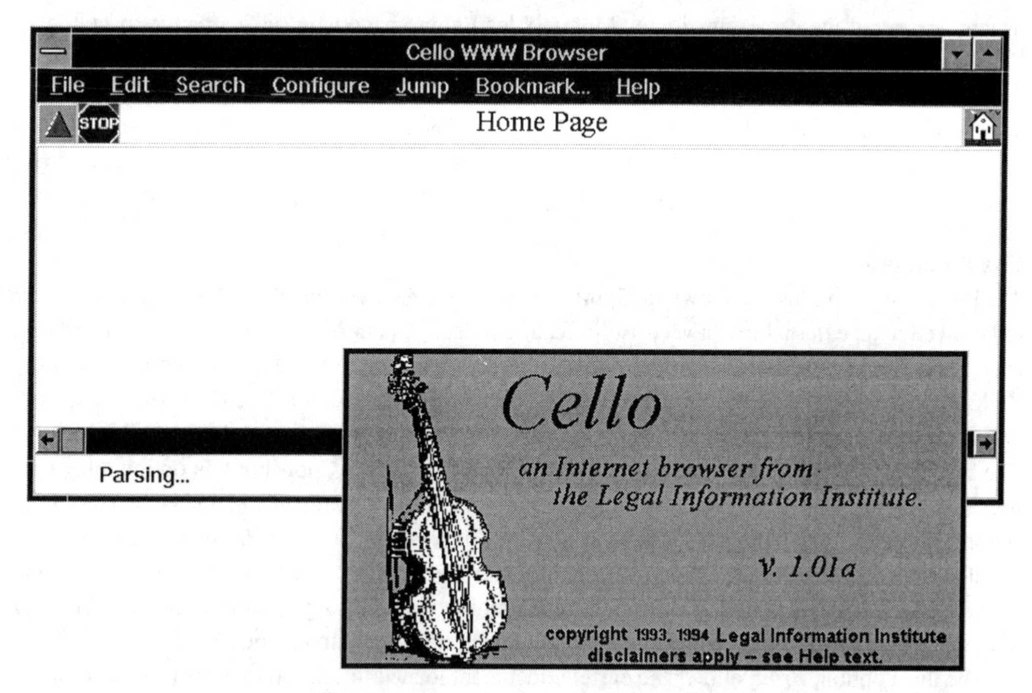

Figure 6.1: Running the Cello browser.

Cello's window. There is no toolbar in Cello; most of Cello's main options must be activated from within an existing menu, which can slow things down a bit.

The first icon is the document movement icon (see below), the equivalent of Mosaic's left-facing arrow to move the user back to the previous page.

Cello only has one direction of movement, so you must either move back to the home page, or to a page referenced using an appropriate HTML hyperlink that has been created for this purpose.

Secondly, we have the *Stop* icon:

which is used to cancel the current network request (Mosaic does this by allowing you to click on its main NCSA logo-icon on the screen, although this isn't documented).

And finally, we have an icon with the picture of a house

which carries out the same function as Mosaic's load home page icon (also a picture of a house). Cello's home page is defined in the `cello.ini` file, to be discussed shortly.

This section examines each of Cello's menus. Cello has seven such menus, namely the *File*, *Edit*, *Search*, *Configure*, *Jump*, *Bookmark* and *Help* menus. Each menu is now examined more closely, and compared against the Mosaic browser for similarities.

The File Menu

The File menu's options are shown in Figure 6.2. The *Save As...* option allows the current document to be saved to an external file, a very useful feature indeed. Under Mosaic, the downloading of files is slightly awkward, mainly since you have to keep toggling the *record-to-file* option on and off. Cello's option simply asks for a file name and then saves the file accordingly. The entire HTML text is saved, so all tags will be written to disk as well. All files are obviously saved in the ASCII format. The second option in the File menu is the *Mail File To...* feature. Choosing this option allows the user to send an email message containing the current HTML document to another person on the Internet. In order to use this option a valid SMTP (Simple Mail Transfer Protocol) server must be installed in your `cello.ini` file. (Mosaic has a similar feature called *Mail-to-developers* which allows feedback to be sent to the NCSA development team for any feedback on their browser, although Cello's email feature is aimed at sending mail to just about anybody.)

The third option, *Print*, allows the current document loaded into Cello to be printed. This option does not ask for confirmation – your file will be printed immediately. Unfortunately, the user has no

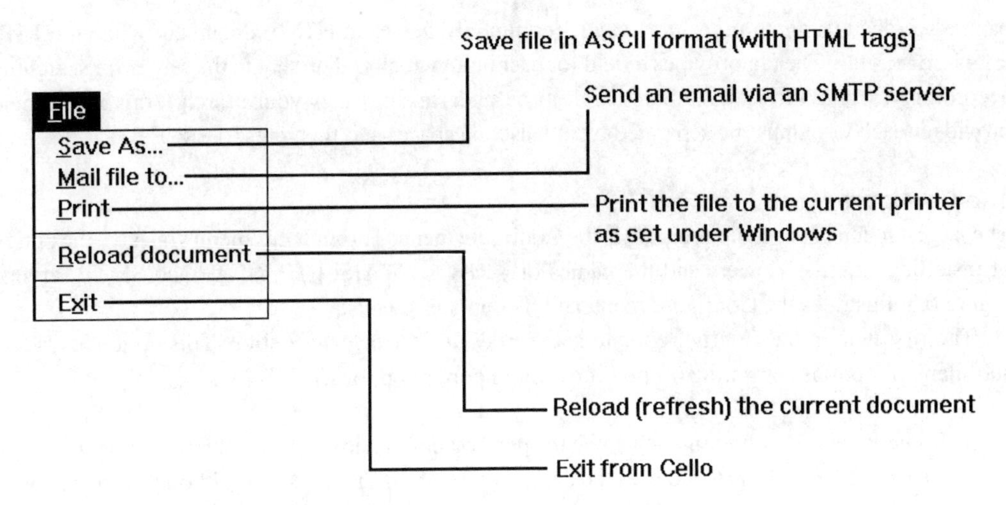

Figure 6.2: The options in Cello's File menu.

control over printer selection, as in the Mosaic browser – Cello's option simply defaults to the currently selected printer. You will therefore have to run the Windows Print Manager if you want to change the printer default. Cello's printer configuration option in the Configure menu also defaults to the current printer and does not allow you to specify a different device. The penultimate option in the File menu is the *Reload* option, which as the name suggests, allows the current document to be re-loaded from disk. If the document is being accessed from a remote URL the option will simply submit request for the file to be re-transmitted. Mosaic has exactly the same option in its toolbar. Finally, we have the *Exit* command, the most self-explanatory option ever. However, Cello asks you if you want to quit first, as opposed to Mosaic which simply exits immediately.

The Edit Menu

Cello's edit menu contains just two options, namely *View Source* and *View Source as Clear Text*, which allow you to view the current HTML document with or without tags. Cello is slightly more flexible here, since it allows you to see the text without the tags, and more importantly you can actually save the results, since it launches the Windows `notepad.exe` program as a viewer/editor. In contrast, Mosaic uses an internal editor that has no save feature. If you are wondering where Cello's search option is, it is located in the Search menu (to be discussed next). Mosaic's search function is found on the toolbar and in its the Edit menu.

The Search Menu

Cello's search menu contains three options, namely *Current File*, *Search Again (F3)* and *Index Document*. The first option conducts a search over the document currently loaded into Cello, and you get a small check-box to enable case-sensitive searches (16 bit Mosaic ignores case on all searches; 32 bit has the same feature as Cello). In order to continue the search over the rest of the document, use the second option, or simply press function key `F3`. The third option is provided to allow the searching of index documents, such as WAIS, Archie or Gopher/veronica servers. Some services on the Web are interfaces to other Internet resources, such as those previously mentioned. Such resources can be searched using an *index-document* – commonly this is an HTML document with an HTML `<isindex>` tag. The tag provides a field for user input which is then sent to the server for searching accordingly. Cello allows a similar search to be undertaken. Enter your search terms in the field provided (each term must be separated by at least one space) and then press `[ENTER]`.

The Configure Menu

The largest menu in the Cello program is the Configure menu. Through this menu you have the option of installing external viewers and the names of URLs for WAIS, FTP, NNTP and SMTP servers. Figure 6.3 illustrates the Configure menu and its four sub-menus.

The first item in the Configure menu is the *Files and Directories* option. This option leads to a sub-menu of options consisting of the following important options:

- *Home Page* – This option allows you to specify a default home page, all input being written to the file `cello.ini`; Cello uses the default name of `default.htm`, although you may want to change this accordingly (include any pathnames as required: for example, you could enter `\windows\cello\mypage.htm`).
- *Book Mark File* – This the equivalent of a Mosaic *hotlist*. Bookmark files have the extension

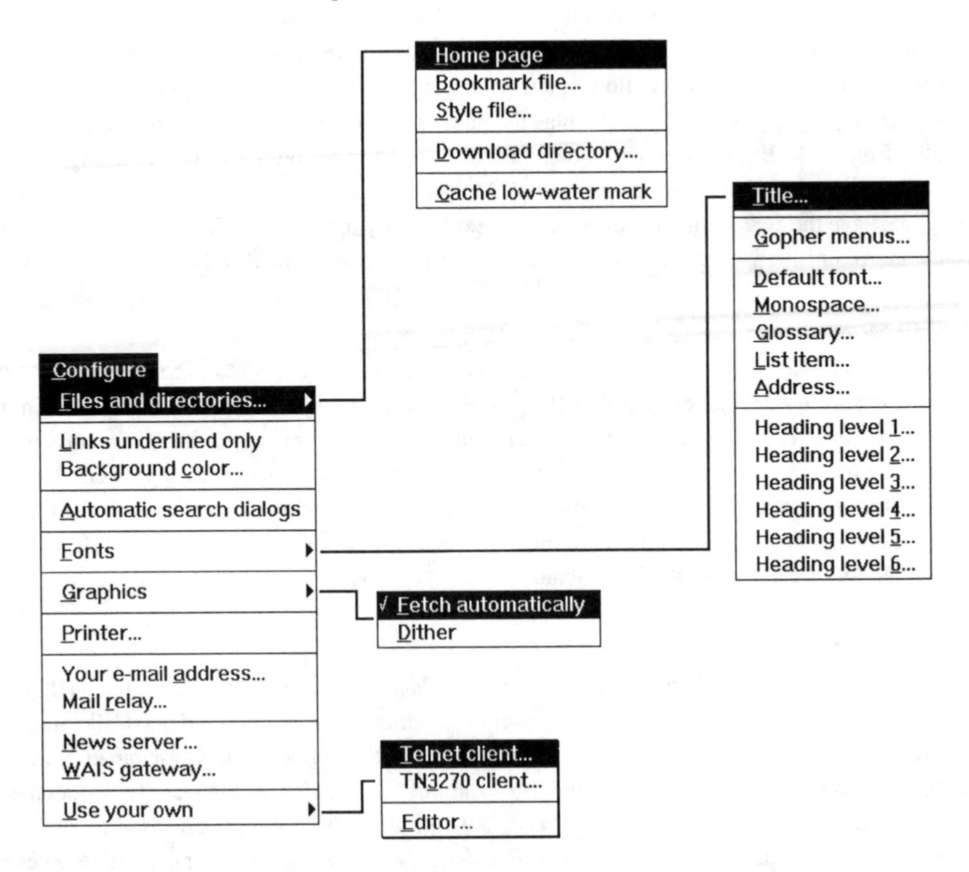

Figure 6.3: Cello's Configure menu and sub-menus.

`.BMK` and should be stored in the same directory as the Cello program. You can have as many bookmark files as you like, perhaps to categorize different URLs and resources. The concept here is the same as in Mosaic.

- *Style File* – Cello presents its HTML text using a template known as a *style-file*. This file sets out the way in which the document is presented and holds details such as the current video configuration (Cello supplies style files for VGA, SVGA (800 × 600) and SVGA (1024 × 768) pixel resolutions, plus details of the various fonts used by the system for HTML text and headers etc. The default style file is called `cello.sty`.
- *Download Directory* – Cello allows you to specify where all downloaded files are kept. By default this is the same directory as where Cello is installed, although you could specify any valid directory. Mosaic has no equivalent; all files are downloaded to the same directory as where Mosaic is installed.
- *Cache Low Water Mark* – This option is similar to Mosaic's page-cache setting. Cello allows you to specify a number that represents the number of bytes that must be left on the hard disk before cache files are erased. Cello caches all pages so that you can follow hyperlinks without re-loading a URL from a remote host that has already been cached to disk or memory. Cache files take up quite a bit of hard disk space, so if Cello finds that the hard disk space has reached the *low water mark* specified, it starts to delete the cache files. By default 500 kbyte (half a megabyte) is used as this amount. Alter this accordingly (all values are in bytes, so 500000 is about 500 kbyte, or roughly half a megabyte).

The second option in the Configure menu is *Links Underlined only*, which controls whether or not hyperlinks are underlined. In Cello, all hyperlinks are enclosed in a dashed box, so enabling this option will make hyperlinks appear similar to that found in Mosaic, i.e. underlined.

Option three in the Configure menu (Background color) allows the background colour (of the Cello window that is) to be altered. A full palette of colours will be shown upon selecting this option, and you can make your choice accordingly. Solid colours are best; by default Cello uses a horrible patterned colour (hard to describe really!) which I advise changing immediately. In contrast, Mosaic can only use the colours white and grey as the background window colour.

Option four, *Automatic Search Dialogs*, is concerned with index pages again. Some pages on Web servers are interfaces to allow searching of resources such as WAIS databases and Archie servers. Some HTML developers use an HTML document with an `<isindex>` tag for this purpose (this is explained in detail in Chapters 2 and 4). Such documents don't look very attractive and are often scarce of any text or instructions for the user. Instead, Cello provides the means of doing away with this screen entirely. When it sees an `<isindex>` tag it replaces the screen with a small dialogue box instead, allowing you to enter your search strings. These are then passed to the server as normal after you commit them by pressing the `[ENTER]` key.

Option five, *Fonts*, allows you to change the fonts used for most of the HTML text styles, such as normal text, header text and blockquote text. A nice option that has been included in the font-selection window is the ability to choose a colour for each of the fonts selected, thus allowing headers and other items to have their own unique colours. Gopher menus can also have their text colour (and font) changed. Mosaic only allows font changes, but not colour selection as yet.

The next option, option six (*Graphics*) is a sub-menu containing just two items (see Figure 6.3), namely *Fetch automatically* and *Dither*. The first option is equivalent to Mosaic's *Display in-line images* option to toggle on and off the display of in-line images within the current document. Mosaic uses a small NCSA logo with the word '*Image*' in place of an image if in-line images are disabled; Cello uses no icon, instead substituting an image with the word `[IMAGE]` instead. A good feature of Cello is its ability to use the `alt=` (alternative text) part of the HTML `<img src>` tag (see Chapter 2 for more details on `<img src>`) when image display is disabled. Mosaic will not show any *alternative text* when in-line images are disabled and the current tag has the `alt=` attribute set. Instead it just shows the standard NCSA logo.

Option seven, *Printer*, configures the current printer. This feature cannot be used to select a different printer device, however: instead you must configure the default device as set up from within Windows. Mosaic has the ability to select any printer device that has already been installed through Windows. If you want to change to a different printer device (or use a different COM port etc.) use the Windows Print Manager icon in the Control Panel (`control.exe`).

The next two options (menu items eight and nine) configure your email settings, the first allowing you to enter your email name, i.e. in the normal `user@host` format, e.g. `fred@somewhere.com`, and the second allowing you to specify an email server to which mail can be sent. Your service provider should have already allocated an SMTP gateway machine for mail forwarding (this will be a machine name, *not* a user name). Ask your service provider for details.

Options ten and eleven are used to specify a news server and WAIS server respectively. In order to use the `wais://` and `news://` URLs you must provide the name of a gateway that Cello can call in order to make a request for some information. No defaults are provided, as with Mosaic, although many NNTP news servers exist (use NCSA's if you like, or see the appendices). The same applies for WAIS servers. Both of these options are configurable through the `cello.ini` file, as are all the options in this menu.

The final menu option, *Use Your Own* is a sub-menu that allows you to specify an alternative telnet interface and editor. Cello has an in-built telnet program, although you can use any suitable third-party alternative (such as WinSock's TELW or NCSA's *WinTel*). When specifying an alternative telnet program be sure to quote the full pathname to the utility concerned. An additional option called *TN3270 Client* allows a separate third-party utility to be used for telnet sessions to mainframes. Mainframe computers use a different telnet emulation (3270 is named after the IBM 3270 mainframe) and you may want to look around for a suitable utility. The standard telnet emulation is 'line-based', whereas some of the larger 3270 class machines (and other mainframes besides) use a 'screen-based' mode of operation. Both telnet interfaces also differ in that they accept different escape codes to control certain function keys and other screen characteristics. In the main you won't have to worry about telnet mainframe emulations since they are rarely found on the Internet.

You may also want to use a different file editor for Cello, the default being `notepad.exe`. Bear in mind that whichever editor you choose should have the ability to save files, since this editor is used for document source operations in Cello's Edit menu (as discussed earlier).

The Jump Menu

This menu is the equivalent of Mosaic's *Navigate* menu. Options in this menu concern document movement and URL launching. The first option is named *Up*, which is the only way you can go in

Cello. Selecting this option moves you back to the parent document (the document previously loaded, that is). Cello also provides an icon (the up-arrow in the upper left-hand corner of the window) for this purpose. Mosaic is more flexible in that previously loaded documents can be moved back and forth into view with its toolbar icons. Secondly, we have the *History* option, which is equivalent to Mosaic's own history feature, allowing the user to click on a previously loaded URL in order to move directly to that entry. This option can be used to move quickly around different HTML documents that have been loaded in an earlier part of the current session. Option three, *Bookmark*, is Cello's equivalent of the Mosaic *hotlist*. Bookmarks hold frequently used URLs which you can select in order to invoke. The next five options are used to launch various sessions with other Internet-based tools. These are somewhat a strange series of options, since all these items are just URLs and could be entered in just one field (as provided by the entry *Launch via a URL*). The Launch TN3270 option is needed, however, since this uses a different utility to conduct the remote session.

Finally in the Jump menu we have the *Send mail message* option, which as the name suggests, does just that. A field is provided for you to enter the body of your message, which is then sent to the SMTP server you have specified in the Configure menu earlier (or via the `cello.ini` file). You can email any person on the Internet using this option. Cello inserts all of the necessary email headers such as `From:`, `To:` and `Subject:` automatically for you.

The Bookmark Menu

This is really an option rather than a menu, since it currently only contains one option, namely to invoke the bookmark editor and launch a particular URL. As mentioned, Cello's *bookmarks* are Mosaic's *hotlists,* and can be used to record all the URLs you most frequently visit, thus saving you time in typing them all in each time. You must click on the option *Mark Current Document* in order to enter a new bookmark (strange name for such an option), although no provision to actually enter the URL for the bookmark is provided other than taking the name of the currently loaded URL. Mosaic's hotlist feature is much better developed in comparison. Bookmark files in Cello have the extension `.BMK` and are stored in ASCII using three lines for each entry, the first being a simple descriptive name, the second a blank line, and the third the actual name of the URL you want to call, for example: `http://www.law.cornell.edu`. This entire option seems to be available in the Jump menu.

The Help Menu

Cello has a fully featured Windows help file, in contrast to Mosaic which has never included a help file, from the very first version right up to version 2 alpha 6. Options that tell you about Cello and its origins are also provided in this menu. Windows help files are not unlike the operation of most graphical web browsers. Simply follow the links provided to get to the information you require. All of the menus in Cello are well documented.

6.2 Configuring the `cello.ini` File

As a Windows application, Cello provides a standard initialization file (`cello.ini`) which contains all of the user settings in operation. Rather than using the menus in the Configure menu to initially configure Cello, you may want to edit the `cello.ini` file directly instead. Make sure you use an

ASCII editor such as Windows' `notepad.exe` or DOS's `edit.com`. The initialization file is itself broken down into a number of sections, each of which is discussed below in detail. Cello looks for its initialization file in its own directory, unlike Mosaic, which expects it to be in the `\WINDOWS` directory.

`[Cello]` Section

This section contains all of the main configuration details for the Cello program. Each option is discussed below.

`NNTPServer=`*`ServerName`*

Specifies the name of an NNTP news server, for example so that you can access USENET via a news: URL; for example: `NNTPServer=news.ibmpcug.co.uk`.

`EMail=`*`name@host`*

Specifies your email name, for example: `Email=somewhere.com`.

`HomePage=`*`drive:\dir\file.htm`*

Specifies the name of your home page. This can be held locally, or it could be a URL on another Internet host. Your home page will be loaded as soon as the Cello program is run, for example: `HomePage=c:\windows\cello\index.htm`

`DLDir=`*`drive:\dir`*

Specifies the name of a local directory on your hard disk where all downloaded files are kept, for example `c:\downloads`.

`AutoSearchBox=`*`yes|no`*

Specifies whether or not a dialogue box is used instead of the normal HTML `<isindex>` screen on a front-end search document. For example: `AutoSearchBox=no`.

`Telnet=`*`drive:\dir\file.exe`*

Specifies the name of a third-party telnet utility for Cello to use, for example `Telnet=c:\windows\viewers\telw.exe`.

`TN3270=`*`drive:\dir\file.exe`*

Same as above, although the utility may be different (for mainframe telnetting where the emulation is different).

`WaisGate=`*`http://waishost`*

A URL that specifies the name of a host that has a WAIS gateway, for example `WaisGate=info.cern.ch:8001`.

`MailRelay=`*`hostname`*

The name of an email gateway host, or its dotted-IP address, for example `MailRelay=127.45.2.132`.

`LowWaterMark=`*`number`*

If the free space on your hard disk drops lower than this amount, all temporary cache files will be deleted to free disk space. Numbers are in bytes. The default is 500000 or roughly half a megabyte. Example: `LowWaterMark=5000000`

`BookmarkFile=`*`drive:\dir\file.bmk`*

The name of the bookmark file currently in use. For example we could specify the file as `BookmarkFile=c:\cello\mybook.bmk`

`StyleFile=`*`drive:\dir\file.sty`*

The name of the Cello style file used to control font settings and video settings, for example `StyleFile=c:\cello\cello.sty`

`FetchGraphics=`*`yes|no`*

Controls whether or not in-line images are displayed (use `no` for slow connections). For example: `FetchGraphics=yes`.

`LocalOnly=`*`yes|no`*

A useful option to control whether or not Cello is used for local access only. Set to `no` for Internet users.

`BackgroundColor=`*`255,255,255`*

Controls the window's background colour. Each number represents Red, Green and Blue levels (0–255). For example, blue background only would be `0,0,255`, while red only would be `255,0,0`.

[Extensions] Section

The `[Extensions]` section is equivalent to Mosaic's `[Suffixes]` section. It is used to specify external viewers to control the display of files that arrive to Cello in different file formats. In-line images already in the `.GIF` format are handled automatically by Cello, as in Mosaic. All other image, sound and text formats (apart from HTML and untagged ASCII) must use external viewers. The use of MIME-formatted names is not required in Cello. Use the format below for all of the viewers that you intend to use with Cello:

```
name=drive:\path\utility ^.extension
```

For example, we could have an `[Extensions]` section structured as follows:

```
[Extensions]
jpg=c:\windows\viewers\lview31.exe ^.jpg
au=c:\windows\viewers\wplany.exe -u -r 8000 ^.au
wav=c:\windows\viewers\wplany.exe -u -r 8000 ^.wav
```

[Geometry] Section

All of Cello's window settings (size and initial x,y position etc.) are specified in this, the smallest section of the cello.ini file. All window settings are specified in pixel units. It is also possible to start Cello in a minimized state (as an icon) or in the normal way within a window using the binary option IsMaximized (binary options are *yes/no* answers). Here is a typical example of a [Geometry] section.

```
[Geometry]
StartupX=50
StartupY=25
StartupHeight=200
StartupWidth=400
IsMaximized=yes
```

These settings are all self-explanatory. Windows' x,y units start from the top left-hand corner, so 0,0 is the upper leftmost corner in this context.

6.3 Mark-up Differences

One of the main reasons for using a different browser is to see your HTML documents presented in a different way. As we have already seen, Cello's ability to use colour for various HTML headings and fonts is a good feature to make documents look more attractive to the end-user. Apart from this, Cello's mark-up of items such as hyperlinks and bullets is also very different from Mosaic's. It seems that Cello's implementation of HTML is far less rigid than Mosaic's. The rules that make up HTML are very rigorously defined. You may remember in Mosaic how multiple paragraph breaks (<p> tags) are ignored when parsed, for example. In Cello they are interpreted literally, so a <p> by itself gives you a blank line. Try getting a blank line in Mosaic – getting blood from a stone would be easier, I would wager.

Hyperlinks in Cello also appear slightly differently. Cello encloses them inside a dashed box (Cello will also change the cursor from a cross-hair into a small arrow when you pass over a hyperlink, the equivalent operation of Mosaic's changing of the default arrow mouse cursor into a small hand). Images (<img src...> tags) that are enclosed within <a href...> tags are left un-dashed; Mosaic, however, would place a blue border (the default colour) around all images enclosed within a hyper-reference. Figure 6.4 shows a typical hyperlink in Cello created using the standard HTML <a href> tag. If HTML is new to you, read Chapter 2 for an introduction.

Cello's bullets are also curious. They appear as a small square with a circle in the middle, as shown in Figure 6.5 which illustrates how a simple <ul> tag (bulleted list) would appear within Cello.

Other differences to note include Cello's implementation of <hr> (horizontal line) which is much thicker than Mosaic's. I also like Cello's adherence to white space, i.e. blank spaces. If you place some blank spaces in a tag, they are kept in the resulting marked-up text. Mosaic hates white space and ignores it in nearly all tags except those such as pre-formatted text (<pre> and the now HTML redundant <xmp> tags). Email support also works flawlessly in Cello. The lesser-known

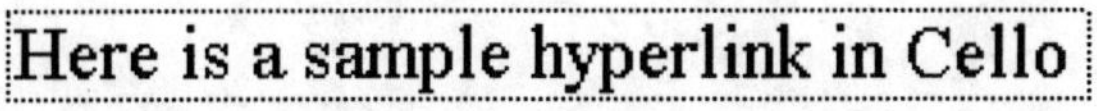

Here is a sample hyperlink in Cello

Figure 6.4 A hyperlink as it appears in Cello.

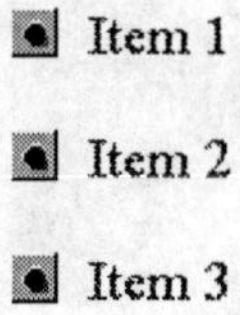

- Item 1
- Item 2
- Item 3

Figure 6.5: A `<ul>` bulleted list in Cello.

`mailto://` URL can be used within a hyper-reference to allow email messages to be sent to individuals while reading an HTML document, for example:

```
<a href="mailto://fred@somewhere.com">Fred Smith</a>
```

would create a clickable region called 'Fred Smith' which when clicked on would launch Cello's *Send Mail Message* option in the Jump menu. Mosaic (both 16 and 32 bit versions) seem reluctant to allow `mailto://` URLs to work at all. This problem will be addressed in the near future, however.

CHAPTER

7

Hyperediting Tools for HTML Authors

7.1 Introduction

Now that publishing on the Net has taken off, software developers are starting to write *hypereditors*, programs that are used to make the creation of HTML documents as easy as possible. Typically, these tools allow tags to be inserted into your text either manually or automatically, as well as offering a variety of text-editing functions useful to the author. This section considers a number of popular freeware and shareware hyperediting systems that are freely available from the Internet, namely:

- The *HTML-Assistant*

- HTML*Ed*
- HTML-HyperEdit
- The HoTMetaL editor

All of these programs run under Microsoft Windows 3.1 and offer a range of different features. If you are publishing large quantities of HTML documents a hypereditor can be an invaluable tool. The *HTML-Assistant* is better suited to the Cello Web browser since a DDE (Dynamic Data Exchange) link into Cello allows the HTML document to be updated as changes are made (known as WYSIWYG mode – What You See Is What You Get). Mosaic will require the *reload* icon to be used, which can be a bit time-consuming to keep on performing every time a change is made to your HTML document (although many editors rely on the reload button to update the HTML text in this way). HTML*Ed* is more extensive in that it has *floating* toolbars that allow features such as character entities (foreign characters) and frequently-used mark-up tags such as headers, hyperlinks and mark-up styles to be chosen by the user without navigating any menus. HTMLHyperEdit is a great program for novices and experts alike. It includes an on-line tutorial and can even convert rich-text to HTML (automatic paragraph tag insertion etc.). Lastly, we have HoTMetaL, a far more extensive HTML editor which has advanced document template support and a whole host of other features besides.

Refer to the appendices for the locations of all these tools if you need to download a copy. Commercial products are also starting to appear. WordPerfect have recently launched their *Intellitag* product, which allows SGML/HTML documents to be written using their well-known WordPerfect word-processing package. Other word processor users, especially those with Microsoft Word, can even use a series of templates and macros that have been specially designed for HTML documents. These are examined later in the chapter.

7.2 The HTML-Assistant

The *HTML-Assistant* is a hyperediting tool written by H. Harawitz (`harawitz@fox.hstn.ns.ca`) that runs with any Web browser, such as Cello or Mosaic. If used with Cello, HTML documents can be created in a WYSIWYG environment because Cello has a DDE capability that hot-links it with the HTML editor. As the actual text and tags that make up a document are entered, the system marks up the text directly so what you see on the screen is the exact representation of the document as it would be viewed using a Web browser.

With Mosaic, the user must press on the *reload* icon in the toolbar, since there is no DDE support for Mosaic (yet). Using a hypereditor can result in a much faster development process altogether, since all the tags and advanced editing functions are available to the author. To install the HTML-Assistant start by decompressing the archive it arrives in, and then move all `.DLL` (Dynamic Link Libraries) to the `\WINDOWS\SYSTEM` directory, and all `.VBX` (Visual Basic) files to the same directory. The main `.EXE` file can be placed in your Mosaic directory if you wish. Create an icon for the program accordingly (under Windows use: ALT-F, New, Program item etc.) and then you can run the program. The *HTML-Assistant* allows the user to work with multiple HTML files using a separate window for each document. The toolbar controls the selection of all the most common

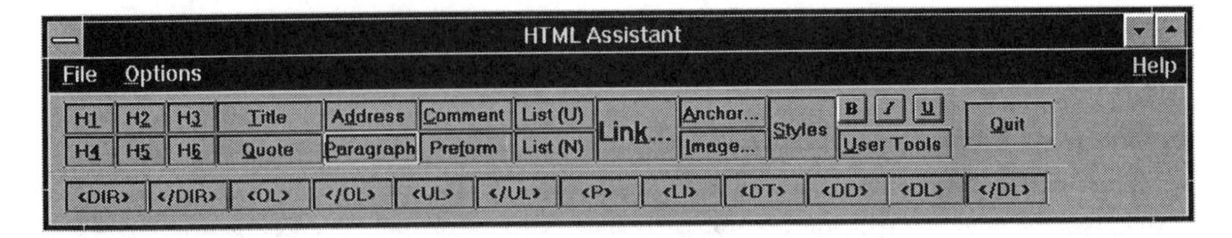

Figure 7.1: The toolbar of the HTML-Assistant.

HTML tags, while the menus above the toolbar contain most of the file-orientated commands, e.g. saving and loading files, all of which are self-explanatory. Figure 7.1 shows the HTML-Assistant's extensive toolbar.

Creating a New Document

When the program starts you are shown a blank window area. Click on the File menu and select *New*, and the HTML-Assistant will open a new window entitled *Untitled:1* (the document will be untitled until you save it to disk – the default extension is `.HTM`, if unspecified). You can then enter your HTML document by hand, using the toolbar to insert the various tags. If you want to open an existing document, simply choose the *Open* option in the File menu and then navigate your way to the appropriate directory and open the required `.HTM` file. The file will then be loaded in its entirety. The toolbar provides the ability to insert a start-tag and an end-tag using separate buttons, although the easiest way of encapsulating such tags around a portion of text is to highlight the area of text and then press the required tag button. For example, in Figure 7.2 a title string has been highlighted by placing the cursor on the very first character of the line and then holding the left mouse key down while highlighting the text. This can also be done using the keyboard by using the `[SHIFT]` key while moving the cursor over the required text.

Now you can click on the tag you require, so in this example we would click on the *Title* button (or press 'T' by itself: notice the underlining of some characters in the buttons for keyboard shortcuts). The HTML-Assistant then encapsulates the tag for us, so our text appears as:

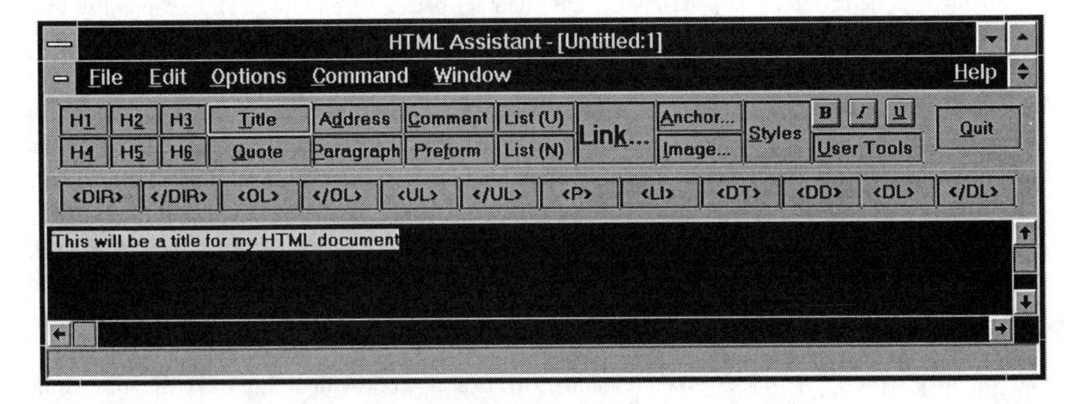

Figure 7.2: Highlighting some text to encapsulate within an HTML tag.

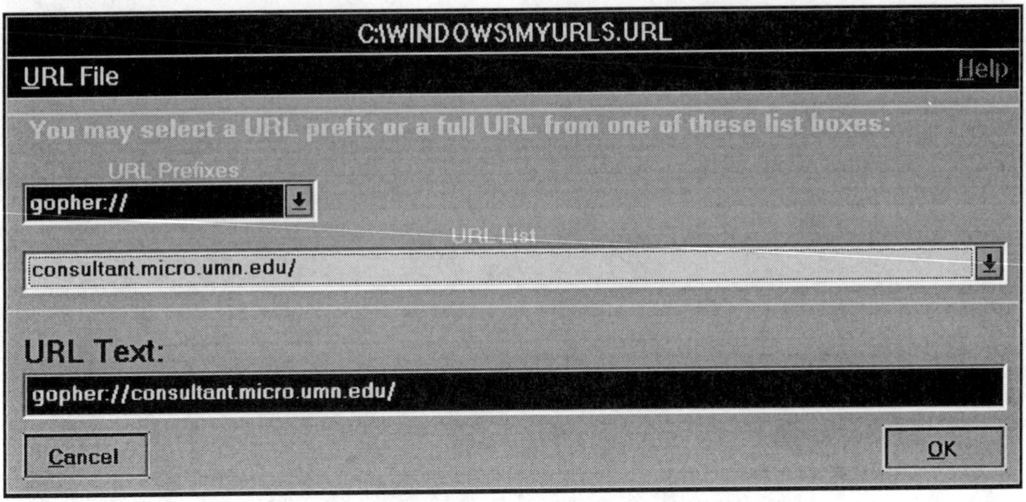

Figure 7.3: Using the HTML-Assistant to create a new hyper-reference tag.

```
<TITLE>This will be a title for my HTML document</TITLE>
```

If we had pressed the *Title* button before highlighting the text, the HTML-Assistant would have simply inserted both tags as `<TITLE></TITLE>` thus leaving it up to the HTML author to insert the text. I have found the best way of creating your documents is to type them in directly without any tags, with the layout that you require e.g. with paragraph breaks and the like, and only then scan through the entire document highlighting the parts you want made into tags in order control the layout and formatting of the document. Highlighting text in this way also works for more complex structures, such as bulleted lists, which really can start to cut down on your typing. The more complex tags such as anchors and hyper-referenced URLs are also dealt with very simply by the HTML-Assistant. For example, inserting an `<a name>` anchor results in the HTML-Assistant asking you for a name for the anchor, which is then inserted into the tag accordingly. Hyper-references to other URLs are selected using the *Link* button. Pressing this results in a window containing a list of acceptable URL resource types, e.g. `gopher://` or `telnet://`, and other fields to allow you to enter the name of the host being called, along with any pathnames etc. The tag is then inserted accordingly. Figure 7.3 shows a typical `gopher://` tag.

The *URL Prefixes* field contains a list of the most common URL resource types, or *prefixes*. After selecting an appropriate resource type The HTML-Assistant places the prefix in the *URL Text* field at the bottom of the window, ready for you to either enter the actual host and file detail, or to select such detail from a URL file. A *URL file* is a feature of the HTML-Assistant, whereby lists of the most common URLs you use can be saved to a file and read in the *URL Text* field as and when required. Notice the option on the menu-bar entitled *URL File*. This option allows you to open an existing URL file, or save a newly created file by saving the file from within the HTML-Assistant (which of course also functions as an enhanced text editor, to all intents and purposes). URL files are completely ASCII, containing one URL per line. The URL should not really include a resource type, e.g. `ftp://`, since this is provided automatically, as described earlier. When creating your ASCII URL files be sure to give them the extension of `.URL`. It is also a good idea to divide the files into different categories according to the resource type. For example, you could have a file called `gopher.url` for all your Gopher hosts, or a file called `ftp.url` for any popular FTP archives. This concept is similar to Mosaic's hotlist feature; indeed you could extract any URL references from the `mosaic.ini` directly, with only minor editing. The end-result of Figure 7.3 would thus be to insert the HTML tag

```
<a href="gopher://consultant.micro.umn.edu/"></a>
```

into the document at the current cursor position. You can now place some text before the end-tag that will represent your actual hyper-reference. Of course, had you highlighted an item of text for the reference beforehand, the tags would have been encapsulated around your text automatically.

Using DDE with the Cello Browser

An interesting feature of the HTML-Assistant is its ability to create a DDE (Dynamic Data Exchange) link with another well-known browser, *Cello* (see Chapter 6). Cello's ability to use DDE makes it an excellent candidate for WYSIWYG development. DDE itself shares many features of the *client/server* methodology, whereby a client maintains links to a server entity and updates it with new information as soon as it becomes available. In DDE parlance, a *hot-link* is maintained by Cello and the HTML-Assistant. Both programs are run side-by-side and soon as any data in the HTML-Assistant is changed (or added etc.) it is immediately passed to the Cello browser which marks up the text directly. The benefit for the user is that development is made much simpler, since the document can be seen as it will actually appear. Mosaic cannot yet handle such a DDE link, so you may consider using Cello and the HTML-Assistant purely as development tools. In fact, many people use a combination of all these tools for their HTML development and publishing.

In order to use Cello and the HTML-Assistant via a DDE hot-link you must firstly tell the HTML-Assistant that you want to use Cello as a client browser. Do this by clicking on the *Enter test program name* option in the HTML-Assistant File menu (you must have already opened a document, or be creating a new document to gain access to this option). You can then enter the name of the browser, e.g. `cello.exe` from the appropriate directory, and then save these details. Next you must click on the Options menu in the HTML-Assistant, and enable the option *Use DDE with Cello*. To see how your HTML looks, simply open the File menu and choose the *Test* option accordingly. Cello will then be launched (arrange your windows so that you can see both the HTML-Assistant and Cello's text window side-by-side – see Figure 7.4) and then try out the feature by entering some HTML text into the HTML-Assistant's screen and then clicking on the *Test* option in the File menu.

▶ TIP

Since Cello has a DDE capability you can in theory call it from any Windows-based application that supports the `DDEExecute` command. As an example, consider the following macro under Microsoft's *Word For Windows*, which opens NCSA's home page using an appropriate URL:

```
Sub MAIN
```

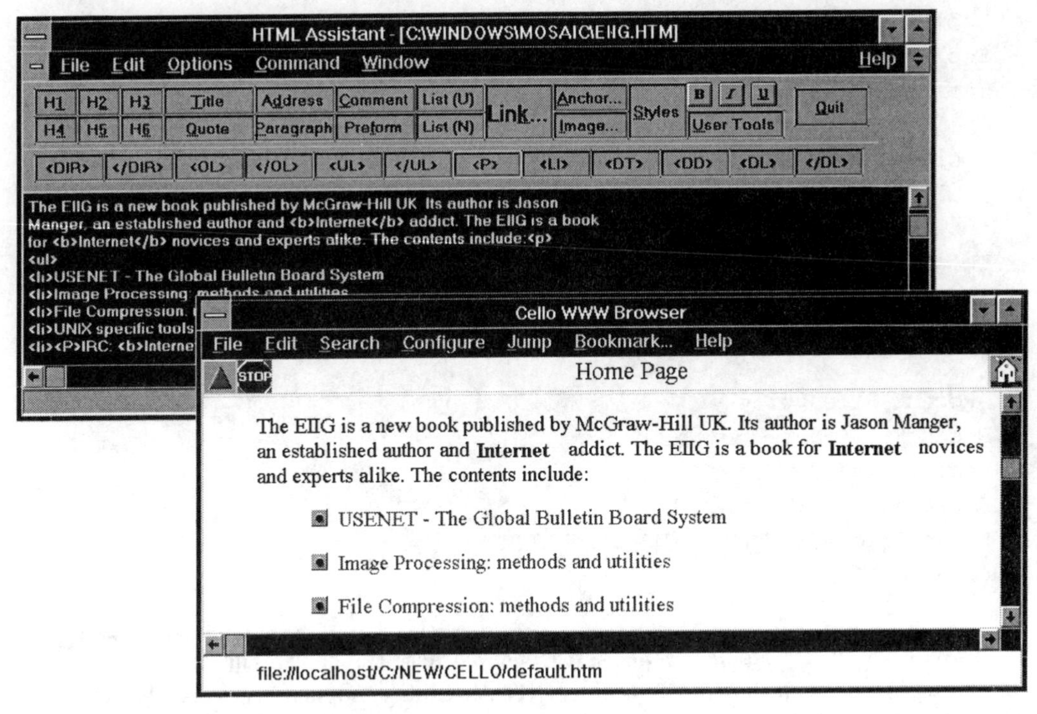

Figure 7.4: The HTML-Assistant and Cello 'hot-linked' together.

```
    ChanNum = DDEInitiate("Cello", "URL")
    DDEExecute(ChanNum, "http://www.ncsa.uiuc.edu")
    DDETerminate(ChanNum)
End Sub
```

Configuring the `htmlasst.ini` File

The HTML-Assistant comes with a small initialization file called `htmlasst.ini`, an example of which is shown below. Sections of interest to the user are: `[Tester]`, which names a program to use as a testing browser (`cello.exe` or `mosaic.exe` perhaps) and `[Custom Tools]`, which defines ten tools that can be defined by the user. This toolbox can be opened in its own window while you are developing using the HTML-Assistant. You are free to place whatever tags and/or text that you like in these ten definitions. The section `[Recent Files]` is used to allow you to quickly open the four most recent HTML files that you have been working on, a useful short cut facility to save re-opening a current project, for example.

```
[Tester]
TestProgram=C:\WINDOWS\CELLO\CELLO.EXE

[Custom Tools]
```

```
Tool1=<a href=" ">
Tool2=</a>
Tool3=<a href="# ">
Tool4=submit
Tool5=action=
Tool6=value=
Tool7=<html>
Tool8=<body>
Tool9=<header>
Tool10=<img src="">

[Recent Files]
RecentFile4=Not Used
RecentFile3=Not Used
RecentFile2=Not Used
RecentFile1=C:\HTTPD\HTDOCS\INDEX.HTM
```

▶ TIP

Why not subscribe to the HTML-Assistant newsletter? This contains dozens of handy tips for use with the HTML-Assistant HTML editing program. To subscribe (the newsletter is delivered via email), simple mail the address:

`harawitz@fox.nstn.ns.ca`

and include the word '`SUBSCRIBE`' in the Subject: line of your message.

7.3 HTMLEd

HTML*Ed*, written by Peter Crawshaw (`inettc@nbnet.nb.ca`) is similar in appearance to the HTML-Assistant in terms of its interface. Once again the user is allowed to open multiple documents in a series of windows, and to cut and paste between them (and between other Windows Applications). A good feature of HTML*Ed* is the provision of *floating* toolbars. These can exist inside or outside of the HTML*Ed*'s main window area. Figure 7.5 illustrates HTML*Ed* in action. Notice that the floating toolbars can be positioned anywhere on the screen, and that one toolbar includes a useful set of HTML character entities (foreign characters).

A number of extensive menus are provided, although nearly all of the commands can be accessed from HTML*Ed*'s toolbar. As a result, one finds that there is not a great need to open that many menus during development. Unlike some of the hypereditors examined in this chapter, HTML*Ed* also provides an *Undo* feature (`ALT-Backspace` – a keystroke found in many Windows programs) that can be used to reinstate the most previous deletion (but not tag insertion, however). Also, the *Undo* feature only works for the most previous deletion.

Text mark-up is provided in much the same way as the HTML-Assistant program previously

Figure 7.5: The HTML*Ed* program with all three *floating toolbars* activated.

discussed. You can enter free-form text in the window provided while positioning tags in the document using the toolbar provided. Tags can be encapsulated around items of text that have been highlighted in order to speed things up. Figure 7.6 illustrates the HTML*Ed* toolbar, and describes the various icons and button functions provided. Standard HTML styles (including some lesser-used tags) are included in the Style menu, e.g. `<TT>` for teletype mode (same as `<PRE>` for preformatted text), and `<EMP>` (which is the same as the `<B>` emboldening tag in most cases). One useful feature in the File menu allows the user to save their documents in either DOS or UNIX format.

UNIX has a thing about carriage return codes that can sometimes corrupt the layout of a DOS-based ASCII document when ported into a UNIX environment (I imagine this is somewhat rare, in any event). DOS-based ASCII documents commonly use ASCII 10 and 13 (linefeed and carriage return codes) to terminate a line in which the user has pressed the `[ENTER]` key. UNIX doesn't always use this combination of codes and the result can be a totally different layout altogether. In order to save the file without carriage return codes, perhaps when moving your HTML files onto a UNIX machine, use the option provided. HTML*Ed* does not run in a WYSIWYG environment, and does not have any *test* option whereby a document can be seen in its actual mark-up. Of course, it is still possible to load Mosaic (or Cello etc.) side-by-side with HTML*Ed* and then load the file you are working on and use the appropriate *reload* button. Future releases of HTML*Ed* may contain a test program-launching facility, however. On the whole, HTML*Ed* is a nice, fast and compact

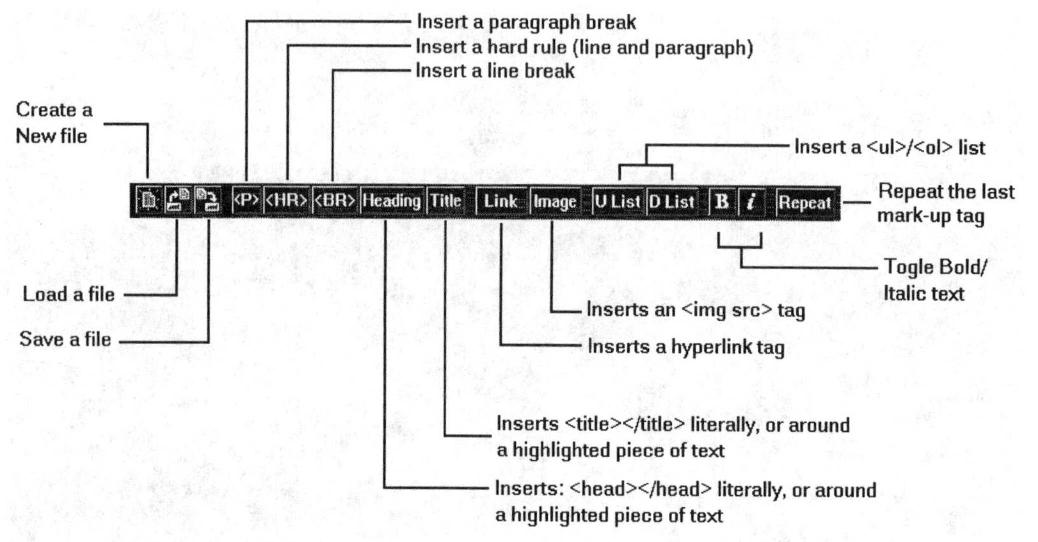

Figure 7.6: HTML*Ed*'s main toolbar.

program. There are no `.INI` or `.DLL` files to worry about and the program can be installed in just a few minutes without any fuss.

7.4 HTML-HyperEdit 

HTML-HyperEdit, written by Steve Hancock (`s.hancock@icarus.curtin.edu.au`), is without doubt the best tool for the novice. It is an extensive system with some unusual, or rather innovative, features that set it aside from many of the other hyperediting tools examined. For a start, the program has two modes of operation, *novice* and *expert* (a small button selects the level of user). Alternating between novice and expert mode simply disables some of the more advanced options, such as specific tag-names, as found in the lower right-hand corner of the program's window. The program opens a default file, which can be changed by the user. Changes such as the name of a file to open and the *novice/expert* mode are all kept in a file called `HTMLEDIT.TBK` (non-editable). Figure 7.7 illustrates the program in action with a sample HTML file, running in advanced mode.

Towards the top of the screen is a small toolbar containing five options, namely: *Load* (to load an HTML file from disk); *Save* (to save the current document to disk); *New* (to create a new file from scratch); *Paragraphs* (used to insert `<p>` codes in rich text); and *Search/Replace* (a facility to find and replace strings within the current document). The last option on the toolbar is useful, since a document without any tags arriving in RTF (Rich Text Format) can have paragraph break tags inserted automatically. Rich Text Format is basically ASCII with all of the carriage return codes (and perhaps others, such as `TAB`s) all in place. RTF documents therefore have a pre-defined structure that the author has used for the document. The program is intelligent enough to know that many ASCII editors require the user to press `[ENTER]` at the end of each line, so the system checks for a blank line after

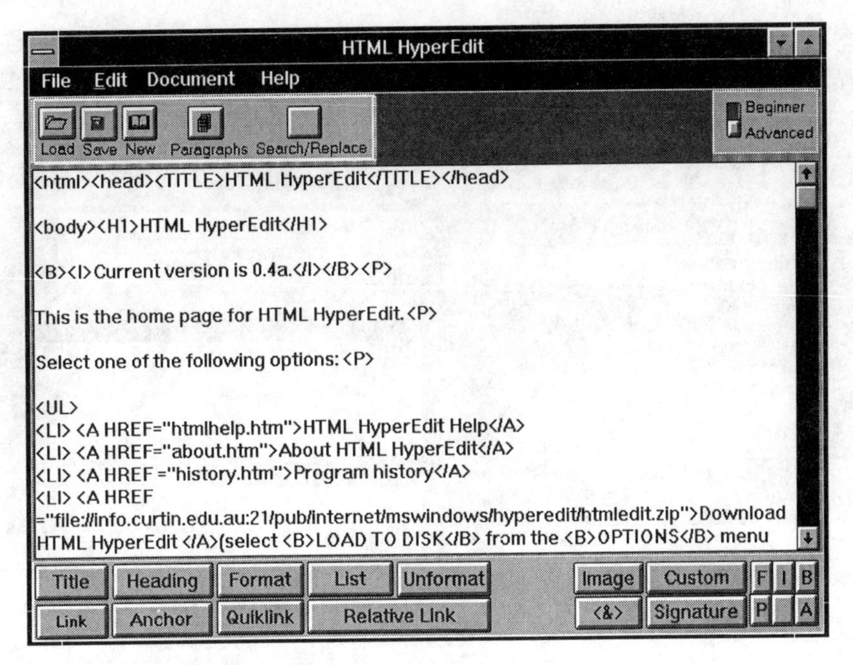

Figure 7.7: A sample HTML-HyperEdit introduction screen.

a paragraph before entering the required `<p>` code. If an area is not highlighted before issuing this command, the system asks you whether or not you want the entire document processed.

Along the bottom of the screen are a series of buttons that control items such as hyperlinks and common HTML tags. Inserting a hyperlink using the *Link* button presents a useful menu of options, as shown in Figure 7.8.

Most of the options in this window are self-explanatory. The upper left-hand window controls the type of URL being selected for the hyperlink you want to insert. Resource types include `ftp://`, `telnet://`, `file://`, `http://` and `news://`, although you can of course type in any value you like. The three field areas immediately below the *Type of Link* area represent the `host/dir/name` of the URL, namely the Internet hostname, directory name and filename respectively, thus building up the URL step-by-step. HTML-HyperEdit allows you to save frequently used hostnames and even directory/filename specifications so that you can insert these into a URL for different hosts, and vice versa.

The

and

buttons provide the option of adding and deleting existing entries for all parts of the URL, and the

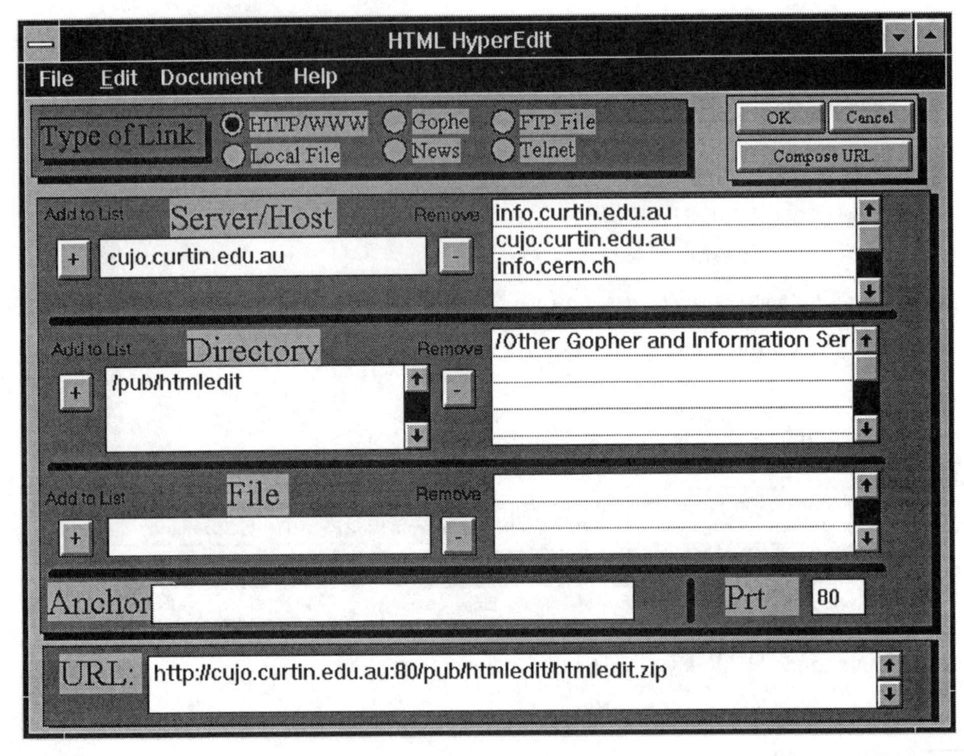

Figure 7.8: Selecting the *Link* button (Hyperlink menu).

right-hand side of the window shows all of the selections that are possible. As you build your URL it is shown at the bottom of the window in the *URL* field. By default all HTTP servers answer on port 80, although there are quite a number of exceptions. When using an `http://` resource type the default port specification of `:80` is appended to the hostname part of the URL automatically by the system. Delete the port number if you do not require this option.

The remaining buttons along the bottom of the screen control the insertion of various HTML tags. The *Format* and *Unformat* buttons allow highlighted text to be encapsulated around a tag of the user's choice. A variety of tags in the *Format* option are provided, as shown in Figure 7.9. The *Unformat* option is like an *Undo* option except that it removes each tag-*layer* from a highlighted area of text, for example the tagged text

```
<h1><b>This is some bold text</b></h1>
```

if highlighted and then *Unformat*ted, would then become just the text:

```
<b>This is some bold text</b>
```

The styles selectable from Figure 7.9 include `<pre>` (preformatted text, e.g. the `Courier` monospaced font), `<b>` (bold), `<i>` (italic), `<code>` (an older style, the same as `<pre>` for

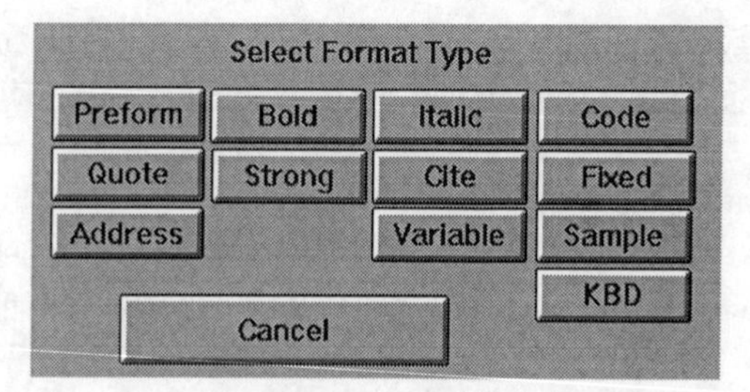

Figure 7.9: Style codes accessed from the *Format* button.

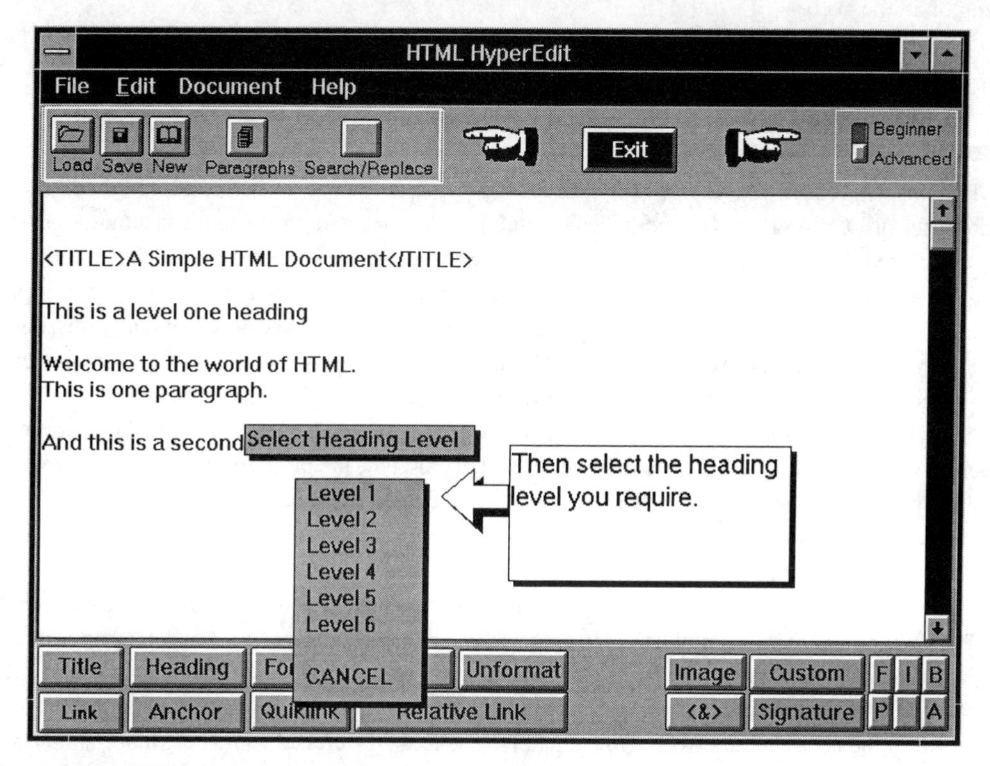

Figure 7.10: HTML-HyperEdit's help tutorial in action.

computer code and computerese text generally), `<blockquote>`, `<strong>` (an older style tag, the same as `<b>` for all intents and purposes), `<cite>`, `<fixed>`, `<sample>` and `<variable>`, which are again older-style tags whose display is dependent on the client browser in use. The address tag `<address>` is used to include details of an author's email address (see Chapter 2), while the `<kbd>` tag is again used for monospaced style *keyboard* text. A browser such as Mosaic may interpret many of these codes as being the same in any event, so many such tags become redundant.

The On-line Help Tutorial

HTML-HyperEdit is one of the few editors that has an in-built tutorial. This tutorial guides the novice user through all of the salient features of the program, as well as offering an introduction to HTML itself. The tutorial option is accessible through the Help menu. Figure 7.10 illustrates the help system in action.

The left and right-facing hands allow the user to move back and forth in the tutorial. You can even interact with the program, since the system will encourage you to get involved as the tutorial develops. The part of the tutorial shown in Figure 7.10 is showing the user a basic mark-up operation using header tags. If you are after a good introduction to the concepts behind HTML, this is the program to try first. A number of extensive Windows help pages are also provided which document most of the program, as well as introducing the user to the 'multimedia revolution' that is currently going on in the Web.

7.5 HoTMetaL

HoTMetaL (from SoftQuad Inc., USA) introduces itself as an HTML+ editor, and, minimal as it is, support for Fill-Out-Forms is included. HoTMetaL is an extensive program that consumes around 5 Mbyte of hard disk space. The file arrives as a self-expanding DOS executable file that should run with the `-D` option (this is probably a PKLITE ZIP archive) in order that the correct directories are installed. Place the file in your root directory (or hypereditors' sub-directory) when doing this, since the archive creates a directory called `HOTMETAL` automatically into which all of the files' components are placed. You can delete the main archive afterwards, although make a back-up first.

So, is HoTMetaL hot? Well, no, not this release anyway. One may expect that such a large program would be overflowing with features, and yet it isn't. To be fair, the program documented here is in fact a slightly *cut-down* version of HoTMetaL-*Pro* which is the full version of the program. All of the standard features are available, including template support. The concept of a template is slightly different in this setting however, since it seems to be just a selection of trial HTML files that implement various document types such as home pages and tag examples. In other settings, such as DTP (desktop publishing), templates control the actual layout of the text, and control the appearance of the document according to the document type using various margin and font settings etc. HTML is, after all, a mark-up language, although such simple extravagances as margin settings do not yet exist within the HTML framework, unfortunately. The main difference with HoTMetaL's interface is that all of the tags in your text are shown graphically as little boxes with the tag code inside them. The actual tags in their native text form are not shown, and this does look quite attractive, to say the least. HoTMetaL is also a very strict editor, in that it requires a document to be properly structured in terms of the `<html>`, `<head>` and `<body>` tags. If you leave out an `<html>` tag it won't allow you to preview the document. *Preview* in this context means to launch a browser such as Mosaic; no in-built WYSIWYG support is provided in this version. Figure 7.11 illustrates the program when initially started (after its introductory screen has been shown).

The opening starts by displaying a *scratch file*, a file in which you can start to enter some HTML text as a the basis of a new document. Multiple windows can be opened, and even minimized so that they appear as icons – a useful feature to unclutter your screen when multiple projects are being prepared. No toolbars exist in the package; all options are selected via the existing menus, or from short cut keystrokes. The menus themselves are well stocked with features. The Markup menu

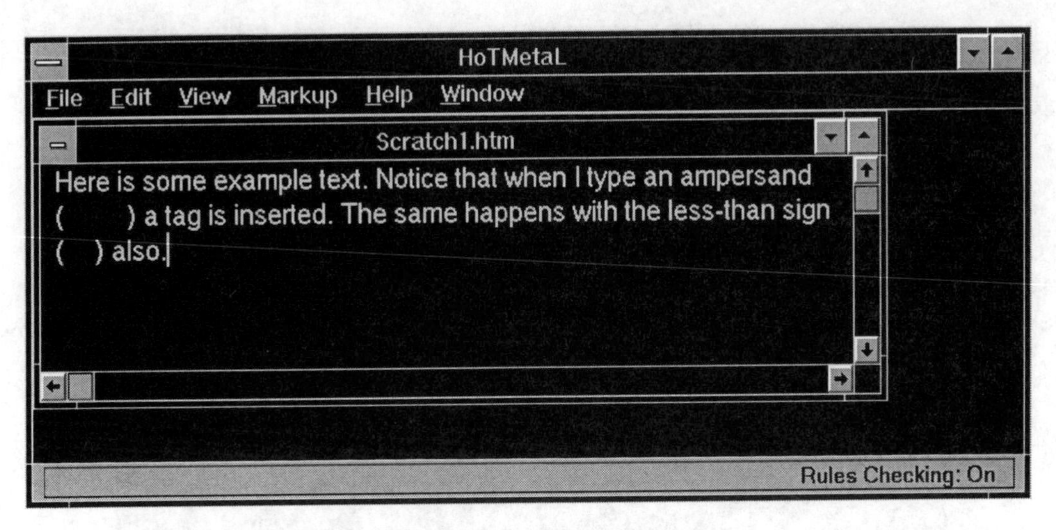

Figure 7.11: HoTMetaL's opening screen.

HoTMetaL - Insert Element

DT	Term to be Defined
EM	Emphasis
FORM	On-line Form (WYSIWYG not supported)
H1	Heading Level 1
H2	Heading Level 2
H3	Heading Level 3
H4	Heading Level 4
H5	Heading Level 5
H6	Heading Level 6
HEAD	Head
HR	Horizontal Rule
HTML	Top Level Document Element

☒ Include Required Elements

Insert Element   Cancel

Figure 7.12: A selection of tags from HoTMetaL's Markup menu.

contains all of the actual HTML tags that you will want to use in your documents, as shown in Figure 7.12. In order to insert a tag you must highlight the text around which you want the tags actually placed. It is probably therefore best to type in your document from scratch and then add the tags as a final stage.

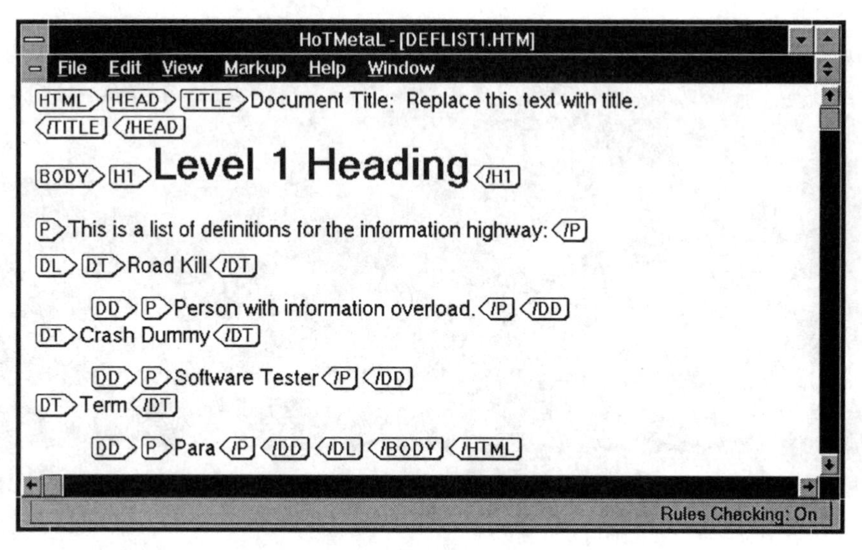

Figure 7.13: How tags look in the HoTMetaL program.

As mentioned, when HoTMetaL displays your HTML document, it does so in an entirely graphical way. All tags are replaced with small icons that represent the various HTML tags, as shown in Figure 7.13.

Most of HoTMEtaL's menus and options are very straightforward to follow. Unlike the other hypereditors already discussed, HoTMetaL cannot insert tags directly into a document unless an area of text is highlighted first (either using the mouse or the cursor keys to highlight the area required). Another useful feature found in HoTMetaL is its *Publish* option. This basically replaces all `file://` URLs with `http://` references. You can enter a hostname and pathname as well when replacing all such entries.

7.6 Microsoft Word HTML Interfaces

If you are a Microsoft Word user you may want to investigate some templates that have been written especially for HTML developers. Working with a powerful word processor such as Word has many advantages, such as the spelling checker, powerful search and replace facilities, and proper cut-and-paste options. This section considers two such templates that are publicly available on the Internet via the Web.

The `GT_HTML.DOT` Template

This template automates the insertion of many common HTML tags and includes support for in-line images. It is available from the URL:

```
http://www.gatech.edu/word_html/release.htm.
```

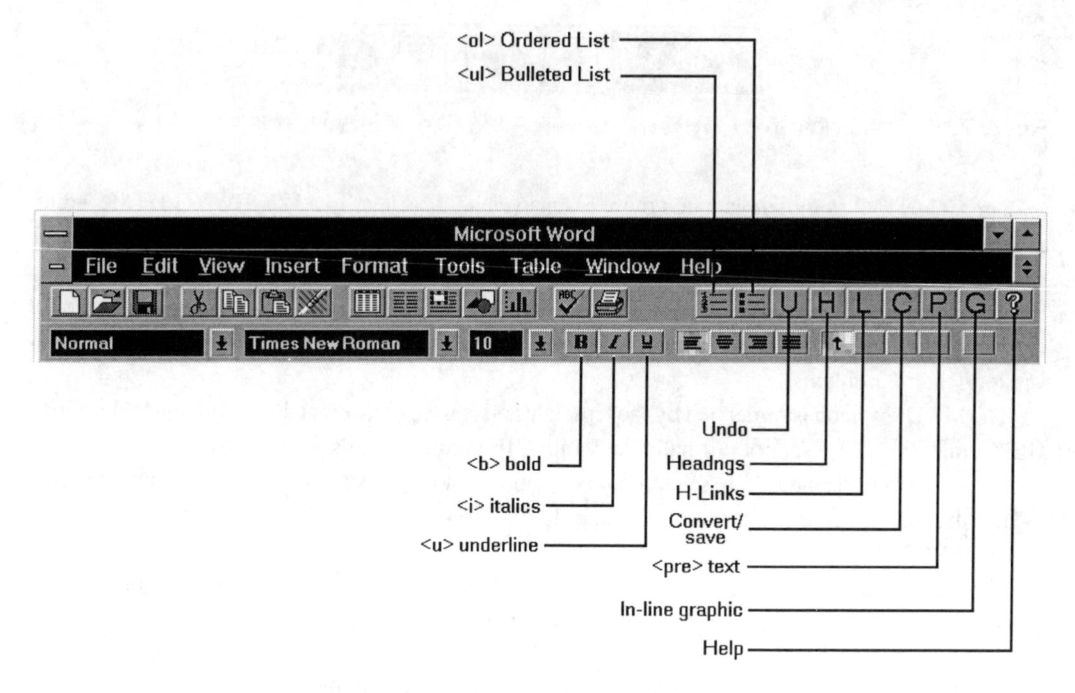

Figure 7.14: Microsoft Word's toolbar after the HTML template has been loaded.

The document at this URL also contains some documentation and an `ftp://` hyper-link in order to download the required files. This template seems to prefer the later versions of Microsoft Word. Using it with Word version 2.0 may cause some unexpected macro problems to occur. Installing the software simply requires you to copy the file `gt_html.dot` into your Microsoft word directory (e.g. `C:\MSWORD`). You can then create a new file in the normal way and Word will ask you for the name of a template to use. Choosing the `gt_html.dot` template provides a number of additional buttons on Word's toolbar that can be used for HTML development. Figure 7.14 shows the Word toolbar after the HTML template has been loaded.

In order to insert a tag, the user must highlight a specific portion of text and then click on the appropriate toolbar button. Word then inserts the required tags and you can continue as normal. Using Word as the basis for your HTML authoring is a clearly beneficial, since you can use all of Word's features. Of course, this does not mean that you can lay text out in a truly WYSIWYG fashion, since HTML has many limitations when it comes to laying out text, although you can get quite near – especially in the case of the next template to be discussed.

The `CU_HTML.DOT` Template

A better alternative to the Word template mentioned above has been written by the Chinese University of Hong Kong, and is called `cu_html.dot`. You can get hold of the ZIP archive it comes in from the URL

```
http://www.cuhk.ck/csc/cu_html/cu_html.htm
```

Figure 7.15: The toolbar in `cu_html.dot`.

The CU_HTML template is much more extensive and is as near to a WYSIWYG HTML editor as you can probably get. This system works in much the same way as the previous system, although the toolbar is different (see Figure 7.15) and support for in-line GIF images (via the `GIF.DLL` that is supplied with it) is included. It also comes in two versions, one for Word version 2.0 and one for version 6.0, so all users can make use of the features without the fear of any macro errors (such as version/feature problems).

The MS Draw icon is remapped by the template and is used to insert an in-line image in the native GIF format. Word 2.0 cannot normally deal with GIF images, so this is a nice touch. Selecting the option results in the standard file selection box, from which you can browse your file system in order to find the relevant file(s). Once a file is selected it is inserted into the page at the current cursor position (WYSIWYG style).

The second icon is used to create hyper-links and references. Files such as other HTML documents, images or sounds can be linked using this icon. In order to use it a word must be highlighted beforehand. The necessary tag-text is then entered. Images can also be made into hyperlinks, as well as a combination of text and pictures if you require.

In order to create a hyper-reference to another server such as a Gopher or FTP server, the search icon should be used. you can type in the name of the URL after the button has been clicked. Highlight a word before clicking on the icon (the word will be used as the clickable-event associated with the link).

Anchors to references within local and external documents are selected using the anchor icon. In order to use this facility you must first insert a *bookmark* for the anchor's reference point (an `<a name>` tag in essence), e.g. a word or other term that you want to move to. The *bookmark* option is in Word's *Insert* menu (or `CTRL-SHIFT-F5` for Word 2.0 users). Type in the name of the bookmark and the template will do the rest. References are marked in blue, as in Mosaic.

If you want to delete a hyperlink simply press on the trash icon and you will be prompted for the hyperlink to be erased. Any item can be deleted by highlighting it and pressing the `[DEL]` key.

Probably the most important icon of all is the Generate icon, which is used to generate the final HTML document. Selecting this icon makes Word convert all the inserted fields into appropriate HTML tags. Make sure that you save your file first. The system will warn you if you have not yet saved. All files are saved in ASCII with an `.htm` extension (although you can change this by selecting the Word *Tools* menu and choosing *HTML options*, where you will find a check-box that toggles on and off the use of `.htm/.html` extensions (the first for DOS, the second for UNIX-based servers).

Inserting styles such as **bold**, *italic* and underlined text is done using the standard Word toolbar icons as normal. Mosaic users cannot use underlined text since it doesn't render properly. *Cello* users will have no problems. Once the template has been loaded you will find that it also makes some changes to Word's *Format* and *Tools* menu. For a start, all of the styles, such as headers and pre-formatted text, can be found in the *Format* menu under the *Styles* option. Word users can access

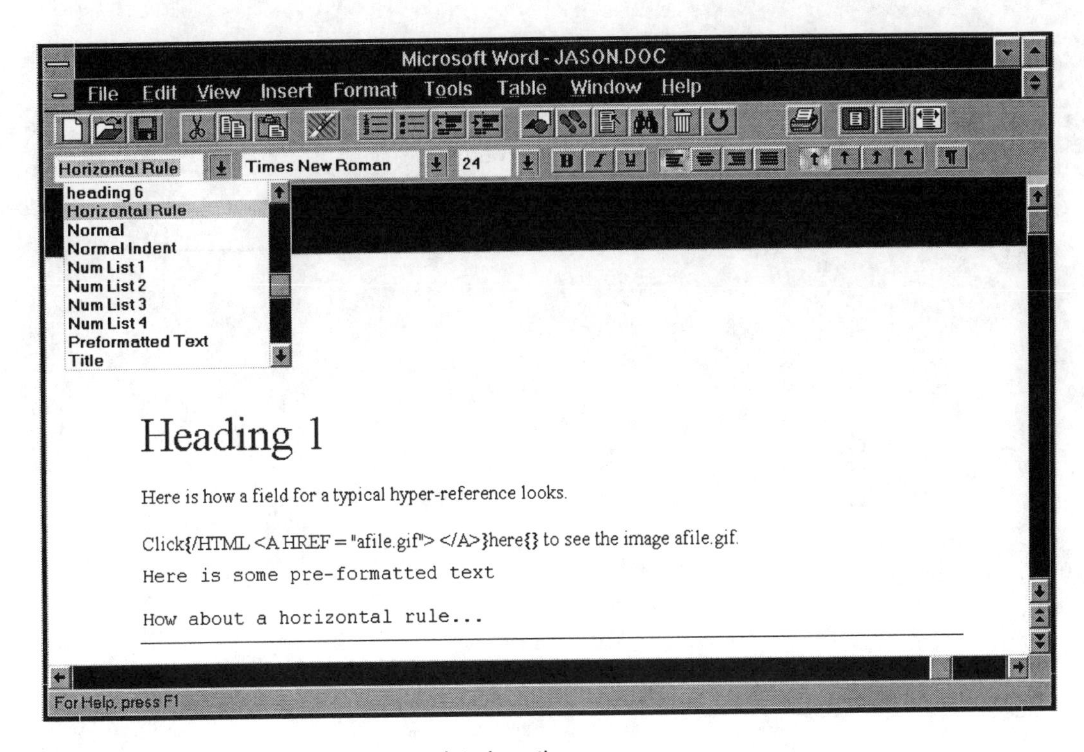

Figure 7.16: The `CU_HTML.DOT` template in action.

all of the HTML styles via the leftmost field in the toolbar area of Word's window, as shown in Figure 7.16 (which also shows some sample Word fields that are used to actually insert the various HTML tags).

▶ TIP

If you want to see the actual tags that are being inserted, simply enable Word's field display option. Select the *Tools* menu and choose *Options* to get at this particular setting.

Working without field codes enabled makes the document resemble Mosaic's interface more accurately.

Fields, such as the `<a href>` tag in Figure 7.16, will be expanded as soon as you click on the generate icon. You can then view the file with your favourite browser. You may be surprised to see how the mark-up of a Word page resembles that of Mosaic. This is due to a number of factors. For a start, all headings have their font size changed according to the same defaults used by Mosaic. Items such as bulleted lists and horizontal rules are also very similar in Word to how they are in the Mosaic system. On the whole this is a good, robust, tool and I recommend it to all HTML developers that have access to Microsoft Word.

▶ TIP

Another template for Word 6.0 users, called the *SGML Tag Wizard*, also exists. This has support for in-line GIF images and can deal with some HTML tags as well. Take a look at the URL

```
http://www.unige.ch/general/tagwiz/taghtm.html
```

for more information on this system.

APPENDIX

A

Interesting Home Pages and Web Servers

This appendix lists home pages of WWW servers located all over the world via the global Internet network. Those entries whose http: reference ends in a '/', or those listed with just a hostname will load a default home page automatically, e.g. index.html. In fact, you can omit any directory name and HTML filename from the URL to access a particular machine's home page in this way (this is a good idea to try if a home page no longer responds, or if it has been changed or moved etc). Entries are marked out of 5 stars for their information content and general usefulness (smileys show the human feelings associated with each star rating) as follows:

★	:(	Yuk!
★★	:-|	Not much to smile about here

★★★	:)	Good
★★★★	:-)	Very good
★★★★★	8-)	A truly net-tastic resource!

URLs are structured as:

```
type://site-name:port/directory/html-filename
```

although default home pages will be loaded by all hosts if you specify just the

```
type://site-name:port/
```

part of the URL.

Web resource name	URL Reference (to home page)
3W Magazine UK ★★★	http://www.3w.com/3W/
Adam Curry (Formerly of MTV) MusicServer ★	http://metaverse.com/vibe/index.html
ALIWEB (an Archie Like Indexing service for the Web) ★★★	http://web.nexor.co.uk/aliweb/doc/aliweb.html
America's Library of Congress ★★★	http://lcweb.loc.gov/homepage/lchp.html
Anglia University UK (education) ★★	http://ultralab.anglia.ac.uk/
Antarctica WWW Server ★★	http://icair.iac.org.nz/
Apollo Advertising UK (WWW advertisers) ★★★	http://apollo.co.uk/
Archie Web Server (at NCSA) ★★★★	http://hoohoo.ncsa.uiuc.edu/
Australian National Botanic Gardens ★★★	http://155.187.10.12:80/anbg.html
'Awsome List' (to various Web facilities) ★★★★	http://www.clark.net/pub/journalism/awesome.html
BBC Networking Club UK ★★★	http://www.bbnc.org.uk/
Birmingham University UK ★★	http://www.cs.bham.ac.uk/
Bradford University UK ★★	http://www.brad.ac.uk/
Brazil National Institute of Space Research ★★	http://www.inpe.br/
Brunel University UK ★★	http://http1.brunel.ac.uk:8080/
BUBL – Bulletin Board for Libraries UK ★★★	http://www.bubl.bath.ac.uk/BUBL/home.html
Cambridge University Press UK ★★★	http://www.cup.cama.ac.uk/
CERN Web Server List ★★★★	http://info.cern.ch/hypertext/DataSources/WWW/Servers.html
CERN's WWW Virtual Library ★★★★★	http://info.cern.ch/hypertext/DataSources/bySubject/overview.html
City University UK Home Page ★★	http://web.city.cs.ac.uk/
CityScape Global On-Line Home Page ★★★	http://www.gold.net/

Coke Machine Web Server (why?!!) ★	http://www.cs.cmu.edu:8001/afs/cs/cmu.edu/user/bsy/www/coke.html
CommerceNet (commerce and industry etc.) ★★	http://www.commerce.net/
Computer Shopper Home Page ★★★	http://www.gold.net/cshop/
Cranfield University UK ★★	http://www.cranfield.ac.uk/
Crash course: writing Web docs (PC Mag) ★★★	http://www.pcweek.ziff.com/~eamonn/crash_course.html*
CUI's W3 Catalog ★★★★	http://cui_www.unige.ch/w3catalog
Dell Computers Home Page ★★★	http://www.us.dell.com/
Demon Internet UK (provider) Home Page ★★	http://www.demon.co.uk/
Dow Jones Industrial Average ★★★	http://www.secapl.com/secapl/quoteserver/djia.html
E-Zines list (electronic texts/magazines etc) ★★	http://www.ora.com:8080/johnl/e-zine-list/
Edinburgh University UK map server ★★	http://www.ucs.ed.ac.uk/General/uk.html
Edward Kennedy's (US Senator) home page ★	http://www.ai.mit.edu/projects/Kennedy/homepage.html
EINET Galaxy Home Page (index to many Web resources and home of WinWeb s/w) ★★★★★	http://galaxy.einet.net/
Elvis's Home Page (*The King* lives on...) ★★	http://tamsun.tamnis.tamu.edu/~ahb2188/elvishom.html*
Encyclopedia Brittanica ★★★★★	http://www.eb.com/
Eye Weekly (Toronto Arts newspaper) ★★	http://io.org:80/eye
Entering the Web: A Guide to Cyberspace ★★	http://www.eit.com/web/www.guide/
Finger Gateway (find information on users) ★★★	http://cism.bus.utexas.edu/cgi-bin/finger
Frequently asked questions about Internet ★★★	http://alfred.econ.lsa.umich.edu:80/FAQs/FAQs.html
FTP "A–Z Monster List of sites" (NCSA) ★★★★	http://hoohoo.ncsa.uiuc.edu:80/ftp-interface.html
GNN – Global Network Navigator ★★★★	http://nearnet.gnn.com/gnn/gnn.html
GNN's 12 best destinations on the Internet ★★★★	http://riskweb.bus.utexas.edu/gnnbest.html
Gopher Information from China ★★	gopher://cnd.cnd.org:70/11/English-Menu
Gopher Jewels ★★★★	http://galaxy.einet.net/GJ/index.html
Guide to Internet Mailing Lists ★★★	http://alpha.acast.nova.edu/listserv.html
Institute of High Energy Physics, Beijing ★★★	http://www.ihep.ac.cn:3000/china.html
Interactive Stock Market Quotes ★★	http://www.secapl.com/cgi-bin/qs
Internet Book Information Centre ★★★★	http://sunsite.unc.edu/ibic/IBIC-homepage.html
Internet Bookshop ★★★	http://www.demon.co.uk/bookshop/index.html
Internet Shopping Network ★★★	http://www.internet.net/
Internet Society (Net statistics etc.) ★★★★	http://info.isoc.org
Internet Web Text Guide ★★★	http://www.rpi.edu/Internet/Guides/decemj/Ttext.html
Information Sources: The Internet and Computer-Mediated Communication (ICMC) ★★★★	http://www.rpi.edu/Internet/Guides/decemj/internet-cmc.html

InterNic (Net miscellany/stats) ★★★★	http://www.internic.net/
Jerusalem's WWW Server ★★	http://shum.cc.huji.il/jeru/jerusalem.html
JewishNet WWW Server (see above also) ★★	http://www.huji.ac.il/www_jewishn/www/t01.html
Developers' JumpStation (HTML editing etc.) ★★★	http://www.stir.ac.uk/jsbin/js
Le Web-Louvre (Paris) ★★★★	http://mistral.enst.fr/~pioch/louvre/*
Learned Information's LI NewsWire ★★	http://info.learned.co.uk/1s/newswire
Leeds University UK (HTML info etc.) ★★	http://www.leeds.ac.uk/
List of Commercial WWW servers (MIT) ★★★	http://tns-www.lcs.mit.edu/commerce.html
Making money on the INTERNET conference ★	http://cism.bus.utexas.edu/Conf.html
MecklerWeb (corporate data and news) ★★★	http://www.mecklerweb.com/MecklerWeb/demo.html
Microsoft Corporation's WWW Server ★★★★	http://www.microsoft.com/
Microsoft Software Knowledge Base ★★★	http://emwac.ed.ac.uk/html/kb/top.html
Mosaic on-line users' guide ★★★	http://www.ncsa.uiuc.edu/SDG/Software/WinMosaic/Docs/WMosToc.html
NASA Space Images ★★★	http://images.jsc.nasa.gov/html/home.htm
Moscow State University ★★★	http://www.npi.msu.su/
NCSA (Home of Mosaic) ★★★★★	http://www.ncsa.uiuc.edu/
NCSA (MS Windows page) ★★★★	http://www.ncsa.uiuc.edu/SDG/Software/WinMosaic/HomePage.html
NETworth Resource For Individual Investors ★★	http://networth.galt.com
Nova-Link's Web Searching Tool ★★★★	http://alpha.acast.nova.edu/start.html
Novell Inc. WWW Home Page ★★	http://www.novell.com/
O'Reilly and Associates (Publishers) ★★★★	http://www.ora.com/
On-line books FAQ ★★	http://cs.indiana.edu/metastuff/book-faq.html
OTIS (Operative Term Is Stimulate) image collection and on-line gallery ★★★	http://sunsite.unc.edu/otis/otis.html
PC Magazine's Favorite WWW sites ★★★★	http://www.pcmag.ziff.com/~pcmag/favehome.htm*
Pipex UK (provider) Home Page ★★	http://www/pipex.net/
Planet Earth Home Page ★★★★	http://white.nosc.mil/info.html
Random URL generator (picks random URLs for you to visit!) ★★	http://kuhttp.cc.ukans.edu/cwis/organizations/kucia/uroulette/uroulette
Recommended Readings on the Internet ★★	http://www.secapl.com/secapl/seminar/readings.html
Russian Information via the Web ★★	http://solar.rtd.ukt.edu/friends/home.html
Sheffield University UK ★★	http://www2.shef.ac.uk/default.html
Standard and Poor's 500 (stock market) ★★	http://www.secapl.com/secapl/quoteserver/sp500.html
Starting Points for Internet Exploration ★★★★	http://www.ncsa.uiuc.edu/SDG/Software/Mosaic/StartingPoints/NetworkStartingPoints.html

Stock Quotes (from QuoteCom) ★★★	http://www.quote.com/demo-chrt.html
Sun Microsystems Home Page ★★★	http://www.sun.com/
The GNN Personal Finance Center ★★	http://nearnet.gnn.com/gnn/meta/finance/bio.html
The Guardian newspaper, UK. *On*Line computer section (with WAIS search) ★★★	http://www.gold.net/online
The Internet's 'Yellow Pages' service ★★★	http://www.cityscape.co.uk/gold/
The Mother of All BBSs – Massive selection of A–Z general information ★★★★★	http://www.cs.colorado.edu/home/mcbryan/ public_html/bb/summary.html
The Johns Hopkins University WWW pages ★★	http://oneworld.wa.com/htmldev/devpage/ dev-page.html
Today in History ★★	http://mtv.com/misc/todayhistory.html
University College London UK map-server ★★	http://www.cs.ucl.ac.uk/misc/uk/intro.html
University of Bath UK ★★	http://www.bath.ac.uk/home.html
Vatican Exhibit Rome Reborn ★★★	http://sunsite.unc.edu/expo/vatican.exhibit/ Vatican.exhibit.html
Virtual Tourist ★★★★	http://wings.buffalo.edu/world
Current Weather Maps ★★★	http://rs560.cl.msu.edu/weather
Weather Server (X-Window, *imagemap* delivery service to your workstation) ★★★	http://rs560.cl.msu.edu/weather/getmegif.html
Web FAQ (Frequently Asked Questions) ★★★	http://siva.cshl.org/~boutell/www_faq.html
Web-search (via EINET Galaxy) ★★★	http://http://galaxy.einet.net/www/www.html
WebCrawler (Web search tool) ★★★	http://www.biotech.washington.edu/WebCrawler/ WebQuery.html
White Sands Missile Base WWW server ★★★★	http://white.nosc.mil/info.htmlc
Whole Internet Catalog (Krol's A–Z services) ★★★★	http://nearnet.gnn.com/wic/newrescat.toc.html
Wired Magazine Home Page ★★	http://www.gold.net/cshop/
World Cup USA '94 (may be off-line soon) ★★	http://www.worldcup.com/
World-Wide Web Servers in Russia ★★★	http://www.npi.msu.su/RUS-other-WWW.html
World-Wide Web Worm (WWWW). Excellent Web searching tool ★★★★★	http://www.cs.colorado.edu/home/mcbryan/ WWWW.html
'Write Your Own Novel' On-line ★★	http://www.awa.com/charter.html
WWW for Instructional Use ★★★	http://www.utexas.edu/world/instruction/index.html
Zambia: Rhodes Unversity ★★	http://www.ru.ac.za/

*DOS browsers may not like the '~'s (tildes) used in UNIX hosts for directory expansion. In the event of an error, use just the hostname as a URL and work your way through the hyperlinks to the required directory.

APPENDIX

B

Interesting Servers to Reference in your HTML Documents

This appendix lists a series of servers that can be incorporated into hyperlinks within your HTML documents. Gopher and veronica servers are included, along with other services, such as X400 and other *white pages* servers. Entries that have HTML pages (i.e. those that end with an `.html` extension) are pages that have hyper-references to the appropriate services. Note down the exact URL of a specific service if you want to call it directly from within your HTML Web page (this basically saves your user from navigating any further menus). Each table below categorizes each server type. In order to use the server facilities (as shown below) within an HTML document you must provide a small user interface routine, perhaps using an `<isindex>` document to send a query string to the server specified. It is best to launch your Web browser and take a look at the server locations below so that you know the exact URL to reference.

Gopher/veronica Servers

Veronica is a tool that allows all of the known Gopher servers to be searched for general information. The Gopher servers listed have links to many other information-searching resources.

Name & type	Location
NCSA **Gopher** server	gopher://gopher.ncsa.uiuc.edu:70/1
PSC **Gopher** server	gopher://gopher.psc.edu:70/1
SDSC **Gopher** server	gopher://gopher.sdsc.edu:70/1
SDSU Sound-file **Gopher** server	gopher://athena.sdsu.edu:71/11/sounds
UIUC **Gopher** server	gopher://gopher.uiuc.edu:70/1
UMN **Gopher** server (The original)	gopher://gopher.micro.umn.edu:70/1
veronica Gopher server	gopher://veronica.scs.unr.edu:70/11/veronica
veronica Gopher server (+ others)	http://www.gold.net/internet-access/
veronica Gopher server (allows *Gopherspace* searching across the whole Internet)	gopher://veronica.sunet.se:2347/7

WAIS Servers

WAIS (Wide Area Information Server) is a database searching tool that allows users to find information on many general topics of interest via a search string.

Name & type	Location
WAIS Web interface	wais://quake.think.com:210/directory-of-servers
WAIS Web interface	wais://archie.au:210/au-directory-of-servers
WAIS Web interface (CERN)	http://info.cern.ch:8001
WAIS Web interface at wais.com	http://www.wais.com/directory-of-servers.html

Miscellaneous Servers

This table lists some miscellaneous servers, such as `finger` and `whois` services.

Name & type	Location
Archie server (file-finding tool)	http://hoohoo.ncsa.uiuc.edu/archie.html
Finger gateway	http://cism.bus.utexas.edu/cgi-bin/finger
Finger gateway server (real-time user lookup)	http://cs.indiana.edu/finger/gateway
Web server directory	http://info.cern.ch/hypertext/DataSources/WWW/ Servers.html
Whois server (user lookup). This is probably a Macintosh machine, so be sure to include all the `%xx` (hex) codes exactly as shown.	gopher://sipb.mit.edu:70/1B%3aInternet%20whois %20servers

APPENDIX

C

The Good Web Software Guide

This appendix lists many dozens of Web/Gopher/WAIS browsers and clients, HTML editors, communications drivers, socket interfaces (and much more besides) that can all be used on the PC, UNIX and Mac platforms. All files are accessible via FTP from the Internet. Make sure that you have a suitable decompressor such as PKUNZIP to handle compressed files, such as `.ZIP` archives (these are the most common format). Items that have been **emboldened** refer to the core software tools for use with Mosaic itself. If any of the files listed below have moved use Archie with any part of the filename to try to locate the file. As with all software, new versions are always forthcoming. Filenames may therefore change also, so you may want to browse an FTP site's directory first before downloading any file(s). Each entry is awarded a star rating (★ = poor, ★★★★★ = excellent) as a guide to help you see at a glance each item's ranking in terms of features, ease of use and robustness. Here are some quick tips:

- If you use Windows to run modem sessions, get hold of the *WfxComm* enhanced driver from Delrina, which replaces the standard Windows 3.1 COMM.DRV communications driver (PCs with UART 16550 serial chips only). See under *WfxComm* below.
- If you are after viewing programs, look under the heading **Viewers** below, which lists an assorted selection of such tools. Refer to Appendix H for an in-depth list.
- If you are a first time user and are looking for the basic utilities, you will want to get all of the items in **bold** type, since these are the essentials e.g. Mosaic, WinSock and some viewers.

Name and platform	FTP site location
Cello Win 3.1 Web browser ★★★★	fatty.law.cornell.edu (/pub/LII/Cello) [b]
Gopher Book (PC Gopher client) ★★★	sunsite.unc.edu (pub/micro/pc-stuff/ ms-windows/winsock/apps)
HGopher (PC/Win 3.1 Gopher client) ★★	lister.cc.ic.ac.uk (pub/wingopher/hgopher.exe) [b]
HTML Assistant – Hypereditor software (PC/Win 3.1 + DDE-Cello support) ★★★	fatty.law.cornell.edu (/Incoming/htmlasst.zip) [b]
HTML*Ed* Hypereditor software (PC/Win 3.1) ★★★	src.doc.ic.ac.uk (/computing/systems/ibmpc/ mosaic/util/htmed09a.zip)
HTML HyperEditor (PC/Win 3.1) ★★★	src.doc.ic.ac.uk (/computing/systems/ibmpc/ mosaic/util/hyperdit.zip)
HTMLMapper (shows all the hyperlinks in a document e.g. for cross-checking) ★★★	s850.mwc.edu (/pub/pc/htmlmap.zip)
HyperWAIS (Macintosh) – Hypercard WAIS browser ★★★	ftp.wais.com (/pub/freeware/mac)
HoTMetaL Editor (HTML hypereditor for DOS/Win 3.1) ★★★	ftp.ncsa.uiuc.edu (/Moasic/contrib/SoftQuad/ hotmetal) [c]
Hytelnet (Hypertext Telnet for PC) ★★★	ftp.usask.ca (/pub/hytelnet/) [b]
MacWAIS (Macintosh) – WAIS client ★★	ftp.einet.net (/einet/mac)
Mosaic for X, PC and Macintosh ★★★★★	ftp.ncsa.uiuc.edu (/Mosaic)
MXQWAIS (X-Window/OSF & Motif window library) ★★★	ftp.eos.ncsu.edu (/pub/mxqwais)
NCSA telnet , TurboGopher, Eudora and Nuntius (Macintosh telnet/ftp/gopher/USENET) ★★★	sumex-aim.stanford.edu (info-mac/comm)
PC Gopher – Gopher client ★★★	sunsite.unc.edu (/pub/packages/gopher/ PC_client) [b]
SerWeb (Web Server for PC/Win 3.1) ★★	sunsite.unc.edu (/pub/micro/pc-stuff/ ms-windows/winsock/serweb03.zip) [b]
tkWWW (X-Window) + HTML editor ★★★	• harbor.ecn.purdue.edu (/pub/tcl/extensions) • info.cern.ch (/pub/www/src)
Viewers for NCSA Mosaic for PC/Windows 3.1 (a miscellaneous selection can be found here including GIF/JPEG/BMP/MPEG/AVI/PostScript viewers etc. – All work with Mosaic et al.) [d]	• www.curtin.edu.au (/pub/internet/mswindows/ viewers) • ftp.ncsa.uiuc.edu (/PC/Mosaic/viewers) • fatty.law.cornell.edu (/pub/LII/Cello)

WAIS Manager (PC/Win 3.1 WAIS client) ★★★	sunsite.unc.edu (/pub/micro/pc-stuff/ ms-windows/winsock/apps) [b]
WAIS-for-Mac (Macintosh) – WAIS client ★★★	ftp.wais.com (pub/freeware/mac)
WFXComm – Windows 3.1 enhanced driver from Delrina software. Replaces `COMM.DRV` and has better UART 16550 support. ★★★	src.doc.ic.ac.uk (/computing/systems/ibmpc/ windows3/ misc/wfxcomm.zip) [c]
Win32s 32 bit extension for Mosaic (Win 3.1) from Microsoft (license free) ★★★	ftp.microsoft.com
WinHTTPD Windows 3.1 HTTP server (run your own HTTP Web server). See *SerWeb also.* ★★★★★	unix.hensa.ac.uk (/contrib/winhttpd/whtp13p1.zip) [b]
Winqvt/net (PC/Win 3.1 telnet/ftp/email/etc.) (sends voice messages across the Net) ★★★★	biochemistry.cwru.edu (/pub/qvtnet) [b]
WinVN (NNTP newsreading software for PC/Win 3.1) ★★★	titan.ksc.nasa.gov (VAX server: [pub. win3.winvn]winvnstd_080.zip [a, b]
WinWAIS (PC/Win 3.1 WAIS client) ★★★	ridgisd.er.usgs.gov (/software/wais) [b]
WinWeb Web browser (NCSA clone) ★★★	ftp.einet.net (/einet/PC/winweb.zip) [b]
WinSock TCP/IP socket interface for Win 3.1 (Version 1.1+) ★★★★	• info.curtin.edu.au (/pub/internet/mswindows/winsock) • ftp.utas.edu (/pc/trumpet/winsock/winsock.zip)
WinSock tools including: WinChat, WinFTP, WinPing and TELW (telnet). Requires the Winsock DLL shown above. ★★★	ftp.utas.edu(/pc/trumpet/winsock/winapps.zip) [b]
WWW Browser (Macintosh) – Web client ★★	info.cern.ch (/pub/www/bin/mac)
WWW browser (X-Windows mostly) ★★★	ftp.ncsa.uiuc.edu (Mosaic/xmosaic-binaries)
XGopher (X-Window) – Gopher client for X-Windows ★★★	boombox.micro.umn.edu (/pub/gopher)
XLibrary (Macintosh) – X network services software interface ★★★	sumex-aim.stanford.edu (/info-mac/comm)
XWAIS (X-Windows) – WAIS client for X ★★★	sunsite.unc.edu (/pub/wais)

[a]VAX machines use different directory names: `[x.y.z]file.txt` is analogous to `/x/y/z/file.txt`.
[b]Requires the Winsock TCP/IP socket interface v1.1, or at least an equivalent PC TCP/IP stack.
[c]This file may arrive as a self-extracting PKLITE archive (`.EXE` file). Use the `-D` option with the utility to preserve the directory structure of the archive. Read any documentation that accompanies the file first.
[d]See Appendix H for an in-depth list of viewers and filters for Mosaic et al.
★ Scoring system (1 star: 20% = poor; 5 stars: 100% = excellent utility). NB: No stars = Score non-applicable.

APPENDIX

D

Entity Codes for HTML Documents

This appendix lists the most common HTML *entity codes* that can be used to display extended characters not normally found on the keyboard. All entity names are prefixed by an ampersand (&) and are followed by a semicolon, as shown below. Characters in the second section are taken from the ISO Latin-1 character set.

1 Common characters with special meanings to HTML

Entity	Description	Literal character
<	The less than sign	<
>	The greater than sign	>

&	The ampersand sign	&
"	The double quote[a]	"

2 ISO Latin 1 character entities

Entity	Description	Literal character
Æ	Capital AE diphthong (ligature)	Æ
Á	Capital A, acute accent	Á
Â	Capital A, circumflex accent	Â
À	Capital A, grave accent	À
Å	Capital A, ring	Å
Ã	Capital A, tilde	Ã
Ä	Capital A, diaeresis or umlaut mark	Ä
Ç	Capital C, cedilla	Ç
Ð	Capital Eth, Icelandic	
É	Capital E, acute accent	É
Ê	Capital E, circumflex accent	Ê
È	Capital E, grave accent	È
Ë	Capital E, diaeresis or umlaut mark	Ë
Í	Capital I, acute accent	Í
Î	Capital I, circumflex accent	Î
Ì	Capital I, grave accent	Ì
Ï	Capital I, diaeresis or umlaut mark	Ï
Ñ	Capital N, tilde	Ñ
Ó	Capital O, acute accent	Ó
Ô	Capital O, circumflex accent	Ô
Ò	Capital O, grave accent	Ò
Ø	Capital O, slash	Ø
Õ	Capital O, tilde	Õ
Ö	Capital O, diaeresis or umlaut mark	Ö
Þ	Capital Thorn, Icelandic	
Ú	Capital U, acute accent	Ú
Û	Capital U, circumflex accent	Û
Ù	Capital U, grave accent	Ù
Ü	Capital U, diaeresis or umlaut mark	Ü
Ý	Capital Y, acute accent	
á	Small a, acute accent	á
â	Small a, circumflex accent	â
æ	Small ae diphthong (ligature)	æ
à	Small a, grave accent	à

å	Small a, ring[a]	å
ã	Small a, tilde	ã
ä	Small a, diaeresis or umlaut mark	ä
ç	Small c, cedilla	ç
é	Small e, acute accent	é
ê	Small e, circumflex accent	ê
è	Small e, grave accent	è
ð	Small eth, Icelandic	
ë	Small e, diaeresis or umlaut mark	ë
í	Small i, acute accent	í
î	Small i, circumflex accent	î
ì	Small i, grave accent	ì
ï	Small i, diaeresis or umlaut mark	ï
ñ	Small n, tilde	ñ
ó	Small o, acute accent	ó
ô	Small o, circumflex accent	ô
ò	Small o, grave accent	ò
ø	Small o, slash	ø
õ	Small o, tilde	õ
ö	Small o, diaeresis or umlaut mark	ö
ß	Small sharp s, German (sz ligature)	ß
þ	Small thorn, Icelandic	
ú	Small u, acute accent	ú
û	Small u, circumflex accent	û
ù	Small u, grave accent	ù
ü	Small u, diaeresis or umlaut mark	ü
ý	Small y, acute accent	
ÿ	Small y, diaeresis or umlaut mark	ÿ

[a]Mosaic does not currently seem to support this entity type.

APPENDIX

E

HTML Quick Reference

This appendix provides a reference guide to all of the most common HTML tags. All entries are ordered in an A–Z fashion. Mark-up operations, such as underlining, italics and emboldening, are very much dependent on the client browser that you use. For example, Mosaic does not always underline text using the <u> tag, although Cello will. You may also find that many tags carry out the same operation, especially those that insert *computerese* text, e.g. pre-formatted monospaced fonts.

Tag entries with a [X] alongside them are obsolete items and are not expected to be carried on into later HTML versions. Such tags can nearly always be replaced by others in order to achieve the desired effect.

<!--**CommentText**-->

Provides the HTML author with a commenting mechanism. Analogous to REM in

BASIC, or /* and */ in C etc. Comments are ignored by the HTML parser. Text may run onto more than one line.

<address>**AddressText**</address>

Provides details of the current document's author, typically the email address of the author.

<a href="**URL**">**LinkText**</a>

Creates a hyper-reference to another Internet resource. `URL` can be the name of a local HTML file, e.g. `file:myfile.htm` or it can be a URL to a remote server, such as a gopher, e.g. `gopher://info.brad.ac.uk`, or it can be the name of an image or audio clip for which Mosaic has the necessary viewing utility installed.

<a name="**myref**">**Word**</a>

Creates an *anchor* for the string `Word` in a document. The `<a href>` tag is used to index the anchor. For example the tag `<a href="#mytag">Click here</a>` would create a hyper-link to the `<a name>` tag with the name "`mytag`", thus moving the user to that entry accordingly. If the anchor entry is in another document, the form of the tag is changed to `<a href="document.htm#anchorname">Click here<a>`, where `document.htm` is the remote document in question, and `anchorname` is the name of the `<a name>` tag in the remote document.

<b>**BoldText**</b> 

Emboldens the text `BoldText`. See also `<emp>`.

<blockquote>**QuoteText**</blockquote>

Inserts a portion of text that is a quote from another source, e.g. from a speech. No quotes (") are placed around the `QuoteText`. Text may run onto more than one line.

<body>**BodyText**</body>

Used to denote the actual *body* (**BodyText**), or part of the HTML document that contains all of the text and associated tags that the reader will actually view on screen (as opposed to the document *header*, which contains tags such as `<title>`, which are not used as body text). This tag is not compulsory. See also `<header>`.

Inserts a line break at the current position (like a carriage return code).

<cite>**CiteText**</cite> 

Inserts some citation text.

<code>**PrefText**</code>

Inserts some pre-formatted text. Analogous to <pre>. A lesser-used tag.

<dd>

See <dl>.

<dt>

See <dl>.

<dl>
<dt>header
<dd>text
</dl>

Inserts a series of tabbed items, known as a *descriptive list*, where <dt> marks the heading and <dd> the sub-heading (tabbed in from the left margin accordingly).

<dir>**Text**</dir>

Directory text (similar to pre-formatted), although typically for entries less than 20 characters (computer directory listings, perhaps).

<emp>**BoldText**</emp>

Same as <b> for all intents and purposes, although Cello may mark up this text as *italic*. This tag is replacing <b>.

<form method="**Method**" action="**Scriptname**">
<input type="**Type**" size=**Size** name="**cName**">
<input type="submit" value="Send details">
</form>

Inserts a Fill-Out-Form (FOF) into the document. Forms are used to send data to a remote Web-server, and basically to allow two-way communication over the Web. The server interfaces to the form using a script file (named by the client in a URL as Scriptname, e.g. http://hostname/dir/script.bat (DOS batch file script). Method controls how the form is encoded by the client; GET and POST are the most common posting methods currently used. The <input type> tag allows input fields to be defined in order to receive the user input. A wide variety of data types are supported including TEXT and NUMBER plus some others called RADIO and CHECKBOX which allow the user to provide *yes/no* type answers. The "submit" input-type is a special attribute that creates a user-defined button, which when clicked upon sends the data in the form to the server identified in the action= part. Forms are the most complicated aspect of HTML and are dealt with in Chapter 2.

<h1>**Header1**</h1> .. <h6>**Header6**</h6>

Denotes a header. Headers are numbered 1 to 6 in HTML (decreasing size as the header number gets larger). Use headers for chapter and section headings, or for titles etc. Headers are the only way of controlling the size of characters.

<head>**HeadTags**</head>

Denotes the header part of a document, where tags such as <title> and <isindex> should ideally be placed within a document. See also <body>.

<hr>

Inserts a horizontal rule (and paragraph break afterwards). Useful for breaking up text into sections and to underline headings etc. See also <u>.

<html>**Document**</html>

Top-level document element. Denotes that the document that follows is in the HTML format. Used to encapsulate the entire HTML document, and should ideally be the first tag used (by convention).

<i>**ItalicText**</i>

Italicizes the text ItalicText.

<img align=**type** src="**ImgName**">

Inserts an in-line image into the current HTML document, where the name of the image is ImgName. The image can be aligned with the text surrounding it using the align type keywords: TOP, MIDDLE or BOTTOM.

<isindex>

This tag makes an HTML file into a *search document*, providing a field within the Mosaic window for a search string allowing user input. This input is encoded (as with a <form> tag) and is sent to a server script to interface with a *back-end* program, e.g. to facilitate a search. See also <form>.

<kbd>**Text**</kbd> 

Inserts some text as entered literally from the keyboard (i.e. pre-formatted). See also <pre>.

<menu>**Text**</menu>

Used to enter menu text, normally pre-formatted text. Hardly used nowadays.

```
<ol>
<li> Bullet 1
```

```
<li> Bullet 2
</ol>
```

Inserts a series of numbered items. See also `<ul>`.

```
<p>
```

Inserts a paragraph break (implied carriage return) and inserts an empty line after the tag.

`<plaintext>`**PlainText**`</plaintext>` 

Inserts some plain text, e.g. pre-formatted. An obsolete tag. See `<pre>`.

`<pre>`**PrefText**`</pre>`

Inserts pre-formatted text, e.g. a monospaced font, by default `Courier`. Used for *computerese* text etc.

`<samp>`**SampText**`</samp>`

Enters some sample text. Yet another pre-formatted equivalent. Use `<pre>`.

`<strong>`**BoldText**`</strong>`

Inserts some bold text. Same as `<b>` and `<emp>` for all intents and purposes purposes. A lesser-used tag, but not obsolete yet.

`<title>`**TitleText**`</title>`

Provides a title on the Mosaic screen which is used to tell the user about the current document that they are reading etc. Mosaic provides a field for the text specified (32 bit Mosaic uses the main window title, note).

`<u>`**UndText**`</u>`

Underlines some text. Mosaic is reluctant to do this, although Cello will underline text without problems. See also `<hr>`.

```
<ul>
<li> Item 1
<li> Item 2
</ul>
```

Inserts a series of bulleted items. See also `<ol>`.

APPENDIX

F

Quick-reference WWW Glossary

This appendix defines the most common terms and acronyms that are currently used in the context of the World-Wide Web.

Cello

A popular Web browser from Cornell University, US. See also Mosaic.

CGI

An acronym for Common Gateway Interface, a standard defining how client applications (such as Mosaic) can interact with a server through an appropriate gateway mechanism, such as using the HTTP protocol. The mechanism is normally a script, or *back end* program, such as a database interface, so that data can be passed from the client and stored or processed by the server. The CGI interface communicates with a client process through a series of environmental variables that hold details of the client's request, e.g. an encoded query string. See also HTTP, FOF.

DOS

An acronym for Disk Operating System. The operating system found on almost all IBM-compatible personal computers, which comes in two flavours: MS-DOS (from Microsoft) and PC-DOS (from IBM).

DTD

An acronym for Document Type Definition, a specific implementation of a document description using SGML. HTML is an SGML DTD. See also HTML, SGML.

Entities

Entities (or *character escape codes*) are part of the HTML tag language. They allow extended characters to be used within a document, typically those from the Latin-1 character set (e.g. ì, Ô, ê) and are inserted into an HTML document at the point required. Refer to Appendix D for a list of such codes.

FOF

An acronym for Fill-Out-Forms. FOFs are regions within a HTML document that allow user input to be passed from the client application (e.g. Mosaic) to a server entity on another Internet host. See also HTML.

FTP

An acronym for File Transfer Protocol (or File Transfer Program, if talking about the *application* itself). FTP is a tool and protocol that defines how files of information are transferred over the Internet. FTP is the principle tool used for moving files between Internet hosts. The World-Wide Web interfaces to FTP via the `ftp://` URL. See also URL, Internet.

GIF

An acronym for Graphics Interchange Format, a ubiquitous image format for still pictures used on the Internet. Web browsers such as Mosaic and Cello use the GIF format for all in-line images within HTML documents. The GIF format was originally developed by CompuServe for use over their network.

Hot region

A hot region is an area of an in-line image which, when clicked upon (using a mouse), activates a particular URL (or hyperlink). See also In-line image, Hyperlink.

HRREFS

A (partial) acronym for Hypertext References, which refers to the hyperlinks embedded within a document that lead to other sources of information. See also Hyperlink.

HTML

An acronym for HyperText Mark-up Language. HTML is a mark-up language for documents, allowing authors to design and create hypermedia documents that can be used over the World-Wide Web. HTML is born out of the ISO SGML standard. The HTML language is made up of a series of *tags* that encapsulate parts of the text within a document and provide document mark-up features such as paragraphs, bold/italic/pre-formatted text, headers, in-line images and so forth. See also SGML, In-line images, Tags.

HTTP

An acronym for HyperText Transfer Protocol, the principle protocol used by the World-Wide Web. HTTP is encapsulated within TCP/IP packets for transmission over the Internet. HTTP is responsible for many things, such as interfacing with other Internet tools (such as FTP and Gopher) using an appropriate URL, as well as actually making requests for information and carrying the information between the client and server. See also URL, TCP/IP, FTP.

HTTPD

An acronym for HyperText Transfer Protocol Daemon, as used in the context of the NCSA httpd Web server program. The term 'daemon' is used heavily on UNIX-based systems when referring to programs that 'listen out' for various requests in order to process them. The Web server software from NCSA is classed as a daemon since it waits passively for incoming HTTP requests. See also HTTP.

Hypereditor

A tool designed for authors that allows HTML mark-up to be automated (albeit to a limited extent). Typically hypereditors allow the insertion of tags and other items via a menu and/or keystroke rather than the user typing them in literally. Some hypereditors also keep track of URLs and other resources so that they can be placed into a document as and when required. Some of the more advanced tools offer WYSIWYG displays so that the mark-up of a document can be seen using a browser of the user's choice. See also WYSIWYG, HTML.

Hyperspace

A collective name referring to the area in which hypermedia and hypertext documents are circulated. Just as 'Cyberspace' is used to refer to the Internet, 'Hyperspace' is really only another name for the World-Wide Web (although these are all the same things in reality). See also WWW, Internet.

Hyperlink

Analogous to hyper-reference. A hyperlink is an item of text (or an image) that the user can click on in order to be led to another item, or source of information. Hyperlinks give the Web its hypertext and hypermedia functionality. See also Hypermedia, Hypertext, Web.

Hypermedia

Hypermedia is similar to hypertext, although bringing together many more forms of media, typically of an audio and visual nature. Hypermedia has been made possible through tools such as Mosaic and the World-Wide Web. See also Hypertext.

Hypertext

Hypertext is a way of cross-referencing and retrieving information. A hypertext document is made up of many cross-references to related items of information. Users can follow a particular reference as they wish, which may lead them on to a completely different, although related, subject. See also Hypermedia.

In-line image

An in-line image is a graphics file that is placed within an HTML document. Mosaic, for example, can handle GIF images and X-Bitmaps within documents (as well as any external image format using an appropriate viewer). See also GIF, viewer, HTML.

Imagemap

An imagemap is an in-line GIF (or X-Bitmap format) image that has one or more hot-regions within it. Each region can be clicked on by the user (with a mouse) in order to activate a particular URL that is associated with that hot-region. See also URL, hot-region, GIF.

Internet

The world's largest computer network; a network of networks all linked together to form one entity, and all of which run the TCP/IP protocol. The Internet is known by many names, including 'The Net', 'The information superhighway' and 'Cyberspace'. See also TCP/IP.

MIME

An acronym for Multipurpose Internet Mail Extensions. MIME defines a number of different internal file formats whose names take the form *file-type/sub-type*. For example, HTML text is specified as `text/html`, whereas plain (or ASCII) text is specified as `text/plain`. MIME allows standard email (which is entirely text-based, and 7 bit only) to carry other file formats (typically binary formats that have 8 bits in each byte). All results passed via the HTTP protocol over the Internet are done via MIME formatted messages. See also Internet, HTTP.

Modem

Modulator/Demodulator. The device that connects you to the Internet (or other service) using a telephone line as a communications medium.

Mosaic

A popular Web browsing tool for Microsoft Windows, X-Windows (UNIX) and the Macintosh platforms. NCSA Mosaic is in essence an HTML-parsing tool that marks up hypermedia documents onto the screen. See also HTML, NCSA.

NCSA

An acronym for National Centre for Supercomputing Applications (at the University of Illinois). This is where those clever people originally developed Mosaic. (Mosaic's full name is normally quoted as 'NCSA Mosaic'). See also Mosaic, Cello.

NNTP

An acronym for Network News Transfer Protocol. A protocol used to send USENET news over the Internet, and used in browsers such as Mosaic to allow access to URLs with resource types such as `news://`.

PC

An acronym for Personal Computer.

Robot

Refers to a program used on the Web that scours the Internet for information (commonly based on some criteria imposed by the user, e.g. a search expression). The term 'Robot' comes from the fact that the process is automated and is carried out electronically. See also The Web, Internet.

SGML

An acronym for Standard Generalized Mark-up Language. SGML is a meta-language that is used to define a wide range of document types. HTML is an *application* of SGML that is used to create such documents. SGML is itself an ISO (International Organization for Standardization) standard. See also HTML, DTD.

SLIP

An acronym for Serial Line Internet Protocol. A communications protocol used over telephone lines via a dial-up connection from the user's computer. SLIP has been superseded by PPP (Point to Point Protocol), although SLIP is still supported since some Mosaic users require this configuration in order to access the Internet. SLIP is essentially an implementation of IP (Internet Protocol) for use over dial-up telephone lines via the serial port on a computer such as a PC (personal computer). See also WWW, TCP/IP, Internet.

Tags

Tags are part of the HTML language. They consist of a series of strings enclosed within < and > characters, and are used to control the mark-up of documents when viewed through a browser such as Mosaic. For example, a sentence could be set in italics using the tags `<i>This is in italics</i>`. Some tags are structured as two separate parts known as a start-tag and an end-tag (as demonstrated), although some tags do not always have to *encapsulate* the text in this way, e.g. `<img src="mygif.gif">` inserts an in-line image and requires no end-tag. See also In-line image, HTML, SGML, Mosaic.

TCP/IP

Transmission Control Protocol/Internet Protocol. The primary communications protocol used over the entire Internet network. HTTP requests are encapsulated within TCP/IP for use over the WWW. See also HTTP, WWW, SLIP.

The Net

Analogous to the Internet. See also Internet, Web.

URL

Acronym for Universal Resource Locator (some say Unique Resource Locator, however). A way of specifying the exact nature and location of a particular resource on the Internet. URLs take the general form `type://hostname/path/file`. For example, `ftp://wuarchive.wustl.edu/simtel20/afile.zip` refers to a file called `afile.zip` that resides in the `/simtel20` directory of the Internet FTP site called `wuarchive.wustl.edu`. The `ftp://` prefix is called the *resource-type*, which in this case is an FTP server, thus this URL would download the file specified. Other resource types include `gopher://`, `telnet://`, and `news://` (for USENET news). See also USENET, FTP, Internet, URN.

URN

An acronym for Uniform Resource Name; an alternative to the URL. There is currently a movement on the Net to introduce URNs . These differ from standard URLs in that they take the user to the nearest resource in order to speed things up, and generally stop all users ending-up at the same point on the Web. See also URL.

USENET

Users' Network. The Internet's 'Bulletin Board', containing over 9000 separate subject areas to which users contribute solely using electronic mail. USENET carries text, image and audio content. See also Internet.

Viewer

A utility program used by a browser such as Mosaic to handle different image and text files. Viewers allow Mosaic to view a myriad of information including audio, visual and textual data. See also Mosaic.

Web

Analogous to the World-Wide Web. The term 'Web' refers to the fact that information is linked together in web-like fashion – all parts of the Web are accessible from any other point, i.e. they all touch one another. See also: World-Wide Web.

WWW

An acronym for the World-Wide Web

World-Wide Web

A hypertext system used over the Internet for cross-referencing and retrieving information over the Internet. See also Internet, Hypertext, Web

WWWW

Acronym for World-Wide Web Worm, a *hypertool* that searches Internet URLs and follows all their links for other information. See Appendix C for its own URL on the Web. See also Web, URL.

WYSIWYG

An acronym for What You See Is What You Get. In the context of the Web and HTML, WYSIWYG refers to fact that the user can see a marked-up version of a HTML document as it will appear in a client browser. Some hypereditors have such a facility, although they are not real-time WYSIWYG, i.e. they require the user to press a *reload* button (as in Mosaic) in order to update the screen. The Cello browser has DDE (Dynamic Data Exchange) support, which allows another Windows application to be update a program with new information in a sort of *client/server* type role.

APPENDIX

G

A–Z of Popular Web Subject URLs

This appendix provides a list of Web pages available on the World-Wide Web organized by their names in an A–Z fashion. Because of the nature of the Web, a single entry may have dozens of other links that point to related items of information. Companies and other organizations running Web servers have also been included in this list. This is by no means an exhaustive list of resources – such a list would fill many books. On-line information should ideally be documented on-line. You may want to examine the URLs listed at the bottom of this list for further information.

Key

[a]This is an FTP archive. You may be given the opportunity to browse a file system to find the file you want, or else the file in question will be down-loaded automatically.

[b]Some MS-DOS browsers may not like tildes (UNIX expansion symbols). Use the home page URL only and browse your way through to the page required instead.
[c]This is a Gopher server, so simply navigate the menus and choose the item(s) that interest you.
[d]This is a VAX machine. Directories take the form `[x.y.z]`, which is the same as `/x/y/z` on UNIX or `\x\y\z` on MS-DOS machines. Web URLs should use '\' for DOS and '/' for Unix.
[e]This a sound file; make sure you have an appropriate viewer installed to handle this format, e.g. `wplany.exe`.
[f]This is a telnetable resource. Mosaic users will need an appropriate telnet program, e.g. `telw.exe`.

A

Abayudaya Jews of Uganda	http://www.intac.com/PubService/uganda/
Aboriginal Studies Electronic Archive	http://coombs.anu.edu.au/SpecialProj/ASEDA/ASEDA.html
Acoustics and Music (IRCAM)	http://www.ircam.fr/
Acoustics Web page	http://www.eng.auburn.edu/department/me/research/acoustics/Acoustics.html
Advanced Microelectronics	http://www.aue.com/
Aeronautics & Electrical Engineering	http://macwww.db.erau.edu/www_virtual_lib/aeronautics.html
Agricultural Genome World Web server	http://probe.nalusda.gov:8000/index.html
Agriculture (general)	• http://moose.cs.indiana.edu:80/internet/agri.html • http://aruba.nysaes.cornell.edu:8000/geneva.html • gopher://gopher.ces.ncsu.edu/
Aircraft Aerodynamics	http://aero.stanford.edu/ADG.html
Algorithmic Image Gallery	http://axpba1.ba.infn.it:8080/
Amateur Radio Page	http://buarc.bradley.edu/
Amdahl Corporation	http://www.amdahl.com/
American Psychological Society	http://www.hanover.edu/pub/aps.html
American Risk & Insurance Association	http://riskweb.bus.utexas.edu/whataria.html
Analytic Philosophy Project	http://www.phil.indiana.edu/ejap/ejap.html
Ancestry: Religion, Death and Culture	http://gort.ucsd.edu/mw/bdl.html
Animal Behaviour	http://www.cisab.indiana.edu:80/index.html
Animations and MPEG files	http://midget.towson.edu:8000/home.html
Animations Index (movie links)	http://midget.towson.edu:8000/home.html
Antarctic Information and Research	http://icair.iac.org.nz/
Anthropology (Aboriginal)	wais://coombs.anu.edu.au:210/ANU-Aboriginal-Studies
Anthropology (miscellaneous)	ftp://coombs.anu.edu.au/coombspapers[a]
Apollo (service-provider), UK	http://apollo.co.uk/
Applied Mathematics	http://fourier.csata.it
Aquatic Ecology	http://davinci.vancouver.wsu.edu/omsi/aquatic.html
Archeology Web server	http://davinci.vancouver.wsu.edu/omsi/arch.html

Archeology section at Cambridge University	ftp://newton.newton.cam.ac.uk/pub/ancient[a]
Archeology of Rome	http://rome.classics.lsa.umich.edu/welcome.html
Archeology (Dead Sea Scrolls)	http://sunsite.unc.edu/expo/deadsea.scrolls/exhibit/intro.html
Archeology (New World)	http://spirit.lib.uconn.edu/HTML/archnet.html
ArchiePlex service	http://www.nexor.co.uk/archieplex-info/info.html
Architecture and Art	gopher://libra.arch.umich.edu/
Architecture Gopher	gopher://gopher.hs.jhu.edu:70/11/%3e...Images/Architecture
Argentina's Ministry of Foreign Affairs	http://www.ar:70/
Art of Japan	ftp://uwtc.washington.edu/pub/Japanese/Pictures/Ukiyo-e/[a]
Art-History-related images	http://rubens.anu.edu.au/
Artificial Intelligence in Design	http://www.arch.su.edu.au/
Artificial Intelligence Research	http://www.cs.washington.edu/research/jair/home.html
Artificial Life On-line	http://alife.santafe.edu/
ArtSource (many Art Web links)	http://www.uky.edu/Artsource/artsourcehome.html
ASCII Clip Art	gopher://cs.ttu.edu/Art%20and%20Images/ClipArt%20%28ASCII%29/
ASSET (Engineering & technology)	http://source.asset.com
Astronomical Institute (U. of Muenster)	http://aquila.uni-muenster.de/
Astronomy & Astrophysics	http://cdsweb.u-strasbg.fr/CDS.html
Astronomy & Astrophysics archive	http://adswww.colorado.edu/adswww/adshomepg.html
Astronomy server (University of Oregon)	http://bovine.uoregon.edu/galaxy.html
Astrophysics Data System	http://adswww.colorado.edu/adswww/adshomepg.html
Astrophysics Division (DAS)	http://www.inpe.br/astro/home
AT & T Web pages	http://www.research.att.com/
Athens High Performance Computing	http://www.hpcl.cti.gr/
Atmospheric Science Group	http://atm21.ucdavis.edu/home.html
Atomic and Solid State Physics	http://www.lassp.cornell.edu/
Australian Environmental Network	http://kaos.erin.gov.au:80/erin.html
Australian Science Archives Project	http://coombs.anu.edu.au/SpecialProj/ASAP/ASAPHome.html
Aviation and Gliding	http://adswww.harvard.edu/MITSA/mitsa_homepg.html
Aviation server (NASA)	http://aviation.jsc.nasa.gov/
Avid Explorer (travel system)	http://www.explore.com/

B

Babylon 5 (TV sci-fi) FAQ on-line	http://www.hyperion.com/b5page.html
Babylon 5 sci-fi series	http://www.hyperion.com/lurk/lurker.html
BBC Networking club (UK)	http://www.bbcnc.org.uk/

Beastie Boys Home Page	http://www.cs.indiana.edu/hyplan/irogers/BeastieBoys/BeastieBoys.html
BEDROCK Systems (Internet solutions)	http://end2.bedrock.com/def.html
Beekeeping	http://alfred1.u.washington.edu:8080/~jlks/bee.html[b]
Berlin and Prague book	http://www-swiss.ai.mit.edu/philg/berlin-prague/book-cover.html
Best of the Web '94 Awards	http://wings.buffalo.edu/contest
Best of the Web 94 book (P. Greenspun)	http://www-swiss.ai.mit.edu/philg/philg.html
Big Dummy's Guide to the Internet	http://www.Germany.EU.net/books/bdgtti/bdgtti-intro.html
Big Time Television	http://daneel.acns.nwu.edu:8082/index.html
Bioinformatics group	http://www.informatics.jax.org/
Biological and Agricultural Engineering	http://www.bae.ncsu.edu/bae/
Biological Sciences server	http://130.17.2.208/wolf/csuwww.html
Bladen Library (University of Toronto)	http://library-www.scar.utoronto.ca/
Botanic Gardens server (Australia)	http://155.187.10.12/index.html
Botany	http://dogwood.botany.uga.edu:80/botany.html
Breast Cancer Information Clearinghouse	http://nysernet.org/breast/Default.html
British Sc-fi archive (scripts etc.)	http://hawks.ha.md.us/
Brunel University, UK	http://http1.brunel.ac.uk:8080/
BSD UNIX Information Server	http://minnie.cs.adfa.oz.au/BSD-info/BSD.html
Building Servers (Mac/DOS/UNIX)	http://www.charm.net/~cyber[b]

C

Cadence Design Systems	http://www.cadence.com/
Canadian Federal Government server	http://debra.dgbt.doc.ca/opengov
Cancer Server (LaJolla)	http://192.231.106.66/default.html
Cancer Server (OncoLink)	http://cancer.med.upenn.edu/
Cell protein server (with imagemaps)	http://siva.cshl.org/
Centre for Atmospheric Science	http://www.atm.ch.cam.ac.uk/
Centre for Landscape Research	http://www.clr.toronto.edu:1080/clr.html
Centre for Renewable Energy, US	http://solstice.crest.org/
Chance Server (maths/probability)	http://www.geom.umn.edu/docs/snell/chance/welcome.html
Chaos in sound	http://www.ccsr.uiuc.edu/People/gmk/Papers/ChuaSndRef.html
Chaos server (Univ. of Georgia)	http://nextworld.cc.gatech.edu:8001/Matt/acl/aclhome.html
Chess information	ftp://chess.uoknor.edu/pub/chess/HTML/homepage[a]
Chinese Communities Web server	http://ifcss.org:8001/index.html
Chinese University of Hong Kong	http://www.cuhk.hk/
Chronicle newsletter (college events)	http://chronicle.merit.edu/

Circuit Theory laboratory	http://www.hut.fi/
Cisco systems (networking products)	http://www.cisco.com/cisco/cisco-home.html
CityScape Internet Services Ltd	http://www.cityscape.co.uk/
Climbing archive	http://www.dtek.chalmers.se/Climbing/index.html
Cognitive and Linguistic Sciences	http://www.cog.brown.edu/
Cognitive and Psychological Sciences	http://matia.stanford.edu/cogsci/
CommerceNet – commerce on the Net	http://www.commerce.net/
Commonwealth Games Web pages	http://freenet.victoria.bc.ca/XVCommonwealth.html
Compilers (free) list	http://cui_www.unige.ch/freecomp
Computer Aided Engineering Network	http://www.engin.umich.edu/college/
Computer Images & Art	gopher://k12.ucs.umacs.edu/11/images
Computer Images & Art	gopher://geneva-acs.uci.edu:1070/11/franklin/multimedia/pictures
Computer Music Journal	ftp://mitpress.mit.edu:/pub/Computer-Music-Journal/Subscribe.t[a]
Computer-Mediated Comm. Magazine	http://www.rpi.edu/~decemj/cmc/mag/current/toc.html[b]
Computerized Ionospheric Labs.	http://www.arlut.utexas.edu/home.html
Cornell Robotics and Vision Laboratory	http://www.cs.cornell.edu/Info/Projects/csrvl/csrvl.html
CPU chips (IEEE study)	gopher://itsa.ucsf.edu/11/.i/.q/.m[c]
CPU Info Center (processor info.)	http://infopad.eecs.berkeley.edu/~burd/gpp/cpu.html[b]
Cryptography, PGP, and Your Privacy	http://draco.centerline.com:8080/~franl/crypto.html[b]
Crystallography server	http://www.unige.ch/
CWI WWW server	http://www.cwi.nl/
CyberCafe (UK)	http://cybercafe.demon.co.uk/
CyberKind magazine	http://sunsite.unc.edu/shannon/ckind/title.html
CyberNet (anarchistic ezine)	http://venus.mcs.com/~flowers/html/cybernet.html[b]
CypherPunks (security/cryptography)	ftp://soda.berkeley.edu/pub/cypherpunks/Home.html[a]

D

Dell Computers	http://www.us.dell.com/
Demographic studies	http://www.psc.lsa.umich.edu/
Demon Internet (service-provider), UK	http://www.demon.co.uk/
Dictionary of Computing Terms	http://wombat.doc.ic.ac.uk/
Digital Image archive (Univ. of Georigia)	http://scarlett.libs.uga.edu/1h/www/darchive.html
Digital's Systems Research Centre (DEC)	http://www.research.digital.com/SRC/home.html
DOS Internet Starters Kit (software)	http://tbone.biol.scarolina.edu/htbin/finger?dean2
Downtown Anywhere ('Virtual City')	http://www.awa.com/
DTP Direct Catalog	http://www.internex.net/DTP/home.html
Dublin City University, UK	http://www.compapp.dcu.ie/DCU_home.html
Dublin Pub Review page (!)	http://www.dsg.cs.tcd.ie:/dsg_people/czimmerm/pubs.html

Dungeons & Dragons Web server	http://www.acm.uiuc.edu/duff/index.html

E

Earth and Planetary Studies (images etc.)	http://ceps.nasm.edu:2020/homepage.html
Earth Resources Laboratory	http://www-erl.mit.edu/
EINet Galaxy Resource Guide	http://galaxy.einet.net/galaxy.html
Electric Propulsion & Plasma Dynamics	http://cougarxp.princeton.edu:2112/eppdyl/eppdyl.html
Elvis Presley Home Page	http://128.194.15.32/~ahb2188/elvishom.html[b]
Encyclopedia Britannica (not free)	http://www.eb.com/
English language and literature	• http://info.cern.ch/hypertext/DataSources/bySubject/Litterature/Overview.html • ftp://mrcnext.cso.uiuc.edu/gutenberg • http://info.cern.ch/roeber/Misc/Gutenberg.html • gopher://world.std.com:70/11/obi • http://english-server.hss.cmu.edu/FrontDoor.html/
Entrepreneurs on the Web	http://sashimi.wwa.com/~notime/eotw/EOTW.html[b]
Environmental Resource Center	http://ftp.clearlake.ibm.com/ERC/HomePage.html
Environmental Resources Info. Network	http://kaos.erin.gov.au/erin.html
EnviroWeb (massive environment site)	http://envirolink.org/
EUnet (major Euroope Internet provider)	http://www.EU.net/
Europe & the global info. society	http://www.earn.net/EC/bangemann.html

F

Fairfax IT centre (EDI protocol et al)	http://axil1.csrc.gmu.edu/
Fax via the Web (FREE!!)	http://linux1.balliol.ox.ac.uk/fax/faxsend.html
Federal Communications Law Journal	http://www.law.indiana.edu/fclj/fclj.html
Federation for Information Processing	http://www.dit.upm.es/~cdk/ifip.html[b]
Fencing (sport) infformation	http://www.ii.uib.no/~arild/fencing.html[b]
Film & Video Resources on the Net	http://http2.sils.umich.edu/Public/fvl/film.html
FineArt Forum	http://www.msstate.edu/Fineart_Online/home.html
Finnish Forest Research Institute	http://www.metla.fi/
FINWeb – Finance and Economics	http://riskweb.bus.utexas.edu/finweb.htm
Fish Information Service (FINS)	http://www.actwin.com/fish/index.html
Florida Mental Health Institute	http://www.fmhi.usf.edu/
Fly Fishing	http://www.geo.mtu.edu/~jsuchosk/fish/fishpage[b]
Food Science & Nutrition	http://fscn1.fsci.umn.edu/
Forensic Laboratory (USFWS)	http://ash.lab.r1.fws.gov/
Forestry Gopher server	gopher://gopher.metla.fi/11/[c]
Forestry Web server	http://www.funet.fi/resources/Capital-area.html

Fractal Database	http://spanky.triumf.ca/
Fractal Movie Archive	http://www.cnam.fr/fractals.html
Fusion research server	http://wwwofe.er.doe.gov/
Fusion studies server	http://w3Fusion.ph.utexas.edu/
Fuzzy Logic archive	http://www.quadralay.com/www/Fuzzy/Fuzzy.html

G

Games Domain	http://wcl-rs.bham.ac.uk/~djh/index.html[b]
Games FAQ	http://wcl-rs.bham.ac.uk/~djh/index.html[b]
Gemini 8m Telescopes Project	http://www.gemini.edu/
Genetics Web server	http://www.cshl.org/
Genome Data Base	http://gdbwww.gdb.org/
Geological Survey, US	http://info.er.usgs.gov/
Geology/Paleontology	http://davinci.vancouver.wsu.edu/omsi/geopal.html
Global Network Navigator	http://nearnet.gnn.com/
Global Prepress Center (DTP etc.)	ftp://ftp.netcom.com/pub/sjledet/www/gpn.html[a]
Greek and Latin classics	http://info.cern.ch:80/hypertext/DataSources/bySubject/Literature/BrynMawr/Overview.html

H

Hang-gliding Mosaic Picture Server	http://cougar.stanford.edu:7878/HGMPSHomePage.html
High Energy Physics	http://slacvm.slac.stanford.edu/find/explist.html
High Performance Computing	http://www.hpcc.gov/
High Performance Computing Centre	http://cs1.soton.ac.uk/
HTML Assistant editor (FAQ)	http://cs.dal.ca/ftp/htmlasst/htmlafaq.html
Hubble Space Telescope images	http://tauon.ph.unimelb.edu.au/home.html
Hubble Space Telescope Team	http://dorrit.as.utexas.edu/
Human Factors in Computing Systems	http://info.sigchi.acm.org/sigchi/chi95.html
Human-Languages Page	http://www.willamette.edu/~tjones/Language-Page.html[b]
Humour server (good for a laugh)	http://www.cs.odu.edu/~cashman/humor.html[b]
HungerNet (Oxfam charity)	http://www.hunger.brown.edu/oxfam/
HyperFiction Dreamscape project	http://daneel.acns.nwu.edu:8082/poeticus/walk/walkhome.html

I

Icon Browser on-line art	http://www.di.unipi.it/iconbrowser/icons.html
Imaging and Distributed Computing	http://george.lbl.gov/ITG.hm.pg.docs/dissect/info.html

India Web Server	http://www.cs.clemson.edu/~nandu/india.html[b]
Indian music server	http://hypatia.ucsc.edu:70/1/RELATED/Batish
Informatics Department (Rutherford, UK)	http://web.inf.rl.ac.uk/
Information Bank (Misc. web-links)	http://www.clark.net/pub/global/home.html
Information centre for the Environment	http://www.ucla.edu/ucservers.html
Informix Software	http://www.informix.com/informix/
InfoVID Outlet: How-To Video outlet	http://branch.com:1080/infovid/c100.html
InfoWorld Magazine	http://www.internet.net/stores/infoworld/index.html
Infrared Processing and Analysis Center	http://www.ipac.caltech.edu/
Institute for Health Informatics	http://www.ihi.aber.ac.uk/index.html
Institute of Meteorology	http://www.met.fu-berlin.de/english/
Intellectual property rights server	http://www.uspto.gov/niiip.html
Internal Auditors Web server	http://www.dartmouth.edu/pages/dhmc/ IAWWW-FOLDER-V1.0/ DARTHOME-IAWWW-EXEC.HTML
International Teletimes (TV listings!)	http://www.wimsey.com/teletimes.root/ teletimes_home_page.html
Internet: Statistics	• ftp://ftp.merit.edu/statistics/nsfnet • http://www.internic.net/internic.html
Internet: Bordering Networks	• http://info.cern.ch:8001/wais.cic.net:210/bitnet%2 fbitearn.nodes? • http://info.cern.ch:8001/kumr.lns.com/nodelist? • http://info.cern.ch:8001/wais.doc.ic.ac.uk:8000/%2 Fpublic%2Fic.doc%2Fwais-indexes%2FNRS-TEXT? • http://info.cern.ch:80/hypertext/DataSources/ bySubject/Internet/ RIPE.html • http://info.cern.ch:80//mailbase.ac.uk/pub/
Internet: Finding people	• gopher://umich.edu:7777/ • http://info.cern.ch:8001/cedar.cic.net:210/ usenet-addresses? • http://info.cern.ch:8001/nnsc.nsf.net:210/ internet-phonebook?"
Internet: Books on-line	• ftp://world.std.com/OBS/The.Internet.Companion • http://www.Germany.EU.net/books/bdgtti/ bdgtti-intro.html • http://src.doc.ic.ac.uk/gbb/wic/newrescat.toc.html
Internet: List of lists	• http://www.internic.net/internic.html • http://info.cern.ch:80//ftp.rpi.edu/pub/ communications/internet-cmc • http://info.cern.ch:8001/nnsc.nsf.net:210/ internet-resource-guide? • http://www.dct.ac.uk/www/fingerinfo/fingerinfo.html
Internet: Miscellaneous documents	• http://info.cern.ch:8001/nnsc.nsf.net:210/

	internet-rfcs? • http://info.cern.ch:8001/nnsc.nsf.net:210/internet-drafts? • http://info.cern.ch:8001/nnsc.nsf.net:210/ietf-documents?" • http://info.cern.ch:80/hypertext/DataSources/Archives/RFC_sites.html
Internet Book Information Center	http://sunsite.unc.edu/ibic
Internet Computer Index (PC/Mac/Unix)	http://ici.proper.com/
Internet RFC searcher	http://web.nexor.co.uk/
Internet Shopping Network	http://shop.internet.net/
Internet Society	gopher://ietf.CNRI.Reston.va.us/
InterNIC Information Services	http://www.internic.net/
InterText Magazine (Web ezine)	http://ftp.etext.org/Zines/InterText/latest.html

J

J. R. Tolkien Web pages	gopher://descartes.uwaterloo.ca/h0/mathSOC/.csc/.www/.relippert/tolkien/rootpage.html[c]
Japanese Information Guide	http://fuji.stanford.edu/
Jayhawk Cyberpunk series (Mary Kuhner)	http://www.klab.caltech.edu/~flowers/jayhawk/[b]
Jerusalem Mosaic	http://shum.cc.huji.ac.il/jeru/hebrew_university_servers.html
Johnson Space Center server, US	http://www.jsc.nasa.gov/jsc/JSC_homepage.html
Journal of Computer-Mediated Comms.	http://www.huji.ac.il/www_jcmc/jcmc.html
Journal of Solar System Studies	http://astrosun.tn.cornell.edu/Icarus/Icarus.html
Judaism Web server	http://sleepless.acm.uiuc.edu/signet/JHSI/judaism.html
Juggling Information Service	http://www.hal.com/services/juggle/

K

Kabbalah Software (Judaic/Hebrew s/w)	http://nysernet.org/~kabbalah/kabbalah.html[b]
Kaleidoscope Communications	http://kaleidoscope.bga.com/
Kaleidospace Arts server	http://kspace.com/
King's College London, UK NeuroNet	http://www.neuronet.ph.kcl.ac.uk/
Knowledge One (fact-finder software)	http://KnowOne_WWW.sonoma.edu/
Korean Martial Art (Taekwondo) server	http://www.bl.physik.tu-muenchen.de/~k2/budo_english/[b]
Krannert Art Museum (on-line)	http://www.ncsa.uiuc.edu/General/UIUC/Krannert/ArtMuseum/KrannertArtHome.html
Krol's Resource Catalogue	http://src.doc.ic.ac.uk/gnn/wic/newrescat.toc.html

L

Languages (Computer)	• http://info.cern.ch/hypertext/DataSources/bySubject/Computing/Languages.html • http://info.desy.de/user/projects/C++.html • http://moose.cs.indiana.edu:80/usr/local/www/elisp/elisp-intro.html • http://asis01.cern.ch/CN/CNTUT/f90/Overview.html • http://vxcrna.cern.ch:80/HELP/PASCAL • http://www.cis.ohio-state.edu:80/hypertext/faq/pfaq/perl-faq-top.html • http://info.cern.ch:80/hypertext/WWW/MarkUp/SGML.html • gopher://ftp.tex.ac.uk:70/11/archive
Law (miscellaneous services)	• ftp://ftp.fcc.gov/ • ftp://ftp.netcom.com/pub/loftus/nocall/home.html • ftp://info2.rus.uni-stuttgart.de/pub/doc/law/german • ftp://netcom8.netcom.com/pub/cchick/scall/home.html • ftp://ra.msstate.edu/pub/docs/history/documents.uk • ftp://wiretap.spies.com/Gov/World • gopher://aclu.org:6601/1 • gopher://garnet.berkeley.edu:1250 • gopher://gopher.eff.org/11/CAF/law • gopher://gopher.law.csuohio.edu:70/ • gopher://holmes.law.cwru.edu:70/1pub/menu • http://143.117.33.25/default.html • http://atlantis.gem.valpo.edu:5000/~jgordon/law.html[b] • http://cali.kentlaw.edu:70/ • http://debra.dgbt.doc.ca:80/opengov/ • http://fuji.stanford.edu/japan_information/japan_legal_info.html • http://galaxy.einet.net/galaxy/Government/Laws-and-Regulations • http://galaxy.einet.net/galaxy/Law.html • http://holmes.law.cwru.edu/ • http://law-gopher.uark.edu/arklaw/home.html • http://risc350b.mdv.gwdg.de/jura/welcome.html • http://www.huji.ac.il/WWW_DIR/ISLAW00.html • http://town.hall.org/patent/patent.html • http://www.csv.warwick.ac.uk/law/default.html • http://www.law.cornell.edu/copyright/copyright.table.html • http://www.law.cornell.edu/source.html • http://www.law.indiana.edu/codes/ca/codes.html

LISTSERV User Guide	http://www.earn.net/lug/notice.html
Literature	• ftp://mrcnext.cso.uiuc.edu/gutenberg • http://info.cern.ch/hypertext/DataSources/bySubject/Litterature/Overview.html
Logic Programming and AI	http://logos.uwaterloo.ca/
London information services company	http://www.tecc.co.uk/public/tqm/
Louvre art exhibit, Paris	http://mistral.enst.fr/~pioch/louvre/[b]
Lycos WWW Server (Web-searcher)	http://fuzine.mt.cs.cmu.edu/mlm/lycos-home.html

M

Macintosh Web archive	gopher://gopher.lcs.mit.edu/h0/HyperArchive.html[c]
Macintosh Networking (*Mactivity*)	http://www.englib.cornell.edu/mactivity/mactivity94.html
Magellan Image Browser (satellite pics)	http://delcano.mit.edu/cgi-bin/midr-query
Manual pages (HTML) for BSD Unix	http://www.bsdi.com/bsdi-man
MapMaker *imagemap* maker	http://tns-www.lcs.mit.edu/cgi-bin/mapmaker
Maricapa Center (Learning & Instruction)	http://hakatai.mcli.dist.maricopa.edu/
Mars exploration	http://esther.la.asu.edu/asu_tes/TES_Editor/MsurveyorMENU.html
Mathematical Software	http://gams.nist.gov/
Maths server (Zentralblatt, Germany)	http://www.zblmath.fiz-karlsruhe.de/
Maxwell Laboratories	http://www.scubed.com:8001/
McDonnell Douglas Aerospace	http://pat.mdc.com/
McDonnell Douglas Modelling System	http://pat.mdc.com/LB/LB.html
Medical Image Processing	http://mipgsun.mipg.upenn.edu/
Microsoft Home Page	http://www.microsoft.com/
MIDI server (synthesizers et al)	http://alf.uib.no/People/midi/midi.html
Ministry of Education (Singapore)	http://www.moe.ac.sg/
Missing Children Forum	http://inept.scubed.com:8001/public_service/missing.html
MKB Music Studio via the Web	http://orpheus.ucsd.edu/mbreen/mkb_music/index.html
Molecular modelling	http://www.nih.gov/molecular_modeling/mmhome.html
Molecular Virology	http://www.bocklabs.wisc.edu/
Morris dancing	ftp://lick.ucsc.edu/pub/www/sla/sms.html[a]
Mosaic "What's New?" page	http://www.ncsa.uiuc.edu/SDG/Software/Mosaic/Docs/whats-new.html
Mother Jones Magazine	http://www.mojones.com/motherjones.html
Movie Database Browser	http://www.msstate.edu/Movies/
Movie Database Browser (MPEG)	http://w3.eeb.ele.tue.nl/mpeg/movies
Movies on TV server	http://www.metronet.com/CGI/HomePages/martin/letterboxed.cgi

Multimedia Information Sources	http://cui_www.unige.ch/OSG/MultimediaInfo/index.html
Music library/sound archive catalogues	http://www.ircam.fr/biblio/query.html
Music on the Web	http://www.cs.cmu.edu:8001/afs/cs.cmu.edu/user/jdg/www/music.html

N

NASA – Kennedy Space Center server	http://www.ksc.nasa.gov/ksc.html
NASA Planetary Data	http://esther.la.asu.edu/asu_tes
NASA Press Releases server	http://krakatoa.jsc.nasa.gov/PressReleases.html
NASA Technical Report server	http://techreports.larc.nasa.gov/cgi-bin/NTRS
National Astronomy & Ionosphere Centre	http://naic.edu/
National Climatic Data Center, US	http://www.ncdc.noaa.gov/ncdc.html
National Inst. of Standards/Technology	http://www.nist.gov/welcome.html
National Institutes of Health, US	http://www.nih.gov/
National Library of Medicine	http://www.nlm.nih.gov/
National Oceanographic Data Center	http://www.nodc.noaa.gov/index.html
National Weather Service, US	http://hpcc1.hpcc.noaa.gov/worldc/mainworl.html
Natural History Museum, London, UK	http://www.nhm.ac.uk/
Netfind gateway to Gopher	gopher://ds.internic.net:4320/1netfind[c]
Network Hardware Suppliers listings	http://www.ai.mit.edu/datawave/hardware.html
NetWorld+Interop 94 Tokyo	http://www.toyo-eng.co.jp/
NEVAlink Co. (St Petersburg, Russia)	http://www.arcom.spb.su/index.html
NewsDay (NY paper) on-line	telnet://HIGHWAY@delphi.com/[f]
NOAA Geosciences Laboratory	http://www.grdl.noaa.gov/
Non-profit organisations on the Net	http://www.ai.mit.edu/people/ellens/non.html
Nonlinear Optics Resource	http://marv.eng.uiowa.edu/
Nonlinear Science e-Print Archive	http://xyz.lanl.gov/form/nlin-sys
NORDUnet (Nordic countries servers)	http://info.nordu.net/
Normandy Invasions / WWII / D-Day	http://192.253.114.31/D-Day/Table_of_contents.html
Not Just Cows (agriculture server)	gopher://snymorva.cs.snymor.edu/hhGOPHER_ROOT1:Y-DOCS.HTML]not_just_cows.html [c,d]
Novell, Inc. (Networking people)	http://www.novell.com/
Novell ND7/NetWare/AppWare database	http://www.novell.com/WaisTitles/nseform.shtml
Nuclear Physics (Moscow University)	http://www.npi.msu.su/
Nursing Information Service	http://crocus.csv.warwick.ac.uk/default.html

O

Obituary page (famous/infamous deaths)	http://catless.ncl.ac.uk/Obituary/README.html

Object-oriented page (Eiffel language)	http://www.cm.cf.ac.uk/CLE
Ocean Engineering	http://take-cover.tamu.edu/
On-line Books Page (bibiliographies etc.)	http://www.cs.cmu.edu:8001/Web/books.html
On-line Dictionary of Computing	http://wombat.doc.ic.ac.uk/
OOP FAQ	http://cui_www.unige.ch/OSG/FAQ/oofaqs.html
OOP Object-Oriented Bibliography	http://cui_www.unige.ch/bibrefs
Open University Web Page (UK)	http://acs-info.open.ac.uk/info-start.html
Oral and Maxillofacial Radiology	http://bpass.dentistry.dal.ca/
Oregon Museum of Science & Industry	http://davinci.vancouver.wsu.edu/omsi/omsiys.html
OS2 FAQ server	http://www.mit.edu:8001/activities/os2/os2world.html

P

Pacific Forestry Center	http://pine.pfc.forestry.ca/
Paleontology Web server	http://ucmp1.berkeley.edu/
Parallel Architectures Center	http://www.npac.syr.edu
Pathology Server	http://www.pathology.washington.edu
PC Week Laboratories	http://www.ziff.com/~pcweek/[b]
Perl HTML developers page	http://www.adp.unc.edu/info/developer.html
Personal Finance Center	http://nearnet.gnn.com/gnn/meta/finance/index.html
Peru Republic WWW server	http://www.rcp.net.pe/rcp.html
Phillips Labs (USAF missile research)	http://www.plk.af.mil/
Pixel Pushers (Web art)	http://www.wimsey.com/Pixel_Pushers/
Planet Earth Home Page	http://white.nosc.mil/info.html
Planetary Data System (NASA)	http://stardust.jpl.nasa.gov/pds_home.html
Plasma Physics Laboratory	http://www.pppl.gov/
Poetry Archive	http://www.ncsa.uiuc.edu:80//sunsite.unc.edu/dykki/poetry/home.html
Poetry on the Web	• http://www.duke.edu/~ap1/homepage.html[b] • http://info.cern.ch:8001/microworld.media.mit.edu:8000/POETRY? • http://english-server.hss.cmu.edu/Poetry.html
Political Science	http://www.uio.no/test/sv/stv/velkommen.html
Population Studies Centre	http://www.psc.lsa.umich.edu/
Positron Emission Tomography	http://pss023.psi.ch/
Postmodern culture	http://jefferson.village.virginia.edu/pmc/contents.194.html
PowerPC News server	http://power.globalnews.com/
Prentice Hall's Gopher Server	gopher://gopher.prenhall.com/[c]
Production and Operations Management	http://rigel.hbs.harvard.edu/
Project Gutenberg (e-texts/audio galore)	ftp://mrcnext.cso.uiuc.edu/etext/NEWUSER.GUT[a]
Psychology server	http://www.psych.rochester.edu/
Purdue University WXP weather server	http://thunder.atms.purdue.edu/

Q

Quarterdeck Office Systems, Inc	http://bear.qdeck.com/qdeckhome.html
Quest Center (Maths/Statistics related)	http://siva.cshl.org/index.html

R

Railroad-related Internet Resources	http://www-cse.ucsd.edu/users/bowdidge/railroad/rail-home.html
RailServer (3000+ German rail stations)	http://rzstud1.rz.uni-karlsruhe.de/~ule3/info-trn.html[b]
Ray-Tracing Web pages	http://www.cm.cf.ac.uk:/Ray.Tracing/
RESUS Server, France	http://ens12.univ-mrs.fr/Us/
Romanian Home Page	http://www.polymtl.ca:8001/zuse/tavi/www/Romania.html
Rosen Sculpture Exhibition	http://www.acs.appstate.edu/art/
RSA Data Security Inc.	http://www.rsa.com/
RUNE: MIT Journal of Arts & Letters	http://www.ai.mit.edu/people/spraxlo/rune/RUNE.html
Runners Web Page (marathons etc.)	http://sunsite.unc.edu/drears/running/running.html
Rush (the heavy-metal group)	http://www.cerf.net/~jlang/rushfan.htm[b]
Russian life culture (English text)	• http://www.arcom.spb.su/index.html • http://www.pitt.edu/~cjp/rees.html[b]
Rwandan Crisis in Africa	http://www.intac.com/PubService/rwanda/

S

Santa Cruz Operation, Inc. (SCO Unix)	http://www.sco.com/index.html
Satellite imagery (ESA/ESRIN satellite)	http://shark1.esrin.esa.it/
Satellite TV listings	http://itre.uncecs.edu/misc/sat.html
Scanner related information	http://www.ideal.com/
Science Fiction	• http://info.cern.ch:8001/turbo.bio.net:210/sf-reviews? • http://www.lysator.liu.se:7500/sf_archive/sf_main.html • ftp://gandalf.rutgers.edu/pub/sfl/sf-resource.guide.html
Scott Yannof's Internet Guide	http://www.dct.ac.uk/www/fingerinfo/fingerinfo.html
Shakespeare server (complete works)	http://the-tech.mit.edu:80/Shakespeare.html
Shortwave and Radio Catalog	http://itre.uncecs.edu/radio/
Silicon Surf (Silicon Graphics)	http://www.sgi.com/
SIMTEL and CICA Archives	http://www.fagg.uni-lj.si/simtel.html
SkyView (NASA flight centre)	http://skview.gsfc.nasa.gov/skyview.html
SNA, an Introduction	http://pclt.cis.yale.edu/pclt/comm/sna.htm

SoftQuad HoTMetaL HTML editor	ftp://ftp.ncsa.uiuc.edu/Web/contrib/SoftQuad/hotmetal[a]
Southern Culture (American)	http://imp.cssc.olemiss.edu/
Space Activism Home Page	http://muon.qrc.com/space/start.html
Space Astrophysics Laboratory	http://www.sal.ists.ca/Welcome.html
Space Physics and Astronomy	http://spacsun.rice.edu/
Space Shuttle Small Payloads Project	http://sspp.gsfc.nasa.gov/
Speleology Information Server	http://speleology.cs.yale.edu/
SQL to Mosaic interface gateway	http://base.ncsa.uiuc.edu:1234/htbin/wmenu1
Stanford Research Institute (SRI)	http://www.sri.com/
Statistics server (programming related)	http://www.stat.washington.edu/index.html
Stock Quote Server (APL)	http://www.secapl.com/secapl/Welcome.html
Sun Microsystems Home Page	http://www.sun.com/
Swedish Language Bank	http://logos.svenska.gu.se/
SYBASE / SQL HTML developers page	http://www.adp.unc.edu/info/developer.html
SYBASE /Perl/VBasic developers page	http://www.adp.unc.edu/info/developer.html
System Integrators, Inc. (SII) Server	http://www.sii.com/

T

Tandem Computers	http://www.tandem.com/
Tango server (dance information)	http://litsun.epfl.ch/tango/welcome.html
Text-to-speech Web server (form-based)	http://utis179.cs.utwente.nl:8001/say/
Textiles Web Server	http://palver.foundation.tricon.com/crafts/index.html
The Global Fund for Women	http://www.ai.mit.edu/people/ellens/gfw.html
The Guide to Network Resource Tools	http://www.earn.net/gnrt/notice.html
The Hub – mathematics material	http://hub.terc.edu/
The Internet Society	http://info.isoc.org/marconi.html
The Lynx (Web magazin project)	http://www.gold.net/lynx/
The Mother of all BBSs Web page	http://www.cs.colorado.edu/homes/mcbryan/public_html/bb/summary.html
The Sisters Of Mercy (pop group)	http://www.cm.cf.ac.uk:/Sisters.Of.Mercy/
The Venom.St Web server (Web links)	http://venom.st.hmc.edu/
ThreeW (3W) Magazine (Internet culture)	http://www.3W.com/3W/index.html
Time server (speaks via audio file!) EST	http://www.yale.edu/cgi-bin/saytime.au[e]
Time server (speaks via audio file!) GMT	http://www.yale.edu/cgi-bin/gmt-saytime.au[e]
TooMuSH (multi user game)	telnet://192.33.116.108:7070[f]
Transformers (the cartoon) server	http://www.vt.edu:10021/other/transformers/
Travels with Samantha	http://www-swiss.ai.mit.edu/samantha/travels-with-samantha.html
Tropical Cyclones (weekly update)	http://web.ngdc.noaa.gov/dmsp/dmsp.html
Tropical Data Base	http://www.ftpt.br/

Turkey information server	http://www.ege.edu.tr/Turkiye/

U

U.S. Department of Energy's server	http://130.20.92.130:8001/esh/home2.htm
U.S. Patent and Trademark Office	http://www.uspto.gov/
UBILAB server (research projects)	http://ubilab.ubs.ch/
UK WWW server list	http://www.ucs.ed.ac.uk/General/uk.html
Under-sea research center (NATO)	http://www.saclantc.nato.int/welcome.html
United Nations Outer Space Office	ftp://ecf.hq.eso.org/pub/un/un-homepage.html[a]
University of Abertay Dundee, UK	http://www.dct.ac.uk/
University of Birmingham, UK	http://www.bham.ac.uk/
University of Chicago	http://www.uchicago.edu/
University of Durham, UK	http://www.dur.ac.uk/
University of Manchester (biology)	http://mbisg2.sbc.man.ac.uk/homepage.html
University of North Carolina, US	http://www.unc.edu/
University of Surrey, UK	http://www.ee.surrey.ac.uk/
University of Twente, Netherlands	http://snmp.cs.utwente.nl/
University of Ulster, UK	http://www.iscm.ulst.ac.uk/
University of York, UK (teaching related)	http://ctipsych.york.ac.uk/ctipsych.html
University of Zurich	http://www-bio.unizh.ch/xmosaic.home
Uruguay Round (trade negotiations)	http://heiwww.unige.ch/gatt/final_act/
USDA Soil Conservation Service	http://www.ncg.scs.ag.gov/
USENET rec.sport.soccer group	http://www.atm.ch.cam.ac.uk/sports
USENET misc.jobs.offered	http://zudock.lerc.nasa.gov:8000/cgi-bin/job-browse/main
USENET rec.arts.movies	http://www.cm.cf.ac.uk/Movies/
USENET rec.guns	http://sal.cs.uiuc.edu/rec.guns/

V

Veterinary Medicine	http://www.vetnet.ucdavis.edu/
Videos on demand	http://tns-www.lcs.mit.edu/vs/demos.html
Viking probe satellite imagery (Mar)	http://barsoom.msss.com/http/vikingdb.html
Virtual Advertising (Web adverts)	http://www.halcyon.com/zz/top.html
Virtual Media Technologies	http://www.onramp.net/virmedia/homepage.html
Virtual Reality information	http://www.jsc.nasa.gov/jsc/JSC_homepage.html
Virtual Reality Markup Language	http://www.wired.com/vrml
Visual Basic HTML Developers page	http://www.adp.unc.edu/info/developer.html

W

WAISGate (WAIS Inc's. interface)	http://server.wais.com/waisgate-announce.html
Weather Radar Laboratory (MIT)	http://graupel.mit.edu/Radar_Lab.html
Web Quiz (University of Hertforshire, UK)	http://altair.herts.ac.uk:8000/html/WebQuiz.html
Web statistics (growth patterns etc.)	http://www.mit.edu:8001/afs/sipb/user/mkgray/ht/web-growth.html
Web traffic analysis	http://white.nosc.mil/sandiego.html
Web Wanders and Robots	http://web.nexor.co.uk/mak/doc/robots/robots.html
WebCalc – WWW/CGI/Perl interface	http://guinan.gsfc.nasa.gov/Web/Calc.html
WebStars – Astrophysics at NASA	http://guinan.gsfc.nasa.gov/WebStars.html
Webster's Weekly ezine	http://www.awa.com/w2/
WebWorld (virtual community)	http://sailfish.peregrine.com/WebWorld/welcome.html
WHO's WHO On-Line	http://www.ictp.trieste.it/Canessa/whoiswho.html
Williams College Astronomy Dept.	http://albert.astro.williams.edu/
Wired Magazine	http://www.wired.com/
Women and computer science	http://www.ncsa.uiuc.edu:80//cpsr.org/cpsr/gender/becoming.comp.sci
Word for Windows 6 SGML Tag Wizard	http://www.unige.ch/general/tagwiz/taghtm.html
Word for Windows HTML template	ftp://ftp.einet.net/einet/pc[a]
World Cup USA '94 WWW Server	http://www.worldcup.com
World Wide Web of Sports	http://tns-www.lcs.mit.edu/cgi-bin/sports
World Wide Web Worm (fact finder)	http://www.cs.colorado.edu/home/mcbryan/WWWW.html

X

Xanadu Australia	http://www.aus.xanadu.com/
Xerox Map Server	http://pubweb.parc.xerox.com/map
XToys server (X-Window tools)	http://penguin.phy.bnl.gov/www/xtoys/xtoys.html

Z

Zimbabwe's stone sculpture	http://www.ncsa.uiuc.edu:80//www.twi.tudelft.nl/Local/ShonaSculpture/ShonaSculpture.html

Other on-line catalogues to check out

Mother of All BBSs
http://www.cs.colarado.edu/home/mcbryan/public_html/bb/summary.html

CERN's Visual Library
http://info.cern.ch/hypertext/DataSources/bySubject/overview.html

CUI's W3 Library
http://cui_www.unige.ch/w3catalog

The 'Awesome List'
http://www.clark.net/pub/journalism/awesome.html

Galaxy Einet Catalogue
http://galaxy.einet.net/

Global Network Navigator (GNN)
http://nearnet.gnn.com/gnn/gnn.html
http://src.doc.ic.ac.uk/gnn/wic/newrescat.toc.html

NCSA's Monster A–Z FTP list
http://hoohoo.ncsa.uiuc.edu:80/ftp-interface.html

NCSA's Starting Points for Internet Exploration
http://www.ncsa.uiuc.edu/SDG/Software/Mosaic/StartingPoints/NetworkStartingPoints.html

The Internet and Computer-Mediated Communication (ICMC)
http://www.rpi.edu/Internet/Guides/decemj/internet-cmc.html

APPENDIX

H

A–Z of Web Viewers and Filters

This appendix provides a list common viewing programs (or *filters*) that can be used with the Mosaic (as well as Cello and the WinWeb browsers etc.). Viewers have been documented for all of the major image, sound and file formats that you are likely to come across in your travels on the Web. Viewers have been awarded a score out of five stars, according to their features, speed and robustness (★ = poor, ★★★★★ = excellent). All of the programs shown run in the Microsoft Windows 3.1 environment only, mostly since this is the main environment for all of the client browsers examined in this book. Viewers are broken down by their type, e.g. `image/audio/text/animation`. This is by no means an exhaustive list; you may want to browse USENET for the latest software releases into the public domain, e.g. `alt.graphics.pixutils` and `comp.graphics`.

Image/picture Viewers

Viewer name/ranking	FTP address
CompuShow (GIF/BMP/MacPaint/Amiga IFF formats) ★★★	• bongo.cc.utexas.edu (/pub/ibmpc/cshw*.zip) • nic.funet.fi (/pub/msdos/graphics/gif/cshw*.zip) • csn.org (/Unidata/giftools/cshow82b.zip)
CView (JPEG file viewer) ★★★★	• wuarchive.wustl.edu (/mirrors/win3/util/CVIEW*.zip) • wuarchive.wustl.edu (/mirrors/win3/desktop/CVIEW*.zip)
ImgFun (GIF, PCX, BMP, JPEG viewer) ★★★	wsmr-simtel20.army.mil (/msdos/graphics/ifse100.zip)
JView (JPEG Viewer) ★★★	• ftp.cica.indiana.edu (/pub/pc/win3/desktop/jview*.zip) • oak.oakland.edu (/pub/msdos/windows)
LView31 (GIF/BMP/RLE viewer/editor) ★★★★	• ftp.law.cornell.edu (/pub/LII/Cello) • ftp.uwp.edu (/pub/picture.viewers) • oak.oakland.edu (/pub/msdos/windows3/lview3*.*)
WinGif (GIF viewer/editor) ★★★★	• wsmr-simtel20.army.mil (/msdos/windows3/wingif*.zip) • ftp.cica.indiana.edu (/pub/pc/win3/util/wingif*.zip) • garbo.uwasa.fi (/win3/gifutil/wingif14.zip) • nic.funet.fi (/pub/msdos/windows/graphics/wingif14.lzh) • ftp.law.cornell.edu (/pub/LII/Cello/wingif*.zip)
WinJPEG (JPEG/TIFF/PCX viewer/editor) ★★★★	• wuarchive.wustl.edu (/mirrors/msdos/windows3/winjp*.zip) • ftp.cica.indiana.edu (/pub/pc/win3/util/winjp*.zip) • oak.oakland.edu (/pub/msdos/windows3/winjp*.zip)

Note: Windows 3.1 has the `pbrush.exe` program, which will show `.BMP` images (although not GIF).

Movie Players/animations

Viewer name/ranking	FTP address
MFW (MPEG player) ★★★	ftp.uwp.edu (/pub/picture.viewers/mfw*.*)
MPEG32w (MPEG player) ★★★★	wuarchive.wustl.edu/systems/ibmpc/win3/nt/[a]
MPEGXing (MPEG player) ★★	• postgres.berkeley.edu (/pub/multimedia/mpeg/Windows3.x/mpegexe.zip) • phoenix.oulu.fi (/pub/incoming/mpeg2_0/mpegexe.zip) • oak.oakland.edu (/pub/msdos/windows3/mpegexe.zip)
VidVue (AVI player) ★★★	wuarchive.wustl.edu (systems/ibmpc/win3/desktop/vidvue*.*)

WAAPlay (FLI viewer) ★★★	• wuarchive.wustl.edu (/mirrors2/win3/desktop/waaplay.zip)

Note: Windows 3.1 has the `mplayer.exe` program that will show `.AVI` movies.
[a]This software requires a 32 bit platform such as Windows 3.11, Windows NT, or Windows 3.1 running the Win32s software. See Appendix A for details of the Win32s software.

Audio/sound Players

Viewer name/ranking	FTP address
Wham (WAV and most other formats) ★★★	• ftp.cica.indiana.edu (/pub/pc/win3/sounds/wham*.*) • ftp.law.cornell.edu (/pub/LII/Cello/wham131.zip)
WPlany (WAV/AU and nearly every other format) ★★★★	wuarchive.wustl.edu (/systems/ibmpc/win3/sounds/wplany*.*)

Note 1: All sounds can be played through the PC speaker with all of the utilities above. This driver is freeware and is available from Microsoft at their FTP site `ftp.microsoft.com` and from numerous other sites such as NCSA's FTP server `ftp.ncsa.uiuc.edu` (as `/PC/Mosaic/viewers/speak.zip`).
Note 2: Windows 3.1 has `soundrec.exe`, which can play `.WAV` format files, although since the program cannot take a command-line argument, you must click on the *Play* button first (this also has the advantage that the sound is kept and can be played multiple times). The `MPLAYER.EXE` movie-player will also play `.WAV` files (this requires a sound card, however).

Telnet Launchers

Viewer name/ranking	FTP address
WinTel (NCSA's telnet program) ★★	ftp.ncsa.uiuc.edu (/pub/telnet)
QVTnet ★★★	wuarchive.wustl.edu (/systems/ibmpc/win3/util/qvtnt94.zip)
TELW (see Note 2 below) ★★★	info.curtin.edu.au (/pub/internet/mswindows/winsock/winapps.zip)

Note 1: Cello has its own telnet client built in and doesn't require a third-party driver, unlike Mosaic.
Note 2: TELW comes as part of the WinSock TCP/IP utilities and is not normally found by itself.

PostScript Viewers

Viewer name/ranking	FTP address
GSView (PostScript viewer) ★★★	ftp.ncsa.uiuc.edu (/PC/Mosaic/viewers/gsview10.zip)
GSWin (PostScript viewer – 'GhostScript') ★★★	ftp.law.cornell.edu (/pub/LII/Cello/gswin.zip)

Note: Windows supplies the `notepad.exe` program as an ASCII viewer (this is an editor as well as a viewer). Any DOS-based ASCII ediror/viewer (such as `EDIT.COM`) can be used if you create a `.PIF` file for the application and ensure that it runs within its own window area. Then call the PIF file as the viewer.

APPENDIX

I

A–Z of Web Service Providers

This appendix provides details on commercial service providers that provide Web-based services. These include the renting of *Web space* so that you can publish your work on-line. Services vary from provider to provider, so the following icons have been used to quickly show you what services are offered:

 Web space offered by service-provider for a monthly/yearly fee.

Provider offers expertise in the Common Gateway Interface.

 Provider offers Fill-Out-Form support (and CGI interface).

<HTML> Provider offers an HTML authoring service, e.g. for home pages.

WAIS Provider has a WAIS interface and/or Web gateway facility.

Name:	**Apollo Advertising, UK**
Internet hostname:	`apollo.co.uk`
Email/contact:	Gordon Wilson (`apollo@apollo.co.uk`)
Services:	CGI <HTML> WAIS
Speed:	64 kbps (ISDN)
Development cost:	Dependent on client requirements
Web space cost:	Dependent on client requirements.
Other services:	Email (+ auto response), Classified advertising
Web demo pages:	`http://apollo.co.uk/`

Name:	**APK, Public Access UNIX™**
Internet hostname:	`wariat.org`
Email/contact:	`gopher@wariat.org`
Services:	<HTML> WAIS
Speed:	56 kbps
Development cost:	Setup cost: $500 (including first 2 Web pages). Further documents: $400.00 (approx. 2 pages each)
Web space cost:	$5 per megabyte per month + per access fee ($0.05 for first 1000 accesses, $0.03 for next 24000, then $0.02 thereafter)
Other services:	Email (+ auto response), Gopher, UUCP and NNTP news feeds

Name:	**Atlantic Computing Technology Corporation**
Internet hostname:	`atlantic.com`
Email/contact:	Rick Romkey (`pokey@atlantic.com`)
Services:	CGI <HTML> WAIS
Speed:	56 kbps
Development cost:	HTML authoring: $50.00 per hour
Web space cost:	$75.00 per month; $50.00 per month for a Gopher server. Setup cost: $1450, or $200.00 for Gopher server
Other services:	FTP, email (+auto response), HTML authoring etc. Publishing generally. Gopher
Web demo pages:	`http://www.atlantic.com/`

Name: **BEDROCK Information Solutions, Incorporated**
Internet hostname: `bedrock.com`
Email/contact: Barry Jackson (`barry@end2.bedrock.com`)
Services: CGI <HTML> WAIS
Speed: T1 speed
Development cost: Depends entirely on client requirements
Web space cost: $50–$1250+ per month depending on features required.
Setup cost: $50–$6000+ depending on features required
Other services: Email (+ auto response), Internet training

Name: **BizNet Technologies**
Internet hostname: `bev.net`
Email/contact: Doug Mauer (`biznet@bev.net`)
Services: CGI <HTML> WAIS
Speed: T1 speed
Development cost: Call directly for details
Web space cost: Call directly for details
Other services: FTP, email (+auto response), HTML authoring. Gopher
Web demo pages: `http://www.biznet.com.blacksburg.va.us/`

Name: **Branch Information Services**
Internet hostname: `b-tech.ann-arbor.mi.us`
Email/contact: Jon Zeeff (`jon@b-tech.ann-arbor.mi.us`)
Services: CGI <HTML> WAIS
Speed: T1 speed
Development cost: Contact directly for details
Web space cost: $40.00 per month. Setup cost: $480.00
Other services: Email, Gopher. Consultancy services available.
Order-to-fax processing.

Name: **Catalog.com Internet Services**
Internet hostname: `catalog.com`
Email/contact: `info@catalog.com`
Services: CGI <HTML> WAIS
Speed: T1 speed
Development cost: Dependent upon requirements
Web space cost: $10.00 per month for 5 Mbyte of disk space
(and 100 Mbyte of transmissions). $50.00 setup cost

Other services:	FTP, email (+auto response), HTML authoring, CGI scripting
Web demo pages:	`http://www.catalog.com/`

Name:	**CERFnet**
Internet hostname:	`cerf.net`
Email/contact:	Rosemarie Al-Amir (`sales@cerf.net`)
Services:	
Speed:	14.4 HST
Development cost:	Contact directly for details
Web space cost:	$20.00 per month (full SLIP dial-up connection). Connect-rates: $5.00 per/hour weekday, $3.00 per/hour weekday. Setup cost: $50.00
Other services:	Email (+ auto response), FTP

Name:	**CityScape Internet Services Ltd UK** (*Global OnLine*).
Internet hostname:	`cityscape.co.uk` *and* `gold.net`
Email/contact:	Tony Jewell (`tony@cityscape.co.uk`)
Services:	
Speed:	2 MB
Development cost:	Contact for details
Web space cost:	£100 sterling a month (per megabyte). Setup cost: £400 sterling (per day)
Other services:	Email (+ auto response), Gopher, MUD multi-user environments etc.
Web demo pages:	`http://www.gold.net/`

Name:	**Computer Engineers Incorporated** (***WorldWide Access***).
Internet hostname:	`wwa.com`
Email/contact:	`info@wwa.com` *or* `support@www.com`
Services:	
Speed:	56 kbps presently; T1 arriving soon
Development cost:	Dependent upon requirements
Web space cost:	$50.00 per month (25 Mbyte of disk space provided)
Other services:	FTP, email (+ auto-response), Gopher
Web demo pages:	`http://www.wwa.com/comm-www.html`

Name:	**Cyberspace Development Incororated**
Internet hostname:	`marketplace.com`
Email/contact:	Andrew Currie (`acurrie@marketplace.com`) or Karyn German (`kgerman@marketplace.com`)

Services: CGI <HTML> WAIS
Speed: T1 speed
Development cost: See: `prices@marketplace.com`
Web space cost: See: `prices@marketplace.com`
Other services: Email (+ auto response), Gopher etc.
Web demo pages: `http://marketplace.cm`

Name: **Demon Internet UK Ltd.**
Internet hostname: `demon.co.uk` *and* `demon.net`
Email/contact: Grahame Davies (`grahame@demon.co.uk`)

Services: CGI <HTML> WAIS
Speed: 256 kbps up to 64 kbps (ISDN)
Development cost: Call directly for details
Web space cost: From £25 sterling a month. Setup cost: £50 sterling
Other services: Email (+ auto response), Dial-up via PPP/SLIP, FTP server
Web demo pages: `http://www.demon.co.uk`

Name: **Digital Marketing, Incorporated**
Internet hostname: `digimark.net`
Email/contact: Gary Goldberg (`og@digimark.net`)

Services: CGI <HTML> WAIS
Speed: T1 speed
Development cost: Call directly for details
Web space cost: $25.00 per month (25 Mbyte of disk space)
Other services: FTP, email (+auto response), HTML authoring. Mailing lists
Web demo pages: `http://www.digimark.net/`

Name: **Downtown Anywhere Incorporated**
Internet hostname: `awa.com`
Email/contact: Sandy Bendremer (`sandy@awa.com`)

Services: CGI <HTML> WAIS
Speed: T1 speed
Development cost: Dependent on client requirements
Web space cost: Dependent on client requirements
Other services: Email (+ auto response), Secure HTTP and credit card transactions etc. FTP.
Web demo pages: `http://www.awa.com/`

Name:	**Electric Press, Incorporated**
Internet hostname:	elpress.com
Email/contact:	Robert Main (Rob_Main@notes.elpress.com)
Services:	
Speed:	T1 speed
Development cost:	Dependent entirely on client requirements
Web space cost:	$1125 per month. Setup cost: $6950 (including 25 HTML pages and own machine for server). Catalogue/product pages: +$6000
Other services:	Email (+ auto response), PR, Turnkey systems, Gopher
Web demo pages:	http://www.elpress.com/

Name:	**Evergreen Internet/Cyberweb/Cybermart**
Internet hostname:	libre.com
Email/contact:	Mark White (mmi@mainsail.com)
Services:	
Speed:	VFast/V34 – 28.8 kbps
Development cost:	Contact directly for details
Web space cost:	Contact directly for details
Other services:	Email (+ auto response), FTP

Name:	**Flightpath Communications**
Internet hostname:	flightpath.com
Email/contact:	Brent Sleeeper (bsleeper@flightpath.com)
Services:	
Speed:	28.8 kbps VFast/V34
Development cost:	Call directly for details. Special rates for non-profit organizations
Web space cost:	$35.00 per month basic rate. Setup cost: $100.00
Other services:	FTP, email (+auto response), HTML authoring, Gopher and IRC
Web demo pages:	http://www.flightpath.com/

Name:	**Great Basin Internet Services**
Internet hostname:	pooh.com
Email/contact:	Bruce Robertson (bruce@pooh.com)
Services:	
Speed:	56 kbps – T1 speeds
Development cost:	By the hour (ask for details)
Web space cost:	$150 - $200 per month. No setup cost

Other services: FTP, email (+auto response), HTML authoring, CGI scripting. Gopher

Name: **InfoMatch Communications Incorporated**
Internet hostname: infomatch.com
Email/contact: John Chapman (john@infomatch.com)

Services:
Speed: 56 kbps up to T2 speed
Development cost: Dependent upon requirements. Contact for details
Web space cost: $40.00 a month per megabyte. No setup cost for new clients
Other services: FTP, email
Web demo pages: http://infomatch.com:70/

Name: **Information Bank**
Internet hostname: clark.net
Email/contact: Kris Herbst (global@clark.net)

Services:
Speed: 28.8 kbps VFast and V34 upto T1
Development cost: Dependent upon requirements
Web space cost: Dependent upon requirements. Contact for details
Other services: FTP, email, HTML authoring
Web demo pages: http://www.clark.net/pub/global/home.html

Name: **Interlink On-Line Services**
Internet hostname: freenet.victoria.bc.ca
Email/contact: Dave Allen (allen@freenet.victoria.bc.ca)

Services:
Speed: 56 kbps
Development cost: $25.00 per hour
Web space cost: $100.00 to set up + $45.00, $90.00 and $180.00 for 1 month, 3 months, and 1 year thereafter (upto 50 kbyte of files). Other pricing options available
Other services: FTP, email (+auto response), HTML authoring etc. Gopher server. FaxBack

Name: **Internet Information Systems**
Internet hostname: internet-is.com
Email/contact: webmaster@internet-is.com

Services:	
Speed:	56 kbps–T1 speed
Development cost:	Dependent upon requirements
Web space cost:	Contact for details
Other services:	Email

Name:	**Internet Media Services**
Internet hostname:	`cdr.stanford.edu`
Email/contact:	Andrew Conru (`conru@cdr.stanford.edu`)
Services:	
Speed:	T1 speed
Development cost:	Dependent upon requirements
Web space cost:	$20–$300+. Setup cost: $200+
Other services:	FTP, email, HTML authoring, On-line maps/imagemaps
Web demo pages:	`http://www.clark.net/pub/global/home.html`

Name:	**Internet Presence & Publishing, Incorporated**
Internet hostname:	`ip.net`
Email/contact:	Keith Basil (`keith@tcp.ip.net`)
Services:	
Speed:	T1 speed
Development cost:	Dependent upon requirements
Web space cost:	Varies upon requirements. Contact directly for details
Other services:	FTP, email (+ auto-response), Gopher, Business Reply™ forms. Internet *ShopKeeper* used for WWW business pages
Web demo pages:	`http://www.ip.net`

Name:	**InterNex Information Services, Incorporated**
Internet hostname:	`internex.net`
Email/contact:	Roger Berger (`rberger@) internex.net`)
Services:	
Speed:	T1 speed and ISDN links
Development cost:	Call for details
Web space cost:	Call for details
Other services:	FTP, email (+auto response), HTML authoring etc.

Name:	**Kaleidoscope Communications**
Internet hostname:	`kaleidoscope.bga.com`

Email/contact: Jim O'Quinn (oquinn@kaleidoscope.bga.com *or* www@kaleidoscope)

Services:
Speed: 256 kbps
Development cost: Depends on features required by client
Web space cost: $170–$1250 per month. Setup cost: $250–$3500
Other services: Email, Gopher, FTP

Name: **Lighthouse Productions – NETCENTER**
Internet hostname: netcom.com
Email/contact: Mike Mathiesen (lite@netcom.com)

Services:
Speed: 115 kbps
Development cost: Dependent upon requirements
Web space cost: $100.00 per month
Other services: FTP, email (+auto response), HTML authoring, InterActive Yellow Pages service, EBook Store, Dating Centre, Business Centre
Web demo pages: http://netcenter.scruznet.com/

Name: **Mainsail Marketing Information, Incororated**
Internet hostname: mainsail.com
Email/contact: Mark White (mmi@mainsail.com)

Services:
Speed: VFast/V34 – 28.8 kbps
Development cost: Contact directly for details
Web space cost: $18.00 per month. $50.00 setup cost
Other services: Email (+ auto response), FTP

Name: **MHVNet**
Internet hostname: mhv.net
Email/contact: Chris Hawkinson (chris@mhv.net)

Services:
Speed: T1 speed
Development cost: Dependent upon requirements. $75.00 per hour
Web space cost: $25.00 per month approx.
Other services: Gopher and Telnet access

Name:	**MicroSystems Internet Services**
Internet hostname:	`powergrid.electriciti.com`
Email/contact:	Brian Knight (`dknight@powergrid.electriciti.com`)
Services:	
Speed:	14.4 HST up to T1 speeds
Development cost:	Call directly for details
Web space cost:	Various (and reasonable) pricing structure
Other services:	FTP, email (+auto response), HTML authoring etc.
Web demo pages:	`http://www.comnet.com/`

Name:	**Net+Effects.**
Internet hostname:	`net.effects.com`
Email/contact:	Jim Hunter (`jshunter@netcom.com`)
Services:	
Speed:	14.4 HST but also access to 56 kbps and T1 connections externally
Development cost:	$75.00 per hour. HTML pages: $50.00. Training: $75.00 per hour
Web space cost:	$50.00 per month (with 10 Mbyte storage space)
Other services:	FTP, email (+auto response), HTML authoring, CGI scripting. Gopher. Training. Turnkey systems
Web demo pages:	`http://www.net.effects.com/`

Name:	**NSTN Incorporated**
Internet hostname:	`nstn.ca`
Email/contact:	Steven Heath (`heath@hawk.nstn.ca`)
Services:	
Speed:	T1
Development cost:	Dependent upon requirements
Web space cost:	$75 upwards
Other services:	FTP, email (+auto response), HTML authoring, secure HTTP access, FOFs, credit card transactions
Web demo pages:	`http://www.nstn.ca/` *and* `gopher.nstn.ca:70`

Name:	**Oslonett, Incorporated**
Internet hostname:	`oslonett.no`
Email/contact:	`info@oslonett.no`
Services:	
Speed:	128 kbps dial-up/28.8 kbps VFast
Development cost:	Call directly for details

Web space cost: $80.00 per year approx + $550 (low usage) or $5000 (high usage)
Other services: FTP, email (+auto response), HTML authoring. Gopher, Telnet, WAIS, USENET
Web demo pages: http://www.oslonett.no/

Name: **Quadralay Corporation**
Internet hostname: quadralay.com
Email/contact: Brian Combs (combs@quadralay.com)
Services: CGI <HTML> WAIS
Speed: T1 speed
Development cost: Dependent entirely on client requirements
Web space cost: $500 per month basic rate (50 kbyte of text and 200 kbyte of graphics)
Other services: Email (+ auto response), FTP server etc. Mosaic sub-licensers
Web demo pages: http://www.quadralay.com/

Name: **QuakeNet**
Internet hostname: quake.com
Email/contact: admin@quake.net
Services: CGI <HTML> WAIS
Speed: 14.4 HST–1.5 Mbps speeds
Development cost: Contact for details
Web space cost: Contact for details
Other services: FTP, email (+auto response), HTML authoring. PPP/SLIP dial-up access

Name: **Quantum Networking Solutions**
Internet hostname: gcr.com
Email/contact: Patrick Linstruth (patrick@ukelele.gcr.com)
Services: CGI <HTML> WAIS
Speed: 14.4 HST currently; T1 speed soon
Development cost: Dependent upon requirements. $75.00 per hour
Web space cost: $350.00 per month for a *shop front* (for your business). Setup cost: $400.00
Other services: FTP, email (+ auto-response), Gopher, Order-processing, On-line catalogues. PPP/SLIP dial-up access
Web demo pages: http:///www.gcr.com/mall

Name: **RTD Systems & Networking, Incorporated**
Internet hostname: `rtd.com`
Email/contact: Rawn Shah (`rawn@rtd.com`)

Services: CGI <HTML> WAIS
Speed: T1 speed
Development cost: HTML Authoring: $50.00 per hour
Web space cost: $1.00 per 100 kbyte of data. Maintenance cost: $50.00. Advertising: $100.00
Other services: FTP, email (+auto response), HTML authoring etc. SLIP dial-up access

Name: ***'Sell-it on the WWW'***
Internet hostname: `powergrid.electriciti.com`
Email/contact: Brian Knight (`dknight@powergrid.electriciti.com`)

Services: CGI <HTML> WAIS
Speed: T1 speed
Development cost: Call directly for details
Web space cost: $5.00 plus storage costs – ask for specific cost details
Other services: FTP, email (+auto response), HTML authoring. Email forms

Name: **South Valley Internet**
Internet hostname: `garlic.com`
Email/contact: `info@garlic.com`

Services: CGI <HTML> WAIS
Speed: 56 kbps presently
Development cost: Dependent upon requirements. Contact for details
Web space cost: $25.00 per month. Setup cost: $15.00
Other services: FTP, email (+ auto-response), Gopher, Image-scanning service. Own domain name provided.

Name: **SSNet, Incorporated**
Internet hostname: `ssnet.com`
Email/contact: Russ Sarbora (`russ@marlin.ssnet.com`)

Services: CGI <HTML> WAIS
Speed: 56 kbps
Development cost: Contact for details
Web space cost: $25.00 per month. Setup cost: $25.00
Other services: FTP, email (+auto response)

Name: **Teleport, Incorporated**
Internet hostname: `teleport.com`
Email/contact: `info@teleport.com`
Services:
Speed: Up to 28.8 kbps VFast/V34
Development cost: Call for details
Web space cost: $5–$35 flat rate. Setup cost: $10.00
Other services: FTP, email (+auto response), HTML authoring etc. Gopher server

Name: **Telerama Public Access Internet**
Internet hostname: `telerama.lm.com`
Email/contact: Peter Berger (`sysop@telerama.lm.com`)
Services:
Speed: T1 speed
Development cost: Dependent upon requirements. $75.00 per hour
Web space cost: $70.00 per month approx. (business rate). $20.00 for just a home page. No setup fee
Other services: FTP, email (+ auto-response), Gopher

Name: **The Computing Support Team, Incorporated**
Internet hostname: `gems.com`
Email/contact: George Boyce (`george@csteam.com`)
Services:
Speed: T1 speed
Development cost: $50.00 per hour
Web space cost: $150 per year (first document).
Additional documents: $20.00 per year
Other services: FTP, email (+auto response), HTML authoring, catalogues. Gopher
Web demo pages: `http://www.gems.com/`

Name: **The Innovation Group**
Internet hostname: Not known
Email/contact: Mike Kovatch (`postmaster@igdell.mk.slip`)
Services:
Speed: Up to 10 Mbps
Development cost: Call directly for details
Web space cost: $50.00 per month. Setup cost: $250.00
Other services: FTP, email (+auto response), HTML authoring. Transaction security

Web demo pages: `http://www.flightpath.com/`

Name: **The New York Web**
Internet hostname: `nyweb.com`
Email/contact: Stephan Moskovic (`mosco@mailhost.nyweb.com`)

Services: CGI <HTML> WAIS
Speed: T1 speed
Development cost: Dependent on client requirements
Web space cost: Dependent on client requirements
Other services: Email (+ auto response), Audio/visual multimedia applications. FTP, Gopher
Web demo pages: `http://nyweb.com/`

Name: **The Sphere Information Service**
Internet hostname: `netcom.com`
Email/contact: Dan Pritchett (`dlp@netcom.com`)

Services: CGI <HTML> WAIS
Speed: 56 kbps–T1 speeds
Development cost: HTML authoring is $50 per hour
Web space cost: $50 per month for the first 5 pages; $10 per page a month for the next 5 pages, and $5 a page per month for pages beyond the first 10 created. No setup cost
Other services: Email (+ auto response), FTP

Name: **The Tenagra Corporation**
Internet hostname: `ssnet.com`
Email/contact: Dr Clifford Kurtzman (`Cliff.Kurtzman@tenagra.com`)

Services: CGI <HTML> WAIS
Speed: T1 speed
Development cost: Contact for details. Hourly charge normal
Web space cost: Contact for details
Other services: FTP, email (+auto response)
Web demo pages: `http://arganet.tenagra.com/Tenagra/tenagra.html`

Name: **Virtual Media Technologies**
Internet hostname: `onramp.net`
Email/contact: Mark Camp *or* Tom Ellis (`markcamp@onramp.net`)

Services:
Speed: 14.4 kbps HST
Development cost: HTML authoring is currently set at $75 per hour
Web space cost: $0.10 a kbyte per month
Other services: Email. Primarily HTML authoring

Name: **XOR Network Engineering/The Internet Plaza**
Internet hostname: plaza.xor.com
Email/contact: plaza@plaza.xor.com

Services:
Speed: T1 speed
Development cost: $150 per HTML document
Web space cost: $275 per month. Setup cost: $250
Other services: FTP, email (+auto response), HTML authoring, CGI scripting. Gopher
Web demo pages: http://plaza.xor.com/

Name: **zNET**
Internet hostname: znet.com
Email/contact: Myron Macleod (info@znet.com)

Services:   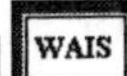
Speed: 28.8 kbps VFast and V34 up to T1
Development cost: Dependent upon requirements
Web space cost: Dependent upon requirements. Contact for details
Other services: FTP, email, Macintosh software support

APPENDIX

J

Questions and Answers

This appendix contains a list of common questions and answers. These have been based on postings from various USENET groups and from the tips scattered throughout this book. Questions are broken down into separate categories, namely: (i) *HTML-related questions*; (ii) *Viewing software questions*; and (iii) *Mosaic-related questions*; (iv) *URL-related questions*; and (v) *CGI-related questions*.

HTML-related Questions

Q1: How can I make an image into a hyper-reference?

A1: Nest the `<img src>` tag inside an `<a href>` hyper-reference tag, for example:

```
<a href="http://somewhere.com/dir/file.htm">
<imm src="image.gif">
</a>
```

Q2: How can I insert comments into an HTML document?
A2: Use the tag <!-- to start the comment and --> to end it. For example, you could have:

```
<!--here is a comment-->
```

Comments can also be carried onto multiple lines, although try not to nest them if at all possible.

Q3: How can I provide user input in an HTML document?
A3: You will need to use a more advanced area of HTML, known as Fill-Out-Forms (FOFs). Mosaic supports such forms using the `<form..>` and `<input..>` tags. Refer to Chapter 4 for an in-depth study of forms and the Common Gateway Interface – a means of interfacing the data from a form with a *back-end* program, such as a database.

Q4: How can I make multiple hot-regions (mouse events) within an in-line image?
A4: You will need to use some Web server software, such as NCSA's httpd (HyperText Transfer Protocol Daemon), that comes pre-installed with the necessary software to allow images to be made into *imagemaps*. Refer to Chapter 4 for more information on imagemaps. Imagemaps require the `ismap` attribute to be included in the `<img src>` tag, for example:

```
<img src="myimage.gif" ismap>
```

Q5: Can I have more than one `<title>` in an HTML document?
A5: Yes, but it is a bad idea. As you move through your HTML document the new title will take effect as planned, although Mosaic will not update it when you move back to an earlier part of the document. Break large subjects up into multiple documents and have one `<title>` tag in each document. See Q6 below also.

Q6: What is the best way of setting out an HTML document?
A6: The internal structure of an HTML document should appear just as if it had been typed into an ASCII text editor so that you can see the layout as you want it to appear on screen to the user. HTML marks up the text differently however, so you will have to insert items such as <p> tags after each portion of text that is a separate paragraph. If you intend to publish work on the Net, use the `<html>` and `</html>` tags to encapsulate the entire document, and use <head> and <body> to divide the document up, so as to keep within publishing conventions on the Web. See Chapter 2 for more details on these tags and their use.

Q7: What is the HTML `<isindex>` tag used for?
A7: A document that has the `<isindex>` tag with in it is used as a front-end into a back-end program such as a database or other search engine. The `<isindex>` tag provides an input field into which the user can type search strings and then submit them to a server named in a particular URL. Refer to Chapter 4 for more on `<isindex>` tags, *back-end* programs and the Common Gateway Interface (CGI).

Q8: How can I insert tables and mathematical equations into my HTML documents?

A8: Such features fall within layer 3 HTML, or the developers' layer (also known as HTML+). At the time of writing Mosaic does not support HTML layer 3 and so such features cannot be used within HTML documents. Tables can, however, be created using conventional keyboard characters in conjunction with the pre-formatted tag `<pre>` (to make the table align properly when viewed on the screen). Mosaic will undoubtedly support some features from HTML+ in the future.

Q9: How can I strip out all of the HTML tags in a document in order to leave the bare ASCII text only?
A9: Mosaic has a *document source* feature, but alas this cannot strip out the HTML tags from a document. *Cello* has such a feature, however, which allows the HTML tags to be stripped from a document and saved accordingly. It is best to keep as many browsers as possible installed to allow such features to be accessed. Mosaic should have this feature built in at a later date.

Q10: How can I access a telnet-based service via Mosaic or Cello?
A10: Use the `telnet://` URL within a hyper-reference. For example:

```
<a href="telnet://archie.ans.net">Telnet to archie.ans.net</a>
```

In order to telnet to the Archie server at the host `archie.ans.net`. Mosaic users will need a telnet-client program to use `telnet://` URLs, e.g. `TELW.EXE`, which comes as part of the WinSock program (see Chapter 3). Cello has an in-built telnet client that requires no third-party software to run. Mosaic users should ensure that their `telnet=` line in the `[Viewers]` section of `mosaic.ini` points to their telnet client.

Mosaic-related Questions

Q1: How can I stop a file transfer or other HTTP request that is currently under way?
A1: Click on the main NCSA logo icon (the one that revolves and animates). This should do the trick, although this feature is more reliable in the later versions of Mosaic, where it is possible to interrupt file and image downloads very easily. You may want to try repetitive clicks to make sure that the request for such an interruption is acknowledged.

Q2: How can I save an HTML file that has been loaded remotely?
A2: Click on the Options menu and choose *Load to Disk* and then click on the reload icon to transfer the document to your machine again. You will then be asked for a filename under which the file will be saved. HTML files are saved in the ASCII format. If you need to obtain an image from a URL, simply note down the URL of the image in question, e.g. `http://host.com/mygif.gif` and use Mosaic's File menu to open a new URL. Type this in as the URL and the images should be downloaded to your machine (you will have to ensure that a viewer for this image type is installed on your system). The image can then be saved using the tool that is displaying it (*WinGif* and *LView31* have save-file options, as do nearly all such picture viewers).

Q3: I have seen an image I like on a server that I was browsing. Can I save it and use it in my own Web pages?

A3: Of course. Press [PrintScrn] while in Windows – this will save the screen to the clipboard where you can then save it in a .CLP file. This file can then be loaded into an application such as Paintbrush (pbrush.exe) using the keystroke [Shift-Insert]. Alternatively, launch an application such as *WinGif* (see Appendix H) and select *Paste* to insert it into the current screen and save it in any format you like, e.g. .BMP format. Ensure that the image can actually be used by third parties, i.e. that it does not contain trade marks of other companies etc.

Q4: Mosaic doesn't refresh the screen sometimes, and I am left with blank window regions. What should I do?
A4: You could press the reload icon to reload the file, although if the file is very large this may take some time. A cure that nearly always works is to minimize the Mosaic window (to an icon) and then maximize it again). The small down-arrow (by itself) in the upper right-hand side of the Mosaic window will minimize the window. To maximize it again, simply double-click on the Mosaic icon.

Q5: I have a slow modem (e.g. 2400 baud). What I can do to improve the speed of my sessions on the Web?
A5: To start with, disable in-line images from Mosaic's Options menu (images are normally quite large and can take time to download). Mosaic users should have at least 9600 baud modems (although 14.4 kbaud would be normal now) in order to handle the large amount of information in Web pages such as images and sound clips. You could also disable *fancy rules* and use hyphens as bullets to increase your speed a bit.

Q6: When I download a file it disappears when I exit Mosaic. Where is the file?
A6: Yes, I've noticed this too. It seems to a be a bug with Mosaic that occasionally deletes the file after you exit the package. Mosaic also seems to keep downloaded files in the directory specified by the DOS TEMP variable (normally this points to somewhere like C:\TEMP, as set in AUTO-EXEC.BAT). The best thing to do is move the file when it is downloaded (from Windows launch a DOS shell and copy the file elsewhere or back up the file). You can also use DOS's UNDELETE command to retrieve files, although this is not guaranteed to retrieve the file as it may have been overwritten by DOS in the meantime.

Q7: I have seen that the X-Windows version of Mosaic can handle multiple windows for different URLs. Can the PC version of Mosaic do this?
A7: Alas, no. (Not while I am writing this, anyway). You cannot start more than one copy of Mosaic under Windows, nor can you open multiple URLs in autonomous windows (although you can of course jump back and forth between different HTML documents). It seems the inherent multi-tasking nature of operating systems such as Unix allows this feature to be used to great benefit, although DOS cannot (bear in mind that Windows is *faking* its multi-tasking in reality, since DOS is still a single-tasking OS). We may see enhancements in later 32 bit Mosaic applications for Windows NT *et al.*, although Mosaic v2.0alpha6 for Windows 3.1 still allows only one main window to be used.

Q8: What is the mailto:// URL, and can I use it with Mosaic and Cello?
A8: The mailto:// URL allows an email message to be sent to a user named in the URL. This

feature was not available in the v2.0alpha6 version of Mosaic (32 bit), but it will be added shortly I understand. Cello users can use this URL resource type without any problems. To use it, embed the URL in a standard HTML hyper-reference tag. For example, in Cello we could have the hyper-reference

```
Mail me, <a href="mailto://joepublic@somewhere.com">joe public</a>
```

so that clicking on the reference *joe public* would invoke Cello's *send email* feature and allow you to enter a message accordingly. An SMTP gateway must be specified in your `cello.ini` file for this to work. See Chapter 6 for more information on Cello's configuration options. Mosaic has a *send mail to developers* feature, although this does not yet interface to a `mailto://` URL.

Q9: What are *annotations*?
A9: Annotations are pieces of text that are attached to HTML documents. They allow descriptive comments to be added (like footnotes, or notes in a margin) to comment a resource or document. To use them make sure that your `mosaic.ini` file is pointing to the correct directory, i.e. one that exists (see the `[Annotations]` section for this setting) and then click on the Annotation option in Mosaic's menu to enter the annotation. The text will then be saved in a file (as HTML text) in the directory specified. Every time you load the current document the annotation will appear at the very bottom. Hyperlinks are provided to link you to the external annotation file. See Chapter 3 for more information, and examples. If you cannot immediately see the annotation, press the Mosaic reload icon and the annotation should appear. You can have as many annotations as you like within a single HTML document.

What has been discussed above refers to *personal annotations* that relate to local HTML documents on your machine. *Group annotations* refer to the same concept of making notes, but they apply to actual URLs (the comments of which are stored in an annotations server – NCSA supply this) so that when you connect to a resource to which a group annotation has been attached, you can see such comments.

URL-related questions

Q1: I am trying to reference a Macintosh machine, but my URL is rejected because I include spaces (Macintosh directories can have spaces in their names). What should I do?
A1: You need to use the code `%20` instead of a space. This is a hexadecimal code that will translate into an ASCII value (32 to be precise) and ASCII 32 is the space you require. For example:

```
http://host.com/List%20of%20WAIS%20servers/
```

translates to the URL

```
http://host.com/List of WAIS servers/
```

Q2: How can I access local files on my hard disk using an appropriate URL (MS-DOS based)?
A2: Use the URL form: `\\\drive-letter|\dir\file`; for example you could use the URL:

`\\\C|\windows\mosaic\myfile.htm`. If you are a *Cello* user ensure that the `LocalOnly=yes` setting is placed in your `cello.ini` file (this will stop nameserver look-ups). Mosaic has no such feature (yet) so incorrect URLs will try to be resolved unfortunately.

Q3: What form of URL do I use for USENET (*netnews*)?
A3: Use the URL form `news:group`; for example: `news:comp.infosystems.www`. You must make sure that an NNTP server is named in your `mosaic.ini` or `cello.ini` files also.

Q4: I am trying to access the URL `http://xyz.com/files:/1/`, but I can't seem to get the URL accepted. Does the use of punctuation symbols matter in URLs?
A4: Yes. All special characters such as punctuation symbols must be changed to hexadecimal form. For example, a colon (`:`) becomes a `%3a` (since a colon is ASCII 58, which in hex is `3a`). The same is true of spaces, which should also be changed within URLs – see Q1 above). Note: a colon in the hostname part of a URL is treated differently (to specify a port number) and does not need changing. Only parts of pathnames e.g. directory names and filenames in URLs need attention.

Viewing software questions

Q1: Why does my viewer crash when I download a file?
A1: This could be caused by many factors. First, ensure that you have your `mosaic.ini` (or `cello.ini`) file configured to handle the file format in question. If you were trying to download a `.GIF` image for example, you would need to configure Mosaic to have an entry in the `[Viewers]` section structured similarly to

```
TYPE0="image/gif"
...
image/gif="c:\windows\viewers\lview31.exe %ls"
```

`mosaic.ini` will come with a number of viewers listed, although none will be pre-installed, so you will have to download the required packages and install them (altering the directory names as required according to your own installation). You will also need to alter the `[Suffixes]` section to ensure that an entry for the file type you want to download is provided.

Q2: How can I play sound without a sound card?
A2: You can use the internal PC speaker if you get hold of Microsoft's speaker driver. This file resides on many hosts on the Internet. See Appendix H for more details.

Q3: What can I do to improve the sound quality with the *Wplany* sound player?
A3: Edit your `mosaic.ini` (or `cello.ini`) file and alter the lines that calls this file and change it to read: `wplany.exe -u -r 8000` (keep the names of any preceding directories, obviously). This should improve the sound significantly.

Q4: When I run Mosaic it automatically runs a viewing program and then complains that it cannot find a viewer for a particular file format? What is happening here?
A4: It seems that the `[Viewers]` section of your `mosaic.ini` file is incorrectly configured. Have you been experimenting with it recently? One common problem concerns the insertion of a `TYPEn=` line in this section for the MIME type `text/html`. There should *not* be such a line, so remove it (keep the line with the `text/html` entry in the `[Suffixes]` section, however). Also ensure that all `TYPEn=` lines are all in order and do not jump a number etc. If this doesn't work, reinstate the original `mosaic.ini` file (from the Mosaic PKZIP archive). It is best to keep copies of all `.INI` files to make this process easier to carry out. In some cases the pathname to a certain viewer may be incorrect. Check everything line-by-line.

Q5: Can I decompress files that are downloaded, e.g. ZIP archives?
A5: Of course you can. There are a number of Windows-based packages that will do this, although most are commercial at the time of writing. Freeware and shareware tools will undoubtedly appear, however (NCSA's 32 bit Mosaic specifies a viewer to de-archive `.ZIP` files, which you may want to search for using Archie, called ZM400). Conventional programs such as PKUNZIP and GZIP can also be used. To do this, run Windows' PIF editor (`pifedit.exe`) and reference the name of your de-archiving tool, e.g. `PKUNZIP.EXE`. You don't want to exit to DOS temporarily, so make sure this entry runs in its own window (select the check-box with this option). Save the entry and then edit your `mosaic.ini` (or `cello.ini` file etc). Now change the `[Viewers]` and `[Suffixes]` section for Mosaic so that it references the PIF file. For example we could have:

```
[Viewers]
TYPE0="application/zip"
...
application.zip="c:\windows\pkunzip.pif %ls"

[Suffixes]
...
application/zip=.zip
```

Now restart Mosaic. When you download `.ZIP` files in the future Mosaic should run the `PKUNZIP.PIF` file on the archive and decompress it accordingly. You can of course handle any archive in this way. Be sure to provide any options to your utility in the PIF file as required. Unfortunately, using a PIF file means that many command-line options cannot be used (some archive files require different options), so it is probably best to use a dedicated tool that will ask you for the options you require.

CGI-related questions

Q1: I try running my CGI script or imagemap but it won't activate. What is wrong?
A1: First of all, check that you are running the NCSA server software. You **must** be running this software in order to use CGI scripts and *imagemaps*. To run the NCSA server program, simply install the `HTTPD.EXE` program and run this before invoking Mosaic (you can do it afterwards, however,

if Mosaic is already running). Then you must ensure that you are accessing all of your HTML pages (which contain forms etc.) through the server. Do this by opening the URL `http://localhost` and you should see the NCSA httpd server icon light up. If the server cannot be reached, shut everything down and restart Windows from scratch. You may also want to try issuing multiple localhost requests, since sometimes the server loses track of the connection with the Mosaic client. You must store all of your HTML files in the directory `C:\HTTPD\HTDOCS`. The first file loaded is normally `index.htm` by default, so ensure that the forms and imagemaps etc. that you are creating are in this file or are called from this file.

Q2: My CGI script keeps on issuing a '*Server Error*' message. What is wrong?
A2: CGI-scripting is a large area, but here are some things to bear in mind. First you must know which type of posting method to use. If your form has a `method="GET"` make sure that you are storing the environment variable `QUERY_STRING`. If a `POST` method is used you should be reading the standard input instead. If your script is displaying any output whatsoever, it **must** have a `Content-type:` field (see Chapter 4) with a blank line after it (very important). For example, to output some HTML text use:

```
Content-type: text/html
[blank line]
```

If you miss out the declaration above and try to output some text, a server error will occur. Another problem you may have encountered if you are **not** displaying any text is the inclusion of a statement to print a single blank line just before your script terminates. The NCSA server needs this line to tell it that your script has finished its duties. See Chapter 4 for numerous examples of this. See Q6 also, below.

Q3: What languages can I program CGI scripts in and what is the best language?
A3: Most languages are sufficient, although some are more sufficient than others. You should make sure that your scripting language can handle environment variables. C, Clipper, Icon and DOS batch files can all handle such variables, as can many other languages. Your language should also be able to read from the standard input (`stdin`) device (C and Icon are very good at this).

UNIX tools such as `awk`, `sed` and `perl` are used extensively for parsing scripts; some of these tools are available for DOS, especially `perl`. It would also be useful if the language you choose can compile programs to `.EXE` format. This will allow you to call the program directly, rather than from a DOS batch file first (see below). Icon can do this (although its `.EXE`s rely on run-time support from an external program); C can of course compile to `.EXE` format, as can many other languages, e.g. Clipper and Visual Basic.

Q4: The `hscript.pif` file is confusing me. What is its purpose?
A4: This file is probably the most important on the system. PIF (Program Interchange File) files are used by Microsoft Windows to customize and configure programs. Typically they are used to control memory requirements and to determine whether or not DOS programs run in a window. The `hscript.pif` file, by default, launches the DOS pre-processor `COMMAND.COM` with the `/C` option

in order to run an external program, which is your script file *interpreter*. Since COMMAND.COM can run any DOS-based program it is suitable mostly for batch file scripts. However, it can also be used to launch many other programs, such as a Visual Basic application. It is advisable to keep the default interpreter as COMMAND.COM and use any DOS-based program, since configuration can be tricky. Chapter 4 shows how to use other interpreters and to how to configure the NCSA httpd's .CNF configuration files.

Q5: I am trying to update the contents of a file but the server cannot find it. What is wrong?
A5: If you reference a file in your script without using a fully qualified name (i.e. you just refer to the file as 'file.txt' etc, the NCSA server will expect to find the file in the directory specified in the hscript.pif file (this is in the directory \HTTPD). This directory location is set to the value of the variable %TEMP%, which should point to a directory such as C:\TMP, as set in AUTO-EXEC.BAT. If you do not have such a variable, create it and reboot your machine (or re-run AUTOEXEC.BAT at least). To avoid this problem in the future, simply reference all files with their full path name.

Q6: How can I see any errors with my script as it is executed?
A6: The NCSA server will run a shell in which your script file is executed. The icon for this process will appear momentarily on the screen, whereupon you can click on it to see what is happening. You can only see program output and error messages in this mode. For a more permanent view of things simply look in the directory specified in the hscript.pif file (e.g. C:\TMP) and you should see a series of .OUT files. These contain any errors that occur in the case of server error.

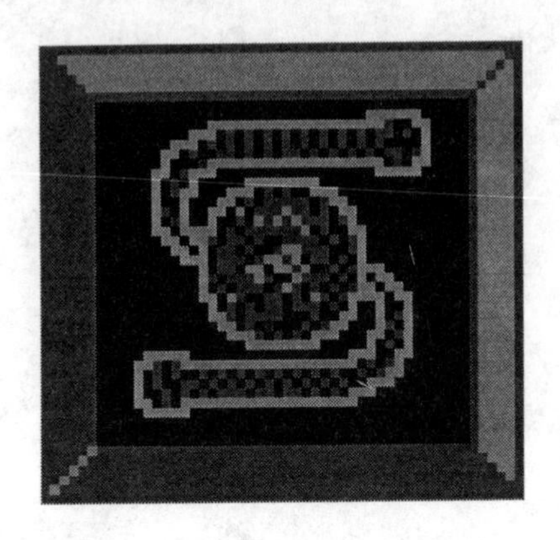

Index

Manger:
The World-Wide Web, Mosaic and More

ISBN 0-07-7091329

Software Disclaimer

Although every effort has been made to ensure the reliability and accuracy of this disk the Publisher cannot guarantee that the disk when used for its intended purpose is free from error or defect.